The Urban Wisdom of Jane Jacobs

Here for the first time is a thoroughly interdisciplinary and international examination of Jane Jacobs's legacy. Divided into four parts: I. Jacobs, Urban Philosopher; II. Jacobs, Urban Economist; III. Jacobs, Urban Sociologist; and IV. Jacobs, Urban Designer, the book evaluates the impact of Jacobs's writings and activism on the city, the professions dedicated to city-building and, more generally, on human thought. Together, the editors and contributors highlight the notion that Jacobs's influence goes beyond planning to philosophy, economics, sociology and design. They set out to answer such questions as: What explains Jacobs's lasting appeal and is it justified? Where was she right and where was she wrong? What were the most important themes she addressed? And, although Jacobs was best known for her work on cities, is it correct to say that she was a much broader thinker, a philosopher, and that the key to her lasting legacy is precisely her exceptional breadth of thought?

Sonia Hirt is Associate Dean of the College of Architecture and Urban Studies and *Diane Zahm* is Co-chair of the Department of Urban Affairs and Planning at the College of Architecture and Urban Studies at Virginia Tech.

Planning, History and Environment Series

Editor:

Ann Rudkin, Alexandrine Press, Marcham, UK

Editorial Board:

Professor Arturo Almandoz, Universidad Simón Bolivar, Caracas, Venezuela and
    Pontificia Universidad Católica de Chile, Santiago, Chile

Professor Nezar AlSayyad, University of California, Berkeley, USA

Professor Scott A. Bollens, University of California, Irvine, USA

Professor Robert Bruegmann, University of Illinois at Chicago, USA

Professor Meredith Clausen, University of Washington, Seattle, USA

Professor Yasser Elsheshtawy, UAE University, Al Ain, UAE

Professor Robert Freestone, University of New South Wales, Sydney, Australia

Professor John R. Gold, Oxford Brookes University, Oxford, UK

Professor Sir Peter Hall, University College London, UK

Professor Michael Hebbert, University College London, UK

Selection of Published Titles

The Urban Wisdom of Jane Jacobs

edited by

Sonia Hirt

with Diane Zahm

Routledge
Taylor & Francis Group

LONDON AND NEW YORK

First published 2012 by Routledge

This paperback edition first published 2015
by Routledge
2 Park Square, Milton Park, Abingdon, Oxfordshire OX14 4RN

and by Routledge
711 Third Avenue, New York, NY 10017

Routledge is an imprint of the Taylor & Francis Group, an informa business

British Library Cataloguing in Publication Data
A catalogue record of this book is available from the British Library

Library of Congress Cataloging in Publication Data

The urban wisdom of Jane Jacobs / edited by Sonia Hirt with Diane Zahm.
  p. cm. — (Planning, history and environment)
Includes bibliographical references and index.
  1. City planning. 2. Urban renewal. 3. Urban policy. I. Jacobs, Jane, 1916–2006. II. Hirt, Sonia. III. Zahm, Diane L.
HT166.U7457 2012
307.1'216—dc23

2012011728

ISBN: 978–0–415–52599–2 (hbk)
ISBN: 978–1–138–82888–9 (pbk)
ISBN: 978–0–203–09517–1 (ebk)

Typeset in Aldine and Swiss by PNR Design, Didcot

Printed and bound in the United States of America by Publishers Graphics, LLC on sustainably sourced paper.

To my family on both sides of the North Atlantic

Contents

Acknowledgements

This book has been in the making for an embarrassingly long period of time. I first read Jane Jacobs's *The Death and Life of Great American Cities* as a master's student in urban planning at the University of Michigan in 1993. I was absolutely smitten! My favourite chapter was the last one, *The Kind of a Problem a City Is*. To this day, I think of it as a statement on philosophy, which uses cities and urban planning only as a case study. And ever since, I wanted to argue somewhere – in a chapter, an article, or even a book review – that Jane Jacobs's contributions touch issues immeasurably broader than urban planning. Then life happened – jobs, kids, a doctorate, and publications on all sorts of other topics. So finally in 2010, I decided to go back to the promise I made to myself nearly two decades ago.

The project initially started as a theme issue of the *Journal of Architectural and Planning Research*. I hoped the issue would come out in 2011, on the 50th anniversary of *The Death and Life*. But it soon became clear that if I included articles by all the wonderful authors who responded to me saying they wished to write on Jane Jacobs's legacy, I would need no less than three journal issues. I am very grateful to the Editor in Chief of the *Journal of Architectural and Planning Research*, Professor Andrew Seidel, for graciously agreeing to let me switch from a journal to a book project.

As the project proceeded, I got to know, personally and via correspondence, a number of truly great scholars. Perhaps needless to say, this book is their book. Among them, I should single out my colleague Diane Zahm, whose insights are integrated throughout the book. I am very grateful to all my other colleagues at Virginia Tech, who have put up with me, with admirable patience, for eight years. As always, I would like to thank my mentors from the University of Michigan, Jonathan Levine and Robert Fishman.

Ann Rudkin, Editor of the Planning, History and Environment series of which this book is a part, did a supreme job organizing and editing the volume. My research assistant, Cynthia Lintz, was another invaluable member of the team.

I want to thank my parents, my husband Oliver and my three daughters, Diliana, Sofia and Maria, and all the other members of my family, on both sides of the Pond, for their love and support. You are the absolute the best!

Sonia Hirt
Blacksburg, 2012

The Contributors

Hassan Abdel-Salam is Professor of Architecture and Environmental Design at Alexandria University, where he teaches theory of architecture, criticism, urban design and sustainability. He is Ex-Dean of the Faculty of Architectural Engineering at Beirut Arab University where he held academic/teaching positions, and participated in several curricular development and quality assurance programmes, developing a broad experience in the fields of local urbanism, housing, and urban regeneration. His research is centred on contemporary architectural trends, environmentalism, local identity and contextualism. He is a member of the Editorial Board of *Urban Design International* and is Chief Editor of the *Architecture and Planning Journal* of Beirut Arab University.

Anirban Adhya is an Associate Professor in Architecture and Urban Design at the College of Architecture and Design at Lawrence Tech where he teaches integrated design studios and urban design theory and methods. He is a founding member of the SYNCH Research Group (synchRG), a systems-based critical research think-tank. He is also an active proponent of the Detroit Studio, the university's community outreach programme in the Detroit metropolitan region. Adhya's research focuses on everyday urbanism and architecture, sustainable placemaking and interdisciplinary approaches to critical questions related to the public realm. Adhya's research has been funded by institutes such as the American Institute of Architects (AIA Research Funding Program) and the University of Michigan (Marans Fellowship).

Jonathan Barnett is a Professor of City and Regional Planning and Director of the Urban Design Program at the University of Pennsylvania. He is also an urban design consultant, specializing in development regulations and other implementation measures. He has been an urban design advisor to more than twenty cities in the United States, as well as the cities of Xiamen and Tianjin in China, and he has prepared large-scale plans and projects in the United States, Cambodia, China and Korea. He is the author of numerous books and articles about urban design and planning, the most recent being: *Redesigning Cities* (2003), *Smart Growth in a Changing World* (2007), and *City Design, Modernist, Traditional, Green and Systems Perspectives* (2011). Jonathan Barnett is a graduate of Yale University and the University of Cambridge. He is a fellow of both the American Institute of Architects and the American Institute of Certified Planners. In 2007, he received the Dale Prize for Excellence in City and Regional Planning and has also been awarded the Athena Medal by the Congress for the New Urbanism.

Paul Cozens obtained a BA in Sustainable Environments in 1997 and was awarded a PhD in Crime and Design in 2000 (University of Glamorgan, UK). He is an environmental criminologist and expert in *Crime Prevention through Environmental Design* (CPTED) with over fifteen years experience in research, policy and practice. He was accredited as an Advanced CPTED Practitioner in 2004. Cozens developed Western Australia's *Designing out Crime Strategy* while working at the Department of the Premier and the Cabinet. He is currently Senior Lecturer at Curtin University's Department of Urban and Regional Planning. His research interests are in environmental criminology, CPTED, urban sustainability, the night-time economy and perceptions of crime. He recently published a book on the process of *Designing out Crime* for use by planners and designers.

Benjamin Fraser is Assistant Professor of Spanish at the College of Charleston and is currently the Managing Editor of the *Arizona Journal of Hispanic Cultural Studies*. A member of the Association of American Geographers (AAG) and the Modern Language Association (MLA), Fraser strives to synthesize approaches from the humanities and the social sciences. He is the author of over thirty published essays, and the monographs *Henri Lefebvre and the Spanish Urban Experience* (2011) and *Encounters with Bergson(ism) in Spain* (2010). He is also the editor/translator of *Deaf History and Culture in Spain* (2009).

Mindy Thompson Fullilove is a research psychiatrist at New York State Psychiatric Institute and a Professor of Clinical Psychiatry and Public Health at Columbia University. She was educated at Bryn Mawr College (AB, 1971) and Columbia University (MS, 1971; MD 1978). She is a board-certified psychiatrist, having received her training at New York Hospital-Westchester Division (1978–1981) and Montefiore Hospital (1981–1982). She has conducted research on AIDS and other epidemics in poor communities, with a special interest in the relationship between the collapse of communities and decline in health. She has published *Root Shock: How Tearing Up City Neighborhoods Hurts America and What We Can Do About It* (2004), and *The House of Joshua: Meditations on Family and Place* (2002). She is a co-author of *Ernest Thompson's Homeboy Came to Orange: A Story of People's Power* (1976) and Rodrick Wallace's *Collective Consciousness and Its Discontents* (2008). She has received many awards, including inclusion in many 'Best Doctors' and two honorary doctorates (Chatham College, 1999, and Bank Street College of Education, 2002). Her work on AIDS is featured in Jacob Levenson's *The Secret Epidemic: The Story of AIDS in Black America*.

David Hillier was until 2006 Professor and Head of Geography at the University of Glamorgan and is now Emeritus Professor attached to the Centre for Police Sciences at the University of Glamorgan. He graduated in 1969 with a BA in Human Geography from University College Wales, Aberystwyth. In 1971 he was awarded the degree of MA in Social Geography from the University of Sussex. In 1975 he was awarded a PhD from the University of Aberdeen for his study of human migration over a period of one hundred years. In 1986 he gained an MA in Criminology from the University of Hull. Hillier has published extensively on the condition and future of the British city over the last thirty years. His research on crime and the design of the city has attracted widespread attention and is currently used by such bodies as the Home Office, the police and the Australian government. This work has appeared in planning, geography, transport, marketing and business and management journals.

Sonia Hirt is Associate Dean of the College of Architecture and Urban Studies at Virginia Tech, where she teaches planning history and theory. She has served as a Visiting Associate Professor at the Graduate School of Design of Harvard University, where she taught Urbanism in Europe. Hirt's research focuses on the relationship between culture and the built environment. She has also published extensively on urbanism in post-socialist Eurasia. She is the author of *Iron Curtains: Gates, Suburbs and Privatization of Space in the Post-socialist City* (2012) and *Twenty Years of Transition: The Evolution of Urban Planning in Eastern Europe and the Former Soviet Union, 1989–2009* (2009, with Kiril Stanilov). Her research has been funded by organizations such as the American Council of Learned Societies, the American Association of University Women and the National Endowment for the Humanities.

Sanford Ikeda is an Associate Professor of Economics at the State University of New York, Purchase. He has contributed his expertise on entrepreneurship to the Mercatus Center's Katrina Project. While serving as President of the Society for the Development of Austrian Economics, Sanford Ikeda wrote *Dynamics of the Mixed Economy* and authored several articles on entrepreneurial activity and urban planning. He earned his PhD in economics from New York University and has previously held academic positions at the University of North Carolina at Chapel Hill and California State University at Hayward.

Paul Kidder is an Associate Professor of Philosophy and Director of the Core Honors Program at Seattle University, where he has taught courses on the history of philosophy, philosophical anthropology, existentialism, philosophy of art and architecture, business ethics, ethics in international development, and ethics in urban affairs. He has published articles in several of these areas. His work as an assistant at the 1987 Jane Jacobs conference at Boston College led to his long-standing interest in philosophy and urban affairs that has been part of his teaching and research ever since.

Marie-Alice L'Heureux is an Associate Professor of Architecture in the School of Architecture, Design, and Planning at the University of Kansas. She is a professional architect and teaches urban design and architecture and a range of seminars on the American cultural landscape, world cities, and urban history and theory. L'Heureux does research on politics, ideology, community, and the built environment and has published articles and presented papers in English and French about space and identity conflicts in the former Soviet Union, racial/ethnic/gender issues in the United States, and energy efficiency and sustainability in architecture and urban design. She has taught at the University of California, Berkeley; at the Ivan Franko University in Lviv, Ukraine; and at the International Ceramics Studio, Kecskemét, Hungary. Her recent research has been financed in part by the Hall Center Foundation and the Fulbright Scholars Program.

Ibrahim Maarouf is Assistant Professor of Architecture in the Department of Architecture at Alexandria University. From 2008 to 2010, he was in the Faculty of Architectural Engineering at Beirut Arab University, where he taught architectural design, construction, history of Islamic architecture, vernacularism, and urban planning. He is also an Assistant Professor in the Architectural Engineering Department at Pharos University, Alexandria. His research covers architectural heritage, urban design, and theory and history of architecture. As a member of the Committee of Higher Education Development in the Alexandria Region, he participates in academic development programmes. He is a referee for articles in the *Architecture and Planning Journal* of Beirut Arab University. Through his private practice, he has wide experience in designing projects in the Middle East.

Kan Nathiwutthikun holds a BA (1987) in Interior Architecture from King Mongkut's Institute of Technology, Ladkrabang and a Master's degree in Economics (2000) from Chiang Mai University. In 2008, she was awarded a PhD from the Faculty of Architecture, Chulalongkorn University. Her dissertation 'The Logic of Multi-Use of Public Open Spaces in Chiang Mai City' was sponsored by the 90th Anniversary of Chulalongkorn University Fund (Ratchadaphiseksomphot Endowment Fund). Presently, she is an instructor at Rajamangala University of Technology, Lanna. Her research interests are in the area of public open space, and sustainable design and planning. She received an award in the Chiang Mai Public Open Space competition in 2006 and in the Revitalize the Old competition in 2008 from the Lanna Association of Siamese Architects.

Saskia Sassen is the Robert S. Lynd Professor of Sociology and Co-Chair of The Committee on Global Thought at Columbia University. Her recent books are *Territory, Authority, Rights: From Medieval to Global Assemblages* (2008), *A Sociology of Globalization* (2007), and the fourth fully updated edition of *Cities in a World Economy* (2011). Her books are translated into twenty-one languages. She is currently working on *When Territory Exits Existing Frameworks*. She contributes regularly to www.OpenDemocracy.net and www.HuffingtonPost.com.

James Stockard is an expert in affordable housing and community development. As a principal for over twenty-five years with the Cambridge, MA consulting firm Stockard & Engler & Brigham, he has worked with non-profit groups and public agencies across the United States on such issues as affordable housing development, property management, and neighbourhood revitalization. Shortly before coming to Harvard, he served as the court-appointed Special Master for the Department of Public and Assisted Housing in Washington DC. Stockard has taught courses on housing policy at MIT's School of Architecture, Tufts University, and the Graduate School of Design at Harvard. He is the co-author of *Managing Affordable Housing*, and wrote the epilogue in

New Directions in Urban Public Housing. He was the Principal Investigator for the *Public Housing Operating Cost Study* commissioned by the U.S. Congress. He has served as a Commissioner of the Cambridge Housing Authority for thirty years (including six terms as chair), and is a founding Trustee of the Cambridge Affordable Housing Trust Fund. He is a past president of the Citizens Housing and Planning Association.

Emily Talen is a Professor of Geography in the School of Geographical Sciences and Urban Planning at Arizona State University, where she is also the Director of the Phoenix Urban Research Lab. She was formerly a Professor of Urban Planning at the University of Illinois, Urbana-Champaign. She is the co-editor of the *Journal of Urbanism*. Talen's books include: *Urban Design Reclaimed: Tools, Techniques and Strategies for Planners* (2009), *Design for Diversity: Exploring Socially Mixed Neighborhoods* (2008), and *New Urbanism and American Planning: The Conflict of Cultures* (2005). She teaches courses on urban form, the history and theory of planning, and environmental design. Her research has been funded by organizations such as the National Endowment for the Arts, the Graham Foundation for Advanced Studies in the Fine Arts, and the Driehaus Foundation.

B.D. Wortham-Galvin is an Assistant Professor in the Department of Architecture at Portland State University and founder and Director of the non-profit Urban Dialogues, Inc. With degrees in American Studies, Anthropology, Historic Preservation and Architecture from Brown University, University of Pennsylvania, University of Maryland and the Massachusetts Institute of Technology, she teaches on a wide variety of subjects including urban and architectural design, history and theory, adaptive reuse, public interest design, and the intersection between sustainability and the everyday American built environment. Her scholarship focuses on how theories of cultural sustainability and the everyday can be applied to the design and stewardship of the built environment. Urban Dialogues, Inc., in partnership with the Eastern Shore Land Conservancy, won the 2009 Outstanding Project of the Year Award from the Heart of Chesapeake Country Heritage Area Program for its place workshops.

Jing Xie is a PhD candidate in architecture and urban design at the University of New South Wales where he teaches design studios. His interests are in the study of mixed-use development in history. He investigates the social meanings of space in a broad historical and cultural context. Jing has been practicing architecture and urban design in Australia and China since 1996.

Diane Zahm is Co-chair of the Department of Urban Affairs and Planning at the College of Architecture and Urban Studies at Virginia Tech, where she teaches land-use planning and policy. Her research examines land use, site layout and facility design, and their long-term impact on crime, fear and neighbourhood viability. She produced a monograph/handbook for the U.S. Department of Justice's Problem-Oriented Policing Center on 'Using Crime Prevention through Environmental Design as a Problem-Solving Tool'. Zahm has served as an Research Associate at Florida State

University's School of Criminology and Criminal Justice; Statistical Analysis Center Administrator for the Florida Department of Law Enforcement (FDLE); Research and Training Specialist for the Florida Attorney General's Crime Prevention through Environmental Design Program; Assistant Professor of Community Development and Instructor at the National Crime Prevention Institute of the University of Louisville; and Grants Analyst for the City of Charlottesville, Virginia.

Chapter 1

Jane Jacobs, Urban Visionary[1]

Sonia Hirt

If the President of the American Planning Association were to follow the example of the British Crown and bestow the honour of a knighthood on the most meritorious community members, Jane Jacobs would have become a Dame long ago.[2] After all, Jacobs is occasionally referred to as 'folk hero', 'Queen Jane', 'Saint Jane' and 'Jane of New York'.[3] Such statements of near-religious worship cannot, of course, be taken seriously. There is, however, little doubt that Jacobs is one of the most influential thinkers who contributed to the revolutionary intellectual currents of the 1960s and 1970s, along with Thomas Kuhn, Ian McHarg, Rachel Carson, Betty Friedan, John Rawls, to name a few. It has become customary to associate these authors with a 'paradigm shift' in some aspect of human thought and practice. According to Max Page, the term applies well to the impact of Jacobs's works and activism: after mistakes in urban renewal practices were laid bare in the 1960s, the city-building paradigm changed 'not slowly and steadily but rapidly and radically, with Jane Jacobs leading the campaign' (Page, 2011, p. 7).

Jacobs is ranked no. 1 on the list of urban thinkers of all time according to *Planetizen*, a popular urban planning website. These rankings were the result of an online poll, in which Jacobs received an 'impossibly wide lead' above her competitors.[4] True, we sometimes hear dissenting voices – 'enough with Jane Jacobs already' (Manshel, 2010) and 'outgrowing Jane Jacobs' (Ouroussoff, 2006) – but these remain in the minority. In fact, based on the number of citations, fifty years after the publication of her most famous book, *The Death and Life of Great American Cities* (1961), Jacobs's influence has only been growing with time (Harris, 2011).

I am saying all this not to advertise Jacobs (she clearly does not need it) or to advertise this book (which clearly does need it), but to ask why, among urban planners, designers and others who claim expertise on cities, her popularity is peculiar, since she was not particularly kind to them. But she was exceptionally kind to their subject, cities, and this may hold the secret to her appeal.

My colleague Diane Zahm and I put this volume together hoping to understand better why Jacobs's legacy persists. Is her reputation warranted? What did she bring to the way we think not 'just' about cities but about society and space?

We organized the contributions in four groups: I. Jacobs, Urban Philosopher; II. Jacobs, Urban Economist; III. Jacobs, Urban Sociologist; and IV. Jacobs, Urban Designer. This disciplinary division was not easy. Jacobs disliked specialized knowledge and what she had to say never fits into neat disciplinary boxes. This may be why so many find her work appealing. We did not include a part on Jacobs as a planner. This is because it seems that her impact on planning – itself an inter-disciplinary field – has been exerted not only directly but also through her influence on philosophy, economics, sociology, design, etc. In this sense, all chapters fit under 'Jacobs, Urban Planner'. We could envision a different, conceptual/empirical division. Some of the chapters discuss Jacobs's influence on an entire discipline (e.g. Jonathan Barnett's chapter on design), or on concepts that permeate the core debates within a discipline (e.g. Sanford Ikeda's presentation on the 'Jacobsonian' view of economic development and Emily Talen's on 'design for diversity'); whereas others attempt – empirically or through a review of the literature – to substantiate or refute particular Jacobs's propositions (e.g. Paul Cozens and David Hillier's critical query into the connection between Jacobs's idea of 'eyes on the street' and safety). We believe, however, that the grouping of chapters we have chosen emphasizes more than other books Jacobs's intellectual breadth.

In short, what do the chapters tell us? To begin with, Jacobs was certainly a philosopher. We could guess this from the fact that she explicitly moved in this direction in her later years; two of her last books, *Systems of Survival* (1992) and *Dark Age Ahead* (2004), are statements on political philosophy. After all, philosophers write about three things: the good, the true and the beautiful and Jacobs hit them all. Paul Kidder argues that Jacobs made a major contribution to philosophy by exploring the balance between the good and the right. In my chapter, I discuss how Jacobs arrived at her notion of what is true. Ben Fraser seeks to prove Jacobs's influence on philosophy by pointing to her influence on two prominent philosophers: Lefebvre and Delgado Ruiz. James Stockard's lively essay is not technically on philosophy but implicitly applies Jacobs's ideas of right and good – the ones discussed by Kidder – to planning and citizen participation.

Part II comprises two chapters: one by Sanford Ikeda showing how Jacobs countered prevailing wisdom in economics by arguing that cities are a major cause of economic development (rather than a spatial artefact that occurs at a certain point of economic development), and one by Saskia Sassen which speculatively explores what Jacobs would have seen in present-day debates of the global city – one of the hottest topics in economic geography today.

The third part on Jacobs and sociology includes two essays dealing with a crucial issue in sociology: race, space and inequality. The authors, Marie-Alice L'Heureux and Mindy Fullilove, somewhat disagree. L'Heureux appears to support Herbert Gans's (1968) claim that Jacobs underestimated the structural obstacles surrounding African Americans, whereas Fullilove takes a more positive view of Jacobs's legacy by focusing on the role that space plays in transforming social relations.

Jacobs's influence on urban design comprises the largest part of the book. Part IV starts with Emily Talen's evaluation of Jacobs's contribution to a key topic in this field: designing cities to promote social diversity. Talen asks a question that has cast a long shadow on designers: if serendipity and flexibility are part of good urban form, much as Jacobs, Christopher Alexander (1965) and Richard Sennet (1970) argued, can it be *designed*? Talen's piece is followed by three empirical attempts to answer this question, all in cities outside of the USA. Jing Xie's essay on medieval China gears towards answering this question in the negative. In Xie's view, there is no straightforward connection between spatial configurations and human activity. The essay implicitly supports Jacobs's claim that rigid intentional ordering of space does not produce better urbanism but challenges her position that space and behaviour are tightly related. By taking us to Beirut and Chiang Mai respectively, Ibrahim Maarouf and Hassan Abdel-Salam, and Kan Nathiwutthikun take a more benign view of Jacobs. Maarouf and Abdel-Salam apply Jacobs's proposition of the four 'generators' of urban diversity (mixed uses, short blocks, aged buildings and concentration) to central Beirut, ultimately claiming that the proposition holds true. Nathiwutthikun's piece offers a perspective that is in short supply in the literature: it concretely operationalizes the diversity of human activities and assesses whether Jacobs's spatial 'generators' of diversity impact these activities in the way she would have expected. Paul Cozens and David Hillier's chapter challenges one of Jacobs's most famous theses: that collective security can be achieved through having people (and their 'eyes on the street') in vibrant public spaces. The next three essays, although technically on urban design, take us implicitly back to the philosophical concepts of the start of the book. Anirban Adhya connects Jacobs's thinking to design paradigms popular today, such as sustainable urbanism and placemaking. But beneath the design focus lurk bigger, philosophical questions of how people know and construct the world around them. Similarly, B.D. Wortham-Galvin's contribution on design as cultural practice touches upon deeper issues of people, power and knowledge. Jonathan Barnett's text comprehensively synthesizes Jacobs's contribution to urban design and planning, which warrants its position as a concluding chapter.

Let us now return to the original questions driving this project. What explains Jacobs's lasting appeal? Is her influence justified? Was she right? What was the most important theme she addressed? Where was she wrong? And, although Jacobs is best known for her work on cities, are we correct in saying that she was a broader thinker and this may be the key to her lasting legacy?

The following partial answers seem to emerge. First, Jacobs was an author of big, paradigm-shifting ideas and not 'just' on cities. Far from being a 'victim' of mere, even 'extreme empiricism' – long the conventional wisdom and still held by some today (Roweis, 2004) – Jacobs was a theory-builder who asked big questions about society and space but gave only a general direction for the answers (Harris, 2011). I am more sympathetic to those who accuse her of unsystematic research than those who accuse her of being averse to theory. Jacobs's work is significant because it produced path-breaking 'starting points' for new research, in the terminology of her contemporaries Glaser and Strauss (1967). It is not the type of work focused on empirical verification/ falsification of existing theories (although she certainly sought to refute some). Xie's and Nathiwutthikun's chapters are examples of verification/falsification work; Jacobs's writings belong in another category. The 'big ideas' along with the fact that Jacobs appears to have proposed several of them generally ahead of others, as Barnett shows, qualifies her for the 'urban visionary' label.

Now, some of her ideas continue to be controversial (e.g. Ikeda illustrates how Jacobs went against conventional wisdom on cities and economic development and her argument is still a subject of controversy). Jacobs proposed but sometimes lacked the rigour to prove her ideas. She overstated the role of space in shaping behaviour (as Xie, Cozens and Hillier, and Wortham-Galvin argue, partially in the footsteps of Gans). But that seems to be the faith of big thinkers: they give the genesis of big and controversial starting points for others to prove or disprove.[5] I am not sure which of Jacobs's ideas was 'biggest'. But from the chapters in this volume, it seems that her 'discovery' of the functional and normative value of diversity as a necessary component of successful, self-organizing and complex systems comes very high on the list. Along with this conceptual contribution, she also made an important methodological one. She shifted the scale of analysis and interpretation: from abstract to concrete; from statistically 'representative' to everyday; from bird's eye view to street level; from coldly 'scientific' to warm and human. She shifted the way we *view* cities and other things around us (as Adhya's chapter explains). No wonder a very good recent volume on Jacobs is titled *What We See* (Goldsmith and Lynne, 2010). Jacobs's humanization of the object of analysis and narration[6] is most evident in *The Death and Life*, but she puts it succinctly in one of her best signature phrases, which she used during a speech at Harvard: 'A store is also a storekeeper' (1956).

Jacobs may have been wrong on some issues (e.g. in overemphasizing the role of local, physical agency in changing societal, structural conditions), but some of her ardent followers have taken this flaw to an extreme (e.g. the New Urbanists in their confidence they can produce better society through better architecture, as argued by Wortham-Galvin). At least Jacobs, even in her old age and having acquired a near-beatification status, retained a sense of modesty. Writing to New York's Mayor, she introduced herself simply: 'Dear Mayor Bloomberg: My name is Jane Jacobs. I am a student of cities.' Perhaps she would have appreciated this label, 'student of cities', more than the 'urban visionary' stuff.

Notes

1. This is also the title of Alexiou's book (2006).
2. This is not just a joke. Lewis Mumford became a Knight Commander of the Order of the British Empire in 1975 and Peter Hall in 1998, both for services to town planning.
3. http://www.theamericanconservative.com/blog/janejacobs/ and http://www.planninghistory.org/JJ_Flyer_mail.pdf. Accessed 13 December 2011. The last label I heard used earnestly by a colleague.
4. http://www.planetizen.com/topthinkers. Accessed 13 December 2011.
5. Think about some of the present-day authors in the socio-spatial professions, say, Andrés Duany, Rem Koolhaas, David Harvey. They are exactly the authors of big, controversial ideas.
6. Of course, Jacobs's narrative style also has a lot to do with her appeal (Rowan, 2011).

References

Alexander, C. (1965) The city is not a tree. *Architectural Forum*, No. 122(1), pp. 58–62 and No. 122(2), pp. 58–62.

Alexiou, A. (2006) *Jane Jacobs: Urban Visionary*. New Brunswick, NJ: Rutgers University Press.

Gans, H. (1968) Urban vitality and the fallacy of physical determinism, in *People and Plans: Essays on Urban Problems and Solutions*. New York: Basic Books, pp. 25–33.

Glaser, B. and Strauss, A. (1967) *The Discovery of Grounded Theory*. New York: Aldine.

Goldsmith, S. and Lynne, E. (eds.) (2010) *What We See: Advancing the Observations of Jane Jacobs*. Oakland, CA: New Village Press.

Harris, R. (2011) The magpie and the bee: Jane Jacobs's magnificent obsession, in Page, M. and Mennel, T. (eds.) *Revisiting Jane Jacobs*. Chicago, IL: Planners Press, 65–83.

Jacobs, J. (1956) In urban design: condensed report of an invitation conference sponsored by the faculty and alumni association of Graduate School of Design, Harvard University, *Progressive Architecture*, August, pp. 97–112.

Jacobs, J. (1961) *The Death and Life of Great American Cities*. New York: Random House.

Jacobs, J. (1992) *Systems of Survival: A Dialogue on the Moral Foundations of Commerce and Politics*. New York: Random House.

Jacobs, J. (2004) *Dark Age Ahead*. New York: Random House.

Jacobs, J. (2005) Letter to Mayor Bloomberg and the City Council. Accessed on 31 July 2011 at http://www.brooklynrail.org/2005/05/local/letter-to-mayor-bloomberg.

Manshel, A. (2010). Enough with Jane Jacobs already. *The Wall Street Journal*, 29 June.

Ouroussoff, N. (2006) Outgrowing Jane Jacobs and her New York. *The New York Times*, 30 April.

Page, M. (2011) Introduction: more than meets the eye, in Page, M. and Mennel, T. (eds.) *Revisiting Jane Jacobs*. Chicago, IL: Planners Press, pp. 3–14.

Rowan, J. (2011) The literary craft of Jane Jacobs, in Page, M. and Mennel, T. (eds.) *Revisiting Jane Jacobs*. Chicago, IL: Planners Press, pp. 43–57.

Roweis, S. (2004) *Jane Jacobs' Déjà Lu: Thoughts and Notes on Jane Jacobs, Dark Age Ahead, 2004*. Available at http://www.oocities.org/planningaction@rogers.com/library/JacobsReviewRoweis.pdf. Accessed 30 April 2012.

Sennet, R. (1970) *Uses of Disorder*. New York: Knopf.

Part I

Jane Jacobs, Urban Philosopher

Chapter 2

The Right and the Good in Jane Jacobs's Urbanism

Paul Kidder

If Jane Jacobs's writings on cities have proved to have a lasting power in American culture, it is not only because they contain helpful ideas on the nature of neighbourhoods, the design of buildings, or the dynamics of the urban economy. On the contrary, the longevity of Jacobs's legacy can to a large extent be explained by the fact that these writings, along with Jacobs herself, have for many years functioned as a powerful moral beacon. In this chapter, I discuss how in her classic trio of urban works *The Death and Life of Great American Cities* (1993, 1961), *The Economy of Cities* (1969) and *Cities and the Wealth of Nations* (1984), Jacobs implicitly addressed issues of what 'right' and what 'good' are in a broad, moral or ethical way. Far from being statements on 'good' or 'right' in cities in the practical sense (e.g. what makes cities wealthier or more pleasant places to be), these books in fact present powerful arguments on the ethical underpinnings of what we call liberal democracy. It is the clarity, integrity and broad appeal of these arguments, I believe, that ultimately endowed Jacobs's activities of civil protest and disobedience with a moral legitimacy so powerful that today her actions are commonly seen as contributing to the justification of civil disobedience itself. Like other great American activists, such as Thoreau or Martin Luther King, Jr, Jacobs will forever remind us of the power of a single person to rekindle the moral conscience of many.

The Death and Life of Great American Cities, *The Economy of Cities*, and *Cities and the Wealth of Nations*, I argue, offer fruitful grounds for discussions in philosophy, political theory, and ethics. In the 1980s, after Jacobs turned to writing explicitly on the subject of ethics, she also came to recognize the implicitly ethical character of the work she had done in this trilogy of urban books. Writing in the 1993 preface to the Modern Library edition of *The Death and Life*, Jacobs gives a definition of a 'city ecosystem' parallel to that of a natural ecosystem:

A natural ecosystem is defined as 'composed of physical-chemical-biological processes active within a space-time unit of any magnitude'. A city ecosystem is composed of physical-economic-

ethical [author's italics] processes active at a given time within a city and its close dependencies. (Jacobs, 1993, p. xvi)

By explicitly pointing to the ethical dimension of urban ecosystems, Jacobs acknowledges that ethical considerations are relevant across the whole range of a city's life and development.

The following pages offer an interpretive study of certain features of the moral theorizing that is implicit in Jacobs's urban writing and activism. I specifically examine the features that pertain to the classic question of the relationship between 'the right' and 'the good' in a liberal democracy.

Liberal democracy is often defined as a system that gives priority of the right over the good; that is, liberal democracy is a system that lays down certain principles of justice, equality, liberty, and certain rights that are necessary for people to live fairly with one another, while seeking to minimize prescriptions as to *how*, in particular, citizens *should* live. Its goal is to allow citizens to decide for themselves how they should make a living, which cultural and religious views they should hold and express, which qualities of character they should cultivate, which associations they should join, and which pastimes they should pursue. These individual choices pertain to 'the good'. They form (in John Rawls's terms) a comprehensive doctrine regarding the nature of a 'good' human life (McCarthy, 1996; Rawls, 1996, pp. 13, 58–61). To say that the right has a priority over the good, then, is to say that no person, organization, or government should prevent a citizen's pursuit of his or her own comprehensive view of the good life unless that pursuit interferes with the ability of other citizens to pursue theirs. In some scholarly formulations, the state is said to be neutral regarding questions of the good except when harm or unjustified infringement is involved (Rawls, 1999, pp. 27–30; Sandel, 1982, pp. 1–7). To give a concrete example: a liberal democratic state cannot (and should not) prescribe a particular religion for its citizens as the 'good' religion; however, it can (and should) guarantee that all citizens can practice freely the religions they deem 'good' and without a fear of penalty.

While the right has priority in a liberal democracy, it is normal to value, in such a democracy, a robust public discourse on what good is. Although some questions regarding the human good are ultimately irresolvable by rational debate, a democratic society should still seek to engage in rational debate to the extent possible. A healthy liberal order, then, generally seeks some balance of the right and the good, giving the right a degree of priority, while seeking to build citizen consensus on the good.

Questions regarding the relationship of the right and the good are familiar to philosophers and political theorists, but they are also relevant to many other fields, including those of urban planning, design, and architecture. The extraordinary diversity of backgrounds, occupations, and interests that come together in cities demands an extraordinary degree of tolerance and mutual respect; hence cities intensify the rationale for defending the priority of the right over a particular version of the good. Yet, it can be argued that it takes much more than neutral tolerance to create a vibrant and appealing urban life. Cities need strong visions of the good. They need a vital public realm where the values expressed in law and cemented in custom are debated. Citizens need interactions that help them build a sense of community, with its potential for mutual support, public discourse, and common action. They need forums where concerns over annoyances, threats, development opportunities, aesthetic improvements, and a host of related issues can be discussed. All of these desirable features of urban life are, arguably, qualities of the good rather than the right. When people live in the kind of close proximity that cities create, they cannot simply leave one another alone; they must take advantage of the ways in which their lives inevitably intertwine and turn these interactions into something positive. Cities, then, augment the need to promote both the right and the good: they must allow for a variety of independent choices but must also serve as a spatial background in which particular common positions are pursued. In other words, cities provide the *right* to choose individual lifestyles, but also the opportunity to pursue some version of a shared *good*.

The fact that Jacobs's urban works contain a complex set of interrelations between the right and the good has often been overlooked. Those who draw upon her works often do so selectively, with an eye to promoting a particular political position or type of urban development rather than engaging with the full and complex range of her thought. Designers often focus on the types of land-use mix she advocates; preservationists often invoke her arguments for urban infill development; environmentalists often praise her call for pedestrian-friendly cities and local economies; and libertarians often repeat her charges against large-scale, government-run projects. As a result, it is not unusual to hear Jacobs's work used to argue both sides of an issue: e.g. to hear her name used by people who, say, support a project that replaces a 'grey' area of the city with a mixed fabric of residences, small businesses and parks, and by people who are opposed to the very same project because the planned development would, ostensibly, cause displacement and has been prepared by government planners rather than the community itself. Note that the proponents of the two sides of this debate interpret Jacobs quite differently. The first side takes Jacobs's ideas of what makes good city form (e.g. mixed land uses), whereas the second side takes issue with the way plans were prepared (i.e. top-down instead of bottom-up). The contradiction is between Jacobs prescribing outcomes as opposed to Jacobs prescribing process. But this is the same as saying that the contradiction is between Jacobs as a theorist of the 'good' (what makes cities good) versus Jacobs as a theorist of what makes them 'right' (what makes them places where the rights of citizens to pursue their individual visions of the good are not threatened by an all-controlling 'big government').

Is this a misuse of Jacobs? Or are her works naturally conducive to such contradicting interpretations? I argue that while Jacobs seemingly sets up the ground for conflicting interpretations of what is primary – the good or the right – she consistently endorses the liberal principles of individual and communal self-determination; she endorses the right over the good. Therefore, she is a clear proponent of liberal democracy. But Jacobs never loses sight of the fact that the right exists for the sake of the good. Liberal principles only come to fruition when visions of the good are realized concretely. In this sense, Jacobs's ethical vision is complex rather than outright contradictory. For her, the right and the good are involved in a complex interaction that relies more emphatically on one or the other at different moments and in different circumstances. These circumstances must always be considered in their specificity; abstract prescriptions of 'right' or 'good', according to Jacobs, are doomed to fail.

The following sections develop my argument. I first focus on these aspects of the right and the good that Jacobs advocates. Specifically, I first review how Jacobs places priority on the right over the good (i.e. I highlight her role as a proponent of liberal democracy). I follow with a discussion on her version of the urban good. Then, I explore some seeming contradictions in Jacobs's thought (i.e. how can she provide detailed prescriptions of the urban good, while at the same time arguing that any such prescription can only be provided by citizens pursuing their individual versions of the urban good?). In the next section, I offer a way of explaining and potentially resolving this seeming contradiction by pointing out that Jacobs criticizes the overly abstract versions of the right and the good as they manifested themselves in the urban practices and policies that she so passionately opposed.

Jacobs as an Advocate for Liberal Democracy

That Jacobs endorses the fundamental principles of liberal democracy can be seen in the stances she takes on a great variety of issues. Not only does she explicitly defend individual and community freedom and autonomy, but she thinks about the social (and even physical) structures that help to preserve that freedom and autonomy in very concrete terms. Jacobs's liberal-democratic convictions are perhaps most fully realized in her advocacy of urban diversity. A city is a vital place when it allows for a diversity of communities, occupations, business ventures, types of buildings, types of uses, etc. Cities which seek cultural assimilation, commercial homogenization, and a bland uniformity in design embrace, in Jacobs's view, a recipe for failure. The vitality derived from diversity makes the city an interesting place to live and work. More importantly, however, diversity carries with it the intrinsic value of freedom; diversity is a consequence of freedom. Diversity is also a means of sustaining and expanding freedoms; genuine freedom requires not merely the absence of constraints, but also the presence of a range of options and opportunities from which to choose. Diversity is, then, also a prerequisite of freedom. From this perspective, the liberal virtue of toleration is not merely a price that is paid for one's own liberty; rather, it reflects recognition of the many values that result from diversity in communities. 'Cities have the capability of providing something for everybody,' Jacobs writes, 'only because, and only when, they are created by everybody' (1993, p. 312).

These liberal-democratic sentiments are evident in Jacobs's opposition to urban developments that are planned in a strict and purposefully non-diverse fashion; i.e. in her opposition to mono-functional and mono-stylistic developments. Her famous claim that 'a city is not a work of art' represents a demand that city dwellers be given the freedom to make their own aesthetic choices and establish their distinctive ways of interacting with the urban environment (1993, p. 485). Designers who try to anticipate and plan for every kind of activity may actually inhibit the very activities that they are trying to promote. Jacobs attributes this failure to the abstract nature of the planning process, which tends to rely on statistical averages (rather than on specific individual and community needs) and has traditionally endorsed the separation of land uses. Jacobs finds that the most synergistic urban forms occur in spaces where different uses and activities intersect. In claiming that the city is not a work of art, Jacobs is of course not saying that the arts are not essential to urban life; rather, she is saying that the city is many works of art rather than one – as many artistic endeavours, indeed, as there are citizens.

In the context of urban politics, Jacobs's advocacy of liberal democracy can be seen clearly from her recommendations of how neighbourhoods and city governments should interact. The residents of city neighbourhoods have unique insights and knowledge of their particular needs; thus, they are the ones who have the capacity to come up with the most appropriate planning visions. However, it is the city administration that often has the power to make these neighbourhood visions happen. Therefore, the political function of what Jacobs calls the 'district' (units composed, she says, of 100,000 people or more in the largest cities) is to mediate these two functions:

Districts have to help bring the resources of a city down to where they are needed by street neighborhoods, and they have to help translate the experiences of real life, in street neighborhoods, into policies and purposes of their city as a whole. (Jacobs, 1993, p. 159)

This model can be said to be democratic in that the political structures give citizens a powerful voice in the distribution of municipal resources. Jacobs emphasizes the importance of strong district organizations that draw together the full range of neighbourhoods. Without these diverse voices, there may be only a representative democracy (in the sense that citizens can vote for city officials and ballot measures) but not a participatory democracy – the type that allows citizens the opportunity to self-govern.

Another, social dimension of liberal-democratic thinking is present in Jacobs's advocacy. It is what sociologists have come to call 'the strength of weak ties'. *The Death and Life* emphasizes the value of casual but regular interactions among neighbours and other citizens – interactions that are substantial enough to generate a sense of care and solidarity but not strong enough to entail the demands of friendship. In such relationships we find the seeds of association that are necessary for collective action in a democracy. According to Jacobs, many elements must be in place for such relationships to develop. Of those, the opportunity for face-to-face contact in the course of conducting everyday activities near the home is among the most essential (1993, pp. 72 ff.). When most activities are done by car, or happen far from home, the opportunities that residents have for getting to know their neighbours are limited.

They must settle for some form of 'togetherness,' in which more is shared with one another than in the life of the sidewalks, or else they must settle for lack of contact … and either [outcome] has distressing results.

The latter option is obviously no basis for building solidarity; the former is limited in this regard because there are only so many connections one can maintain with that degree of purposefulness.

Jacobs's subsequent two books could be said to explore the economic implications of her liberal democratic ideals. Perhaps the strongest emphasis in *The Economy of Cities* is on the importance of fostering an urban environment that permits citizens to chart their own economic course and pursue innovation. Cities where people find the freedom and opportunity to begin new ventures on a shoestring budget will not only have a more satisfied creative class, but will reap the economic rewards from those ventures. In *Cities and the Wealth of Nations*, Jacobs includes an analogous case for the importance of economic freedom and autonomy for cities themselves. Cities function as economic units and engines in ways that a national economy, taken as a whole, does not (1984, pp. 31–44). Therefore, Jacobs makes a case for the freedom of city administrations to consider their internal economies in terms of imports and exports, set their own economic agendas, and seek to interact with the higher levels of government with an eye towards urban economic and political autonomy (1984, pp. 156 ff.). The routine way in which we think of state and federal policies as having an overriding, controlling and homogenizing role falls far short of Jacobs's notions of freedom and self-rule as the building blocks of democracy.

These examples (which are by no means exhaustive) clearly show that Jacobs is an advocate for liberal democracy who consistently asserts the priority of the right over the good. For her, individual, local and community decisions and the diversity that they produce take primacy over any general prescription of how cities function or should function. But matters become more complicated when she approaches the question of the good. After all, if a diversity of individual and local choices is always to be welcome, how can one decide which are the 'good' choices? How can one be sure that anything – including Jacobs's own views of mixed land uses, street patterns, etc., and even the very notion of diversity itself – is 'good'?

Jacobs and the Question of the Urban Good

A good city, for Jacobs, is one that builds upon the vitality that is unique to concentrated urban populations. At the heart of this vitality is an active public realm. The ordinary, decent ways in which people conduct their daily business, when done in public, shape relationships and establish standards of community conduct. Everything that Jacobs says about designing streets, organizing districts, providing local amenities, and creating economic opportunities serves to promote a vital urban community. The vitality that stems from urban concentration is, according to Jacobs, what makes the city a great and fascinating place, what makes it able to undertake forms of production requiring a complex set of inputs and leading to a complex set of outputs, and what makes it capable of sustaining copious and ambitious forms of artistic enterprise (1969, pp.188–190). For example, it is for the sake of the vital community that Jacobs advocates mixed uses and architectural designs that put 'eyes on the street' (1993, pp. 44–51). Such physical features activate public space in ways that allow neighbourhoods to accommodate strangers without sacrificing safety. For the sake of the vital community, Jacobs stresses the important role of 'public characters' – the shop owners, the neighbourhood regulars, the 'hop-and-skip' neighbours who know many different people for many different kinds of reasons – in creating a network of communication and mutual trust (1993, pp. 91–92, 174–178; Byrne, 1989).

In addition to her particular view of the public realm and community life, Jacobs also offers commentaries on the 'good' as it pertains to the structure of family life. The emergence of purely residential zones, for example, separates work life from family life. Further, it tends to separate the genders: men spend their days in downtowns, rather than in the (suburban) neighbourhoods where their children are raised; whereas women remain excluded, to some extent, from active participation in civic and business life by virtue of their place of residence (1993, pp. 109 ff.). There is certainly more than a hint of feminism in Jacobs's criticism of the suburban isolation of women in the strictly zoned metropolis. She anticipates the charge of liberal feminism that to be separated out in this way is not to be spared the urban world of work, but to be denied it.

If feminism can be discerned in Jacobs's vision of the urban good, so, too, can environmentalism. Cities use fewer resources when neighbourhoods have places of work, services, retail, and residences mixed together and accessible by foot or public transportation. Jacobs critiqued, at a very early point, the low-density and single-use settlement patterns that have caused unsustainable resource use, pollution, and natural habitat destruction across the United States. One should note that Jacobs was also quite focused on the potential benefits of recycling. In the *Economy of Cities*, she praises examples of the use of solid waste in creating building materials, the processing of garbage into compost, the recovery of sulphuric acid and fly ash from factory emissions, and the recycling of waste paper (1969, pp. 107–117). In the late 1960s, recycling efforts of this sort were relatively rare – a point that illustrates, once again, Jacobs's pioneering vision.

Jacobs values good cities because of the immediate and practical benefits they deliver to their citizens, but also because they serve as settings where people can attain intrinsic values of mutual respect and sacrifice. In this line of thought, Jacobs echoes a long tradition of virtue ethics that goes back to Plato and Aristotle, and was revived in the late twentieth century by diverse thinkers such as Alasdair MacIntyre (1981; 1988), Bernard Lonergan (1996), and Martha Nussbaum (2000). For Jacobs, the city is a place where characters are formed, or as Hadley Arkes has put it, 'a place where people learn the lessons of propriety and self-control' (Arkes, 1981, p. 3). From friendships with people who contribute to the success of the community one learns not only practical but also intrinsic values related to pursuing lives dedicated to worthwhile, altruistic goals (see Arendt, 1958; Byrne, 1989; Honohan, 2002; McCarthy, 1996).

Distinctive in Jacobs's work, however, is the consistent pattern of seeing values, habits, and qualities of character as tied to specific patterns of interaction and exchange. In her 1993 introduction to *The Death and Life*, she made this point by distinguishing between 'car people' and 'foot people'. Jacobs's books seem to be written with a heavy preference towards 'foot people' – people who tend to organize their lives around pedestrian and mass-transit travel (if circumstances permit it).

This book was instantly understood by foot people... They recognized that what it said jibed with their own enjoyment, concerns, and experiences, which is hardly surprising, since much of the book's information came from observing and listening to foot people. They were collaborators in the research. Then, reciprocally, the book collaborated with foot people by giving legitimacy to what they already knew for themselves... Conversely, the book neither collaborated with car people nor had an influence on them. It still does not, as far as I can see. (1993, p. xii)

In her later, explicitly ethical writings, Jacobs broadened her idea of the interconnection of values and ways of life by identifying two fundamental systems of values: one set, called 'commercial values', is cultivated in lives dominated by patterns of commercial exchange; the other set, 'guardian values', is found in lives engaged in the task of governing and collaborating with others in ways to promote some version of a shared, community good. According to this typology, the values that Jacobs first witnessed among her Greenwich Village neighbours are associated with the 'commercial' ways of life. But once that way of life came under attack by governing interventions, neighbours turned into political activists and 'traders' eventually learned to embrace the values of the guardian way of life (Jacobs, 1989a, p. 274; Jacobs, 1992; Kidder, 2008).

The above examples show that Jacobs takes a clear normative stand; she advocates very specific positions regarding what comprises the urban good. Far from being neutral, she in fact endorses particular types of urban structure (e.g. integrated urban neighbourhoods that are rich in public spaces) and particular social values (e.g. those aligned with feminism, environmentalism, and an active public realm).

A Contradictory Position?

Much of the value that Jacobs's works have had for planners, designers, and architects derives from the fact that her vision of the urban good is a very detailed one. This is because Jacobs's advocacy of particular physical structures translates so easily into prescriptions for urban development projects, building designs, blocks and street layouts, strategies for transportation, and historic preservation initiatives. Over time, Jacobs's ideas regarding preservation, mixed use, short city blocks, etc., have appeared in neighbourhood and citywide plans, as well as in federal projects. They have worked their way into city design guidelines and building codes and have influenced all sorts of planning paradigms: New Urbanism, downtown revitalization, historic preservation, transit-oriented development, etc. (see, for example, Calthorpe, 1993; Carmona et al., 2003; Downs, 1994; Garvin, 1996; Gratz, 1994 and 1998). Indeed, in some American cities, a striking amount of what I have characterized as Jacobs's vision of the urban good has been virtually written into law.

But here is where one encounters the curious phenomenon of Jacobs being argued on two sides of an issue. In the example used earlier, a city may be seeking to revitalize a 'grey area' filled with parking lots, car dealerships, and half-used warehouses by acquiring properties that will be dedicated to mixed-use public-private development. The new development may be carefully planned to integrate uses and allow for 'eyes on the street'-type of observation that would, ostensibly, improve urban safety. In remodelling the old buildings while preserving affordable housing opportunities, the development may well qualify as an urban infill at its best. The design of new buildings may fit well with the older ones, may incorporate the best elements of regional architectural styles, and may include the most appealing local building materials. The planned public spaces may work well for 'foot people', may facilitate the kind of interaction that makes urban neighbourhoods desirable places to live, and may promote the type of active public realm that Jacobs hoped for. At the same time, the process by which this project is envisioned, designed, approved and contracted out may have little to do with those who are being displaced, their wishes and ideals. May one say that if these people protest, they express only the interests of relatively few small businesses? May one argue that the project will serve many citizens and will stimulate the establishment of many new kinds of small businesses (Kelbaugh, 1997, pp. 161–173)? Further, what if the people who would be displaced are 'car people', what if they don't like mixed use, what if they don't like the proposed architecture? Should the project be implemented because it follows Jacobs's version of the urban good, or should it be overturned because it does not correspond to the version of the urban good embraced by the existing residents and property owners, the ones to be displaced? Which is primary: product or process?

In such a case, Jacobs's prescriptions on the urban good may be reflected in all physical details of the project, but her advocacy of liberty and autonomy may only come alive in the voices of those who oppose the project. Does this suggest that Jacobs's views on the right and the good are contradictory? Is her political liberalism undermined by her overly specific recipes for the urban good? Is this contradiction deeply embedded in her thought, or does it exist only because her thought is misinterpreted by her ardent followers? I believe that Jacobs proposes a complex way of integrating the right and the good, which avoids such blatant dichotomies and seeming paradoxes. Three observations may serve to bring this complexity to light.

First, when it comes to the political process of urban development, Jacobs gives priority to process over product. As I argued earlier in the chapter, being a liberal democratic thinker, Jacobs clearly recognizes the priority of the right over the good. There are in fact plenty of projects that make heavy use of Jacobs's design principles that Jacobs herself would likely oppose because of the manner in which they are imposed on the public. Jacobs's emphasis on process (much as her recipes for particular physical outcomes) has also become the norm. Architectural critic Paul Goldberger recently wondered whether New York City has not gone so far in the opposite direction from the autocratic pragmatism of the Robert Moses era as to let too many good projects become mired in endless stakeholder disputes (Goldberger 2007; see also Ballon and Jackson, 2007; Flint, 2009, pp. 189–190).

Second, much of Jacobs's advocacy for her vision of the urban good can be characterized as drawing on the idea that liberty reaches its limits where actions interfere with the freedom and well-being of others. Postwar urban renewal programmes gained public support by means of a moral and political rhetoric reassuring everyone that those who were displaced or otherwise had their lives disrupted would be compensated and that, in the end, the inconveniences suffered by a few citizens would be balanced by the many great benefits to the broader public. The apothegms of Moses (e.g. that one cannot make an omelette without breaking eggs, or that if the interests of everyone affected were taken into account nothing would ever get built [Caro, 1974, p. 218]) exhibit a political pragmatism, but also an element of utilitarian moral principle: harms are outweighed by benefits. But Jacobs made clear that leaders like Moses were hiding the very real harms they were causing to individual citizens. The works of Robert Caro and others have indeed subsequently shown that Moses was simply blind to such harms (Alexiou, 2006; Caro, 1974; Flint, 2009, pp.186–189; Gratz, 1994, 2010). Jacobs created an additional vivid image of a more subtle but perhaps more devastating harm: the damage done to the fabric of city life. The consequences of demolishing neighbourhoods and replacing diversity with urban monoculture may not be immediately recognizable or palpably felt as an individual injury. In the long run, however, it may do the most decisive kind of harm, the kind of harm that bestows unsafe streets, poorly used parks, choked highways, and many other obstacles to urban vitality upon whole generations of future citizens. Still, Jacobs never argues that everyone should live in the kind of bounded, high-density, mixed-use urban environments that she extols. She only writes from the perspective of someone who has seen dense urban neighbourhoods obliterated.

Third, many of Jacobs's appeals are not intended as specific policy or design prescriptions. In most instances, they are only attempts to influence the sensibilities and preferences of her readers (i.e. she tries to legitimate the preferences of 'foot people', to make an aesthetic case for the mixing of old and new buildings, etc.). These appeals come under the heading, then, of the kind of rational discourse on the good that is encouraged in a society where members are given freedom to make these kinds of choices for themselves. They are arguments for a vision of the good meant to be embraced freely by those who choose, by those who see the reasonableness of her case. In other words, Jacobs argues for *her* point of view on the urban good; she does not claim that her vision is the only acceptable version.

For Jacobs, the question as to how the right and the good should be balanced is one that is worked out in complex, particular ways. It should not be surprising then, as I argue further, that her work contains explicit and implicit critique of all approaches in ethics, politics, and design that take an overly abstract approach to questions of freedom and value. Jacobs does not attack only abstract liberalism or abstract theories of the good; she attacks both, showing that her primary opponent is abstract mentality in whatever theoretical or practical context it may occur.

The Critique of Overly Abstract Forms of Liberalism

Jacobs is critical (at least implicitly) of any liberal-democratic point of view that would take an overly abstract approach to the question of basic individual needs or goods. John Rawls's classic *A Theory of Justice* argued that while political liberalism is fundamentally neutral regarding the individual good, it must nevertheless be committed to a 'thin' conception of the good. This 'thin' conception must guarantee not only basic freedoms, but also a level of health and wealth necessary for a basic equality of opportunity among citizens (Rawls, 1999, pp. 54, 347–355). The difficulty that Jacobs would see in such a position is that it normally comes in abstract categories such as 'jobs', 'housing', 'retail', 'transportation', and 'parks'. Further, the provision of such goods is often based on some abstract averages: retail per person, parks per person, as if humans and neighbourhoods are some statistical units (1993, pp. 569–573). Notice how the very formulation of these concepts already moves the mind towards images of the kind of separation and uniformity that Jacobs considers detrimental to cities – jobs go here, housing goes there, transportation runs between them. In *Death and Life* she calls this the view of the city a set of 'two-variable problems' wherein the goal is to isolate particular variables and relate them one by one to other variables. But in fact, she says, cities present problems of organized complexity – problems with too many variables to isolate. Such problems must be approached not through bivariate statistical methods, but with a view towards discovering the complex patterns of organization emerging in the data – much as it is done in the life sciences (1993, pp. 558–570). Notice, too, how the word, 'basic' has a 'utilitarian' and 'unadorned' flavour that can easily lead to the dull, bland, grey urban districts that Jacobs so eloquently critiques. Imagine, finally, how an abstractly conceived basic good such as 'public housing' is likely to be realized if the governmental agency overseeing its design is attempting to be as neutral as possible, making sure to apply a 'thin', rather than a 'thick' notion of the human good. One can perhaps see how the 'thin' conception of the good can find its aesthetic corollary in International-Style architectural uniformity.

Another kind of oversimplified and abstract application of liberal democratic principles occurs, in Jacobs's view, when 'liberty' comes to be disproportionately associated with the private realm of life at the expense of the public realm. The ideal of freedom that is at the heart of American political culture is a surprisingly ambiguous notion. It can be conceived primarily as a freedom from public constraint; i.e. as freedom to do what one wants and acquire what one desires. It can be conceived, alternatively, as something that can only be realized in the public realm; i.e. in political activities by which the citizenry engages in self-governance. While in any given real-life worldview these two notions (along with other variants) will combine, typically one of them would be more important. The privately minded person may see public political processes as valuable mostly as a means to protect and facilitate the exercise of private freedoms. He or she may prefer spending time in a private place of work and a private home, commuting between them in a private automobile. Because of these preferences and patterns of behaviour, the privately minded person may not be too interested in spending public resources on public amenities and public buildings, yet may consider it perfectly appropriate to spend lavishly on private amenities and private symbols of the good life. A publicly-minded person, by contrast, sees an intrinsic value in the public, civic life, the life by which citizens form a community and shape their future together. He or she will seek to improve the quality of public interactions and the conditions under which they occur. The publicly minded person may be willing to make substantial investments in public amenities and programmes, perhaps embracing the idea that public architecture and monuments must be ambitious symbols of the greatness of the city, the state, or the nation (cf. Benhabib, 1992; Calthorpe, 1993; Habermas, 1991; Madanipour, 2003; Squires, 1991; Warner, 1968, pp. 3–21). The sensibilities of the city dwellers that Jacobs describes as 'foot people' are mostly publicly minded sensibilities, for to be on foot (or bus or subway) is to be in public. Hence one finds Jacobs continuously defending public space from private encroachments: opposing the widening of roads for private vehicles, opposing the suburban transformation of public streets into semi-private culs-de-sac, opposing the relocation of street uses into hallways and elevators, opposing the shift from street markets and neighbourhood stores to supermarkets and shopping malls, etc. For those who associate freedom with private life there is nothing wrong with these social and spatial changes, but for Jacobs they threaten the freedom of self-rule by making it harder for citizens to form associations, build social ties and develop political solidarity.

To stay neutral regarding the human good allows an overemphasis on private goods, at least in US culture. This is why, for Jacobs, this approach represents an overly abstract form of the right. Liberal democracy in its fullest sense requires and allows for both public and private freedoms. In Jacobs's view, cities are the unique setting in which both types can flourish.

The Critique of Overly Abstract Conceptions of the Good

Jacobs's resistance to generalized notions of the good goes back to her battles with city officials in New York City. The 'common good' was a phrase often used by urban renewal leaders to belittle people like Jacobs who opposed them. Highways and large-scale developments, they said, inconvenience some residents but benefit 'the common good'.

One of [Robert Moses'] favorite sayings was, 'You cannot make an omelet without breaking eggs', and the omelet was the common good, and the eggs were the people who were broken. If you protested that people were not eggs, and that this was a false analogy – however you tried to reason about this – you were called selfish. And there has been quite a long era when people who really are concerned concretely with the common good, in a way that was understandable and tangible to them … were called selfish because they were concerned with those things instead of some abstract 'common good' that was defined by the omelet makers. (Jacobs, 1989b, pp. 186–187).

If abstractions such as 'the common good' are inevitable, Jacobs suggests, they should at least be scaled down and replaced with more particular terms, such as the 'neighbourhood good' (Jacobs, 1989b, p. 187).

There is another level of abstraction that Jacobs constantly worked against: the idea of the 'good of the nation'. For Jacobs, this notion is both artificially separate and falsely higher than what is good for individual cities. This concern is illustrated in *The Economy of Cities*, where Jacobs argues against prioritizing rural development over urban development. Such prioritization ignores the special role of cities in making a prosperous nation (Jacobs, 1969, pp. 3–48). In *Cities and the Wealth of Nations,* this argument is extended to challenge the very notion of a national economy – a notion, which in Jacobs's view may distort the unique and independent ways in which cities must function to sustain their role as economic engines. In such cases, the 'common good' of nations is too abstract to reflect the complex and unique nature of the good, which includes local and national interests all at the same time (Jacobs, 1984, pp. 29–44).

Jacobs's critiques of abstractions, both with regard to the right and the good, echo debates that have occurred, since the late 1970s, in the field of moral theory. Rawls's commitment to a 'neutral' liberal-democratic political framework, along with his 'thin' conception of the good was criticized by theorists such as MacIntyre (1981, 1988), Nussbaum (2000), Sandel (1982), Sen (1992), and Walzer (1983, 1994) as being too abstract and minimalist to reflect the very 'thick' and particular ideas of the good by which people actually live. In response, Rawls later recast his theory by asserting that the liberal-democratic framework of principles is not neutral but is the product of an 'overlapping consensus'. Citizens live by 'thick' conceptions of the good, but when the many differing thick notions intersect and overlap, one may argue that shared moral and political principles of justice are formed (Rawls, 1996, pp. 48–54, 58–71, 212–227). It might be said, then, that one of Jacobs's greatest achievement is to provide exceptionally vivid illustrations of the concrete patterns by which such 'overlapping' occurs in cities.

Conclusion: The Theoretical Relevance of Jacobs's Urban Ethics

It was never Jacobs's ambition to see her ideas integrated into the academic study of urban sociology, planning and design. While she regularly collaborated with academics (famously, with William H. Whyte and Charles Abrams [Fishman, 2007]), she was fundamentally suspicious of the way experts are credentialed. Mastery of an academic discipline, for her, too often locks the mind into a narrowly disciplinary way of viewing the world, drawing one into the very kinds of abstractions that she opposed. Yet academic interpretations of Jacobs's thinking – such as the present effort to interpret Jacobs as a thinker on traditional philosophical questions regarding the right and the good – reveal the rich nuances of her positions, whose complexity is not at all undermined by the fact that she preferred to couch them in popular, rather than academic, prose.

In the context of urban ethics, and I believe in so many other contexts, Jacobs's principal role is to offer a concrete way of viewing and interpreting the evidence that city life puts before us. If moral and political philosophers choose to ignore the concrete patterns of urban life, they can easily fall prey to the same sort of misleading abstractions that Jacobs found among planners and governmental leaders in the heyday of her activism. In seeking to make cities good, these officials succeeded only in making them less city-like; they didn't save cities, Jacobs audaciously posited, they ended up 'sacking' them (Jacobs, 1993, p. 6). Against such anti-urban approaches that are pursued so often even with the best of intentions, Jacobs stands for the ethical integrity of the genuinely complex life of North American cities. She does so with powers of ethical insight and moral passion uniquely her own. In her method of argumentation, i.e. in the thick description of everyday, real-life urban experiences, Jacobs ultimately showed herself as the liberal democratic thinker and activist that she truly was – the kind of thinker and activist who fought against abstract totalizing visions for the sake of the human, the lived, and the particular.

References

Alexiou, A.S. (2006) *Jane Jacobs: Urban Visionary*. New Brunswick, NJ: Rutgers University Press.

Arendt, H. (1958) *The Human Condition*. New York: Doubleday.

Arkes, H. (1981) *The Philosopher in the City: The Moral Dimensions of Urban Politics*. Princeton, NJ: Princeton University Press.

Ballon, H. and Jackson, K. (eds.) (2007) *Robert Moses and the Modern City: The Transformation of New York*. New York: Queens Museum of Art.

Benhabib, S. (1992) Models of public space: Hannah Arendt, the liberal tradition, and Jürgen Habermas, in Calhoun, C. (ed.) *Habermas and the Public Sphere*. Cambridge, MA: MIT Press.

Byrne, P. (1989) Jane Jacobs and the common good, in Lawrence, F. (ed.) *Ethics in Making a Living: The Jane Jacobs Conference, Lonergan Workshop*, Volume 7 (supplement). Atlanta, GA: Scholars Press, pp. 169–189.

Calthorpe, P. (1993) *The Next American Metropolis: Ecology, Community, and the American Dream*. New York: Princeton Architectural Press.

Carmona, M., Heath, T., Oc, T. and Tiesdell, S. (2003) *Public Places – Urban Spaces*. Oxford: Architectural Press.

Caro, R. (1974) *The Power Broker: Robert Moses and the Fall of New York*. New York: Alfred A. Knopf.

Downs, A. (1994) *New Visions for Metropolitan America*. Washington, DC: The Brookings Institution.

Fishman, R. (2007) Revolt of the urbs: Robert Moses and his critics, in Ballon, H. and Jackson, K. (eds.) *Robert Moses and the Modern City: The Transformation of New York*. New York: Queens Museum of Art, pp. 122–129.

Flint, A. (2009) *Wrestling with Moses: How Jane Jacobs took on New York's Master Builder and Transformed the American City*. New York: Random House.

Garvin, A. (1996) *The American City: What Works, What Doesn't*. New York: McGraw-Hill.

Goldberger, P. (2007) Eminent dominion: rethinking the legacy of Robert Moses. The New Yorker, **82**(48), p. 83.

Gratz, R.B. (1994) *The Living City: How America's Cities are being Revitalized by Thinking Small in a Big Way*. Washington DC: Preservation Press.

Gratz, R.B. (1998) *Cities Back from the Edge*. Washington, DC: Preservation Press.

Gratz, R.B. (2010) *The Battle for Gotham: New York in the Shadow of Robert Moses and Jane Jacobs*. New York: Nation Books.

Habermas, J. (1991) *The Structural Transformation of the Public Sphere*. Cambridge, MA: MIT Press.

Honohan, I. (2002) *Civic Republicanism*. London: Routledge.

Jacobs, J. (1993, 1961) *The Death and Life of Great American Cities*. New York: Modern Library.

Jacobs, J. (1969) *The Economy of Cities*. New York: Random House.

Jacobs, J. (1984) *Cities and the Wealth of Nations: Principles of Economic Life*. New York: Random House.

Jacobs, J. (1989*a*) Systems of economic ethics, in Lawrence, F. (ed.) *Ethics in Making a Living: The Jane Jacobs Conference, Lonergan Workshop*, Volume 7 (supplement). Atlanta, GA: Scholars Press, pp. 211–286.

Jacobs, J. (1989*b*) Jane Jacobs's response to Patrick Byrne's presentation, in Lawrence, F. (ed.) *Ethics in Making a Living: The Jane Jacobs Conference, Lonergan Workshop*, Volume 7 (supplement). Atlanta, GA: Scholars Press: 186–187.

Jacobs, J. (1992) *Systems of Survival: A Dialogue on the Moral Foundations of Commerce and Politics*. New York: Random House.

Kelbaugh, D. (1997) *Common Place: Toward Neighborhood and Regional Design*. Seattle, WA: University of Washington Press.

Kidder, P. (2008) The urbanist ethics of Jane Jacobs. *Ethics, Place, and Environment*, **11**(3), pp. 253–266.

Lawrence, F. (ed.) (1989) *Ethics in Making a Living: The Jane Jacobs Conference, Lonergan Workshop*, Volume 7 (supplement). Atlanta, GA: Scholars Press.

Lonergan, B. (1996) *Method in Theology*. Toronto: University of Toronto Press.

McCarthy, M. (1996) Liberty, history, and the common good: an exercise in critical retrieval. *Lonergan Workshop*. Volume 12, pp. 111–145.

MacIntyre, A. (1981) *After Virtue*. Notre Dame, IN: University of Notre Dame Press.

MacIntyre, A. (1988) *Whose Justice? Which Rationality?* Notre Dame, IN: University of Notre Dame Press.

Madanipour, A. (2003) *Public and Private Spaces of the City*. London: Routledge.

Nussbaum, M.C. (2000) *Women and Development*. Cambridge: Cambridge University Press.

Rawls, J. (1996) *Political Liberalism*. New York: Columbia University Press.

Rawls, J. (1999) *A Theory of Justice*, revised edition. Cambridge, MA: Harvard University Press.

Sandel, M.J. (1982) *Liberalism and the Limits of Justice*. Cambridge: Cambridge University Press.

Sen, A. (1992) *Inequality Reexamined*. Cambridge, MA: Harvard University Press.

Squires, G.D. (1991) Partnership and the pursuit of the private city, in Goettdiener, M. and Pickvance, C. (eds.) *Urban Life in Transition*. Newbury Park, CA: Sage, pp. 123–140.

Walzer, M. (1983) *Spheres of Justice*. New York: Basic Books.

Walzer, M. (1994) *Thick and Thin*. Notre Dame, IN: University of Notre Dame Press.

Warner, S.B. (1968) *The Private City: Philadelphia in Three Periods of Its Growth*. Philadelphia, PA: University of Pennsylvania Press.

Chapter 3

The 'Sidewalk Ballet' in the Work of Henri Lefebvre and Manuel Delgado Ruiz

Benjamin Fraser

This chapter argues for a philosophical treatment of Jane Jacobs's work by focusing on her deployment of the metaphor of the 'sidewalk ballet'. The implicit and explicit re-appropriation of this metaphor by two noted urban scholars, Henri Lefebvre (France, 1901–1991) and Manuel Delgado Ruiz (Spain, 1956–), testifies both to the extensive influence of Jacobs's work outside of North America and also, perhaps more importantly, to the originality and philosophical potential of her thought to highlight the city as a mobile phenomenon. The felicitous metaphor of 'the sidewalk ballet' perhaps best expresses the complex approach to urban life articulated by Jacobs. Introducing the metaphor in her classic book *The Death and Life of Great American Cities* (1992, 1961), she penned the following characteristically elegant description:

Under the seeming disorder of the old city, wherever the old city is working successfully, is a marvelous order for maintaining the safety of the streets and the freedom of the city. It is a complex order. Its essence is intricacy of sidewalk use, bringing with it a constant succession of eyes. This order is all composed of movement and change, and although it is life, not art, we may fancifully call it the art form of the city and liken it to the dance – not to a simple-minded precision dance with everyone kicking up at the same time, twirling in unison and bowing off en masse, but to an intricate ballet in which the individual dancers and ensembles all have distinctive parts which miraculously reinforce each other and compose an orderly whole. The ballet of the good city sidewalk never repeats itself from place to place, and in any one place is always replete with new improvisations. (Jacobs 1992, p. 50; see also p. 96, on the 'ballet' of Rittenhouse Square in Philadelphia, and p. 153, once again pertaining to the author's own Hudson Street)

Recourse to this sort of poignant metaphor is hardly a rarity in Jacobs's writing. She was, after all, also able to breathe fresh life into one of the most stale metaphors of modern city planning – that of the city as an organism (Jacobs, 1992, p. 433).[1] Just as Jacobs's famous re-appropriation of the organic metaphor is a salvo launched as part of 'an attack' (*Ibid.*, p. 3) on planning practices, her coining of 'the sidewalk ballet' reflects an extensive and largely philosophical defence of those aspects of urban life that have persistently been subjected to strict control by urban designers and planners seeking to outlaw the unpredictable. Her work consistently highlighted a multiplicity of themes that she felt had been neglected by orthodox urban planners and designers: motion, spontaneity, diversity and community. She stressed the city as a lived space and a complex living creature (*Ibid.*, p. 433) just as she argued for an understanding of the urban experience rooted in the realm of the senses and not merely in the intellectual notion of a static plan. In the process, she questioned a planning practice that Richard Sennett has described in terms of a 'visual technology of power' that alienated planners from their work (*Ibid.*, p. 61). Like subsequent thinkers such as David Harvey (1989, pp. 1–2) and Michel de Certeau (1988, pp. 91–93), she sought to complement the structural or theoretical view of the city from the high modernist towers of urban design with a practical perspective drawn from the level of the streets themselves (see also Alexiou 2006, pp. 43,72). Her 'sidewalk ballet' metaphor concisely stresses the importance of that street-level vision, and its qualities (mobility, spontaneity, sensuality) stand as a reminder of all that has been lacking from urban visions which have insufficiently grappled with the notions of diversity and community.

The notion of the 'sidewalk ballet' is in many respects the heart of Jacobs's famous treatise on the city. The metaphor is captivating because it is both quite accessible and quite apt. In an increasingly urbanizing society where the city constitutes the centre of the contemporary world – drawing even 'the most remote parts of the world into its orbit' as Louis Wirth of the Chicago School of Urban Sociology once noted (Wirth, 1938, p. 2) – there are relatively few who would find it difficult to envision a bustling urban scene. Jacobs's metaphor grounds itself in this powerfully modern imagery of the crowded city in order to convey a deep respect for the life of its sidewalks. In the process, she manages to reference both the beauty of art (while concertedly avoiding the reduction of life to art) and the nature of everyday activities as performance. Most importantly, given her urban activism, she imbues this multivalent and 'improvisational' performance taking place on the city sidewalk with the quality of community. Her own explanation of the characteristics that make her ballet metaphor appropriate suggests that the city dance is not the meandering of the modern *flâneur* engaging individually in a nonetheless socio-cultural practice (as perhaps Benjamin [2002] and de Certeau [1988] would have it), but an orchestral (although decidedly not orchestrated), collective movement comprised of multiple participants. As the aforementioned quotation from *The Death and Life* makes clear (1992, p. 50), this urban ballet tends not towards simplistic movements but towards improvisation, towards unpredictability rather than serialized repetition. Instead of imagining that there might be one central organizational principle or 'conductor' of this ballet, we do well in imagining each individual dancer as a conductor of sorts. At the root of the complex unity of the sidewalk ballet there is, simply put, a community in movement.

Jacobs's work squares with a long line of theorists in positing an understanding of urban communities that are defined precisely by difference, spontaneity and motion. 'The city is the place where difference *lives*', writes Don Mitchell (original emphasis, 2003, p. 18; cf. Harvey, 2000; Young, 1990). This perspective emphasizes that people have the 'right' to be strangers in public spaces, expecting no friendship or commitment from one another. Although there is reason to be wary of simplistic notions of a public sphere into which private interests do not intrude – Mabel Berezin reminds us that 'the terms *public* and *private* are used with more frequency than with precision' (original emphasis, 1999, p. 358; see also Fraser, 2007a; Madanipour, 2003; Marston, 1990; Mitchell, 2003, pp. 130–134; Staeheli, 1996) – we do well to recognize the potential of certain 'public' spaces of the city to engender diverse communities. This point is well made by Lyn Lofland (1991), for example, who reiterates Anselm Strauss's development of the concept of a 'locale' – a place where strangers of diverse backgrounds are likely to gather with no expectations. Importantly, 'there can occur at such locales a more sociable, more lasting kind of contact between peoples drawn from different social worlds' (Strauss, 1961, pp. 63–64; quoted in Lofland, 1991, p. 198).

The image of the 'sidewalk ballet' is useful because it in fact underscores not merely the complexity but also the fluid nature of the urban phenomenon. Since at least Georg Simmel's famous early twentieth-century characterization of the chaos of the modern urban experience ('The Metropolis and Mental Life', 2000 [first published in 1903]) – and subsequently of the extended debate surrounding the progressive 'urbanization of consciousness' (e.g. Harvey, 1989) – the city has been seen in terms of movements and flows (e.g. Latham and McCormack, 2004). This perspective has become increasingly *de rigueur* in new and intriguing critical views on space and place, as evidenced by the emerging discipline of Mobility Studies (and perhaps also the recent establishment of the journal *Mobilities*; see Hannam *et al.*, 2006). Cities are, as Jacobs observed in the 1960s, insufficiently served by contemporary perspectives that reduce them to a static planar geometry. Instead, they are better seen as living organisms, constituted by a plurality of factors, riddled with contradiction and defined by a constant tension between order and disorder that – just as in the mathematical problem of squaring the circle – cannot be resolved without recourse to movement.[2] The importance that Jacobs ascribes to movement, of course, can be seen also in her other works: in her dialectical *Systems of Survival* (1994), where fictional perspectives are embodied in the unfolding dialogues amongst the characters of Armbruster, Kate, Hortense, Jasper, Quincy, and Ben; and also in her support for the notion of 'drift' as outlined in *Cities and The Wealth of Nations* (1984). 'A city sidewalk by itself is nothing. It is an abstraction', writes Jacobs (1992, p. 29) – it is rather the movement, the hustle and bustle, the very life of the sidewalks that matters.

In what follows, I explore a small but important part of Jane Jacobs's legacy. There is, in her novel phrase – the 'sidewalk ballet' – a philosophical premise whose originality has not escaped the attention of prominent urban critics outside North American contexts. This chapter traces Jacobs's resonance with and influence on two such critics in particular. Both Henri Lefebvre and contemporary Lefebvrian thinker Manuel Delgado Ruiz have zeroed-in on this single metaphor thus testifying both to the lasting power of Jacobs's ideas and the captivating elegance of her prose. Their tribute to Jacobs also points to the exceptional originality of her thought, warranting her reconsideration not only as an admired (if controversial) urban critic and activist, but even more fundamentally, as an urban philosopher. In returning to her thinking, reinterpreting and expanding her ideas and engaging throughout with her notion of the 'sidewalk ballet', Lefebvre and Delgado Ruiz have proved the extraordinary philosophical potential of her metaphor. Although Jacobs's influence is more extensive in the case of Delgado Ruiz, it is Delgado's folding of Jacobs's metaphor into a decidedly Lefebvrian framework (specifically, into the method of 'rhythmanalysis') that makes it necessary first to interrogate Lefebvre's philosophical position.

Henri Lefebvre

It is no trivial detail that Jacobs was mentioned by name several times in the works of urban geographer and self-proclaimed Marxist philosopher Henri Lefebvre (see Elden, 2001). A prolific writer, whose life spanned almost the entire twentieth century and whose ideas intersected with those of the Situationists (among them, notably, Guy Debord), subsequently influencing a generation of critics who are perhaps more widely recognized in the United States than even he is (first and foremost, David Harvey), Lefebvre authored over sixty books on topics related to cities, as well as on capital and spatial production. Although Lefebvre perhaps arrived at an understanding of the life of city streets quite similar to that of Jacobs on his own terms and around the same time (Merrifield, 2006, p. 64; Fraser, 2009a), he nonetheless references her in his foundational works *The Urban Revolution* (2003)[3] and *The Production of Space* (1991),[4] thus making it clear he is aware of and sympathetic to her contribution to urban studies.

The two thinkers undoubtedly share many ideas – among the most important ones are their respect for the complexity of the urban experience. They also share creative re-appropriations of the organic metaphor underpinning modern urban planning (see Fraser, 2009b, 2010, 2011a, 2011b). Lefebvre's own concerns as he expressed them in *The Right to the City* (along with *The Urban Revolution*), specifically in the distinction he maintains between the 'planned city' and the 'practiced city' (Lefebvre, 1996; also maintained in Delgado, 1999, p. 182), closely parallel Jacobs's straightforward denunciation of top-down city-building practices. In the aforementioned works, the French urban scholar explored the distance between two opposing understandings of the city. On one hand there was the geometrical if not abstract notion of the city so often engaged by urban planners from the nineteenth century onwards (e.g. Baron Haussmann), a notion Lefebvre labelled the 'planned city'. On the other hand was the 'practiced city'; that is, the city as it was commonly experienced at the scale of everyday life by its inhabitants, people who historically have had very little input as to what shape the city is to take. A similar distinction can also be found in Lefebvre's critique of the 'city' as practico-material and architectural fact (a closed system), which exists in opposition to the 'urban'. The latter, he says, 'is more or less the oeuvre of its citizens instead of imposing itself upon them as a system, as an already closed book' (Lefebvre,

1996, p. 117). Generally speaking, both Lefebvre and Jacobs were concerned that the city was being designed by specialists such as planners who were out of touch with how it was experienced on the streets.

While this distinction between the ideas of the city held by planners and those commonly held by urban dwellers is more clearly linked to Jacobs's metaphor in the work of Lefebvrian critic Manuel Delgado Ruiz, what deserves more attention here is the Lefebvrian concept (also continued by the Spaniard) of 'rhythmanalysis'.[5] This term strongly resonates with the notion of the 'sidewalk ballet' that the French philosopher would have necessarily encountered in Jacobs's classic work. As if channelling the main thrust of *The Death and Life*, Lefebvre makes it clear that the shifting and changing nature of life on the streets presents the strongest challenge to a static conception of the city. In his words, 'The urban phenomenon is made manifest as movement' (Lefebvre, 2003, p. 174). Recognizing the living character of cities is an important tactic in combating the largely static model of the city touted by modern urban planning – a fragmentary bourgeois science of the nineteenth century (Lefebvre, 1996, pp. 94–99) that allowed the city as 'exchange-value' to trump the city as 'use-value'.[6] Ultimately, this planning tradition has failed to create 'an urban reality for users and not [merely for] speculators, builders, and technicians' (Lefebvre, 1996, p. 168). Lefebvre's denunciation of the static vision of urban planning parallels Jacobs's; he, too, takes planners to task for ignoring the mobile nature of the urban. Within this context, he asserts the potential of 'rhythmanalysis' as a method of reappraising the value of urban life in works originally published in 1961, 1981 (in his *Critique of Everyday Life*, Vols. 2 and 3, 2002, 2005) and posthumously in 1992 (*Rhythmanalysis*, 2006).

Whereas the 'sidewalk ballet' is a concise metaphor that speaks to the widely held perception that the urban is a movement, rhythmanalysis is a method more concertedly directed towards making sense of that movement. The trope of rhythm for Lefebvre is a way of underscoring the complexity of the city (Lefebvre, 2006, p. 37). He outlines this method in this way:

The rhythmanalyst calls on all his senses. He draws on his breathing, the circulation of his blood, the beatings of his heart and the delivery of his speech as landmarks. Without privileging any one of these sensations, raised by him in the perception of rhythms, to the detriment of any other. He thinks with his body, not in the abstract, but in lived temporality. (Lefebvre, 2006, p. 21)

The city that Lefebvre observes from his window (Lefebvre, 2006, chapter 3) is full of multiple rhythms. Each individual rhythm is moving and alive, thus implying 'complex (dialectical) relations' (Lefebvre, 2006, p. 78). Immersed in this living temporality, the rhythmanalyst goes beyond the visual in his or her assessment of the city, towards the olfactory (Lefebvre, 2006, p. 21) and also towards the auditory (Lefebvre, 2006, pp. 19–22, 60). Lefebvre underscores that such an 'embodied thinker' 'listen(s) to "a house, a street, a town" (above) as an audience listens to a symphony' (Lefebvre, 2006, p. 22).

The insights Lefebvre elaborated so carefully in *Rhythmanalysis* – the volume he intended to be the fourth of his *Critique* (Elden, 2006, p. viii; see also Fraser, 2008) –

were, however, already anticipated in Jacobs's classic text and more specifically in her fine-arts metaphor for street life. Talking about her home neighbourhood in New York, she writes in musical terms (*Rhythmanalysis* too is riddled with references to music) of how 'after work, the ballet [on Hudson Street] is reaching its crescendo' (Jacobs, 1992, p. 52, emphasis added), for example. Her description is grounded not merely in the visual splendour of the present but in bodily memories of the deep enduring (Bergsonian) past. On her ritual farewell with Mr Lofaro she writes, 'We have done this many a morning for more than ten years, and we both know what it means: All is well' (Jacobs, 1992, p. 51). Anticipating Lefebvre's advice to 'listen to "a house, a street, a town"' (above), Jacobs writes compellingly in 1961 of the singing, the weeping, the roars, bellows, conversations and even bagpipes of the 'deep night ballet' (Jacobs, 1992, p. 53) of Hudson Street.

While the above connections between Jacobs and Lefebvre are among the most prominent ones, this discussion should not be taken as exhaustive. What is important is to recognize that their respective attacks on contemporary urban planning coincided in significant ways. Each of the two authors denounced existing practices of urban design as overly abstract and geometrical, each called for an acknowledgment of the way the city was experienced on the ground by urban dwellers, and each defined the very nature of the city in terms of complexity and movement. Lefebvre's explicit mention of Jacobs's work in two of his most important works (1991, 2003) both conveys his esteem for her work *The Death and Life* and signals that a more thorough comparison of the two might be even more fruitful. The case of Lefebvrian thinker Manuel Delgado Ruiz further shows that Jacobs's influence outside of North America has been extensive and direct.

Manuel Delgado Ruiz

Delgado's return to Jacobs's work can only be properly understood by situating the Spanish theorist within the Lefebvrian tradition. Delgado begins his book *Sociedades movedizas* [Mobile societies] with a reference to Lefebvre (Delgado, 2007a, p. 11; see also 1999, pp. 19, 29, 33, 38, 55, 70–72, 191, 193, 199; 2001, pp. 34, 36, 37, 39, 41, 48; 2007a, pp. 16, 179–180, 196, 267; 2007b, pp. 105, 217). He writes of 'rhythmanalysis' specifically in his publications *Memoria y lugar* [Memory and place] (Delgado 2001, p. 36; in fact, he devotes a subsection to it) and *El animal público* [The public animal] (Delgado 1999, p. 71), employing a Lefebvrian/Jacobsian conception of space-movement to link 'streets and bodies [la calle y el cuerpo]' (Delgado, 2001, p. 26; also 'each body is a space and has a space, a space for relation and for movement', *Ibid*., p. 35, my translation).[7] As Lefebvre before him, Delgado highlights the distinction between 'planned city' and 'practiced city' (Delgado, 1999, p. 182) just as that between 'city' and 'urban' (Delgado, 2007a, p. 11). He also refers to Jacobs explicitly much more frequently than does the French thinker (e.g. Delgado, 1999, pp. 19, 38, 74) and uses her metaphor more extensively (Delgado, 2001, p. 27; 2007a, pp. 129, 135, 245; see also Fraser, 2007b).

At the start of his prize-winning book *El animal público*, Delgado underscores the foundational importance of Jacobs's work for his own theorizations of the urban.

My readings of *The death and life of great American cities*, by Jane Jacobs ([published in Spanish translation by] Península, Barcelona, 1973), and *The fall of public man*, by Richard Sennet [*sic*] (Península, Barcelona, 1974), were for me revelations, and the present book [El animal público] would neither seek to, nor could it, hide this fact. (Delgado, 1999, p. 19, my translation)[8]

Eight years later, in *Sociedades movedizas* [Mobile societies], still captivated by Jacobs's book, he writes of 'the "life of the sidewalk" [la "vida de acera"]', similarly pronouncing that *The Death and Life* is 'a fundamental text [un texto fundamental]' (Delgado, 2007a, p. 245), and once again invoking and unpacking Jacobs's metaphor of street activities as dance:

It is worth insisting upon the aforementioned – and time-honoured – analogy between pedestrian activity and a certain form of choreography. In effect, dance expresses perfectly that language of multiple, at times microscopic reciprocities, proclamations of an extreme lightness, mutual – frequently peripheral – vigilances, and other manifest visual activities produced by a variety of realizations and socio-organizational formats in urban spaces. Dance is that class of artistic creation most grounded in taking maximum advantage of the expressive possibilities of the body, deploying its energy at a given time and space, a time and space that might seem to have already been there prior to human action, but that in reality emanate from it. Dance carries to a logical conclusion the embodiment of the social actor's initiatives, a comprehension in corporeal terms of the interaction he maintains with his social environment, with the things surrounding him and with other human beings, the uninterrupted interpellation of person and world. The time–energy–body of the dancer expresses all of its possibilities through everyday activity in urban settings in which words become accustomed to being worth relatively little in the relations between partial or total strangers and in which all seems to depend on superficial eloquence, not in the trivial sense, but rather in terms of acts that take place on the surface, that function through slippages, that avoid or extract the maximum utility from the contours of the land, that seek out and create grooves and folds, that conceal any regularities on the skin of the social [body]. (Delgado, 2007a, pp. 135–136, my translation).[9]

For Delgado, the importance of the metaphor of the sidewalk ballet seems to lie in its potential to account for difference and multiplicity in the representation of urban spaces and activities. This quality was, of course, already present in Jacobs's lengthy 'rhythmanalysis' of Hudson Street (Jacobs, 1992, pp. 50–54), which highlighted multiple sets of eyes as well as multiple actors of different socio-economic backgrounds – even 'strangers' who may or may not be the same from day to day (Jacobs, 1992, pp. 53–54). But the Spanish urban theorist recuperates Jacobs's metaphor en route to a more explicitly radical urban politics. As such, he succeeds in drawing out aspects of public space that were also important to Jacobs. In *El animal público* he writes of how streets (if they are by definition places constituted by 'the integration of incompatibilities [la integración de las incompatibilidades]' that shift over time) create conditions favourable to 'the most effective exercises of thinking through questions of identity, where political commitment takes shape as a consequence of the possibilities for action and where social mobilization allows the potential of the current of sympathy and solidarity among strangers to be known' (Delgado, 1999, p. 208, my translation).[10]

Despite his marked suspicion of the way the notion of 'public space' has been turned into a contrived marketing tool (Delgado, 2006, 2007*b*, pp. 225–226), the theorist nonetheless believes in the importance of a city's sidewalks, where pedestrians may 'become walking absences, nullified profiles, hypertransitive beings, lacking a state, that is to say they cannot be contemplated statically, but only in excitation, bustling about from one place to another' (Delgado, 1999, p. 201, my translation).[11] 'Those beings,' he writes later in *Sociedades movedizas*, 'have declined to declare who they are. They refuse to be identified' (Delgado, 2007*a*, p. 188, my translation).[12] In implicit agreement with theorists such as Anselm Strauss (1961; also Lofland, 1991), Delgado sees a link between the unencumbered exercise of what he terms the 'right to anonymity' (Delgado, 2007*a*, p. 188) and the way in which public spaces bring people of varying circumstances and subjectivities together, ultimately aiding in the cultivation of possible political solidarities.[13]

Significantly, in fact, this reconciliation of 'strangers' was already formulated in Jacobs's notion of the sidewalk ballet, which hinges on difference as the building block of successful sidewalks. The qualities of 'intricacy' and 'complexity' that are at the heart of the sidewalk ballet (Jacobs, 1992, p. 50; above), are a way of expressing what was, for her, one of the defining features of contemporary cities – diversity. In her words, 'Diversity is natural to big cities' (quoted in Alexiou, 2006, p. 77). For both Jacobs and Delgado, the constantly shifting and mobile, unpredictable and living character of the sidewalk has the potential to be a place in which diversity may thrive and engender inclusive, democratic forms of community. This community is not one, but multiple; it is not univocal but is instead the product and the producer of difference and disorder – or in Jacobs's words, of 'a complex order'. 'There is nothing simple about that order itself,' she says, 'or the bewildering number of components that go into it' (Jacobs, 1992, pp. 50, 54). Delgado also testifies to the power of Jacobs's complex vision of the city, when he writes that:

Sidewalks, as urban spaces par excellence, should therefore rightly be considered the terrain for a dynamic and shifting culture, elaborated and re-elaborated constantly by the practices and discourses of its users. (Delgado 2007a: 129, my translation).[14]

In a sense, for both Delgado and Jacobs, city streets and sidewalks constitute a microcosm of the city itself – a place of constant movement and even performance, where a complex notion of community may be formed and reformed.

Jacobs's Legacy Today

Jacobs, Lefebvre and Delgado all share distaste for the simplistic plans that reduced the city to a flat geometry and attempted to conceal the essential nature of the urban as a movement. If Lefebvre and Delgado are any indicators, Jacobs's body of work is perhaps even more relevant today than it was in 1961. It is no less necessary today than it was 50 years ago to resist the facile solutions to social problems touted by some proponents of urban design. It could be said that contemporary urban design approaches, such as those advocated by the New Urbanists for example, continue to rely on large-scale and strictly ordered planning schemes that do little to encourage the type of spontaneous and complex interaction that Jacobs (and Lefebvre and Delgado, for that matter) advocated.

Sonia Hirt (2009, p. 249), for example, points out that New Urbanism has on the whole neglected its self-proclaimed rhetorical commitment to pluralism and diversity and has ended up replicating modernist architecture's preference for controlled functional make-up (Hirt, 2009, p. 263). The Lefebvrian-inspired urban scholar David Harvey (2005, p. 23), too, has echoed this perspective in his critique of New Urbanism, asking 'does it not perpetuate the idea that the shaping of spatial order is or can be the foundation for a new moral and aesthetic order?' Noting that differing notions of community may function as either barriers to or facilitators of progressive social change (2005, pp. 24–25), Harvey's essay suggests that a diverse and inclusive community is not something that can be made-to-order and added on to the production of a new built environment. His view is that the intentions of New Urbanism have been limited by what he calls a 'communitarian trap': 'it [New Urbanism] builds an *image* of community and a *rhetoric* of place-based civic pride and consciousness for those who do not need it, while abandoning those who do to their "underclass" fate' (emphasis added; Harvey, 2005, p. 25).

Jacobs's lifelong activism and published remarks stressing the importance of community action over the implementation of highly publicized urban plans suggest she would be sceptical of contemporary 'mixed-use' designs and other pre-packaged, sidewalk-heavy communities. Jacobs consistently complained of the superficial way in which planners would make a point of including a corner grocery store in their public projects, a practice she denounced as 'a thin, patronizing conception of city diversity' (quoted in Alexiou, 2006, p. 77). Reminiscent of Harvey's point regarding the superficiality of urban solutions targeting the spatial order alone, Jacobs wrote against the idea that neat manicured parks were an easy solution to urban problems. In chapter five of *The Death and Life* she notes that:

Conventionally, neighborhood parks or parklike open spaces are considered boons conferred on the deprived populations of cities. Let us turn this thought around, and consider city parks deprived places that need the boon of life and appreciation conferred on them. This is more nearly in accord with reality, for people do confer use on parks and make them successes – or else withhold use and doom parks to rejection and failure. (1992, p. 89; cf. Fraser 2007a)

As evidenced in this quotation, Jacobs's 'attack' (1992, p. 3) on urban planning rejected the notion that simple changes to the built environment alone, uninformed by a more complex grasp of social relations, would in themselves result in better cities. If the above views of Hirt and Harvey on New Urbanism are any guide, this criticism is still appropriate even a half-century after the publication of *The Death and Life*.

What this shows is that the distance Lefebvre pointed out between the 'planned city' and the 'practiced city' has not yet been overcome. In this context, the notion of the 'sidewalk ballet' stands as a reminder that the city is a lived, human space more than it is a geometrical, abstract space. Furthermore, even though the built environment cannot substitute for the real actions of urban dwellers, it can nonetheless restrict those actions. As a consequence, any orchestrated production of city space that ignores the urban landscape's socio-cultural, human component abrogates its potential for forming diverse communities. In short, as Jacobs well understood neither the mere construction of new buildings nor neatly renovated city infrastructures can stand in place of the real democratic processes and inclusive notions of community that might be formed on the city sidewalks.

Jane Jacobs's elegant prose underscored the mobile and improvisational nature of city life. She recognized that successful urban communities have great potential for reconciling differences and building communities. Rereading Jacobs's classic text today reminds us not only that the complex problems of cities require complex solutions, but also that the life of city streets is still something worth celebrating. It also reminds us that we should all take a minute to stop and applaud the beautiful and orchestral complexity of the 'sidewalk ballet'. This metaphor cuts to the heart of Jacobs's work by emphasizing the everyday practices that comprise the city as a living process.

Notes

1. This organic metaphor has held wide currency in urban planning from the nineteenth-century designs of Baron Haussmann in France and Ildefons Cerdà in Spain, although Richard Sennett has persuasively linked the practice to the seventeenth-century discovery of the circulation of blood (see Choay, 1969; Harvey, 2006; Fraser, 2009a, 2010, 2011a, 2011b; Sennett, 2008).

2. Jacobs's philosophical complement may arguably be found in aspects of Bergsonism, as Fraser (2009b) explores, in a number of shared emphases, including the desire to avoid simplistic definitions and abstractions, applaud the concrete, return to the real world, and start all analysis with experience (cf. Fraser 2010).

3. 'The work of Jane Jacobs has shown that, in the United States, the street (highly trafficked, busy) provides the only security possible against criminal violence (theft, rape, aggression)' (Lefebvre, 2003, p. 19).

4. 'As long ago as 1961, Jane Jacobs examined the failures of "city planning and rebuilding" in the United States. In particular, she showed how the destruction of streets and neighborhoods led to the disappearance of many acquired characteristics of city life – or rather, characteristics assumed to have been permanently acquired: security, social contract, facility of child-rearing, diversity of relationships, and so on. Jacobs did not go so far as to flatly incriminate neocapitalism, or as to isolate the contradictions immanent to the space produced by capitalism (abstract space). But she did very forcefully demonstrate how destructive this space can be, and specifically how urban space, using the very means apparently intended to create or re-create it, effects its own self-destruction' (Lefebvre, 1991, p. 364). In his review essay prompted by the publication of the English translation of *The Production of Space*, another renowned urban scholar, Harvey Molotch, phrases it a bit more strongly, proposing that Lefebvre 'draws on Jane Jacobs's writings to point out the superiority of absolute space as a kind of organic to human need, versus the abstracted hell laid on by planner's schemes' (Molotch, 1993, p. 890).

5. Lefebvre admits the notion of rhythmanalysis is borrowed from Gaston Bachelard (and before that from Portuguese writer Lucio Alberto Pinheiro) (Lefebvre, 2006, p. 9; also Elden, 2006, p. xiii).

6. Lefebvre's use of the terms use-value and exchange-value are a testament to the Marxian roots of his urban thinking. As discussed in Marx's *Capital* (1977), the change in social relations prompted by the rise of the bourgeoisie produced a schism between 'use-value' (the object's worth as defined by its utility) and 'exchange value' (the object's worth as defined by its price on the market, which is clearly dependent on a number of circumstances that vary across space and time). A novelty of Lefebvre's work was to apply this tenet of Marxian thinking to the built environment of the city. Thus the city has a 'use-value' for the people who live in it and walk its streets, while it has an 'exchange-value' stemming from the processes of investment and speculation (e.g. rent, tourism, what urban scholars have called 'intercity competition'; see Harvey, 2000).

7. The original Spanish reads: 'cada cuerpo es un espacio y tiene un espacio, espacio para la relación y para el movimiento' (*Ibid.*).

8. The original Spanish reads: 'La lectura de Muerte y vida de las grandes ciudades, de Jane Jacobs (Península, Barcelona, 1973), o El declive del hombre público, de Richard Sennet (Península, Barcelona, 1974), tuvieron para mí una virtud reveladora y este libro no quiere ni puede disimularlo' (*Ibid.*).

9. The original Spanish reads: 'Cabe insistir en la ya apuntada – y vieja – analogía entre las actividades peatonales y una determinada forma de coreografía En efecto, el baile expresa a la perfección ese lenguaje de reciprocidades multiplicadas, a veces microscópicas, proclamaciones de una extrema levedad, vigilancias mutuas – con frecuencia de soslayo – y otras actividades visuales manifestas, que producen una diversidad de realizaciones y de formatos socio–organizativos en los espacios urbanos. La danza es ese tipo de creación artística que se basa en el aprovechamiento al máximo de las posibilidades expresivas del cuerpo, ejerciendo su energía sobre un tiempo y un espacio, tiempo y espacio que podría parecer que ya estaban ahí antes de la acción humana, pero que en realidad es de ésta de la que emanan. El baile lleva hasta las últimas consecuencias la somatización por el actor social de sus iniciativas, la comprensión en términos corporales de la interacción que mantiene con su medio espacial, con las cosas que le rodean y con los demás humanos, la interpelación ininterrumpida entre persona y mundo. El cuerpo–energía–tiempo del danzante expresa todas sus posibilidades en una actividad cotidiana en marcos urbanos en que las palabras suelen valer relativamente poco en la relación entre desconocidos absolutos o parciales y en la que todo parece depender de elocuencias superficiales, no en el sentido de triviales, sino en tanto actos que tienen lugar en la superficie, que funcionan por deslizamientos, que evitan o extraen el máximo provecho de los accidentes del terreno, que buscan y crean las estrías y los pliegues, que desmienten cualquier univocidad en la piel de lo social' (*Ibid.*).

10. The original Spanish reads: 'los más eficaces ejercicios de reflexión sobre la propia identidad, donde cobra sentido el compromiso político como consciencia de las posibilidades de la acción y donde la movilización social permite conocer la potencia de las corrientes de simpatía y solidaridad entre extraños' (*Ibid.*).

11. The original Spanish reads: 'devenir nadas ambulantes, perfiles nihilizados, seres hipertransitivos, sin estado, es decir que no pueden ser contemplados estáticamente, sino sólo en excitación, trajinando de un lado para otro' (*Ibid.*).

12. The original Spanish reads: 'Esos seres han renunciado a proclamar quiénes son. Se niegan a identificarse' (*Ibid.*).

13. Delgado writes of the emancipatory potential of public space: 'For example, "immigrants" or those making up cultural, ethnic or religious "minorities". All of these are subject to conceptualizations that do not reflect an objective reality, but that are rather derogatory attributes applied with the goal of signalling the presence of someone who is "different"', who is "the other" in a context in which everyone in the world is – or should be – recognized as different or as the other. Those persons who are labelled "ethnic" or "immigrant" are systematically obliged to give explanations, to justify what they do, what they think, what the rites they perform are, what they eat, what their sexuality is, what religious sentiments they have or what their vision of the universe is'. The original Spanish reads: 'Por ejemplo, los "inmigrantes" o los componentes de "minorías" culturales, étnicas o religiosas. Todos ellos reciben conceptualizaciones que no reflejan una realidad objetiva, sino que son atributos denegatorios aplicados con la finalidad de señalar la presencia de alguien que es "el diferente", que es "el otro", en un contexto en el cual todo el mundo es – o debería ser – reconocido como diferente y otro. Estas personas a las que se aplica la

marca de "étnico" o "inmigrante" son sistemáticamente obligadas a dar explicaciones, a justificar qué hacen, qué piensan, cuáles son los ritos que siguen, qué comen, cómo es su sexualidad, qué sentimientos religiosos tienen o cuál es la visión que tienen del universo' (Delgado, 2007a, p. 192).

14. The original Spanish reads: 'Las aceras, como espacios urbanos por excelencia, deben ser consideradas por tanto terreno para una cultura dinámica e inestable, elaborada y reelaborada constantemente por las prácticas y discursos de sus usuarios' (*Ibid.*).

References

Alexiou, A.S. (2006) *Jane Jacobs: Urban Visionary*. New Brunswick, NJ: Rutger's University Press.

Benjamin, W. (2002) *The Arcades Project* (translated by H. Eiland and K. McLaughlin). Cambridge, MA: Harvard University Press.

Berezin, M. (1999) Political belonging: emotion, nation, and identity in fascist Italy, in Steinmetz, G. (ed.) *State/Culture: State-Formation After the Cultural Turn*. Ithaca, NY: Cornell University Press, pp. 355–377.

de Certeau, M. (1988) *The Practice of Everyday Life* (translated by S. Rendall). Berkeley, CA: University of California Press.

Choay, F. (1969) *The Modern City: Planning in the 19th Century* (translated by M. Hugo and G.R. Collins). New York: George Braziller.

Delgado Ruiz, M. (1999) *El animal público* (The Public Animal). Barcelona: Anagrama.

Delgado Ruiz, M. (2001) *Memoria y lugar: El espacio público como crisis de significado* (Memory and Place: Public Space as Crisis of Meaning). Valencia: Ediciones Generales de la Construcción.

Delgado Ruiz, M. (2006) Espacio público (Public space). *El País*, 29 May.

Delgado Ruiz, M. (2007a) *Sociedades movedizas: pasos hacia una antropología de las calles* (Mobile Societies: Steps Toward an Anthropology of the Streets). Barcelona: Anagrama.

Delgado Ruiz, M. (2007b) *La ciudad mentirosa: Fraude y miseria del 'modelo Barcelona'* (The Deceitful City: The Fraud and Misery of the 'Barcelona Model'). Madrid: Catarata.

Elden, S. (2001) Politics, philosophy, geography: Henri Lefebvre in recent Anglo-American scholarship. *Antipode*, **33**(5), pp. 809–825.

Elden, S. (2006) Rhythmanalysis: an introduction, in Lefebvre, H. *Rhythmanalysis: Space, Time and Everyday Life* (translated by S. Elden and G. Moore). London: Continuum, pp. vii–xv.

Fraser, B. (2007a) Madrid's Retiro Park as publicly-private space and the spatial problems of spatial theory. *Social & Cultural Geography*, **8**(5), pp. 673–700.

Fraser, B. (2007b) Manuel Delgado's urban anthropology: from multidimensional space to interdisciplinary spatial theory. *Arizona Journal of Hispanic Cultural Studies*, **11**, pp. 57–75.

Fraser, B. (2008) Toward a philosophy of the urban: Henri Lefebvre's uncomfortable application of Bergsonism. *Environment and Planning D*, **26**(2), pp. 338–58.

Fraser, B. (2009a) Narrating the organic city: a Lefebvrian approach to city planning, the novel & urban theory in Spain. *Journal of Narrative Theory*, **39**(3), pp. 369–390.

Fraser, B. (2009b) The 'kind of problem cities pose': Jane Jacobs at the intersection of pedagogy, philosophy and urban theory. *Teaching in Higher Education*, **14**(3), pp. 265–276.

Fraser, B. (2010) *Encounters with Bergson(ism) in Spain. Reconciling Philosophy, Literature, Film and Urban Space*. Chapel Hill, NC: University of North Carolina Press.

Fraser, B. (2011a) Ildefons Cerdà's scalpel: A Lefebvrian perspective on nineteenth-century urban planning. *Catalan Review*, **25**.

Fraser, B. (2011b) *Henri Lefebvre and the Spanish Urban Experience: Reading the Mobile City*. Lewisburg, PA: Bucknell University Press.

Hannam, K., Sheller, M. and Urry, J. (2006) Editorial: mobilities, immobilities and moorings. *Mobilities*, **1**(1), pp. 1–22.

Harvey, D. (1989) *The Urban Experience*. Baltimore, MD: Johns Hopkins University Press.

Harvey, D. (2000) *Justice, Nature and the Geography of Difference*. Oxford: Blackwell.

Harvey, D. (2005) The New Urbanism and the communitarian trap: on social problems and the false hope of design, in Saunders, W.S. (ed.) *Sprawl and Suburbia*. Minneapolis, MN: University of Minnesota Press, pp. 21–26.

Harvey, D. (2006) *Paris, Capital of Modernity*. London: Routledge.

Hirt, S. (2009) Pre-modern, modern, postmodern? Placing New Urbanism into a historical perspective. *Journal of Planning History*, **8**(3), pp. 248–273.

Jacobs, J. (1984) *Cities and the Wealth of Nations: Principles of Economic Life*. New York: Random House.

Jacobs, J. (1992, 1961) *The Death and Life of Great American Cities*. New York: Vintage.

Jacobs, J. (1994) *Systems of Survival: A Dialogue on the Moral Foundations of Commerce and Politics*. New York: Vintage.

Latham, A. and McCormack, D. (2004) Moving cities: rethinking the materialities of urban geographies. *Progress in Human Geography*, **28**(6), pp. 701–724.

Lefebvre, H. (1991) *The Production of Space* (translated by Donald Nicholson-Smith). Oxford: Blackwell.

Lefebvre, H. (1996) The right to the city, in Kofman, E. and Lebas, E. (eds. and translators) *Writings on Cities*. Oxford: Blackwell, pp. 63–181.

Lefebvre, H. (2002) *Critique of Everyday Life*, Vol. 2 (translated by J. Moore). London: Verso.

Lefebvre, H. (2003) The Urban Revolution (translated by R. Bononno). Minneapolis, MN: University of Minnesota Press.

Lefebvre, H. (2005) *Critique of Everyday Life*, Vol. 3 (translated by G. Elliott). London: Verso.

Lefebvre, H. (2006) *Rhythmanalysis: Space, Time and Everyday Life* (translated by S. Elden and G. Moore). London: Continuum.

Lofland, L. (1991) The urban milieu: locales, public sociability and moral concern, in Maines, D.R. (ed.) *Social Organization and Social Process: Essays in Honor of Anselm Strauss*. New York: Aldine de Gruyter.

Madanipour, A. (2003) *Public and Private Spaces of the City*. London: Routledge.

Marston, S. (1990) Who are 'the people'? Gender, citizenship and the making of the American nation. *Environment and Planning D*, **8**, pp. 449–458.

Marx, K. (1977) *Capital*, Vol. 1 (translated by B. Fowkes, introduction by E. Mandel). New York: Vintage.

Merrifield, A. (2006) *Henri Lefebvre: A Critical Introduction*. London: Routledge.

Mitchell, D. (2003) *The Right to the City*. New York: Guilford Press.

Molotch, H. (1993) The space of Lefebvre. *Theory and Society*, **22**(6), pp. 887–895.

Sennett, R. (1992) *The Conscience of the Eye: The Design and Social Life of Cities*. New York: Norton.

Sennett, R. (2008) *The Craftsman*. New Haven, CT: Yale University Press.

Simmel, G. (2000) The metropolis and mental life, in Farganis, J. (ed.) *Readings in Social Theory: The Classic Tradition to Post-modernism*, 3rd ed. New York: McGraw Hill, pp. 149–157.

Staeheli, L. (1996) Publicity, privacy and women's political action. *Environment and Planning D*, **14**, pp. 601–619.

Strauss, A.(1961) *Images of the American City*. New York: Free Press.

Wirth, L. (1938) Urbanism as a way of life. *The American Journal of Sociology*, **44**(1), pp. 1–24.

Young, I.M. (1990) *Justice and the Politics of Difference*. Princeton, NJ: Princeton University Press.

Chapter 4

Jane Jacobs,
Modernity and Knowledge

Sonia Hirt

If we imagine the philosophical discussion of the modern period reconstructed as a judicial hearing, it would be deciding a single question: how is reliable knowledge (Erkenntnis) possible.

Jürgen Habermas

Although best known as a theorist of urbanism and a critic of urban planning, Jane Jacobs made important contributions to economics, politics, and philosophy. Out of her eight books, only the second but most popular one, *The Death and Life of Great American Cities*, is specifically about urbanism and urban planning. Of the others, three (*The Economy of Cities, Cities and the Wealth of Nations,* and *The Nature of Economies*) are explicitly on economics (admittedly, with emphasis on *cities* and economics), three can be said to be political (*Constitutional Chaff, The Question of Separatism,* and *Dark Age Ahead*), and one is clearly on ethics (*Systems of Survival*). Jacobs is not, however, normally considered an epistemologist, a philosopher of knowledge. Yet, we can perhaps infer from the fact that *The Death and Life's* synthesis chapter is dedicated not to the social or spatial features of the city but, rather, to *The Kind of a Problem a City Is,* that she was deeply interested in the problems of knowledge and how it is generated.[1] In this chapter, I explore Jacobs's take on knowledge and knowledge-building. I argue that Jacobs's writings are an exemplary critique of the epistemological premises of technocratic 'high modernism' – a philosophical paradigm which reached its culmination in the middle of the twentieth century (Scott, 1998). I base my argument mainly on a read of *The Death and Life* and the other two books from Jacobs's urban trilogy, *The Economy of Cities* and *Cities and the Wealth of Nations,* lighter references to some of her other publications, and some archival materials available at Boston College's Jane Jacobs Papers collection.

Epistemology is of course a complex subject which has been debated, at least in Western thought, since the times of Plato and Aristotle. A typical definition refers to the 'study or theory of the nature and grounds of knowledge especially in reference to its limits and validity'.[2] The definition is deceivingly simple: it is pretty difficult to grasp the 'nature and grounds of knowledge'. One way to organize the debate is to pose three related questions – what, how and who: What about the world can be known? How can we know it? and Who can know it? (e.g. White, 1982). For the purposes of this chapter, I take these questions to relate to *extent, evidence* and *expertise*: 1. What can be the extent of our knowledge of the world? 2. What constitutes sufficient evidence for knowing? and 3. Who has the capacity to know?

From the Enlightenment all the way to the era of mid-twentieth-century high modernism, these questions in Western thought tended to be answered in a particular way: 1. reality, natural and social, operates under objective and universal laws that can be fully known and applied for the purposes of human betterment; 2. knowledge-building occurs through the construction and verification of logical hypotheses pertaining to the laws of reality, hypotheses which can be tested through formal empirical observation; and 3. a cadre of highly trained individuals possess superior capacity to attain knowledge (e.g., Reiss, 1982; Harvey, 1989; Havel, 1992; Healey, 1997; Scott, 1998). This specific way of answering the questions, which forms the core of Enlightenment-modernist thought, has been under heavy fire since the 1960s with the advent of post-positivist and post-modern thinking. The critique of modern epistemology is central to broader critiques of modernity – one good reason why Jean-François Lyotard (1984) wrote about the 'postmodern condition' as a 'report on knowledge' and why Jürgen Habermas chose to open his *Knowledge and Human Interests* with a depiction of an imaginary judicial hearing on the achievements (and failures) of modernity focused on a single question: How is reliable knowledge possible? (1972, p. 3).

What and how does Jacobs *know*? To what extent does she think the world can be known? How does she think she gets to know what she claims to know? And, who does she think can know? What would she have said at the Habermasian judicial hearing? My argument is that although Jacobs criticizes modernist epistemology, she also works to improve it instead of rejecting it (which in fact makes her a potential, if implicit, early ally of Habermas, who defends the 'modern project'[3] and an opponent of Lyotard, who denounces it). Clarifying Jacobs's take on 'how is reliable knowledge possible' is important in order to better understand what Jacobs claims and why she claims it. It also allows us to find her rightful place in the line of twentieth-century philosophers of knowledge.

Jacobs and the Question of Extent: What Can Be Known About the (Urban) World?

It perhaps goes without saying that Jacobs believed reality, urban or other, can be generally known and understood.[4] Despite common charges that she was a commonplace observer and not a 'real' scientist (i.e. one that is interested in law discovery and theory-building), Jacobs was in fact deeply driven by poignant scholarly questions which aimed to uncover fundamental issues pertaining to the 'nature of things' (cities in her case)[5] such as the factors that explain how cities grow or what makes them successful (see also Harris, 2011).[6] In Jacobs's view, urban reality operates as a coherent, if complex 'system' guided by a set of immanent and logical principles or laws that can and should be grasped through human reasoning and observation – an utterly modern proposition. The second paragraph of *The Death and Life* (1961, pp. 3–4) conveys this point clearly: Jacobs writes that her principal intent in the book is to *generate theory from facts* (Harris, 2011): specifically, to discover the causal mechanisms that drive urban spaces to behave the way they do in real life (e.g. 'why some parks are marvelous and others are vice traps and death traps; why some slums stay slums and other slums regenerate themselves', etc.). She posits that once the causal factors are discovered, they can be applied directly towards practical progress:[7] e.g. to 'promote the social and economic vitality of cities' – again, an utterly modern idea. Had she not believed that these factors can be derived and well-understood, it would have been impossible for her to spend most of the book discussing them under the headings of 'conditions of diversity' and 'forces of decline and regeneration'. But any further, even superficial reading reveals that Jacobs's views of what can be known are not fully within the high modernist epistemological tradition, which dominated her time.

Vaclav Havel (1992) claims that modernist epistemology can be summed up as the belief in a 'wholly knowable system governed by a finite number of universal laws that man can grasp'. If so, I would argue that Jacobs's view of what we can know about the world allows way too much room for doubt and for contingency to fit comfortably in this definition. True, in each of her urban books, Jacobs speaks of discoverable 'universal laws' that apply to cities, development, or even more generally to all 'systems': natural, urban, economic, etc. For example, in the last chapter of *The Death and Life*, she argues that cities like other 'systems of organized complexity' (e.g. human bodies, natural habitats) are governed by a 'number of factors which are interrelated in an organic whole' and that the interconnected working of these factors is an 'essential feature of [any] organization' (1961, pp. 432–433). In *The Economy of Cities*, she makes a similar attempt to extract universal tenets of development common to all 'systems' (e.g. 'We find reciprocating systems all about us, in nature as well as in man-made contrivances'; 1969, p. 126). And in *Cities and the Wealth of Nations*, she posits that certain economic principles are universal ('[although] history does not repeat itself in details, but patterns of economic history are so repetitious as to suggest they are almost laws'; 1984, p. 206). She also quite often makes the case for natural-human systems crossover: 'Many of the root processes at work and in human and natural ecologies are amazingly similar' (1984, p. 224); e.g. cataclysmic events ('transactions of decline') that shake human and natural systems in fairly similar ways:

In nature, for example, stresses and instabilities gradually build up in various portions of the earth's crust. When the accumulating stresses reach a certain point they are abruptly disposed of by a discontinuity. The same phenomenon is at work in human affairs. A city enterprise that moves out because of accumulating stresses – say, congestion, makeshift space, rising costs – is experiencing an abrupt discontinuity. (1984, pp. 206–208)[8]

Such statements can potentially be taken as illustration of her viewpoint that the world consists of fully 'knowable systems' governed by universal laws that 'man can grasp'. But, this is true only to an extent. Where Jacobs deviates from the modernist tradition – a fact she herself emphasizes consistently – is the extent to which she believes that the 'systems' are so complex as to make it impossible for humans to grasp all the factors that affect them in all their interconnections, thus rendering futile any human attempts to master fully the causal combinations and thus design wholly new systems successfully. This in fact seems to be the chief lesson from *The Death and Life*'s last chapter, in which she famously lambasts the knowledge-seeking approach of her predecessors and contemporaries. Knowledge of the urban world, she argues, cannot be achieved by taking it either as a bivariate problem or even as a multivariate problem that includes many unrelated independent variables. So even though the urban world could theoretically be fully known if we choose to study it as the 'problem of organized complexity' that it is, any effort to derive anything but the broadest possible principles of what makes cities (and other types of systems) successful or not is doomed to fail. So, yes, diversity is a common trait of all successful systems; thus, we can call it a rule that, say, mono-functional arrangements do not work (e.g. cities where residences and commerce are far apart) and multi-functional ones do seem to work better (e.g. cities where residences and commerce are more integrated), but it is impossible to calculate the 'proper' level of land-use mix because this would depend on a vast variety of factors that we can only understand in very unique, particular (rather than widely generalizable) contexts. Hence a statement like: 'I have generalized about these forces and processes considerably but let no one be misled that these generalizations can be used routinely to declare what the particulars, in this or that place, *ought* to be' (1961, p. 441) – is a sort of a general law against generalizability, which she rehearses throughout her writings. And hence another Jacobs's 'general law': that small-scale, incremental adjustment, dynamic flexibility, innovation and experimentation are the hallmarks of a successful system; and that disallowing such innovation and sticking to pre-emptively determined, rigid rules of how a system should work are the hallmark of bad policy.

Although these perpetual trial-and-error adjustments of the urban realm were misconstrued as chaotic by some of her contemporaries, whom she heavily criticized, for Jacobs they were examples of the creative but not wholly knowable and predictable internal forces that allowed a complex system perpetually to evolve and self-correct. This appreciation of the relative 'unknowability' of systems is the root of Jacobs's passionate assertion that the 'city is not art' (i.e. it cannot be successfully created from blueprints, with a stroke of a pen or a paintbrush) and her adamant opposition to static, preordained programmes of how to create new systems of any kind, which permeates all of her writings. Here is a lesser known but very clear example from a draft speech entitled *The Failure and Future of American Housing Programs*,[9] in which she ridicules efforts to design neighbourhoods from scratch: 'First a plan has to be made for the whole, in advance. Second, it has to be executed in its entirety, in unity. Third, once executed it has to be protected ever after from changes at cross purposes to it'. Pointing to the absurdity of this method, she then argues for a 'careful filling-in approach', in which '[t]he end result cannot be worked out at the beginning'. She reiterated this view in an especially vivid way in one of her last media interviews:

I love New York so much still… Like all cites, it's self-organizing… The most properly designed place cannot compete. Everything is provided which is the worst thing that we can provide. There's a joke that the father of an old friend used to tell, about a preacher who warns children, 'In Hell there will be wailing and weeping and gnashing of teeth'. 'What if you don't have teeth?' one of the children asks. 'Then teeth will be provided', he says sternly. That's it – the spirit of the designed city: Teeth Will Be Provided for You. (cited by Gopnik, 2007)

In short then, while Jacobs searched for and claimed to have attained knowledge of certain broad laws and principles that operate within the urban realm and, potentially, of laws and principles that work across systems, she also recognized the limited capacity of human reason to conquer reality's complexity in full.

Jacobs and the Question of Evidence: How to Know?

Now, what kind of evidence allows us to claim reliable, even if incomplete, knowledge of the world around us? Jacobs lays out the cornerstone of her philosophy of how to know the urban realm in the same second paragraph of *The Death and Life* that I already quoted. She starts this paragraph with: 'In setting forth different principles, I shall mainly be writing about common, ordinary things' and ends it with 'In short, I shall be writing about *how cities work in real life because this is the only way to learn* [my italics] what principles of planning and what practices in rebuilding can work to improve cities and what will work to 'deaden' them' (1961, pp. 3–4). In other words, she proposes that reliable knowledge is possible only through direct observation of everyday, actually occurring phenomena (as opposed to through abstract models of how reality ought to work according to 'pure reason'). In this sense, her thought fits in the empiricist and inductive, Darwinian school of modern knowledge-building rather than, say, in the Descartes's wing of deductive reasoning.[10] Not surprisingly, one of her favourite mottoes, which she borrowed from Deng Xiaoping, was 'Seek truth from facts' (Hospers, 2006). Perhaps needless to say, Jacobs carries on this method consistently throughout *The Death and Life*. In the last chapter, she summarizes her knowledge-building philosophy, or what she calls 'habits of thought', in the following terms:

1.   To think about processes;

2.   To work inductively, reasoning from particulars to the general, rather than the reverse;

3.   To seek for the 'unaverage' clues involving very small quantities, which reveal the way larger and more 'average' quantities are operating. (1961, p. 440)

Jacobs's favourite example of the wrong way of gathering knowledge, the wrong 'habits of thought', comes alive in the introductory chapter of *The Death and Life*, where she recounts a conversation with a Boston planner who had been educated to think of cities according to academic theories and models. The planner was shocked that Boston's North End seemed like a rather vital place, even though its formal attributes – population densities, land-use ratios, street measurements, etc. – were all 'wrong' according to the theories the planner had learned (1961, pp. 8–11). The planner's education must have been in line with the philosophy of, say, Le Corbusier – perhaps the most rigid of the high-modernist architect-planners (Scott, 1998), whom Jacobs especially detested. In his 1929 book *The City of To-morrow and Its Planning*, Le Corbusier offers a version of epistemology that runs exactly contrary to that of Jacobs: he thought that cities can be modelled to resemble highly idealized versions of eternal urban order and that they should be planned once and for all in 'search for perfection' (1987, p. xxii). He also thought that statistics give an 'exact picture of our present state' and even of some 'eternal verities' to the point that 'statistics is the Pegasus of the town planner' and 'jumping-off ground for poetry' (1987, pp. 107–126).[11] Jacobs ridicules this school of thought for being *a priori* and normative; i.e. for assuming knowledge before the fact; for being independent of real-life, empirical evidence; and for being based on irrelevant abstract models and false analogies:

Cities are an immense laboratory of trial and error, failure and success, in city planning and design. This is the laboratory in which city planning should have been learning and forming and testing its theories. Instead the practitioners and teachers of this discipline (if such it can be called) have ignored the study of success and failure in real life, have been incurious about the reasons of unexpected success, and are guided instead by principles derived from the behavior and appearance of towns, suburbs, tuberculosis sanatoria, fairs and imaginary dream cities – from anything but cities themselves. (1961, p. 6).

Planners, architects of city design … have gone to great pain to learn what the saints and sages of modern orthodox planning have said about how cities ought to work and what ought to be good for people and businesses in them. They take this with such devotion that when contradictory reality intrudes, threatening to shatter their dearly won learning, they must shrug reality altogether. (1961, p. 8)

She returns to the failure of abstract and normative reason in the last chapter of the book bringing up once again the example of the bewildered Boston planner torn between his learned theories and his lived experiences:

Why reason inductively? Because to reason, instead, from generalizations ultimately drives us into absurdities – as in the case of the Boston planner who knew (against all the real-life evidence he had) that the North End had to be a slum because the generalizations that make him an expert say it is… This is an obvious pitfall because the generalizations on which the planner was depending were themselves nonsensical. However, inductive reasoning is just as important for identifying, understanding and constructively using the forces and processes that are actually relevant to cities, and therefore are not nonsensical. (1961, p. 441)

She continued to champion empirical knowledge versus normative, *a priori* knowledge with the same vigorous rhetoric two decades later in *Cities and the Wealth of Nations*. The book's opening chapter, 'Fool's Paradise' (1984, pp. 3–28), is preoccupied with the 'dismal science of economics' which managed to reduce the complexity of the world to neat graphs and curves. Her second chapter is called, perhaps not surprisingly, 'Back to Reality'. Clearly, Jacobs's idea of knowledge-formation heavily favours *a posteriori* knowledge: 'The way to get at what goes in the seemingly mysterious and perverse behavior of cities, I think, is to look closely, *and with as little previous expectation as possible* (my italics), at the most ordinary scenes and events...' (1961, p. 13). This statement comes quite close to what, some half a dozen years after *The Death and Life* was written, Barney Glaser and Anselm Strauss (1967) called 'grounded' theory-making.

Keeping in mind Jacobs's insistence on studying real-life, factual evidence on the ground, it is peculiar that one of the most persistent critiques against her – a critique dating back to Robert Moses's assessment of her work as 'sloppy' and 'inaccurate' – has been precisely the one that she *lacks* this type of evidence and, thus, cannot claim that her findings are generalizable. This view was well articulated in a recent piece in *The Wall Street Journal*, which stated that 'Jacobs had a tendency toward sweeping conclusions based on anecdotal information, and some of them were overblown and/or oblivious to the facts' (Manshel, 2010).

The charge does not appear to imply that Jacobs distorted facts but, rather, that she chose them in an unsystematic way to support her pre-conceived theories (in this sense, the statement accuses Jacobs of doing exactly what she accused her adversaries – constructing *a priori* theory). In a positivist world, Jacobs is quite vulnerable to the charge. Indeed, observing everyday people going about their everyday activities in the city (as she does in *The Death and Life*) without explaining how these people (which social scientists like to call 'subjects') were selected to achieve representation is dubious. If selection is haphazard, can Jacobs claim to make generalizable conclusions? (If asked, Le Corbusier's followers would likely expect random statistical selection to ensure generalizability.) Furthermore, even in the urban books in which she does not focus on the experiences of everyday people but rather on the behaviour of cities as basic units of analysis, Jacobs does not articulate how 'subject' or case selection was made. I would argue, though, that even without explicit articulation of sampling method, Jacobs actually followed what today is considered a perfectly mainstream methodology: case-study research. Take for example *The Economy of Cities*. Does Jacobs have a method? She moves from city to city with the same ease and seeming frivolousness as she moves from person to person and from neighbourhood to neighbourhood in *The Death and Life*. On just two pages (1969, pp. 130–131), we find references to some dozen cities, old and new, spread all over the world: Venice, London, Paris, Hamburg, Osaka, Chicago, Dinant, Mohenjo-daro, Harappa. Is there research logic behind these case choices? Is this scientific selection or some sloppy, rambling sequence? I would argue that far from rambling, Jacobs is perhaps subconsciously following the research logic of the classic qualitative methodologies that Robert Yin (1984) outlined some 15 years after Jacobs wrote *The Economy of Cities*. Her analytic tactic is in fact commonly used in multiple case-study research design: the researcher makes case selection expecting similar results from a series of cases – a method Yin (1984, p. 46) calls 'literal replication'. (In this particular instance, Jacobs is using multiple case-study design to extract a particular theoretical proposition for the importance of export-oriented growth in urban development – something which she believed her contemporary urban theorists had neglected.)

Now, one can argue that the evidence she accumulated and presented on cities as diverse as Harappa and Hamburg may have been superficial and, in contrast to the evidence used in *The Death and Life*, certainly based entirely on secondary sources. But her research logic – selecting cases in which a number of circumstances (i.e. independent variables) are quite different (hence the value of the diverse selection across time and space), yet outcomes (in this case, explosive urban development) are common, thus pointing to the significance of at least one shared independent variable – falls quite in line with case-study technique. A more substantially researched example – this time of the second major logic underlying multiple case studies, that of 'theoretical replication' based on analysis of contrasting cases (Yin, 1984, p. 46) – can be found on the preceding pages of *The Economy of Cities*. There, Jacobs contrasts industrial-era Birmingham and Manchester – two cases in which almost all pertinent independent variables seem quite similar, yet one – the extent to which the urban economy was diversified – was different. Hence, as Birmingham and Manchester follow contrasting trajectories (the former ultimately falters, the latter prospers), they speak to the importance of urban economic diversity as an explanatory factor (1969, pp. 86–93).

One can find many similar examples in *The Death and Life* too. In comparing Boston's thriving and untouched-by-planning North End versus various not-so-vibrant planner-produced districts as extreme and contrasting examples, Jacobs was again employing textbook case-study research logic. No wonder that she explicitly searched for precisely what statistics do not offer: 'unaverages'. Indeed, qualitative methodology, and the case study method especially, involve analytical instead of statistical generalization; they extract knowledge from the workings of non-average, non-typical cases that best illustrate a theory (Yin, 1984). In short then, Jacobs seems to have clearly sided with the empiricist tradition of knowledge-building. Furthermore, even when she lacked in-depth access to primary sources (as is in *The Economy of Cities*), she worked using what we now would consider legitimate ways of extracting theories about reality from observation.

Jacobs and the Question of Expertise: Who Can Know

From the three aspects of knowledge-formation discussed in this chapter, Jacobs's view on experts and expertise has been the most widely discussed. Her views on that matter are closely related to her views on how knowledge can be generated, which I addressed in the previous section of this chapter. In a nutshell, Jacobs was the 'nonexpert expert' (Kinkela, 2009): she lacked formal education or an official title, professorial or other, in the disciplines to which she ultimately contributed. Indeed, she often scoffed at academic credentials, refused to be referred to as an 'expert' in print, and rebuffed the universities which sought to give her honorary degrees, as all of her recent biographies have emphasized (Alexiou, 2006; Flint, 2009; Gratz, 2010). Jacobs's lack of official training was commonly used as a source of sneer by her decorated adversaries. Robert Moses referred to *The Death and Life* as 'junk'. In a 1961 letter, Lewis Mumford declined to comment on the book since this would amount to 'an old surgeon giving public judgment on the work of a confident but sloppy novice'. A year later he wrote his famous scathing book review ridiculing 'Mother Jacobs' for her 'schoolgirl howlers' and her 'homemade poultice for the cure of (urban) cancer' (Mumford, 1962). The then-President of the American Institute of Planning Officials was equally dismissive: 'Mrs. Jacobs clearly knows so little about planning' (still he feared the impact of the book enough as to call: 'So batten down the hatches, boys, we are in for a big blow!'; cited by Alexiou, 2006). The patriarchal overtones of such statements directed at Jacobs's ostensible ignorance are quite obvious (and strong enough to warrant a separate article) but not surprising. As earlier said, Jacobs consistently praised practical, everyday knowledge over theory-led, propositional knowledge – an approach which has been historically associated with women and has thus been routinely degraded as knowledge of a lower rank.[12]

A closer scrutiny of Jacobs's life and writings, however, hardly suggests aversion to either experts or expertise per se. As a matter of fact, Jacobs received a rather rigorous training at Columbia University even though she was not granted a degree (since the university would only issue diplomas to males); read obsessively on various scientific subjects; engaged closely with many of the best-known experts of her time (e.g. William Whyte); and while being unafraid to critique scholars of the magnitude of Marx and Keynes (she does so in *Cities and the Wealth of Nations*), relied heavily on the theories of rising scholars to advance her own assertions (e.g. Kevin Lynch in *The Death and Life*; see Klemek, 2007; Harris, 2011). True, a book like *Cities and the Wealth of Nations* starts with a brutal critique of science and expertise and the theme occurs repeatedly in *The Death and Life*. (The above-cited story of the Boston planner, obviously misled by his schooling, is one among many obvious examples.) But Jacobs's opposition only targets science and expertise that *misrepresent* how reality works. Jacobs is opposed to nonsensical 'expertise' much as any sane person would be opposed to, say, the medieval science of healing through bloodletting – one of Jacobs's favourite examples of harmful expertise. She has no problem with science and the search for expertise per se. In *The Kind of a Problem a City Is* Jacobs puts forward a consistent argument for understanding cities as a scientific problem, as long as the problem is correctly defined (i.e. as long as cities are seen as problems of 'organized complexity'). She speaks passionately of the need for scientific progress and advocates learning specifically from the life sciences, which she views as most advanced. Jacobs thus attacks not expertise, but false expertise, not training, but bad training:

Planners have been trained and disciplined in deductive thinking, like the Boston planner who learned his lessons only too well. Possibly because of this bad training, planners frequently seem to be less equipped intellectually for respecting particulars than ordinary people, untrained in expertise, who are attached to the neighborhood, accustomed to using it, and so are not accustomed to thinking of it in a generalized or abstract fashion. (1961, p. 441)

Expertise is quite necessary in Jacobs's view because it has the unique capacity to inform action (e.g. '… we need desperately to learn and apply as much knowledge as it is true and useful to cities as fast as possible'; 1961, p. 16) – a position quite in line with modern epistemology, as I mentioned earlier. But Jacobs deviates from modern epistemology in that she does not believe that the formal training of 'enlightened' elites makes them better experts than people going about their daily lives in the city. To Jacobs, anyone armed with the powers of observation and reflection can know. In fact, people who have been spared indoctrination into certain false theoretical constructs and rely on their common sense would be positioned to know much better. As other critics of modernity, Jacobs eradicates the distance between 'high' and 'low' knowledge, between learned expertise and experiential expertise. Not only does she put trained experts and common-sense experts on the same footing but, in fact, she often switches their hierarchical positions, as the previous quote demonstrates. *The Death and Life* includes many other citations to that effect, yet I find one of Jacobs's last letters, from 2005, written to New York's Mayor Michael Bloomberg, as the most artful example. Jacobs, by that time 88 years old and widely considered an Olympian authority on cities, starts by framing her expertise in terms of studentship (not scholarship): 'My name is Jane Jacobs. I am a student of cities, interested in learning why some cities persist in prospering while others persistently decline…'. The letter addresses two competing plans which were put forward for New York's Greenpoint-Williamsburg waterfront: the first was prepared by 'experts' and included proposals for large redevelopment projects, and the second was the product of grassroots activism and focused on small-industry retention and the provision of affordable housing. Jacobs briefly examines the arguments of each side and ends in a truly Jacobsonian manner: 'Dear Mayor Bloomberg… Come on, do the right thing. The community really does know best' (Jacobs, 2005).

Conclusion

If Lyotard was correct in that post-modernism is 'incredulity toward meta-narratives' (Lyotad, 1984, p. xxiv), then Jane Jacobs wrote the textbook on how to challenge the prevailing urban meta-narrative of her time. Lacking Lyotard's unbounded relativism, however, Jacobs did not seem to think of all meta-narratives as flawed at inception. She did in fact search to discover some immanent, general principles that guide urban development (shall we call them meta-narratives?), even though she was wise enough to recognize the imperfect capacity of humans to grasp these principles and their interconnections in full. Thus, the most important meta-narrative that Jacobs contributed may be that urban systems are so complex as to permit only modest interventions, interventions that leave sufficient room for ongoing adjustments and experimentation.

In her belief that urban reality can be known (at least to an extent) and that this knowledge can and should be applied to facilitate human progress (that is, to build better, more vibrant, just and efficient cities in her case), Jacobs appears to have carried on what Habermas called the 'extravagant expectation' of Enlightenment-modern thinkers to use knowledge for 'understanding of the world and of the self, for moral progress, the justice of institutions and even the happiness of human beings' (1997, p. 9). In this pursuit, Jacobs does not aim to negate the role of science and expertise but rather to expand their realms in ways to include knowledge that builds on the stories of 'small', common people. If 'science has always been in conflict with narratives' (Lyotard, 1984, p. xxiii), Jacobs brings narrative back into science. And while searching for the broad patterns that may make a meta-narrative, she tells, especially in *The Death and Life*, many diverse and delightful human, everyday mini-narratives that captured the imagination of several generations of readers. In so doing, Jacobs shifts the basic units of analysis used by the urban sciences of her time – ratios, populations, jobs, land uses, housing – back to people. 'A store', she said while addressing an urban design conference at Harvard, 'is also a storekeeper' (1956, p. 102) – a statement which suggests that in addition to her legacy in epistemology, Jane Jacobs also contributed to ontology, the study of what kinds of entities and categories exist and are worth knowing. But that should be the subject of another essay.

Notes

1. In fact, I would posit that *The Death and Life* is more a critique of the epistemology of urban planning than of any other of its aspects.
2. According to the Merriam-Webster Dictionary.
3. I refer, of course, to Habermas's *Modernity: An Unfinished Project* (1997 [1980]).
4. This may sound like a very commonplace observation. However, many important philosophers, from René Descartes to George Berkeley, have doubted that the world can be known, thus expressing various degrees of scepticism and agnosticism (this is true even if we put aside the question whether the world exists at all; that is, outside our minds – a solipsistic position that can be traced to the Roman thinker Sextus Empiricus).
5. In my view, Harris (2011) finally puts to rest the myth that Jacobs was antagonistic towards theory-building.
6. The point that Jacobs believed in discovering and then applying the 'laws of reality' directly towards the systematic betterment of human conditions (as obvious as the idea may seem to most of us today) is not entirely trivial. The idea of using systematically derived knowledge for the widespread improvement of society emerged in Western thought only during the Enlightenment (Scott, 1998).
7. According to Lyotard (1984, p. 12), this type of modernist assumption spans from Comte to Luhman. Lyotard gives the following example from Talcott Parsons: 'The most essential condition of successful dynamic analysis is a continual and systematic reference of every problem to the state of the system as a whole… A process or set of conditions either 'contributes' to the maintenance (or development) of the system or it is 'dysfunctional' in that it detracts from the integration, effectiveness, etc, of the system'.
8. In another example, Jacobs argued that despite differences between cultures and even between types of systems (human, natural, etc.), 'cities obey the same basic laws of life'. This is according to the typewritten draft of the foreword to the Japanese edition of *Cities and the Wealth of Nations* dated April 1986 and available in the Jane Jacobs Collection at Boston College (file # MS 02-13[1/4]).
9. From the Jane Jacobs Collection at Boston College (file # MS 95-29 [525-29]).
10. For example, Achinstein (2011) on 'kinds of knowledge'.
11. For a fuller account of Le Corbusier's ideas on this subject, see Guiton (1981).
12. For a good account of the intersection of gender politics and types of knowledge see, for example, Tanesini (2011).

References

Achinstein, P. (2011) Scientific knowledge, in Bernecker, S. and Prichard, D. (eds.) *The Routledge Companion to Epistemology*. New York: Routledge.

Alexiou, A.S. (2006) *Jane Jacobs: Urban Visionary*. New Brunswick, NJ: Rutgers University Press.

Flint, A. (2009) *Wrestling with Moses: How Jane Jacobs took on New York's Master Builder and Transformed the American City*. New York: Random House.

Gopnik, A. (2007) From 'Cities and Songs', in Mennel, T., Steffens, J. and Klemek, C. (eds.) *Block by Block: Jane Jacobs and the Future of New York*. Princeton, NJ: Princeton Architectural Press.

Glaser, B. and Strauss, A. (1967) *The Discovery of Grounded Theory*. New York: Aldine.

Gratz, R. (2010) *The Battle for Gotham: New York in the Shadow of Robert Moses and Jane Jacobs*. New York: Nation Books.

Guiton, J. (1981) *The Ideas of Le Corbusier on Architecture and Urban Planning*. New York. Braziller.

Habermas, J. (1972) *Knowledge and Human Interests* (translated by J. Shapiro). London: Heinemann.

Habermas, J. (1997 [1980]) Modernity: an unfinished project, in Passerin d'Entrèves, M. and Benhabib, S. (eds.) *Habermas and the Unfinished Project of Modernity: Critical Essays on the Philosophical Discourse of Modernity*. Cambridge, MA: MIT Press.

Harris, R. (2011) The magpie and the bee: Jane Jacobs's magnificent obsession, in M. Page and Mennel, T. (eds.) *Revisiting Jane Jacobs*. Chicago, IL: Planners Press.

Harvey, D. (1989) *The Condition of Post-modernity: An Enquiry into the Origins of Cultural Change*. Oxford: Blackwell.

Havel, V. (1992) The end of the modern era. *The New York Times*, 1 March.

Healey, P. (1997) *Collaborative Planning: Shaping Places in Fragmented Societies*. Vancouver: University of British Columbia Press.

Hospers, G.-J. (2006) Jane Jacobs: her life and work. *European Planning Studies*, **14**(6), pp. 723–732.

Jacobs, J. (1941) *Constitutional Chaff: Rejected Suggestions of the Constitutional Convention of 1787*. New York: Columbia University Press.

Jacobs, J. (1956) Urban design: condensed report of an invitation conference sponsored by the faculty and alumni association of Graduate School of Design, Harvard University. *Progressive Architecture*, August, pp. 97–112.

Jacobs, J. (1961) *The Death and Life of Great American Cities*. New York: Vintage Books.

Jacobs, J. (1969) *The Economy of Cities*. New York: Random House.

Jacobs, J. (1984) *Cities and the Wealth of Nations: Principles of Economic Life*. New York: Random House.

Jacobs, J. (1992) *Systems of Survival: A Dialogue on the Moral Foundations of Commerce and Politics*. New York: Random House.

Jacobs, J. (2005) Letter to Mayor Bloomberg and the City Council. Available at http://www.brooklynrail. org/2005/05/local/letter-to-mayor-bloomberg. Accessed 31 July 2011.

Kinkela, D. (2009) The ecological landscapes of Jane Jacobs and Rachel Carson. *American Quarterly*, **6**(4), pp. 905–928.

Klemek, C. (2007) Placing Jane Jacobs into the transatlantic urban conversation. *Journal of the American Planning Association*, **73**(1), pp. 49–67.

Laurence, P. (2011) The unknown Jane Jacobs: geographer, propagandist, city planning idealist, in Page, M. and Mennel, T. (eds.) *Revisiting Jane Jacobs*. Chicago, IL: Planners Press.

Le Corbusier (1987 [1929]) *The City of Tomorrow and Its Planning*. New York: Dover.

Lyotard, J-F. (1984) *The Postmodern Condition: A Report on Knowledge* (translated by G. Bennington and B. Massumi). Minneapolis, MN: University of Minnesota Press.

Manshel, A. (2010) Enough with Jane Jacobs already. *The Wall Street Journal*, 29 June.

Mumford, L. (1962) Mother Jacobs' home remedies for urban cancer. *The New Yorker*, 1 December.

Reiss, T. (1982) *The Discourse of Modernism*. Ithaca, NY: Cornell University Press.

Scott, J.C. (1998) *Seeing like a State: How Certain Schemes to Improve the Human Conditions have Failed*. New Haven, CT: Yale University Press.

Tanesini, A., (2011) Feminist epistemology, in Bernecker, S. and Prichard, D. (eds.) *The Routledge Companion to Epistemology*. New York: Routledge.

White, A. (1982) *The Nature of Knowledge*. Totowa, NJ: Rowman & Littlefield.

Yin, R. (1994) *Case Study Research: Design and Methods*. Thousand Oaks, CA: Sage.

Chapter 5

Jane Jacobs and Citizen Participation

James Stockard

Cities have the capability of providing something for everybody, only because, and only when, *they are created by everybody*.

Jane Jacobs

The Debate

Everybody loves Jane Jacobs. Really. In fact, so many people have loved her ideas for so long that the edgy and innovative thing to say now is 'Enough with Jane Jacobs Already', as a recent headline in the *Wall Street Journal* proclaimed (Manshel, 2010). Nowhere are the competing claims to True Discipleship more urgent than in conversations about citizen participation. New Urbanists assure us they have incorporated Jacobs's ideas through form-based codes so their plans should be baptized as is. Planners working for their mayor say they have reformed their profession as Jane taught them and engage in active participatory processes. So they now carry the true mantle. Neighbours clamour that the only way to honour Jacobs is to give them veto power over any proposal that would change any element of their turf. It's the product that counts. No, it's the process that matters. Product. Process. Product. Process.

In this chapter, I will argue that none of these positions is absolutely right or absolutely wrong. It is the product and the process. Cities are incredibly complex places. Jacobs understood that and described that complexity as well as anyone before or since:

Among those responsible for cities, at the top, there is much ignorance. This is inescapable, because cities are just too big and too complex to be comprehended in detail from any vantage point ... or to be comprehended by any human; yet detail is of the essence. (1961, pp. 121ff)

It would be folly to think she, or any other thoughtful person, would prescribe a single narrow definition of who or what should 'rule' in the shaping and re-shaping of our urban environments. Jane Jacobs clearly believed that among the wonderful things about cities are their diversity, unpredictability, serendipity and adaptability. She would have left room for all that in the ideal process of planning for the future of her beloved streets and districts. She would have acknowledged that good planning would be a messy, uneven, unique-to-its-place-and-time process. But she would have insisted on a few very fundamental principles of engagement that should be honoured by all. In the paragraphs that follow I will suggest what some of those principles might be.

Two Assumptions

I want to posit two basic assumptions I believe are important in understanding Jane Jacobs's ideas about urban planning. First, let's be clear that Jacobs was not opposed to 'city planning' as a discipline. She just had a strong distrust of the mid-twentieth-century state of the art. In the first paragraph of her seminal *Death and Life of Great American Cities* she says her book is an 'attack on *current* city planning and rebuilding... It is an attack, rather, on the principles and aims that have shaped *modern, orthodox* city planning and rebuilding' (1961, p. 3) (emphasis added). She was mad about the way city planning was practised by the official leaders of American cities. She didn't care for Urban Renewal. She couldn't tolerate wholesale demolition of entire neighbourhoods. She disliked intensely the idea of blasting highways through, over, and around lively city districts. And she absolutely hated the idea that these plans were cooked up in back rooms by people who had probably never walked the streets of those neighbourhoods, much less lived in them. In short, urban leaders of that time were using a very bad *process* to produce an equally bad *product*.

After all, Jane Jacobs *was* a planner. You can't be a citizen activist and build an opposition movement against powerful political and development interests without being a planner. You can't be a member of a family with children to raise, homes to purchase and maintain, and bills to pay without being a planner. And you certainly can't be an author with texts to outline, research to complete and deadlines to meet without being a planner. So Jane Jacobs was certainly a planner. After all, what is the alternative to planning? Not planning? Allow randomness and anarchy to rule? There may be those who would answer 'yes', but the unavoidable result of that approach is outcomes that favour those who enter the arena with power. The developers will rule. No... planning is necessary. But it must be 'good' planning. What Jane Jacobs fought so relentlessly against (and she often won because she was so obviously right) was *bad* planning – planning that was poorly conceived and even more poorly executed. She fought against uninformed, uneducated, wrongly influenced, single-minded, simplistic planning. I believe she would have supported and even enthusiastically participated in a different form of city planning. After all, in that same first paragraph she says '(this book) is also, and mostly, an attempt to introduce new principles of city planning and rebuilding, different and even opposite from those now taught in everything from schools of architecture and planning to the Sunday supplements and women's magazines' (1961, p. 3). So there will be no denunciation of the city planning craft in this chapter.

The second critical concept on which we must agree and which I believe Jacobs understood in a fundamental way is that cities are constantly changing. There is no such thing as a static state for the city. Some neighbourhoods change more rapidly than others. But all parts of cities change constantly. I love the following quote from *The Death and Life* that expresses this idea:

Under the seeming disorder of the old city, wherever the old city is working successfully, is a marvelous order for maintaining the safety of the streets and the freedom of the city. It is a complex order. Its essence is intricacy of sidewalk use, bringing with it a constant succession of eyes. This order is composed of movement and change, and although it is life, not art, we may fancifully call it the art form of the city and liken it to dance – not to simple-minded precision dance with everyone kicking up at the same time, twirling in unison and bowing off en masse, but to an intricate ballet in which the individual dancers and ensembles all have distinctive parts which miraculously reinforce each other and compose an orderly whole. *The ballet of the good city sidewalk never repeats itself from place to place and in any one place is always replete with new improvisations.* (1961, p. 50, emphasis added)

So the question is: how shall that change be shaped? And what should the role of the everyday citizen be in that process? In many places we have seen what happens when we do *nothing* and let the inevitable change occur as the market dictates. It often produces places not very many of us like. Disinvestment condemns certain neighbourhoods and the residents, who cannot escape them, to unattractive, dangerous, underserved environments, which are not desirable in any sense. Or gentrification causes dislocation of the less affluent along with all the pain and cost that creates. The winners are those with property and money and influence. The losers are the people of modest means that are the lifeblood of the city. And that means the city loses.

Another alternative is to let the 'government' take care of all the change. This matrix of elected political leaders, career civil servants, public agencies, and special commissions is officially charged with the responsibility for much of this change through their policies, laws, regulations, decision-making authority and organizational procedures. Perhaps we should just let them exercise their judgment and live with the results. After all, we elected some of them and the rest were appointed by the ones we elected. This, too, is likely to produce city districts and streets not very many of us will like. It was one of Jacobs's central points. She argued that the 'planners' and others in these agencies were ill-equipped to make all these decisions:

So many of the problems need never have arisen. If only well-meaning officials in departments of the city government or in freewheeling authorities knew intimately, and cared about, the streets or districts which their schemes so vitally affect – or if they knew in the least what the citizens of that place consider of value in their lives, and why. (1961, p. 406)

Or later:

Aims of this kind cannot be pursued unless [officials] ... know what they are doing ... not in some generalized way, but in terms of precise and unique places... Much of what they need to know they can learn from no one but the people of the place, because nobody else knows enough about it. (1961, p. 409)

In addition, one might argue that public officials (in some ways just like private developers) have other agendas than simply making parts of the city better. They have re-election concerns, budget concerns, constituency concerns, staff capacity concerns, personal advancement concerns, professional principles, and much more. If we leave city growth entirely to the people who are 'charged with it', we are not likely to be totally pleased either.

How about letting the citizens decide? Each neighbourhood or district could determine a way of making decisions (an elected council, lots of voting about various plans, an online polling arrangement à la American Idol). The district could be granted a certain amount of budget and decision-making authority over things that will happen in their part of the city. We could eliminate the city's planning staff and neighbourhoods could decide whom they wanted to turn to for advice, if anybody. Alas, as appealing as this idea will be to some, I'm not sure even Jane Jacobs would have embraced it. Listen to her words regarding some citizens who speak at public hearings in New York City:

To be sure, foolish things are said too, and untrue things, and things brazenly or suavely self-seeking... (1961, p. 407)

Just because someone is a 'regular neighbour' doesn't mean he or she is free of the personal agenda (e.g. increase my property values, keep 'those' people out of the neighbourhood, ban bars because I am religiously opposed to alcohol) that would get in the way of making good decisions about healthy future growth for the district.

Second, there exists some actual knowledge about how cities work – knowledge that Jacobs describes and illustrates at length – that would be helpful in shaping change. There is no guarantee that ordinary citizens possess this knowledge to any greater extent than city officials or developers. They certainly know more about their part of the city and how it works (or doesn't work) in relation to their own values. What is not so clear is whether they know how to sustain it, fix it, or accurately analyze the implications of a new proposal for these values. In fact, there is some anecdotal evidence that what neighbours like best is no change, even when the change might get them more of what they want. For example, it is a well documented fact that certain levels of residential density are essential to sustain various types of retail establishment. These levels are often greater where a 'mom and pop' store is involved as opposed to a chain outlet. Yet in my own home community many of the same people who bemoan the loss of locally owned, single-store enterprises will simultaneously argue vociferously to down-zone the adjacent neighbourhoods, thus robbing 'mom and pop' of the pedestrian traffic they need to survive.

In fact, many of the most beloved neighbourhoods in the nation would not be able to be built today. Were someone to propose a Beacon Hill, a Georgetown, a South End in Boston, or a Nob Hill in San Francisco it would never get off the ground. Why not? The current zoning regulations would not allow it. Neighbours would fight the variance applications for increased density. Developers wouldn't want to go through the resulting lengthy process to get their approvals. Politicians would not support it for fear of losing the next election. Local planners would not suggest it because they would anticipate the lack of political will. And lenders would not fund it for all of the above reasons. In summary, creating the diverse, active, interesting, sustainable neighbourhoods Jane Jacobs liked so much is a challenge and nobody has a lock on how to do it.

So I suggest there is no silver bullet in the quest for the perfect process of shaping the change constantly occurring in great cities. Rather, I believe Ms Jacobs would advocate a few principles that ought to shape any process that determines how our cities will grow. Let me suggest some of those principles.

Five Principles

First, the process should be dominated by people who have a true understanding of what makes a city work:

In setting forth different principles (for city planning) I shall mainly be writing about common, ordinary things: for instance, what kinds of city streets are safe and what kinds are not; why some city parks are marvelous and others are vice traps and death traps; why some slums stay slums and other slums regenerate themselves even against financial and official opposition; what makes downtowns shift their centers; what, if anything, is a city neighborhood, and what jobs, if any, neighborhoods in great cities do. In short, I shall be writing about how cities work in real life, because this is the only way to learn what principles of planning and what practices in rebuilding can promote social and economic vitality in cities, and what practices and principles will deaden these attributes. (1961, p. 3)

These principles are not always obvious. To learn them one must be a constant observer of cities in the present moment and over time. What changed and what did that change lead to? What did that intervention by some actor (public, for-profit or non-profit) lead to? What happened gradually and naturally and what happened as a result of some initiative? What changed quickly and what seems to stay the same forever? What does well-grounded research say about the changes you are interested in? It goes without saying that a wide range of people observes in this way and learns from their observations. Jacobs, herself, with no college degree and no professional training, but an incredibly sharp eye and a remarkable ability to learn from her observations, is one of the best examples. Some local residents are great at this, others not so. Some journalists get it, some don't. Some academics are terrible at it, a few are brilliant. Politicians may be good at it when it relates to their re-election chances, not so good when it comes to the long-term health of a neighbourhood. The best planners have learned how to do it, but many are satisfied to stay in their offices at City Hall and read the census or look at their wonderful new GIS tools. So who should lead planning processes in a particular place? The ones who understand how cities work in those places.

In some of her most famous fights, I think Jane Jacobs would say she and her allies found these people and called them together. The 'official' planners in those cases did not have this expertise and did not know how to find those who did. But is it conceivable that planners in a different setting could collect such a wise group of observers – a mix of the people who use a neighbourhood and those who study such places and understand how they work? Sure. But putting such people in key leadership roles has to be a fundamental principle of the planning process.

Second, Jane Jacobs would say you need detailed information about the particular place you are planning for. No matter how much you understand in general about how cities work, every neighbourhood, every district, every block, every street is different. Yes, diversity is essential. But if the neighbourhood bar that adds that diversity is a scene for loud music late at night, dangerous fights that sprawl out into the street and a blatant drug-selling operation targeted at the youth of the area, it has to go. Yes, active sidewalks are key to the vitality of a place. But if the activity can be attributed to several brothels on the street (a real case from my professional life), something needs to change. Yes, large public housing developments isolating poor families in one district are usually a bad idea. But if the management of a particular property cares deeply about the residents and generates programmes that help them develop the skills they need to become part of the economic mainstream, perhaps that place is a positive part of the city. So local, specific knowledge is a critical part of any planning effort.

Who knows this? As in the quote above, neighbourhood residents and merchants are almost always the best source for this type of information. But when good public servants spend important hours in the district over a substantial period of time, they may add to this knowledge. Police officers, neighbourhood schoolteachers and principals, mail carriers, and even planners who walk the streets regularly and get to know people can add important specific information to the planning conversations. And some developers, who realize their projects will be more successful in every way if they work hard to understand how cities work and what districts need in order to be vital, contributing parts of the city, can be helpful in these planning efforts.

Third, the process must be led by people who truly care about the future of the district. Not empire builders. Not bureaucrats waiting for retirement or scouting for a promotion. Not political leaders anxious to raise funds or curry voters' favour so they can move to the next office. Not profiteers, looking to maximize their bottom line. And not even neighbourhood residents or merchants with a personal axe to grind or a quick profit to turn. No, I think Jane Jacobs would say that the process should be led by those who truly want the district to thrive – to work better for its current residents, workers and merchants, to grow and change in ways that secure a healthy future for those people and their successors, and to play a vital and strategic role in the city of which it is a part.

Fourth, the process should reach as far into the neighbourhood as possible. The more people are involved, the better the chance that widely observed realities will be accurately reported (rather than the sometimes skewed perspectives of those who mostly like to hear themselves speak in public). Jacobs was famous for writing letters, calling people, holding meetings, activating young people and employing other tactics to enlarge the number of individuals participating in the conversations about neighbourhood change. The good news is we have a rapidly increasing set of tools to help with this task. Citywide and special focus web sites, instant polling devices for large public meetings, neighbourhood blogs, Facebook pages and Tweeting citizens are among the new tools that have the capacity to engage more people on a regular basis in the shaping of their cities. While I'm not so sure Ms Jacobs would have loved the technology *per se*, I'm pretty certain she would have rather quickly seen how it could be used to deepen and broaden citizen involvement. These same tools can also be used to provide data that can inform planning processes. For example, if the city posts accurate data about the actual arrival and departure times of city buses, it will either support local anecdotal observations or call them into question.

Finally, I believe Jane Jacobs would say that any planning process should be weighted towards the current users of a neighbourhood. But not absolutely stacked in their favour via a 'veto' on change, by any means. That is the way racially isolated neighbourhoods get to stay that way. But I think she would say that people who have committed themselves to a place, have been there for a while and who plan to stay there, should have a large say in how that place changes. Forcing people to move their home or their enterprise, or taking steps which makes that dislocation inevitable should be a last resort, and one taken for overwhelmingly important reasons with substantial benefits for those who bear the negative brunt of the change. Such standards would encourage cities to truly weigh the benefits of the proposals. If the change seems so vital to the future of the city or the health of its citizens (e.g. changes in New Orleans to avoid the deaths and losses from the next Hurricane Katrina – but not changes like central city highways that save suburbanites five minutes on their commute), then the large expenditures of money and services for those who must sacrifice to secure a better future for the larger community should be easy to authorize.

What Would Jane Do?

So what would a planning process that Jane Jacobs would endorse and be pleased to participate in look like? It would be a process that follows all the principles above. It would be a planning process that is *not* – I repeat, *not* – project-based. Our current processes are heavily weighted in this direction and many of them violate several of the principles above. Most importantly, by the time they enter the public domain, some parts of the plans that are afoot are already set and a number of people already have stakes in them. If the proposal is a development project, chances are the developer has already determined certain aspects of his or her project, has discussed them with city officials and with political actors. Those people have all formed their viewpoints and will have a difficult time coming to a planning process with an open mind. If the proposal is a new planning study or revision of a regulatory regimen, someone has probably gone to some trouble to define the 'area of study' and the presumed outer edges of the work to be done. Again, positions are already staked out, definitions are posited and certain powers are aligned to support this work. In many of these cases, it is unlikely that local stakeholders have been consulted for their wisdom or insights about the proposals. This means these folks may well be on the defensive as soon as the conversations do start. It is exactly this sort of misguided initiation of the planning process that made Jane Jacobs so angry. It's a process that has begun on paper, in an office, and in the minds of people who typically have little local knowledge. It has not begun on the street, which is where all planning should start. Let me suggest another approach.

Suppose 'planning' was a continuous process that engaged a wide variety of people in learning about a particular part of the city and discussing its future on a regular basis. Imagine that professional planners met neighbourhood groups on a regular basis (quarterly? monthly?) to exchange information, discuss issues, and formulate ideas about things that would make the neighbourhood a better place to live. Planners would bring neighbourhood statistics and information about citywide, regional or national trends that might affect the district. Residents and merchants would bring their descriptions about what was happening in the neighbourhood – including a great deal of information that would likely have flown well under the radar of the professionals based at city hall. An important part of these regular conversations would be education. Planners would be taught about the relationships, the street life, the information flow, the important actors and the concerns of the area. People who live and work in the district would be taught about the ways in which cities and neighbourhoods work – the relationship of density to retail success, the importance of mixed uses for successful sidewalks, the effect of one-way traffic on congestion and active street life. In the best case, there would not be any decisions to make at many of the meetings. There would simply be information to exchange, and discussions to conduct.

Meetings would always be held in the neighbourhood. While the sessions would be open to the public, there might be a smaller set of people (elected?) who committed to always coming to the meetings so that a certain continuity of discussion would be maintained and a core knowledge of the place would be built up by all the actors – citizens and planners together. City staff would be assigned to neighbourhoods rather than topics. Ideally, as Jacobs describes in Chapter 21 of *The Death and Life*, all city departments would be organized in this manner.

Administrative districts in a big city would promptly begin to act as political creatures, because they would possess real organs of information, recommendation, decision and action… Citizens of big cities need fulcrum points where they can apply their pressures, and make their wills and their knowledge known and respected. Administrative districts would inevitably become such fulcrum points. (1961, p. 422)

This would mean that if there were a traffic issue on the agenda, the person from the Traffic Department who was working in this neighbourhood would be at the meeting. Or the staff person for this neighbourhood from the Parks Department, or the Fire Department, or whoever else was needed. And the city staff would not have to say

'I'm not really familiar with the North Side, but Department policy is...'. This place would be their territory. They would know the people from the other departments who worked in their area and they would share knowledge easily. All the city staff would know the leaders of the neighbourhood and whom to consult when a particular issue arose.

Now occasionally, a specific project will come up. Someone will want to build on that empty lot. A property owner will want to convert this or her home into a store. An outside developer will want to purchase several parcels, tear down some houses and put up a new office building. The university or the hospital on the edge of the district will want to expand. The local Community Development Corporation will want to build some affordable housing. There will be a proposal to create more bike lanes on the streets. The public works department will propose a major renovation of the sewer lines in the area, requiring excavation of many streets. How would Jane Jacobs handle that?

I believe there might be several requirements for having a project considered by neighbourhood gatherings. First, and most important, the proposal would have to be very transparent. What is suggested? Who are the principals involved? What are the goals of the project? When will it start? How long will it take? Will it require any relocation, either temporary or permanent? Where will the financing come from? It would be important to explain the links between the proposal and the widely shared goals for the neighbourhood.

Second, the proposal would need to come to this neighbourhood gathering at a very early stage in the process. The authors of the proposal would need to be very open to changes so the project could be modified to better fit the shared hopes for the future of the district.

Third, the proposal would need to deal with related neighbourhood issues. So, if the community had set a priority for more street-level retail uses, a proponent of an office building with nothing but a security lobby on the first floor, would have to explain why he or she was ignoring the neighbourhood priorities or why this building would meet some larger goals in ways that were similar to, or better than, street-level retail.

Ideally, in this scenario, many proposals will arise from the neighbourhood planning meetings. Current residents or merchants will offer proposals that aim to accomplish some of the goals discussed at the meetings. Such proposals should move through the review process easily. Outsiders would be well advised to attend these meetings for a while before making a proposal so they can tailor their ideas to the wishes of the neighbourhood.

One last important detail of the neighbourhood review process is to have a specific and time-limited process for the discussion and decision-making about a project. This is meant to serve all parties. Nobody is well served by discussions which go on for years. Proposal authors see their projects become infeasible as the process drags out. Neighbours get bored hearing the same discussions over and over. City officials spend too much of their time on projects that eventually die. It might be that the neighbourhood groups have three time frames for considering a proposal. Routine matters are taken care of in three months, more complex proposals get a six-month review period and large-scale projects with neighbourhood-wide implications get a nine-month or one-year review. When a proposal first comes to the group, a decision would be made about which schedule would be followed. Extra meetings might need to be scheduled. Predictability would help all parties.

I would not advocate these meetings have the right to formal approval for the project. We have plenty of evidence that granting such power to a very localized body, no matter how representative or thoughtful, is an invitation to small thinking and exclusion of any ideas that will bring change. On the other hand, if these local meetings become occasions for sound and rational discussions with many viewpoints gaining consideration and attendees being careful to balance current and future goals, they will begin to have a power of their own. Political leaders and appointed officials who fail to heed their decisions and ideas do so at their peril.

In order for this to occur, there will need to be several factors acknowledged by these neighbourhood meetings. First, all neighbourhoods change constantly as a result of many factors that are not subject to public 'approvals'. People move. Stores thrive and expand or fail and close. Kids grow up and head off to college or work elsewhere. Technology changes the way we use the neighbourhood (e.g. air conditioning and TVs took people off the streets in the middle of the twentieth century; cell phones freed them from the land lines in their homes and brought them back out). A new pastor at the local church starts youth programmes that activate that corner of the neighbourhood. A beloved principal at the elementary school retires and the PTA ceases to be a strong neighbourhood institution. Greenwich Village is a very different place today from what it was when Jane Jacobs walked its streets, and much of the change is a result of individual decisions and changes brought about by larger societal forces. All parties to these conversations need to agree that change is natural and the goal is not to stop all change, but to reinforce the change that is healthy and work to minimize the change that is undesirable.

It is also important to acknowledge that time in a place counts for a lot. People and merchants who have been a part of a place for a long time should be listened to carefully. If you will, they are the 'elders' of the neighbourhood, and every effort should be made to acknowledge the wisdom they bring to conversations about the future direction of the district. Again, I don't think even Jane Jacobs would give them a veto. Some of their ideas will *not* be wise. But I think she would say they ought to be listened to very carefully. Further, if plans do go forward that adversely impact them, they ought to be compensated in a fulsome manner. When the hardware store that has been in the neighbourhood for 40 years has to move in order to enlarge the park in a way that has wide support, the owner deserves more than the appraised value of his or her real estate and enough money to put the stock in a truck and take it somewhere else. Some value has to be placed on all that a merchant has contributed to the area over all those years. Such valuations would make local and citywide decision-makers think twice about the decision to force the relocation. Perhaps it would cause them to work harder for a solution that accomplished both goals – enlarge the park and preserve a valued neighbourhood business.

Finally, and I'm not quite sure how Jane Jacobs would have stated this, I believe it is important to acknowledge the importance of long-range goals. Too many neighbourhood conversations focus on what will happen tomorrow or next month or, worst of all, before or after the next election (which doesn't have anything to do with building great neighbourhoods). My own city of Cambridge has been very badly affected by an initiative taken by a small group of people who only wanted to maximize their own property values. Once they achieved their goals, they sold their buildings and left town, leaving us behind to struggle with the loss of many of our middle-class families who fought to make our public schools excellent for their children. Had true understanding of the economics of our unusual housing market been on the table and had people considered the long-range consequences of this action, our city would be healthier today.

This planning regimen is demanding. It requires planners to spend much more time physically engaged in the neighbourhoods they are serving. It demands they study carefully how cities work and truly commit to learning about the part of the city their work will impact. It requires citizens to participate more actively in the change taking place in their part of the city and to learn more about how cities work and consider data that describes the changes that are taking place. It requires developers or others with proposals for change to be much more transparent in their process, much more open to altering their ideas and much more forthcoming with the information they are accustomed to keeping private. It's not clear any of these parties are prepared to take these steps.

But I would argue that each of these changes in 'business as usual' has at its core some of the most important principles Jane Jacobs stood for. She wanted us to be smarter about cities, more observant about what is actually happening on our streets and more thoughtful about the kinds of initiatives which will make them healthier. She wanted us to truly love our cities. And if we are to do that, we must commit ourselves to a deeper engagement with their lives. That's what real planning – the kind of city planning Jane Jacobs would have embraced – is about.

References

Jacobs, J. (1961) *The Death and Life of Great American Cities*. New York: Random House.
Manshel, A. (2010) Enough with Jane Jacobs already. *The Wall Street Journal*, 29 June.

Part II

Jane Jacobs, Urban Economist

Chapter 6

Economic Development from a Jacobsian Perspective[1]

Sanford Ikeda

And I hear, from your voice, the invisible reasons which make cities live, through which perhaps, once dead, they will come to life again.

Italo Calvino

The ideas of Jane Jacobs, while highly influential in the fields of urban planning and other urban fields, have as yet made few inroads into economics.[2] I think Jacobs found this situation frustrating because she believed her main intellectual contribution was to economic theory. Four of her books deal primarily with economics,[3] especially *The Economy of Cities* (1969) and *The Nature of Economies* (2000) (Jacobs 1961, 1969a, 1984, 2000).[4]

Jacobs's most famous book, *The Death and Life of American Cities* (1961), galvanized the growing opposition to the kind of heavy-handed urban planning practised for decades by the likes of Robert Moses in New York City. But she did more than simply criticize. Based on keen observation of how people actually use urban spaces, she used a kind of common-sense genius[5] to explain how a successful city works, or doesn't work, at the micro-level. And she explained how policies that ignore the 'locality knowledge' of its inhabitants and the 'social capital' that make its streets safe and liveable can produce a deadly 'dynamics of decline'.

But it is her next book, *The Economy of Cities*, which focused exclusively on the nitty-gritty of economic development, that will be my main focus here. I will outline in brief and offer my interpretations of what I believe are Jacobs's fundamental contributions to the theory of economic development, illustrating with Jacobs's examples and some of my own.

A Note on 'Economic Development'

The concept of 'development' implies change. Economic development implies not simply change, however, but in some sense 'change for the better'. There is a long tradition in economics that takes tastes (i.e. opinions of what 'better' is) as given. This tradition regards what constitutes 'better' as purely subjective; i.e. in this view, the category 'better' may not bear any systematic relation to anything objectively measureable at all. That said, to the extent that subjective betterment is related to wellbeing, and that it is related to material welfare, and to output available for consumption, per-capita GDP or another similar standard could become a useful measure of betterment. But there are severe limitations to this approach.

Measured economic growth has two sources. One is the production and consumption of 'more of the same' goods and services, while the other is the production and consumption of 'more different (and better) things'. The latter, for which the term 'economic development' is more apt, refers to material improvement that comes about because things are being done significantly differently, innovatively; or because novel goods and services are being produced. This type of development certainly has a more profound impact on the human condition and social evolution. Since 'doing things differently' entails change, the focus of economic development, perhaps more than any other area of economics, is on the causes and conditions that promote or retard change for the better.

Cities and Economic Development

I will begin, as Jacobs (1969a) does, with an analysis of how cities first emerged in the Neolithic period. It may seem odd to frame a discussion of economic development relevant for today this way, especially since material welfare rises significantly only after 1500AD, and then really gets going after 1800. But in its own way the Neolithic period was one of radical social change and innovation. It saw the discovery of agriculture, animal husbandry, literacy, numeracy, calendrical sciences, organized religion, markets, large-scale engineering, government, and, of course, the first cities. By some estimates the population of the world between 10,000BC and 5,000BC rose five-fold, from 1 million to 5 million.[6] So, I believe studying this period goes to the heart of the nature and significance of the city, and clearly reveals the role of the city in economic development today.

It has almost become a truism that beyond some point economic progress is tied to urbanization. To gauge the level of material prosperity, look for cities. 'There is a near perfect correlation between urbanization and prosperity across nations' (Glaeser, 2011, p. 159). But, to put it perhaps too simply, this begs the question of whether cities are the cause or the consequence of early cultural and economic development.[7] Here, Jacobs's conclusion is sharply at odds with the conventional view.

The belief that cities, as centres of culture and material prosperity, are the consequence of the accumulation of sufficient capital and material wealth, has led to the conventional belief that cities, both logically and historically, must have been preceded by small towns, which had to have been preceded by smaller, isolated settlements that were founded by bands of hunter-gatherers. According to this view,

Homo sapiens scratched out a nomadic existence living on wild food until eventually they established more or less permanent settlements where they gradually learned how to practice farming and domesticate animals. As knowledge of agriculture and animal husbandry grew, they were able to accumulate surpluses large enough to support a labour force that could build the physical infrastructure (walls, streets, and irrigation) and to establish the social infrastructure (laws, norms, and conventions) that are necessary for even larger settlements. Small towns then became convenient places to buy and sell surplus goods, the wealth from which could then be used to construct the first real cities.[8]

According to this view, a city is more or less the same kind of social phenomenon as a small village, only with many more people and buildings – a kind of luxury good collectively affordable only after income has risen past a certain threshold. This is consistent with the 'more of the same' aspect of economic growth. Cities enter the picture in the relatively late stages of social development and only then do they play an undeniably major role in economic and cultural progress.

However, it is also pretty much accepted, even among those who adhere to the conventional view, that one of the most important functions of a city is to serve as a market, even if it originated as a shrine or fortress or the like (Weber, 1958). The alternative thesis that sees cities as the cause of economic development, must resolve a paradox obvious to anyone holding the conventional perspective: if cities are the essential drivers of economic development, how can they play this role if they arise only at its later stages? Logically, a city cannot be both the original cause and also the product of robust economic development.[9] A city, a large economically and socially vibrant settlement that presupposes a very high level of social cooperation, cannot itself be the source of that cooperation. Or can it?

The Problems of Discovery and Diffusion

Although Jacobs does not use these terms, I think it is helpful to frame her analysis in terms of discovery and diffusion. In other words, economic development, creating new things or making old things in a different way, requires people to solve two problems. The first is for an agent to gather enough information – hints or clues – and, with the aid of his experience and intelligence, to manipulate them mentally and see them in a novel and useful way. In a word: discovery. Doing this can take a lot of work or a lot of luck or both. But it does not have to.

If the agent is placed in an environment in which new problems are regularly presented to him in a fairly clear way, it would be easier to make discoveries, in the form of solutions to those problems, that are useful to himself or others that he knows. Ordinary people under these circumstances can make more discoveries or become better able to use their faculties to their full potential. They could in this sense be more creative. Frequent contact with a large number of people with diverse knowledge, skills, and tastes is the sort of environment in which these kinds of opportunities may emerge. It is also important that these contacts take place in a context of relative peace, because the proximity of so many diverse people may produce opportunities for violent conflict, which would obscure gains from trade or other forms of free association. What we want is a 'clash of culture' in which the clashers can resolve their differences peacefully and to their mutual advantage. Economic freedom is important here because people driven by profit seeking are more apt to tolerate or overcome differences with others in just this way, as well as to enforce norms of fairness (Heinrich, *et al.*, 2010).

The second problem that people have to solve, or rather their environment has to enable them to solve, in order for development to take place, is to maximize the likelihood that the useful knowledge that is discovered can spread to those for whom that knowledge – of new goods, markets, techniques, concepts, networks – would be profitable. In a word: diffusion. This can happen either because of or despite the existence of rules, norms, or conventions regarding intellectual property. That is, the prevention of free-riding on discoveries is necessary to encourage profit-seeking agents to make those discoveries, and so it would be good if there were some way for the agents to sell the discovery and capture enough net benefit at reasonably low transactions costs to make it worthwhile.[10] At the same time, a lot of economic development is the result of word-of-mouth, imitation, and various other kinds of behaviour that might be called free riding. Competition that results from other buyers or sellers seeing someone exploit a net gain from trade has well-known benefits for material prosperity. It is precisely the impossibility of a fully specified, clearly defined, and enforceable system of property rights, however, that leaves room for such free riding. (But this gets us into a very complicated area of discussion regarding the optimal framework of property rights that I need not get bogged down in here.)

Neither the problem of discovery nor the problem of diffusion is very likely to be solved by nomads or farmers in small, isolated settlements. A person in either situation would have very little to work with, very few sources of new information with which to make a discovery. Hints, clues, and new ways of looking at the world would be in very short supply. Innovation and invention by such a person would take a level of creative and independent thought far beyond the norm of his community, especially in places where dealing with familiar persons and ideas almost always trumps dealing with the new and unfamiliar. And even if an extraordinarily creative and independent-minded individual in a small settlement were to make an important discovery that his kinsmen were willing to adopt (e.g. three-field crop rotation or a new variety of grain), how, in the absence of regular contact with distant settlements (in which resistance to change is probably staunch), would the discovery be diffused? Who, in the absence of regular contact with outsiders, would be willing to take on the risky task of spreading the good news, and what incentive would they need to do so?

Considered in this way, the conventional assumption that rural growth must historically precede cities is itself paradoxical. Cities not only foster economic development in its later stages; economic development, beyond the most rudimentary level, cannot even begin unless large, diversely populated settlements, cities, appear near the very beginning of the story. This means that some places must have transitioned from being inhabited by nomadic hunter-gatherers to being inhabited by urban hunter-gatherers very quickly in human social evolution.[11]

Such a seemingly counter-intuitive hypothesis becomes plausible if we imagine this kind of urbanization as the product of market formation. Archaeological evidence indeed suggests that hunter-gatherer groups in Neolithic times did trade with one another in large settlements.[12] In this sense a person from the Neolithic era is no different from Mark Zuckerberg in that both will strive to improve their situation, as they see it, through mutually beneficial exchange. In the early Neolithic period, before the emergence of cities, the potential gains from trade must have been enormous, but the uncertainty and danger of coming face-to-face with strangers outside one's own tight social network, must have been very great as well. Other things being equal, under these circumstances, where one trades would seem to be just as important as what one trades. As with real-estate markets, the three most important factors would be location, location, and location.

Jacobs's contribution in this line of thought is significant. First, she discusses how a trading location is situated so that it is relatively accessible to members of two or more hunter-gatherer groups (Jacobs, 1969a, p. 19). Such places usually have certain physical characteristics, such as proximity to waterways or other travel routes which lower transactions costs. They must also be perceived as safe. However, their exact siting may simply be the result of chance selection from among several suitable alternatives. Next, persons from hunter-gatherer (HG) groups that may never have traded before must start doing so. HG1 and HG2, may use an intermediary, HG3, with whom members of each group may be familiar, who sets the time and location of the trade. Next, if trade among these groups proves successful and regular, other hunter-gatherer groups with some connection[13] to HG1, HG2, or HG3 would probably then find the trading area an attractive option as well. Then, as traders from these groups return to this location for more frequent and extended visits, they build temporary dwellings that become more permanent with time, and the trading post evolves into a settlement with an ever-growing population of people from different groups. Thus, not only are cities 'market cities' in Max Weber's (1958) sense, but their genesis is very often in trade, or they become market cities perhaps after being established for other (e.g. religious or military) reasons.[14]

Jacobs (1969a, p. 262) defines a city as 'a settlement that consistently generates its economic growth from its own local economy'.[15] In her sense, then, these early settlements were on the verge of being cities, but not because they contained historically large numbers of people living fairly close together (otherwise a prison or a military encampment would have to be called a city).[16]

What the trading settlement did have that hunter-gatherer groups lacked, in addition to a large population, was an enormous and increasing diversity of knowledge, skills, and tastes that traders and their families brought with them, as well as an unprecedented opportunity to make new connections and utilize existing connections when the opportunity arose. While some social ties weaken and dissolve, or even sometimes become a source of disadvantage (to at least one side of the relation), on the whole the rate at which advantageous new ties form among strangers in such social environments is typically much higher, resulting in a growing and increasingly complex network of relations.[17]

James Coleman (1990) points out that it is through such 'relations of trust' that complementarities among human capital can be utilized. A typical urban dweller under these circumstances may encounter more people in a year than he would have in an entire lifetime as a nomad or a farmer living near an isolated village. This dweller will also encounter more opportunities to buy and sell, make friendships or acquaintances, trust or distrust, than he could have imagined elsewhere; and in the process his knowledge, attitudes, skills and tastes, will change faster and more dramatically than he would have thought possible (or perhaps desirable).

In an environment such as this, then, things do not stay the same, inside the mind of the individual or in his social surroundings. There are several dimensions along which it is possible to speculate that change takes place – psychological, moral, and of course cultural – but Jacobs focuses on the economic (although she does later develop the related moral considerations in Jacobs (1992)). For example, people will find new uses for already-existing goods. Leather pouches used to carry precious volcanic stones to be sold in the city make, with some modifications, fine purses for carrying personal items, adding to the pouch's value. But, more importantly, people will discover new ways of doing old tasks as well as new tasks, new kinds of work, based on their exposure to the variety they see daily around them. Again, this tends to enhance the value of the goods and their complements. Crucially, it raises the value of their own work. The expectation of increasing one's value productivity through contact with a diverse range of people is what attracted and continues to attract people to urban life, although this may not always happen in the way they expected it to. In Jacobs's view, it is when the settlement is able consistently to generate net increases in wealth in this fashion that the settlement becomes what I like to call a 'living city'. This is, again, the starting point of all significant economic progress.

Solving the Problems of Discovery and Diffusion

A living city (with its high population density,[18] diversity of knowledge and tastes, and dynamic networks that give coherence to these disparate elements) solves the problem of discovery and diffusion. Innovation depends much less on the lone creative genius (and his great deal of luck). It is sometimes said that markets economize on altruism by harnessing the power of self-interest. Creative genius, like altruism, is also very rare and markets economize on it, too. Richard Florida (2004) argues that if cities today wish to rejuvenate themselves, they need to pursue policies that attract creative people. He is partly right. But the marvel of the living city is that it makes ordinary people extraordinary by placing them in a network in which information and opportunities, conducted by dense social ties, come at them from many and often unexpected directions. And dense social networks also make it much more likely that useful novelty spreads to those for whom it has net value, even if they do not know the innovator (and whether they pay for the knowledge or free ride). And as Glaeser (2011, p. 455) notes: 'An abundance of local employers also provides implicit insurance against the failure of any particular start-up'. So if city dwellers augment serendipitous discovery with deliberate research and experimentation, they can do so at much lower cost than their brethren in the countryside.

Jacobs explains how this works by speculating on how agriculture and animal husbandry originally emerged unplanned within the boundaries of a city. She first explains how a large trading settlement is established by hunter-gatherers and then grows and develops spontaneously along the lines I have sketched. Now, one of the locational advantages of the city already mentioned is that it lowers the cost of transport, so that goods can be traded there from much farther away than would otherwise be possible. But location does a great deal more than simply lowering transactions costs.

Jacobs uses the example of seed grains from distant areas, perhaps with significant variations in flavour or heartiness, which are brought together in unprecedented proximity. The chances of deliberate, or more likely, accidental mixing of seeds are thus much greater in a city than in a nonurban setting. Those responsible for storing wild seed grain, itself a new business invented in the city, are, out of self-interest, much more likely than isolated farmers to notice which seeds produce what characteristics. Moreover, unlike farmers in rural settlements, for whom experimenting is extremely costly (since there is typically little surplus to spare and failure could mean starvation), seed-storers need only notice the properties of the different varieties as well as any hybrids that might serendipitously emerge in the normal course of business in the city. They become experts in a brand new area; an expertise they share with rival seed-storers, whose interest is, among other things, to keep a sharp eye out for new developments in their trade in the hopes of profiting from them. The fundamental lesson here is that none of this was done deliberately: the seed-storers-turned-hybridists were not aware that they were inventing agriculture but that is what they did. A new business and the invention of systematic hybridization were an unintended consequence of urban life.

Jacobs tells essentially the same story about animal husbandry. Some former hunter-gatherers specialize in feeding and minding wild animals, goats for example, whose owners live with him until they are ready to be slaughtered. Again, a new business. In a small village the gatherer would rarely, if ever, see so many varieties of sheep. In the city, however, he could not help but notice differences in size and temperament. In time, he might out of convenience to self and clients add slaughtering to the business. When this happens, wild sheep owners who deposited their wild animals with the gatherer for care are replaced by, or themselves become, suppliers of wild sheep for the business. He will now be in a position to pick and choose which sheep will be slaughtered first and which later, and which he will retain for breeding. (He will also likely need new kinds of tools or additional kinds of labour to engage in the new work.) As in the case of seed-storers, purely out of self-interest he will probably slaughter the most difficult-to-keep sheep first and retain the more docile and easier-to-care-for for breeding. After several generations, a new breed of domesticated sheep will emerge. Again, in the milieu of urban diversity and density, the breeder and his competitors have invented animal husbandry without consciously trying to do so.

The knowledge of and benefits from this discovery will spread rapidly through the dense social network of the city. Although I have treated these problems and their solutions as separate phenomena, discovery and diffusion are not really separate processes. Without the lines of contact that bring new opportunities to urban entrepreneurs few discoveries and little diffusion would take place. The knowledge is diffused over dense social networks only because agents are entrepreneurially alert to profits that can accrue from, in essence, buying and selling knowledge.[19]

Once again, both the business and the invention of animal husbandry emerge spontaneously within the walls of the city (which itself is a self-generating and self-regulating order). The knowledge and skill that the seed expert and the sheep breeder created would have been nearly impossible to discover and then to diffuse in a region of small, relatively isolated settlements. Urban processes simply cannot be replicated in a rural setting. A city is, indeed, not simply a village or town only many times larger. It is an utterly different kind of social phenomenon.

Although perhaps interesting in itself, these stories of the 'spontaneous order' of the origin of the city and the innovations that happen within it tell us something about the fundamental nature of all living cities, including those of today. For instance, in order to be 'incubators of ideas' and generators of prosperity, cities require an ever-changing diversity in knowledge and tastes. Just as important is flexibility in land use so that the actions that constitute this diversity can happen. That 'action space' (Ikeda, 2007) is filled with social networks. And all this requires economic freedom.

Social Networks and Economic Freedom[20]

I have already made a number of references to social networks and concepts related to social networks. Although Jacobs was one of the first to point out the nature and significance of trust and social networks in economic development and political activism, even coining the term 'social capital' (Jacobs, 1961, p. 138), she does not use those terms very much in her 1969 book. It is not only possible, but I think very useful, to introduce those concepts explicitly into her analysis, and especially the extensions that Mark Granovetter and Robert Putnam have made to them.

Granovetter (1973) in his path-breaking study of the way relevant information is transmitted argues that 'weak ties' are more important than 'strong ties'. The strength of a tie is a (probably linear) combination of the amount of time, the emotional intensity, the intimacy (mutual confiding), and the reciprocal services which characterize the tie (1973, p. 1361).

In researching how survey participants learned about jobs, Granovetter found evidence corroborating his hypothesis that weak ties are better able to do this than strong ties. This is because weak ties are what connects the strongly-tied network that agent A belongs to with other, more distant networks that have information relevant to A and that A is unlikely to know about since its source is socially distant.

Putnam (2001) defines social capital as 'networks of trust and norms of reciprocity'. He makes a very useful distinction between 'bonding social capital' and 'bridging social capital'. The former use strong ties of kinship, religion, or language and culture mainly to exclude outsiders from trust relationships. Bridging social capital generates weak ties, and is based on norms such as tolerance and criticism that extend to relative strangers many of the conventions of friendship, fair-play, and reciprocity in a given social network.

Now, the diversity and density that give rise to economic development evolve together, as individuals make contact and form weak ties with strangers outside their relatively closed, strongly tied networks. Diversity breeds more diversity in a living city. Links form and dissolve, creating a complex, intricate, and dynamic web of personal contacts. As noted, it is through these ties, especially the weak ones, that relevant information (though certainly not all relevant information) gets conveyed to alert individuals; information about where prices are lower, whose grains are heartier, what new lines of work are profitable; information that, interpreted in the right context, can transform a sheep-minder into a meat-seller and a sheep-minder's customer into a sheep-slaughterer's supplier; information, in other words, that can enable an ordinary person to do very creative things. None of this density- and diversity-generating discovery and development happens unless people feel secure in their person and property, and feel generally free to pursue gains from trade where and when they see them.

Indeed, the original market places do not get off the ground unless representatives of the various hunter-gatherer groups feel safe and secure enough to trust one another. Part of that security, as I noted earlier, comes from the limited familiarity that may already exist among members of different networks. But the gap between the level of security a given representative would need to have in order to be willing to engage in an exchange and the amount of confidence he actually has can be bridged, if it can be bridged at all, by a 'leap of faith'.[21] It is this kind of trust, the willingness to rely on a stranger who might make a sucker out of you (or worse), that is the basis of the formation of weak ties, and it is weak ties that serve as conduits of new information, of clues and feedback, that so greatly accelerates the pace of economic development. Strong ties, on the other hand, form in family and kinship groups, or in stable and long-standing personal relationships. As Malcolm Gladwell (2010) has noted, strong ties are particularly useful when individuals are called upon to make significant personal sacrifices, such as in the military or in political revolutions. But for the polycentric networks that typify dynamic markets, weak ties are essential. Both the need to trust (i.e. making oneself vulnerable to strangers) and the opportunity to trust, which bring the potential gains from harnessing human capital and diverse tastes, are greatest in the tremendous diversity and high density of a living city. Again, none of this can happen without economic freedom.

Economic freedom does more, then, than promote market formation by lowering transactions costs. Economic freedom enables the formation of trust and the emergence of weakly tied social networks – Putnam's 'bridging social capital' – that are essential for robust, long-term economic development. And to the extent that trusting produces positive outcomes for trusters and trustees, it bolsters the willingness of people to trust. Thus, the markets at the heart of economic development are not placeless, abstract phenomena. Their location is not arbitrary and the emergent social infrastructure that supports them differs from city to city. These locational and infrastructural differences really matter. Action space evolves and adjusts to changing conditions in the context of economic freedom.

The Process of Innovation: New Work Piggybacks on Old Work

Jacobs sees innovation, or what she likes to call the creation of 'new work', as growing out of existing or 'parent work'. In this special sense, then, innovation proceeds incrementally. But being creative, it is inherently unpredictable:

To be sure this process is full of surprises and hard to predict – possibly it is unpredictable – before it has happened… It is analogous, I think, to a form of logic, or intuition if you prefer, that artists use. Artists often comment that although they are masters of the work they are creating, they are also alert to messages that come from the work, and act upon them. (1969a, p. 59)

The new work represents a dramatic departure from the parent work. That is because, while an innovation depends on the intelligence, awareness, and connections of someone within an established business, the new product or service created tends to serve a completely different set of customers from that served by the parent business or perhaps even by the industry in which the parent operates. So if you are trying to understand this essentially dynamic process, static categories, such as 'local services' or 'light manufacturing' are not helpful (1969a, p. 61).

For this reason, while the new work may have originated in an established firm, it is more likely to break away or spin-off from the parent. Henry Ford was a young mechanic for a Detroit firm that made engines for ships before he broke away and designed and produced his first working automobile; and local carriage makers provided the first body frames for Ford and others (Glaeser, 2011, p. 848). It is true that some businesses, even very big ones (Apple Inc. being the outstanding contemporary example), are able to reinvent themselves over time in order to serve a shifting customer base or enter new markets. But radical innovations are typically the initiative of relatively small, relatively poor individuals or groups. Indeed, the very tendency to equate entrepreneurship with start-up companies may reflect an empirical tendency that supports the spin-off model.

Without a wide variety of skills and tastes readily at hand that will serve to complement and support new start-ups, what Jacobs (1961) refers to as 'pools of efficient use' and later as 'co-development',[22] new projects may never get off the ground. Diversity in this sense both inspires and enables innovation. It generates multiplier effects in the local economy as employment and investment rises in the new business as well as in the new domestic (and foreign) suppliers of that business.

But the freedom to convert existing space to new uses at low cost is crucial. Flexibility of land use means businesses can more easily expand or contract, and it enables a wider range of land-use diversity. Its absence retards innovation and creative urban development. Thus, if the innovation that drives economic development is made up chiefly of new firms springing up among the old, the legal-institutional framework must be flexible enough to let this happen; if, that is, economic development is an aim of public policy. Beyond the formal legal environment, however, the customs, norms, and networks operating within this environment should encourage, or at least not discourage, new ways of doing old things, new products and services, and, just as importantly, new consumption behaviours and lifestyles of those whose diverse tastes drive the dynamic demand side of economic development. People need to be allowed, and to allow themselves, to experiment with and adopt new tastes and attitudes, and to welcome into their communities socially distant outsiders.

To prevent this inevitable clash of cultures from bursting into violent conflict there must prevail a general attitude of tolerance and trust. These are values of the commercial system (Jacobs, 1992) that develop in the context of economic freedom (Ikeda, 2002, 2008).[23]

The Mechanics of Economic Development at the System Level

To avoid misunderstanding in this section, it is important to realize that a city in Jacobs's sense is a 'spontaneous order', an undersigned, unplanned set of complex relations that adjust to changing conditions over time (Hayek, 1967). Like the individual agent, household, or business firm, the city is an emergent phenomenon and a natural unit of economic analysis. In this it is fundamentally different from the artificial construction of the nation-state.

Now, in Jacobs's analysis, while at the level of the individual firm, innovation typically builds on old work, at the level of the system as a whole, the city, economic expansion happens in discontinuous, often explosive leaps. This is as true of the modern city as it was for the Neolithic city. Regular expansion tends to be the result of businesses and their customers making and consuming more of already existing goods and services – more of the same. Economic development as we have seen takes place as the result of diversification and differentiation on the part of producers and consumers. For both, but especially for development, imports and exports into and out of the city are obviously central players.

Recall that in the Neolithic city, wild food is at first imported as hunter-gatherers bring goats with them to the settlement. Caring for them requires, in addition to the goats, other inputs such as someone to tend them, water and feed, and a pen to hold them. When the tender adds domesticating and butchering to the business, this also adds new work, new divisions of labour, to the old process. This also means that less wild food needs to be imported into the city – imports will be replaced. The new product, say butchered meat or a new breed of sheep, is added to the tables of local consumers. But the new product is an improvement over the original, having been filtered through a process, accidentally or deliberately, to better suit local tastes. As such, it may be something that is attractive to consumers in other cities, foreigners, who do not have direct access to this new breed. The export of a new product then brings added wealth into the city.

Part of the new wealth, according to Jacobs, will increase the demand for existing goods and services, and in the competitive environment of a living city, it will elicit a response from domestic and foreign suppliers of those things. This, in turn, will induce local suppliers of finished products to increase their demand for those foreign inputs needed to make more of these domestic goods. It will also increase the importation of finished goods from outside the city. Some of the new wealth and spending will also go to cover the costs of the newly multiplied division of labour.

The other part of the added wealth, however, will be spent on goods from other cities that are not available domestically. Exposure to novel cultures, customs, and ways of thinking, will expand local residents' taste for novel foreign products: foods, books, clothing, entertainment, house wares, styles, and the like. Also, the new kinds of work added to the previous division of labour may require some tools, materials, and know-how not available locally, so these too will have to be imported with the help of the added wealth. The importation of these new goods and services, however, sets into motion the same process of input replacement, greater complexity of the local division of labour, additional exports, and increases in local wealth, and so on. And when domestic entrepreneurs imitate successful innovators, local output, employment and consumption are further expanded.

In living cities, this process repeats itself again and again. Imports and exports grow together over time and are what drives the dynamics of economic development at the system level. There is no upper boundary to this process, no limit to the size of the living city, economically or demographically.[24]

Cities can also decline – after all, the title of Jacobs's most famous book is *The Death and Life of Great American Cities* – owing either to 'natural' or 'man-made' causes. For Jacobs, the single most important natural or endogenous cause of urban decline is over-specialization in a particular industry, giving rise to a city's heavy dependence on a single, dominating use. Then, the process produces a 'dynamics of decline' that is very difficult to reverse. Modern-day Detroit might be a good example.[25] This can also occur as the result of public policy; for example, when tariffs and quotas are imposed on foreign imports to favour domestic industries. (See below for more discussion on policy.)

In this regard, Jacobs is careful to distance her discussion of 'import replacement' from the familiar-sounding but very different policy of 'import substitution'. The latter is associated with legal import barriers and protections to local, usually politically connected, businesses or industries. In Jacobs's framework, economic development cannot take place unless locals are free to import and export as they please. And, mindful of knowledge problems and the unpredictability of innovation, she does not advocate a policy of picking winners via subsidies, tariffs, and quotas. For Jacobs, far from being a problem to be removed, imports are what drive the process of economic development.

A final thing to bear in mind here is that, because the essence of economic development is a creative and therefore radically unpredictable process, the standard categories of efficiency and inefficiency are not helpful.[26] Moreover, while greater static efficiency via economies of scale, economies of scope, and the like, or a more extensive division of labour within an already existing production process will all produce 'more of the same' and contribute to economic growth, they are irrelevant for economic development in the sense used here.

Division of labour is a device for achieving operating efficiency, nothing more. Of itself, it has no power to promote further economic development. And because it does not, division of labour is even extraordinarily limited in improving operating efficiency in any given work. All further increases in efficiency, once existing work has been suitably divided into tasks, depend upon the addition of new activities. (Jacobs, 1969a, pp. 82–83)

For Jacobs a better measure of the vitality of an economic system is the ratio of new work to total work. She replaces the norm of efficiency with the norm of new work,[27] which is measured by how much the division of labour multiplies, by how it becomes more complex over time (1969a, p. 57). This concept deserves further consideration.

Policy Implications

Because it would be too difficult to trace in this chapter what I believe are the important policy implications of this discussion to all relevant topics in economic development, I will limit myself to the following areas:

Implications for Developed Countries with Mixed Economies

1. *The Role of Prices*. One of the glaring weaknesses of Jacobs's early work on economics is the absence of any mention of the role of prices. Indeed, in Jacobs (1961), in which she discusses various reasons for the decline of cities and their neighbourhoods, conspicuous by its absence is any mention of rent control, although it is clear from her proposal for addressing housing for the poor that she is no proponent of rent control (Jacobs, 1961, pp. 321–337). By the time of *The Nature of Economies* (2000), however, she had filled in that lacuna:

New York City failed to abandon rent controls instituted after civilian construction was halted during the Second World War; then, as anachronisms, ironically, rent controls depressed construction. (Jacobs, 2000, p. 117)[28]

For Jacobs, in general trying to promote economic development via subsidies is a mistake because 'subsidies falsify both costs and prices' (2000, p. 111) Moreover, 'the most pervasive and tenacious falsifications of costs and prices tend to be imposed institutionally' (*Ibid.*). And once again, for Jacobs, the process of import replacement that fuels local expansion presupposes free trade: no subsidies for local businesses and no tariffs and trade barriers on imports.

2.   *Enable Spin-Offs.* Reducing red tape and regulations, which in large cities such as New York are so costly, should be high on Jacobs's agenda because spin-offs that piggyback on old work are so central to her analysis. Excessive labour regulations, health and safety regulations, as well as building codes and land-use restrictions, especially strict zoning for use (rather than for size), all discourage entrepreneurial spin-offs.

This is consistent with Gordon and Ikeda (2011) who argue that 'flexible land markets' allow voluntary actions spontaneously to adjust levels of density as appropriate to local conditions. Again, this is especially important in encouraging the diversity of land use that is central to the Jacobsian theory of economic development and is examined empirically by Glaeser *et al.* (1992).

Policies that target low-density development (e.g. federal subsidies for single-family housing, exurban highway and infrastructure construction, which have been a political objective of the United States since at least the 1930s) should be stopped. The suburban lifestyle has been a desideratum of the rich for millennia, but only in the twentieth century have markets and free trade enabled ordinary people to pursue this dream. Artificially stimulating this movement, however, threatens to disrupt the balance between diversity and density needed for robust economic development. Cheap exurban land made accessible by the interstate highway system has produced super-sized malls and elephantine big-box stores that probably would not have seen the light of day, had government policy and private-public developments not underwritten urban sprawl.[29]

3.   *Encourage Mobility.* Ease of both pedestrian and vehicular movement not only reduces time-costs of travel and the search for gainful trades, it also allows for neighbourhoods and districts within a city to maintain a more stable population. Jacobs points out that in order to encourage people to move to and remain in a particular city location, it is necessary to make them feel that the rest of the city, or at least those parts that contain commercial, financial, and entertainment attractors, are easily accessible. Mobility promotes stability. A stable core population in a given neighbourhood is needed in order to preserve and pass-on the social capital conducive to the perception of safety, security, and trust that enables contact among the myriad of strangers that pass through every day.

Although Jacobs is usually interpreted as being in favour of mass transit over the automobile, this was not necessarily the case. What was important for her was the preservation of mobility in and around the city, by foot, by car, or by transit. Today, policy prescriptions for expensive public spending on transit, overwhelmingly funded by federal tax money channelled through state governments, is chronically inefficient and subject to rent-seeking. On the other hand, massive investments in freeways, while generating tremendous benefits in moving from one macro location to another, have generally disrupted local micro destinations and undermined local networks and social capital. They have, thus, had a depressive effect on local economies.

A small but growing trend in the Netherlands, Germany, other parts of Northern Europe, and the UK has been to eliminate almost completely automobile and pedestrian traffic regulations at certain urban intersections, including some with high traffic volume. This has: 1. reduced traffic and pedestrian injuries and fatalities; 2. reduced congestion and created a smoother, more common-sense flow of traffic; and 3. shown some potential to reduce air pollution from needlessly idling cars. Such traffic deregulation, combined with cut-backs in cataclysmic spending on transit and highways, may hold the key to mobility in the future. Some form of congestion pricing may also be appropriate, although whether drivers or parkers should be charged (but probably not both) is open for discussion (Shoup, 2005).

4. *Avoid 'Monstrous Hybrids'*. In *The Death and Life*, Jacobs does not explicitly comment on the moral foundations of economic development, although one could argue that it was implicit in her discussion (1961, p. 35). Later, in her *Systems and Survival* (1992), she explicitly addresses this question, and cautions against 'monstrous hybrids' of what she terms moral 'syndromes' or practices that occur together. In Jacobs's analysis, there are two moral syndromes, the Commercial Moral Syndrome[30] and the Guardian/ Governmental Syndrome,[31] which are in turn based on her observation that:

[w]e have two distinct ways of making a living, no more no less… First, we're able to take what we want – simply take, depending of course, on what's available to be taken. That's what all other animals do. (1992, p. 51)… But in addition, we human beings are capable of trading – exchanging our services for other goods and services, depending, again, on what's available, but in this case what's available for exchange rather than taking. (p. 52)

According to Jacobs, 'You can't mix up such contradictory moral syndromes without opening up moral abysses and producing all kinds of functional messes' (1992, p. 81). A mix deteriorates the moral foundations of politics and commerce and reduces the effectiveness of both. Jacobs's example of a commercial enterprise that injects Guardian morality into its operations is the Mafia; her example of a governmental organization that attempts to engage in commerce is central economic planning in communist regimes.

Jacobs's firm resistance to being ideologically pigeonholed notwithstanding, there is an unmistakable libertarian flavour to the moral framework she outlines, although she does not argue that government is unnecessary, but only that agents in the public sphere shun the practices of the private sector in order to seek gain and that profit-seekers in the private sphere likewise avoid the practices of the Guardians. Ultimately, the monstrous hybrids that are produced in either sphere lead to a state in which 'public good succumbs to private gain' (1992, p. 205).

5. *Liberalize Immigration*. One of the most important sources of new firms in the

United States has been foreign immigrants. In this relatively free environment, immigrants have not only contributed small businesses that cater to particular ethnic groups, but have also brought with them different ways of seeing and doing things that come from having been raised in a different culture. This does not always contribute to economic development and social cooperation, of course, and domestic redistribution policies often exacerbate this problem by attracting non-industrious persons to the USA. Liberalized immigration, therefore, would need to be accompanied by reform of these policies.

That said, just as free immigration from different regions of the United States, such as from the South to the North-East, has helped address labour shortages in the past, surplus housing, and dwindling populations, the same dynamic should be encouraged internationally.

6.   *Creative Cities*. One of Jacobs's most visible proponents today is Richard Florida. Florida argues that if contemporary cities want to encourage the kind of creativity that will result in long-term economic development, urban policy must promote 'talent, tolerance, and technology', the 'Three Ts'. Attracting members of the 'Creative Class', as Florida terms it, is a possible strategy for rejuvenating failing cities.[32] Creative people who come to a city tend to attract other creative people, and less creative people tend to be more creative when they work with creative people (Glaeser, 2011). But the idea that what has made cities engines of discovery and incubators of ideas is the presence of a creative class, is, I believe, somewhat at odds with a Jacobsian attitude. As I argued earlier, the marvel of living cities is not that they attract extraordinary people, they do, but that they enable ordinary people to do extraordinary things. However, whether or not there is an important philosophical disagreement here, from the point of view of policy, promoting Florida's Three Ts is probably consistent with Jacobs.

Implications for Less-Developed Countries: The 'Charter City' Proposal

Paul Romer, who is widely recognized for his work on the theory of economic growth and the idea of increasing returns with knowledge or 'ideas' as a factor of production, has proposed Charter Cities as a way to jump-start chronically under-developed economies.

The Charter Cities[33] concept derives from the experience of politically autonomous cities located in countries other than their source of governance. Just as Hong Kong, a former British colony established on the Chinese mainland, has spurred the People's Republic of China to create Special Economic Zones with greater economic freedom than other parts of China, it has also inspired the Charter Cities concept. With the host country's blessing, a highly developed 'guarantor' country, such as the United States, or a group of guarantor countries, may establish a legal framework and basic infrastructure, patterned after their own, by leasing and chartering a city-sized tract of undeveloped land within the host country. With the promise of a stable, market-friendly legal and social environment in place, the guarantors arrange for private business investment from abroad to create jobs and housing, and for a liberal immigration policy for anyone who would like to move to the Charter City.

Charter Cities promise rapid development by letting portions of a developing country start off with a clean slate and side-step the frustrating complexities of reforming an ineffective system hampered by entrenched interests, excessive restrictions on business and immigration, and unpredictable intrusions into domestic life. The concept promises a legal system that preserves economic freedom and creates new infrastructure conducive to commercial expansion. It also holds the possibility of inculcating norms of behaviour sympathetic to entrepreneurship, openness, and trade; i.e. norms consistent with Jacobs's Commercial Moral Syndrome. Populated by those who self-select for ambition, tolerance, resourcefulness, and energy, a Charter City is proposed as a way of quickly overcoming political, economic, and social obstacles that block economic development and allow the emergence of effective action spaces.[34]

On the face of it, a Charter City confronts a number of problems, even assuming a host country and guarantor government can be found. First, the entire concept smacks of colonialism. Suppose the concept is successful and gains popularity among governments worldwide. It is easy to imagine at least some of these governments chartering cities not to promote the economic interests of the citizens of the host and guarantor countries, but strategically to invest in such cities for geopolitical reasons.

Similarly, such a scheme would seem to be vulnerable to public-choice considerations as rent-seeking businesses and politicians vie for privileged investment positions in the provision of infrastructure or in new businesses. There is also the threat of post-contractual opportunism by the host government, especially should the Charter City become, as it is hoped, a thriving metropolis. Companies and productive workers would appear to be attractive cash cows. More seriously, should the host engage in large-scale post-contractual opportunism against investors from guarantor countries who have sunk large sums in location-specific investments – say, by threatening to nationalize businesses – what would be the appropriate response of guarantor countries? An armada of warships?

Finally, the Charter City proposal, contrary to the spirit of Jacobs, especially in the final chapter of her 1961 book ('The kind of problem a city is'), has troubling constructivist (Hayek, 1978) overtones. That is, trying to design complex systems is what Jacobs refers to as a problem of 'organized complexity'. The attempt will inevitably frustrate the designers' intentions owing to a lack of 'locality knowledge'. As with those of mice and men, the best-laid plans of even benevolent planners usually come to naught.[35] That is not necessarily a bad thing; what is a failure to some may turn out in the long-term to be a success. But how the host and guarantor countries would respond to plan failure is critical, and their responses will probably be driven by political expediency rather than considerations of the general welfare. There is an element of what Hayek (1988) has called a 'fatal conceit' in the way Romer has conceived Charter Cities.

Conclusion

To the extent that current thinking about economic progress, whether in developing or mature economies, does not take adequate account of the centrality of cities, entrepreneurial discovery, the non-market foundations of economic development such as trust and social networks, and the importance of demand- and supply-side diversity, Jacobs offers a valuable alternative perspective. Hers is a narrative of a dynamic process in which, in the context of economic freedom, diversity and density give rise to discovery and development. In this process, innovations based on old work depend crucially on co-development. Their genesis is rooted in the ever-growing range of knowledge and tastes, and their diffusion is reliant on the dense, weakly tied social networks that emerge in action space. The social networks and the norms that support innovations can in turn generate explosive economic expansion.

Given problems of knowledge and political incentives, governments should not engage in interventionist policies that stand in the way of new uses of space that would enable cities to evolve and adjust locally to changes in tastes, technology, and resources; and in the longer term to changes in demography, environment, and geography. The inherently unpredictable and evolutionary character of economic development should especially caution against large-scale 'giga-projects', especially when public authorities are the ones making the big decisions and when the need for creative adjustment inevitably arises.

Notes

1. For their comments I wish to thank Bill Butos, Gene Callahan, Young-Back Choi, Peter Gordon, David Harper, Andreas Hoffmann, Chidem Kurdas, Thomas McQuade, Maria Pia Paganelli, Mario Rizzo, Joe Salerno, and Loic Sauce. The usual caveat applies.
2. There are three notable exceptions. Jacobs published an article dealing with the subject-matter in the *American Economic Review* (1969*b*). Robert Lucas explicitly credits Jacobs for his article on 'The Mechanics of Economic Development' (1988) in the *Journal of Monetary Economics*. And Edward Glaeser, et al. (1992) confirmed the explanatory power of a version of 'Jacobs spillovers' in *The Journal of Political Economy* (1992).
3. They are Jacobs 1961, 1969*a*, 1984.
4. The former details her theory of economic development. I suppose the best advice I could give to someone who wants to learn about that theory is to read those books (after reading this much shorter chapter).
5. I first used the phrase 'commonsense genius' in a tribute to Jane Jacobs published in *National Review Online* (27 April 2006), which is similar to the book title later used by Lang and Wunsch (2009).
6. See http://www.census.gov/ipc/www/worldhis.html.
7. To clarify, it is neither my contention, nor was it Jacobs's, that cities have to be either exclusively one or the other. The object here is to use Jacobs's analysis of how historically agriculture and animal husbandry may have first arisen in cities, as a framework for understanding how other essential elements of culture – writing, numeracy, etc. – could also have had their genesis in cities.
8. Some might expect to see Jacobs's definition of 'city' at this point, but it would be best first to present the conventional view of the evolution of cities.
9. Again, here I am speaking of the historical emergence of the first cities. What below I term as 'living cities' are both a cause and consequence of economic development.
10. Whether these property rights are formal or informal I will not discuss here, except to note

that formal property rights would seem to be most important when people live and work close together and have frequent contact with strangers, rather than living dispersed across smaller settlements. Glaeser (2011, Loc400): 'The commercial cities developed the legal rules regarding private property and commerce that still guide us today'.

11. Although this may (or may not) have taken several intermediate steps.

12. Archaeological evidence at Çatal Höyük lends some support for this hypothesis. See Mellaart (1967) and the website: http://www.catalhoyuk.com/. Also, Algaze (2008, chapter 6) provides evidence on 'import replacement' (which for Jacobs plays a central role in the urban development process) in the economic growth in Lower Mesopotamia in the middle to late Uruk period (4000– 3100BC), particularly with respect to flint, wool, metals, and other products not indigenous to that area.

13. Probably 'weak ties' in Granovetter's sense. See below.

14. Again, what later becomes a 'living city' need not have originated in trade, but to become a living city trade must be the essential element of a settlement. Thus, it is no contradiction to point out that ancient Romans planted cities across Europe as military outposts (e.g. Milan) that later became living cities.

15. Also, '… cities are places where adding new work to older work proceeds vigorously. Indeed, any settlement where this happens becomes a city' (Jacobs, 1969a, p. 50).

16. Large collections of people such as the latter are sometimes, of course, referred to metaphorically as cities, but they are not cities in almost anyone's sense. Edward Glaeser's remark that 'cities are the absence of physical space between people and companies' (Glaeser, 2011, Loc131) is not particularly useful in this regard.

17. A good discussion of the pros and cons of social networks is Christakis and Fowler (2009). Also, in research sponsored by the Netherlands Organization for Scientific Research, Gerald Mollenhorst reported (2009): 'Over a period of seven years the average size of personal networks was found to be strikingly stable. However, during the course of seven years we replace many members of our network with other people. Only thirty percent of the discussion partners and practical helpers still held the same position seven years later. Only 48 percent were still part of the network.'

18. The role of population density is the subject of much debate among urbanists. Particularly since the invention of the car and high-speed communication, the demand for living and working in proximity has fallen. But this is not the same thing as saying that the need for personal or face-to-face contact has been reduced. Quite the contrary, I think. Density, in the sense of being able to interact easily with large numbers of persons outside one's own strongly tied network, is still as important as it ever was for economic development. I have coined the term 'Jacobs Density' to refer to this idea (Gordon and Ikeda, 2011), and I am currently developing it, using the concepts of social networks and 'social distance'.

19. The standard reference for the role of entrepreneurship is, of course, Kirzner (1973).

20. I am using the term 'economic freedom' in the sense used by the authors of the Economic Freedom of the World Annual Reports at http://www.freetheworld.com/index.html. The four cornerstones of economic freedom are:
    - personal choice
    - voluntary exchange coordinated by markets
    - freedom to enter and compete in markets
    - protection of persons and their property from aggression by others.

21. Traders might also bridge the gap with sufficient knowledge of the trustworthiness of the 'other', though this could take some time. However, at some point early on, a leap of faith would seem to be necessary to overcome ancient suspicions among hunter-gatherer groups. This sort of dynamic must still take place to some degree among agents in a modern market process. I have found Seligman (1997) very helpful for clarifying the nature of trust.

22. This is a concept she explicitly borrows from ecology.

23. Jacobs devotes an entire chapter to economic development, in which she nicely summarizes these thoughts in three points:
    1. Differentiation emerges from generality.
    2. Differentiations become generalities from which further differentiations emerge.
    3. Development depends on co-development.

The first two points refer to new work arising from parts of old work and to new work over time becoming the old work from which new, new work will emerge. The third point refers to the milieu of cities, especially the diverse ecosystems that they represent, in both fostering innovation, by providing sources of ideas, inputs, and customers, and by providing a kind of safety net (i.e. alternative jobs and customers) when the economic environment shifts…

24. The size of cities follows a 'power-law distribution'. See Krugman (1996, pp. 39–46).
25. Indeed, Glaeser (2011) gives precisely this reason for Detroit's decline.
26. One can go further and say that they are completely irrelevant. Efficiency has to do with the ability to achieve a given end using means at the least cost. Because no one can possibly know what new products, procedures, or forms of organization the city economy will generate over time, the 'ends' are never given and so the 'means' will not be known beforehand either (Ikeda, 2010).
27. Jacobs (2000) adds what is perhaps another evaluative norm, that of 'dynamic stability'.
28. See also: 'Price feedback is inherently well integrated … the data carry meaningful information' (p. 110).
29. There are many references here, but one of the most balanced is Bruegmann (2005).
30. Components of the Commercial Moral Syndrome: Shun force, come to voluntary agreements, be honest, collaborate easily with strangers and aliens, compete, respect contracts, use initiative and enterprise, be open to inventiveness and novelty, be efficient, promote comfort and convenience, dissent for the sake of the task, invest for productive purposes, be industrious, be thrifty, be optimistic (p. 215).
31. Components of the Guardian Moral Syndrome: Shun trading, exert prowess, be obedient and disciplined, adhere to tradition, respect hierarchy, be loyal, take vengeance, deceive for the sake of the task, make rich use of leisure, be ostentatious, dispense largesse, be exclusive, show fortitude, be fatalistic, treasure honor (p. 215).
32. Edward Glaeser (2005), however, has found the evidence for this ambiguous, since creativity, as defined by Florida, is hard to disentangle empirically from ordinary human capital.
33. See http://www.chartercities.org/.
34. As of this writing, there has been serious discussion by the Honduran government on establishing a Charter City in their country. See http://online.wsj.com/article/SB10001424052748704775604576119931268333632.html.
35. To misquote Robert Burn's poem, 'To a Mouse', 1785: 'The best-laid schemes o' mice an' men gang aft agley'.

References

Algaze, G. (2008) *Ancient Mesopotamia at the Dawn of Civilization: The Evolution of an Urban Landscape*. Chicago, IL: University of Chicago Press.

Bruegmann, R. (2005) *Sprawl: A Compact History*. Chicago, IL: University of Chicago Press.

Christakis, N.A. and Fowler, J.H. (2009) *Connected: The Surprising Power of Our Social Networks and How They Shape Our Lives*. New York: Little, Brown.

Coleman, J.S. (1990) *Foundations of Social Theory*. Cambridge, MA: Harvard University Press.

Florida, R. (2004) *Cities and the Creative Class*. London: Routledge.

Gladwell, M. (2010) Small change: why the revolution will not be tweeted. *The New Yorker*, 4 October. Available at http://www.newyorker.com/reporting/2010/10/04/101004fa_fact_gladwell.

Glaeser, E.L. (2005) Review of Richard Florida's *The Rise of the Creative Class*. *Regional Science and Urban Economics*, **35**(5), pp. 593–596.

Glaeser, E.L. (2011) *The Triumph of the City: How Our Greatest Invention Makes Us Richer, Smarter, Greener, Healthier and Happier*. New York: Macmillan, Kindle edition. *Note*: 'LocX' refers to the Location Number in this book where the appropriate text may be found.

Glaeser, E.L., Kallal, H., Sheinkman, J. and Shleifer, A. (1992) Growth in cities. *Journal of Political Economy*, **100**, pp. 1126–1152.

Gordon, P. and Ikeda, S. (2011) Does density matter, in Andersson, D.E., Charlotta Mellander, C. and Andersson, Å (eds.) *Handbook of Creative Cities*. Cheltenham: Edward Elgar.

Granovetter, M. (1973) The strength of weak ties. *The American Journal of Sociology*, **78**(6), pp. 1360–1380.

Hayek, F.A. (1967) The results of human action but not of human design, in *Studies in Philosophy, Politics and Economics*. Chicago, IL: University of Chicago Press.

Hayek, F.A. (1978) The errors of constructivism, in *New Studies in Philosophy, Politics, Economics and the History of Ideas*. Chicago, IL: University of Chicago Press.

Hayek, F.A. (1988) *The Fatal Conceit: The Errors of Socialism*. Volume 1, The Collected Works of F.A. Hayek, edited by W.W. Bartley III. Chicago, IL: University of Chicago Press.

Heinrich, J. *et al.* (2010) Markets, religion, community size, and the evolution of fairness and punishment. *Science*, **327**(5927), pp. 1480–1484.

Ikeda, S. (2002) The role of social capital in the market process. *Journal des Economistes et de Etudes Humanines*, **12**(2/3), pp. 229–240.

Ikeda, S. (2007) Urbanizing economics. *Review of Austrian Economics*, **20**(4), pp. 213–220.

Ikeda, S. (2008) The meaning of 'social capital' as it relates to the market process. *Review of Austrian Economics*, **29**, pp. 167–182.

Ikeda, S. (2010) The mirage of the efficient city, in Goldsmith, S.A. and Lynne, E. (eds.) *What We See: Advancing the Observations of Jane Jacobs*. Oakland, CA: New Village Press.

Jacobs, J. (1961) *The Death and Life of Great American Cities*. New York: Vintage.

Jacobs, J. (1969a) *The Economy of Cities*. New York: Vintage.

Jacobs, J. (1969b) Strategies for helping cities. *American Economic Review*, **59**(4), pp. 652–256.

Jacobs, J. (1984) *Cities and the Wealth of Nations: Principles of Economic Life*. New York: Vintage.

Jacobs, J. (1992) *Systems of Survival: A Dialogue on the Moral Foundations of Commerce and Politics*. New York: Vintage.

Jacobs, J. (2000) *The Nature of Economies*. New York: Modern Library.

Kirzner, I.M. (1973) *Competition and Entrepreneurship*. Chicago, IL: University of Chicago Press.

Krugman, P. (1996) *The Self-Organizing Economy*. Oxford: Blackwell.

Lang, G. and Wunsch, M. (2009) *Genius of Common Sense*. Boston, MA: Godine.

Lucas, R. (1988) On the mechanics of economic development. *Journal of Monetary Economics*, **22**(1), pp. 3–42.

Mellaart, J. (1967) *Catal Huyuk: A Neolithic Town in Anatolia*. New York: McGraw-Hill.

Mollenhorst, G. (2009) http://www.alphagalileo.org/ViewItem.aspx?ItemId=58115&CultureCode=en.

Putnam, R. (2001) *Bowling Alone: The Collapse and Revival of American Community*. New York: Simon & Schuster.

Seligman, A.B. (1997) *The Problem of Trust*. Princeton, NJ: Princeton University Press.

Shoup, D.C. (2005) *The High Cost of Free Parking*. Washington, DC: American Planning Association.

Weber, M. (1958) *The City*. Translated by D. Martindale and G. Neuwirth. New York: Free Press.

Chapter 7

What Would Jane Jacobs
See in the Global City?
Place and Social Practices

Saskia Sassen

The master images in the currently dominant account of economic globalization emphasize hypermobility, global communications, and the neutralization of place and distance. There is a tendency to take the existence of a global economic system as a given, a function of the power of transnational corporations and global communications. This underlines both the power and the technical attributes of the global corporate economy.

But there is much more at work in these processes. Thinking about what Jane Jacobs asked us to see in the city, leads me to a focus on the making of these conditions – the enormous diversity of workers, their living spaces and working spaces, the multiple sub-economies involved. Many of these are typically seen as irrelevant to the global city, or as belonging to another era. A close look shows us that this is wrong. Jane Jacobs would also ask us to look at the consequences of these sub-economies for the city, for its people, for its neighbourhoods and for the visual orders involved. She would ask us to see all the other economies and spaces mobilized by the massive gentrifications, and the resulting massive displacements of modest households and modest profit-making neighbourhood firms.

This is what I want to explore here – how to see these articulations rendered invisible by narratives of development and the competitiveness of cities. I first examine the role of place and production in analyses of the global economy. Next is a discussion of how the city was at one point, in the early 1900s, a lens for understanding larger processes, a role it had lost by the 1950s. It was Jane Jacobs who taught us once again to see the city in a deeper, more complex way. Based on this recovery of place-based activities in a global economy, the third section posits the formation of new cross-border geographies of centrality and marginality constituted by these processes of globalization. Returning to the consequences of these processes for the specific types of places involved in these geographies, the ensuing section discusses the encounter between global processes and the thick 'placeness' of cities, the remaking of the socio-spatial order in global cities, and the localizations of the global – from finance capital to immigration. I conclude with a discussion of the global city as a nexus where these various trends come together and produce new political alignments.

No Matter How Electronic and Global, It Needs to be Made

The capabilities for global operation, coordination, and control contained in the new information technologies and in the power of transnational corporations need to be produced. By focusing on the production of these capabilities, we add a neglected dimension to the familiar issue of the power of large corporations and the new technologies. The emphasis shifts to the practices that constitute what we call 'economic globalization' and 'global control': the work of making and reproducing the organization and management of a global production system and a global marketplace for finance, both under conditions of economic concentration (Sassen, 1991, 2001).

A focus on practices draws the categories of place and production process into the analysis of economic globalization. These are two categories easily overlooked in accounts centred on the hypermobility of capital and the power of transnationals. Developing categories such as place and production process do not negate the centrality of hypermobility and power. Rather, they bring to the fore the fact that many of the resources necessary for global economic activities are not hypermobile and are, indeed, deeply embedded in place, notably often in global cities and export-processing zones.

Why is it important to recover place and production in analyses of the global economy, particularly as these are constituted in major cities? Because they allow us to see the multiplicity of economies and work cultures in which the global information economy is embedded (Harvey, 2007; Abu-Lughod, 1994, 1999; Burdett, 2006; Lloyd, 2005; Banerjee-Guha, 2010). They also allow us to recover the concrete, localized processes through which globalization exists and to argue that much of the multiculturalism in large cities is as much a part of globalization as is international finance (Herzog, 2006; Krause and Petro, 2003; Nashashibi, 2007; Weinstein and Ren, 2009; Ribera-Fumaz, 2009; King, 1996).

Focusing on cities also allows us to specify a geography of strategic places at the global scale, places bound to each other by the dynamics of economic globalization (Taylor *et al.*, 2007; Amen *et al.*, 2006; Brown *et al.*, 2010; McCann and Ward, 2010). I refer to this as a 'new geography of centrality', and one of the questions it engenders is whether this new transnational geography is also the space for new transnational politics (Sassen, 2012, chapters. 7, 8 and 9; see also Heine, 2011). Insofar as an economic analysis of the global city recovers the broad array of jobs and work cultures that are part of the global economy, though typically not marked as such, it allows us to examine the possibility of new forms of inequality arising out of economic globalization (Sassen, 2001, Part 3, 2012, p. 6; Fiscal Policy Institute, 2010; Heine, 2011).

And it allows us to detect new types of politics among traditionally disadvantaged workers; that is to say, it allows us to understand in its empirical detail whether operating in this transnational economic geography, as it materializes in global cities, makes a difference to the disadvantaged (Bartlett, 2007; Ong and Roy, 2010; Soysal, 2010; INURA, 2003). This would be a politics arising out of economic participation in the global economy among those who hold the 'other' jobs in the global economy – whether factory workers in export-processing zones in Asia, garment sweatshop workers in Los Angeles, or janitors on Wall Street.

One specific sociological question organizing my research on these issues is whether we are actually seeing the formation of new social forms among old social conditions. Power, capital mobility, economic and political disadvantage, homelessness, gangs, all have existed long before the current stage of globalization. And Jane Jacobs (1993; Goldsmith and Elizabeth, 2010) gave us some great insights into all of this. My question is whether the types of power, mobility, inequality, homelessness, professional classes and households, gangs, politics, we see emerge in the 1980s are sufficiently distinct that they are actually novel social forms even though in a general sense they look the same as always?

The next section examines the possibility that the city, a complex type of place, has once again become a lens through which to examine major processes that unsettle existing arrangements. Jane Jacobs (1970, 1985) developed a vocabulary and foci for observation that made the city into a condition that told a story larger than itself. Today many of the conditions in our cities have changed considerably: but are they, once again, helping us see a larger condition than the city itself?

The City: Its Return as a Lens for Social Theory

The city has long been a strategic site for the exploration of many major subjects confronting society and sociology. But it has not always been an heuristic space – a space capable of producing knowledge about some of the major transformations of an epoch. Thus, in the first half of the twentieth century, the study of cities was at the heart of sociology. This is evident in the work of Simmel, Weber, Benjamin, Lefebvre, the Chicago School, especially Park and Wirth, both deeply influenced by German sociology. These sociologists confronted massive processes – industrialization, urbanization, alienation, a new cultural formation they called 'urbanity'. Studying the city was not simply studying the urban. It was about studying the major social processes of an era.

But by the 1950s, the study of the city had gradually lost this privileged role as a lens for the discipline and as producer of key analytic categories. There are many reasons for this, most important among which are questions of the particular developments of method, data, and the major questions driving social science. The social sciences, we might say, lost their capacity to 'see' the city and all it made visible. By the 1960s, most of what remained of the traditions of 'seeing' was focused on 'social problems'. This focus was not unrelated to the beginnings of economic restructuring and the loss of manufacturing and other industrial service jobs in major northern cities which together led to massive unemployment especially among men from ethnic minorities.

Jane Jacobs (1970) brought back the capacity to see larger worlds in the city. She gave us an economic analysis that allowed us to understand something not only about 'the' economy, but also about the specific ways in which cities were distinctive economic spaces and distinctive social spaces. One effect of this was a positive recoding of what were commonly seen as social problems and backward economic formats.

Today, the city is once again emerging as a strategic site for understanding some of the major new trends reconfiguring the social order. The city and the metropolitan region emerge as one of the strategic sites where major macro-social trends materialize and hence can be constituted as an object of study. Among these trends are globalization, the rise of the new information technologies, the intensifying of transnational and translocal dynamics, and the strengthening presence and voice of specific types of socio-cultural diversity. Each one of these trends has its own specific conditionalities, contents, and consequences. The urban moment is but one moment in often complex multi-sited trajectories. But it is an important one: the urban moment of a major process makes the latter susceptible to empirical study in ways that other phases of such a process might not.

At the same time, this partial urbanization of major dynamics repositions the city as an object of study. What is it we are actually naming today when we use the construct 'city'? The city has long been a debatable construct, whether in early writings (Lefebvre, 1974; Castells, 1977; Harvey, 1982) or in recent ones (Brenner, 1998; Lloyd, 2005; Paddison, 2001; Drainville, 2004; Fainstein, 2010; Zukin, 2010). Today we are seeing a partial unbundling of national space and of the traditional hierarchies of scale centred on the national, with the city nested somewhere between the local and the region (Ross, 2009; Xu and Yeh, 2010; Brenner and Keil, 2005). This unbundling, even if partial, makes it problematic to conceptualize the city as nested in such hierarchies. Major cities have historically been nodes where a variety of processes intersect in particularly pronounced concentrations. In the context of globalization, many of these processes are operating at a global scale that cuts across historical borders, with the added complexities entails.

Cities emerge as one territorial or scalar moment in a trans-urban dynamic.[1] This is, however, not the city as a bounded unit, but the city as a complex structure that can articulate a variety of cross-boundary processes and reconstitute them as a partly urban condition (Sassen, 2001, 2008). Further, this type of city cannot be located simply in a scalar hierarchy that puts it beneath the national, regional and global. It is one of the spaces of the global, and it engages the global directly, often by-passing the national. Some cities may have had this capacity long before the current era; but today these conditions have been multiplied and amplified to the point that they can be read as contributing to a qualitatively different urban era. Cities have also long been sites where major trends interact with each other in distinct, often complex manners, in a way they do not in just about any other setting. Today all of this holds also for studying the global in its urban localizations.

There is a challenge in the effort to recover place in the context of globalization, telecommunications, and the proliferation of transnational and translocal dynamics. It is perhaps one of the ironies at the start of a new century that some of the old questions of the early Chicago School of Urban Sociology and later Jane Jacobs should resurface as promising and strategic to understand certain critical issues in today's global cities. One might ask if their methods might be of particular use in recovering the category 'place' at a time when dominant forces such as globalization and telecommunications seem to signal that place and the details of the local no longer matter.

But that is only part of the challenge of recovering place. Large cities around the world are the terrain where multiple globalization processes assume concrete, localized forms. These localized forms are, in good part, what globalization is about. Recovering place means recovering the multiplicity of presences in this landscape. The large city of today has emerged as a strategic site for a whole range of new types of operations – political, economic, 'cultural', subjective (Abu-Lughod, 1994; Bridge and Watson, 2011; Yuval-Davis, 1999; Krause and Petro, 2003; Bartlett, 2007; Hagedorn, 2007; Fainstein and Campbell, 2011; Ren, 2011). Immigration, for instance, is one major process through which a new transnational political economy is being constituted both at the macro-level of global labour markets and at the micro-level of translocal household survival strategies.

The city is one of the nexus where the formation of new claims materializes and assumes concrete forms. The loss of power at the national level produces the possibility for new forms of power and politics at the subnational level. Further, insofar as the national as container of social process and power is cracked, it opens up possibilities for a geography of politics that links subnational spaces across borders. Cities are foremost in this new geography. One question this engenders is how and whether we are seeing the formation of a new type of transnational politics that localizes in these cities. Global capital and the new immigrant workforce are two major instances of transnationalized actors with features that constitute each as a somewhat unitary actor overriding borders while at the same time in contestation with each other inside cities (Ehrenreich and Hochschild, 2003; Banerjee-Guha, 2010; Weinstein and Ren, 2009; Nashashibi, 2007).

Place and Production in the Global Economy

Globalization can be deconstructed in terms of the strategic sites where global processes and the linkages that bind them materialize. Among these sites are export-processing zones, offshore banking centres and on a far more complex level, global cities. This produces a specific geography of globalization and underlines the extent to which it is not a planetary event encompassing the entire world.[2] It is, furthermore, a changing geography, one that has transformed over the last few centuries and over the last few decades.[3] Most recently, this changing geography has come to include electronic space.

The geography of globalization contains both a dynamic of dispersal and of centralization, a condition that is only now beginning to receive recognition.[4] The massive trends towards the spatial dispersal of economic activities at the metropolitan, national and global level that we associate with globalization have contributed to a demand for new forms of territorial centralization of top-level management and control operations. This is due to continuing concentration in control, ownership and profit appropriation that characterizes the current economic system.[5]

National and global markets as well as globally integrated organizations require central places where the work of globalization gets done.[6] Furthermore, information industries also require a vast physical infrastructure containing strategic nodes with a hyperconcentration of facilities. We need to distinguish between the capacity for global transmission and communication and the material conditions that make this possible. Finally, even the most advanced information industries have a production process that is at least partly bound to place because of the combination of resources it requires even when the outputs are hypermobile.

The vast new economic topography that is being implemented through electronic space is one moment, one fragment, of an even vaster economic chain that is in good part embedded in non-electronic spaces. There is no fully dematerialized firm or industry. Even the most advanced information industries, such as finance, are installed only partly in electronic space. And so are industries that produce digital products, such as software designers. The growing digitalization of economic activities has not eliminated the need for major international business and financial centres and all the material resources they concentrate, from state-of-the-art telecommunications infrastructure to brain talent.

In my research, I have conceptualized cities as production sites for the leading information industries of our time in order to recover the infrastructure of activities, firms, and jobs that is necessary to run the advanced corporate economy, including its globalized sectors. These industries are typically conceptualized in terms of the hypermobility of their outputs and the high levels of expertise of their professionals. I am far more interested in recovering the production process involved and the requisite infrastructure of facilities and non-expert jobs that are also part of these industries. A detailed analysis of service-based urban economies shows that there is a considerable articulation of firms, sectors, and workers who may appear as though they have little connection to an urban economy dominated by finance and specialized services but, in fact, fulfil a series of functions that are an integral part of that economy. They do so, however, under conditions of sharp social earnings, and often racial/ethnic segmentation (Sassen, 2012, chapters 4–7).

In the day-to-day work of the leading services complex dominated by finance, a large share of the jobs involved is low paid and manual, many held by women and immigrants. Although these types of workers and jobs are never represented as part of the global economy, they are in fact part of the infrastructure of jobs involved in running and implementing the global economic system, including such an advanced form as international finance.[7] The top end of the corporate economy – the corporate towers that project engineering expertise, precision, 'techne' – is far easier to mark as necessary for an advanced economic system than are truckers and other industrial service workers, even though these are a necessary ingredient.[8] We see here a dynamic of valorization at work that has sharply increased the distance between the devalorized and the valorized, indeed overvalorized, sectors of the economy.

Elements of a New Socio-Spatial Order

The implantation of global processes and markets in major cities has meant that the internationalized sector of the urban economy has expanded sharply and has imposed a new set of criteria for valuing or pricing various economic activities and outcomes. This has had devastating effects on large sectors of the urban economy. It is not simply a quantitative transformation; we see here the elements for a new economic regime.

These tendencies towards polarization assume distinct forms in 1. the spatial organization of the urban economy; 2. the structures for social reproduction; and 3. the organization of the labour process. In these trends towards multiple forms of polarization lie conditions for the creation of employment-centred urban poverty and marginality and for new class formations.

The ascendance of the specialized services-led economy, particularly the new finance and services complex, engenders what may be regarded as a new economic regime because, although this sector may account for only a fraction of the economy of a city, it imposes itself on that larger economy. One of these pressures is towards polarization, as is the case with the possibility for super profits in finance, which contributes to devalorize manufacturing and low-value-added services insofar as these sectors cannot generate the super profits typical of much financial activity. The super-profit-making capacity of many of the leading industries is embedded in a complex combination of new trends: technologies that make possible the hypermobility of capital at a global scale and the deregulation of multiple markets that allows for implementing that hypermobility; financial inventions such as securitization which liquefy hitherto illiquid capital and allow it to circulate and hence make additional profits; and the growing demand for services in all industries along with the increasing complexity and specialization of many of these inputs, which have contributed to their valorization and often over-valorization, as illustrated in the unusually high salary increases beginning in the 1980s for top level professionals and CEOs. Globalization further adds to the complexity of these services, their strategic character, their glamour and therewith adds to their over-valorization.

The presence of a critical mass of firms with extremely high profit-making capabilities contributes to bid up the prices of commercial space, industrial services, and other business needs, thereby making survival for firms with moderate profit-making capabilities increasingly precarious. And while the latter are essential to the operation of the urban economy and the daily needs of residents, their economic viability is threatened in a situation where finance and specialized services can earn super profits. High prices and profit levels in the internationalized sector and its ancillary activities, such as top-of-the-line restaurants and hotels, make it increasingly difficult for other sectors to compete for space and investments. Many of these other sectors have experienced considerable downgrading and/or displacement; for example, the replacement of neighbourhood shops tailored to local needs by upscale boutiques and restaurants catering to new high-income urban elites.

Inequality in the profit-making capabilities of different sectors of the economy has always existed. But what we see happening today takes place on another order of magnitude and is engendering massive distortions in the operations of various markets, from housing to labour. For example, the polarization of firms and households in the spatial organization of the economy contribute, in my reading, towards the informalization of a growing array of economic activities in advanced urban economies. When firms with low or modest profit-making capacities experience an ongoing, if not increasing demand for their goods and services from households and other firms in a context where a significant sector of the economy makes super profits, they often cannot afford the higher costs, even though there is an effective demand for what they produce. Operating informally is often one of the few ways in which such firms can survive; for example, using spaces not zoned for commercial or manufacturing uses, such as basements in residential areas, or space that is not up to health, fire and other such standards. Similarly, new firms in low-profit industries entering a strong market for their goods and services may only be able to do so informally. Another option for firms with limited profit-making capabilities is to subcontract part of their work to informal operations.[9] The recomposition of the sources of growth and profit-making entailed by these transformations also contributes to a reorganization of some components of social reproduction or consumption. While the middle strata still constitute the majority, the conditions that contributed to their expansion and politico-economic power in the postwar decades – the centrality of mass production and mass consumption in economic growth and profit realization – have been displaced by new sources of growth.

The rapid growth of industries with strong concentrations of high- and low-income jobs has assumed distinct forms in the consumption structure, which, in turn, has a feedback effect on the organization of work and the types of jobs being created. The expansion of the high-income workforce in conjunction with the emergence of new cultural forms has led to a process of high-income gentrification that rests, in the last analysis, on the availability of a vast supply of low-wage workers.

In good part, the consumption needs of the low-income population in large cities are met by manufacturing and retail establishments which are small, rely on family labour, and often fall below minimum safety and health standards. Cheap, locally produced sweatshop garments, for example, can compete with low-cost Asian imports. A growing range of products and services, from low-cost furniture made in basements to 'gypsy cabs' and family daycare, is available to meet the demand for the growing low-income population.

One way of conceptualizing informalization in advanced urban economies today is to posit it as the systemic equivalent of what we call deregulation at the top of the economy (see Sassen, 2012, pp. 257–259). Both the deregulation of a growing number of leading information industries and the informalization of a growing number of sectors with low profit-making capacities can be conceptualized as adjustments under conditions where new economic developments and old regulations enter in growing tension.[10] 'Regulatory fractures' is one concept I have used to capture this condition.

We can think of these developments as constituting new geographies of centrality and marginality that cut across the old divide between poor and rich countries, and new geographies of marginality that have become increasingly evident not only in the less developed world but within highly developed countries. Inside major cities in both the developed and developing world, we see a new geography of centres and margins that not only contributes to strengthen existing inequalities but also sets in motion a whole series of new dynamics of inequality.

The Localizations of the Global

Economic globalization, then, needs to be understood also in its multiple localizations, rather than only in terms of the broad, overarching macro-level processes that dominate the mainstream account. Further, we need to see that some of these localizations do not generally get coded as having anything to do with the global economy. The global city can be seen as one strategic instantiation of such multiple localizations.

Here I focus on localizations of the global with these two features. Many of these localizations are embedded in the demographic transition evident in such cities, where a majority of resident workers today are immigrants and women, often women of colour. At the same time, many of the jobs that matter for the globalized sectors do not fit the master images about globalization, yet are part of it. The fact that they are low wage and held by minoritized workers obscures the importance of these jobs. This, in turn, contributes to the devalorization of these types of workers and work cultures and to the 'legitimacy' of that devalorization.

This can be read as a rupture of the traditional dynamic whereby membership in leading economic sectors contributes conditions towards the formation of a labour aristocracy – a process long evident in Western industrialized economies. 'Women and immigrants' come to replace the Fordist/family-wage category of 'women and children' (Sassen, 2008).[11] One of the localizations of the dynamics of globalization is the process of economic restructuring in global cities. The associated socioeconomic polarization has generated a large growth in the demand for low-wage workers and for jobs that offer few advancement possibilities. This occurs amidst an explosion in the wealth and power concentrated in these cities – that is to say, in conditions where there is also a visible expansion in high-income jobs and high-priced urban space.

'Women and immigrants' emerge as the labour supply that facilitates the imposition of low wages and powerlessness under conditions of high demand for those workers and the location of those jobs in high-growth sectors. It breaks the historic nexus that would have led to empowering workers and legitimates this break culturally.

Another localization which is rarely associated with globalization, informalization, re-introduces the community and the household as an important economic space in global cities. I see informalization in this setting as the low-cost – and often feminized – equivalent of deregulation at the top of the system. As with deregulation (e.g.

financial deregulation), informalization introduces flexibility, reduces the 'burdens' of regulation and lowers costs; in this case, especially the costs of labour. Informalization in major cities of highly developed countries – whether New York, London, Paris or Berlin – can be seen as a downgrading of a variety of activities for which there is an effective demand in these cities, but also a devaluing and enormous competition, given low entry costs and few alternative forms of employment. Going informal is one way of producing and distributing goods and services at a lower cost and with greater flexibility. This further devalues these types of activities. Immigrants and women are important actors in the new informal economies of these cities. They absorb the costs of informalizing these activities.

Immigration and ethnicity are too often constituted as 'otherness'. Understanding them as a set of processes whereby global elements are localized, international labour markets are constituted and cultures from all over the world are deterritorialized, puts them right there at the centre of the stage – along with the internationalization of capital. Further, this way of narrating the migration events of the postwar era captures the ongoing weight of colonialism and post-colonial forms of empire on major processes of globalization today and, specifically, on those binding emigration and immigration countries. While the specific genesis and contents of their responsibility will vary from case to case and period to period, none of the major immigration countries is an innocent bystander.

The centrality of place in a context of global processes engenders a transnational economic and political opening in the formation of new claims and hence in the constitution of entitlements, notably rights to place and, at the limit, in the constitution of 'citizenship'. The city has indeed emerged as a site for new claims: by global capital which uses the city as an 'organizational commodity' but also by disadvantaged sectors of the urban population, who are often as international a presence in large cities as capital. Cities one of the key sites where people from many different countries are most likely to meet and a multiplicity of cultures can come together. The international character of major cities lies not only in their telecommunication infrastructure and international firms: it lies also in the many different cultural environments in which these workers exist. One can no longer think of centres for international business and finance simply in terms of the corporate towers and corporate culture at its centre.

Conclusion

Large cities around the world are the terrain where a multiplicity of globalization processes assumes concrete, localized forms. These localized forms are, in good part, what globalization is about. If we consider further that large cities also concentrate a growing share of disadvantaged populations – immigrants in Europe and the United States, African-Americans and Latinos in the United States, masses of shanty dwellers in the mega-cities of the developing world – then we can see that cities have become a strategic terrain for a whole series of conflicts and contradictions.

We can then think of cities also as one of the sites for the contradictions of the globalization of capital. On one hand, they concentrate a disproportionate share of corporate power and are one of the key sites for the over-valorization of the corporate economy; on the other hand, they concentrate a disproportionate share of the disadvantaged and are one of the key sites for their devalorization. This joint presence happens in a context where (1) the transnationalization of economies has grown sharply and cities have become increasingly strategic for global capital, and (2) marginalized people have found their voice and are making claims on the city as well. This joint presence is further brought into focus by the sharpening of the distance between the two.

These joint presences have made cities a contested terrain. Inequality, high unemployment, homelessness, police abuse all can coexist with the new high-end corporate sectors. The global city concentrates diversity. Its spaces are inscribed with the dominant corporate culture but also with a multiplicity of other cultures and identities, notably through immigration. The slippage is evident: the dominant culture can encompass only part of the city. And while corporate power inscribes non-corporate cultures and identities with 'otherness', thereby devaluing them, they are present everywhere. The immigrant communities and informal economy in cities such as New York and Los Angeles are only two instances.

As earlier said, the centrality of place in conditions of globalization leads to the formation of new claims and the constitution of new entitlements, especially rights to place. It also brings about the constitution of new forms of 'citizenship' and enhances the multiplicity of citizenship practices. The global city has thus become a site for new contestations: by transnational capital which uses it as an 'organizational commodity', and by disadvantaged segments of the urban citizenry, which are often as internationalized in their composition as capital itself. The denationalizing of urban space and the formation of new claims centred on transnational actors and involving contestation constitute the global city as a frontier zone for a new type of engagement. In short, cities have once again become a key lens through which to understand major emerging social dynamics. And Jane Jacobs would have gone in there and captured the good and the bad.

Notes

1.   I have theorized this in terms of the network of global cities, where the latter are partly a function of that network. For example, the growth of the financial centres in New York or London is fed by what flows through the worldwide network of financial centres given deregulation of national economies. The cities at the top of this global hierarchy concentrate the capacities to maximize their capture of the proceeds, so to speak.

2.   Globalization is also a process that produces differentiation, only that the alignment of differences is of a very different kind from that associated with such differentiating notions as national character, national culture and national society. For example, the corporate world today has a global geography, but it does not exist everywhere in the world: in fact, it has highly defined and structured spaces; secondly, it also is increasingly sharply differentiated from non-corporate segments in the economies of the particular locations (e.g. a city such as New York) or countries where it operates. There is homogenization along certain lines that cross national boundaries and sharp differentiation inside these boundaries.

3.   We need to recognize the specific historical conditions for different conceptions of the 'international' or the 'global'. There is a tendency to see the internationalization of the economy as a process operating at the centre, embedded in the power of the multinational corporations today and colonial enterprises in the past. One could note that the economies of many peripheral countries are thoroughly internationalized due to high levels of foreign investments in all economic sectors and heavy dependence on world markets for 'hard' currency. What centre countries have are strategic concentrations of firms and markets that operate globally. This is a very different form of the international from that of peripheral countries. But what both types of countries increasingly have is global cities with the capability of global control and coordination.

4.   This proposition lies at the heart of my model of the global city (see Sassen, 2001, p. 1, 2011, p. 1).

5.   More conceptually, we can ask whether an economic system with strong tendencies towards such concentration can have a space economy that lacks points of physical agglomeration. That is to say, does power, in this case economic power, have spatial correlates?

6.   I see the producer services, and especially finance and advanced corporate services, as industries producing the organizational commodities necessary for the implementation and management of global economic systems (Sassen 2012, chapters 4 and 5). Producer services are intermediate outputs; that is, services bought by firms. They cover financial, legal, and general management matters, innovation, development, design, administration, personnel, production technology, maintenance, transport, communications, wholesale distribution, advertising, cleaning services for firms, security and storage. Central components of the producer services category are a range of industries with mixed business and consumer markets; they are insurance, banking, financial services, real estate, legal services, accounting and professional associations.

7.   A methodological tool I find useful for this type of examination is what I call circuits for the distribution and installation of economic operations. These circuits allow me to follow economic activities into terrains that escape the increasingly narrow borders of mainstream representations of 'the advanced economy' and to negotiate the crossing of socio-culturally discontinuous spaces.

8.   This is illustrated by the following event. When the first acute stock market crisis happened in 1987 after years of enormous growth, there were numerous press reports about the sudden and massive unemployment crisis among high-income professionals on Wall Street. The other unemployment crisis on Wall Street, affecting secretaries and blue-collar workers was never noticed nor reported upon. And yet, the stock market crash created a very concentrated unemployment crisis, for example, in the Dominican immigrant community in Northern Manhattan where a lot of the Wall Street janitors live.

9.   More generally, we are seeing the formation of new types of labour market segmentation. Two characteristics stand out. One is the weakening role of the firm in structuring the employment relation; more is left to the market. A second form in this restructuring of the labour market is what could be described as the shift of labour market functions to the household or community.

10   Linking informalization and growth takes the analysis beyond the notion that the emergence of informal sectors in cities like New York and Los Angeles is caused by the presence of immigrants and their propensities to replicate survival strategies typical of Third World countries. Linking informalization and growth also takes the analysis beyond the notion that unemployment and recession generally may be the key factors promoting informalization in the current phase of highly industrialized economies. It may point to characteristics of advanced capitalism that are not typically noted.

11.   This newer case brings out more brutally than did the Fordist contract, the economic significance of these types of actors, a significance veiled or softened in the case of the Fordist contract through the provision of the family wage.

References

Abu-Lughod, J.L. (1994) *From Urban Village to 'East Village': The Battle for New York's Lower East Side.* Oxford: Blackwell.

Abu-Lughod, J.L. (1999) *New York, Chicago, Los Angeles. America's Global Cities.* Minneapolis, MN: University of Minnesota Press.

Amen, M.M., Archer, K. and Martin Bosman, M. (eds.) (2006) *Relocating Global Cities: From the Center to the Margins*. Lanham, MD: Rowman & Littlefield.

Banerjee-Guha, S. (ed.) (2010) *Accumulation by Dispossession: Transformative Cities in the New Global Order*. Thousand Oaks, CA: Sage.

Bartlett, A. (2007) The city and the self: the emergence of new political subjects in London, in Sassen, S. (ed.) *Deciphering the Global: Its Spaces, Scales and Subjects*. London: Routledge, pp. 221–243.

Brenner, N. (1998) Global cities, glocal states: global city formation and state territorial restructuring in contemporary Europe. *Review of International Political Economy*, **5**(1), pp.1–37.

Brenner, N. and Keil, R. (2005) *The Global Cities Reader*. London: Routledge.

Bridge, G. and Watson, S. (2011) *The New Blackwell: Companion to the City*. Oxford: Wiley-Blackwell.

Brown, E., Derudder, B., Parnreiter, C., Pelupessy, W., Taylor, P.J. and Witlox, F. (2010) World city networks and global commodity chains: towards a world systems integration. *Global Networks*, **10**(1), pp. 12–34.

Burdett, R. (ed.) (2006) *Cities: People, Society, Architecture*. New York: Rizzoli.

Castells, M. (1977) *The Urban Question: A Marxist Approach*. Translated by A. Sheridan. Cambridge, MA: MIT Press.

Drainville, A. (2004) *Contesting Globalization: Space and Place in the World Economy*. London: Routledge.

Ehrenreich, B. and Hochschild, A. (eds.) (2003) *Global Woman*. New York: Metropolitan Books.

Fainstein, S. (2010) *The Just City*. Ithaca, NY: Cornell University Press.

Fainstein, S. and Campbell, S. (2011) Theories of urban development and their implications for policy and planning, in Fainstein, S. and Campbell, S. (eds.) *Readings in Urban Theory*, 3rd ed. Oxford: Wiley-Blackwell, pp. 1–15.

Fiscal Policy Institute (2010) Grow Together or Pull Further Apart? Income Concentration Trends in New York. Available at http://www.fiscalpolicy.org/archivepages/publication2010_archive.html. Accessed 13 December 2010.

Goldsmith, S.A. and Elizabeth, L. (eds.) (2010) *What We See: Advancing the Observations of Jane Jacobs*. New York: New Village Press.

Hagedorn, J. (ed.) (2007) *Gangs in the Global City: Exploring Alternatives to Traditional Criminology*. Chicago, IL: University of Illinois Press.

Harvey, D. (1982) *The Limits to Capital*. Oxford: Blackwell.

Harvey, D. (2007) The subnational constitution of global markets, in Sassen, S. (ed.) *Deciphering the Global: Its Spaces, Scales and Subjects*. London: Routledge, pp. 199–216.

Heine, J. (ed.) (2011) *The Dark Side of Globalization*. Tokyo: United Nations University Press.

Herzog, L.A. (2006) *Return to the Center: Culture, Public Space, and City-Building in a Global Era*. Austin, TX: University of Texas Press.

INURA (ed.) (2003) *The Contested Metropolis*. Zurich: Birkhauser.

Jacobs, J. (1970) *The Economy of Cities*. London: Vintage.

Jacobs, J. (1985) *Cities and the Wealth of Nations*. New York: Vintage.

Jacobs, J. (1993, 1961) *The Death and Life of Great American Cities*. New York: Modern Library.

King, A.D. (ed.) (1996) *Re-presenting the City. Ethnicity, Capital and Culture in the 21st Century*. London: Macmillan.

Krause, L. and Petro, P. (eds.) (2003) *Global Cities: Cinema, Architecture, and Urbanism in a Digital Age*. New Brunswick, NJ: Rutgers University Press.

Lefebvre, H. (1974) *The Production of Space*. Paris: Éditions Anthropos.

Lloyd, R. (2005) *Neo-Bohemia: Art and Commerce in the Postindustrial City*. London: Routledge.

McCann, E. and Ward, K. (2010) *Mobile Urbanism: Cities and Policy-making in a Global Age*. Minneapolis, MN: Minnesota University Press.

Nashashibi, R. (2007) Ghetto cosmopolitanism: making theory at the margins, in Sassen, S. (ed.) *Deciphering the Global: Its Spaces, Scales and Subjects*. London: Routledge, pp. 241–262.

Ong, A. and Roy, A. (eds.) (2010) *Worlding Cities: Asian Experiments and the Art of Being Global*. Oxford: Blackwell.

Paddison, R. (ed.) (2001) Introduction, in *Handbook of Urban Studies*. London: Sage.

Ren, X. (2011) *Building Globalization: Transnational Architecture Production in Urban China*. Chicago, IL: University of Chicago Press.

Ribera-Fumaz, R. (2009) From urban political economy to cultural political economy: rethinking culture and economy in and beyond the urban. *Progress in Human Geography*, **33**, pp. 447–465.

Ross, C. (2009) *Megaregions: Planning for Global Competitiveness*. Washington DC: Island Press.

Sassen, S. ([1991] 2001) *The Global City: New York, London, and Tokyo*, 2nd ed. Princeton, NJ: Princeton University Press.

Sassen, S. (2008) *Territory, Authority, Rights: From Medieval to Global Assemblages*. Princeton, NJ: Princeton University Press.

Sassen, S. (2012) *Cities in a World Economy*, 4th ed. Pine Forge, PA: Sage.

Soysal, L. (2010) Intimate engagements of the public kind. *Anthropological Quarterly*, **83**, pp. 373–389.

Taylor, P.J., Derudder, B., Saey, P. and Witlox, F. (eds.) (2007) *Cities in Globalization: Practices, Policies and Theories*. London: Routledge.

Taylor, P.J., Ni, P., Derudder, B., Hoyler, M., Huang, J. and Witlox, F. (eds.) (2010) *Global Urban Analysis: A Survey of Cities in Globalization*. London: Earthscan.

Weinstein, L. and Ren. X. (2009) The changing right to the city: urban renewal and housing rights in globalizing Shanghai and Mumbai. *City & Community*, **8**(4), pp. 407–432.

Xu, J. and Yeh, A.O.H. (2010) *Governance and Planning of Mega-City Regions: An International Comparative Perspective*. London: Routledge.

Yuval-Davis, N. (1999) Ethnicity, gender relations and multiculturalism, in Torres, R., Miron, L. and Inda, J.X. (eds.) *Race, Identity, and Citizenship*. Oxford: Blackwell, pp. 112–125.

Zukin, S. (2010) *Naked City: The Death and Life of Authentic Urban Places*. Oxford: Oxford University Press.

Part III

Jane Jacobs, Urban Sociologist

Chapter 8

Infrastructure, Social Injustice, and the City: Parsing the Wisdom of Jane Jacobs[1]

Marie-Alice L'Heureux

In *The Death and Life of Great American Cities* (1961), Jane Jacobs does not use the word 'infrastructure'. Nevertheless, infrastructure underlies her subject – the configuration of streets and sidewalks, the un-zoning of districts and neighbourhoods, the opposition to urban highways, and the retention and reuse of old buildings. Her book is ultimately about what is built or un-built, where, by whom, and how: who pays and who benefits. Through her activism, Jacobs showed that even small groups of people can promote change if they can network from the street (which is where neighbourhood identities are formed), through the district, to the city as a whole (where the power to cause change typically resides) (Jacobs, 1961, pp. 128–129). Jacobs does not seem to realize that people who are poor or lack resources, especially African Americans, are challenged in multiple ways (because of historic and lingering racism) in mobilizing at the district and city levels unless their concerns overlap with those of more powerful or connected people (Gotham, 1999; Issel, 1999; Mohl, 2004; Mollenkopf, 1983).

My thesis is that infrastructural projects that have been used to revitalize US cities with significant African-American populations historically have had a pronounced racial bias. Even though Jane Jacobs does not fully recognize this in *The Death and Life*, she argues for planning approaches that are based on the careful study of urban contexts, on local participation in decision-making, and on the value of incremental growth, which would benefit minority residents more than the policies that most US planners and city leaders pursue. The racial bias in urban infrastructural development has become less explicit over time. In fact, in their planning documents, cities tend to embrace rhetorically the principles that Jacobs promotes including walkability, diverse communities, lively mixed-use developments, incremental growth, mass transit, and even 'eyes on the street'. However, rhetorical endorsement and practical implementation have not gone together. The strategies of city officials often lead them to spend *cataclysmic* money on large infrastructural projects such as urban arenas and convention centres that, on the whole, not only contradict Jacobs's tenets but also appear to prolong the embedded racial inequalities in urban centres.

This chapter is structured as follows. First, I discuss the intimate intersection between historic urban development (including large infrastructural projects such as highways and Urban Renewal)[2] and racial inequality in the United States. I then elaborate on the ways cities have tried to promote development in the 1990s and 2000s. Approaches have certainly changed over time but the racial underpinnings of urban development have not gone away. Next, I turn to my case study, Kansas City, Missouri. I first outline the early-twentieth-century strategies that private entities used to prevent non-white infiltration into white neighbourhoods and the impact of these strategies on African Americans. I then discuss the way Kansas City has used legal and financial tools to promote developments that have often failed to counteract the negative effects of earlier racial segregation, urban highways, and Urban Renewal on the city centre. The third section picks up the narrative in the 1970s, in a supposedly post-segregation society when racial segregation was no longer considered a 'problem' and disappeared from the national agenda. The last section analyzes the contemporary scene in Kansas City: specifically, I review the manipulation of images and representation in the depiction of historically black neighbourhoods. Ultimately, although I focus on Kansas City, Missouri, I believe the issues apply to other cities I have studied recently such as Little Rock, Arkansas; Cincinnati, Columbus, and Cleveland, Ohio; Louisville and Lexington, Kentucky; Indianapolis, Indiana; and Nashville and Memphis, Tennessee.

Infrastructure and Racial Inequity in the Twentieth Century

People and city neighbourhoods are never equally or even equitably served (Castells, 1989; Harvey, 1973; Kirsch, 1995). The decisions of what type of transportation, water, and energy systems to use; where buildings, roads, pipes, wires, and networks should go and flow; what kinds of schools, entertainment districts, and parks to fund; and who should pay and who should benefit are made under evolving economic and varying ideological conditions (Tarr, 1984). They invariably favour some people over others. Infrastructure also creates a framework that generates greater wealth accumulation in some areas of cities than in others (Harvey, 1973).[3] Scholars have shown that in cities with a large African-American population, the negative aspects of infrastructure (highways, high-tension electric lines, etc.) have tended to impact their neighbourhoods more so than others (Bullard, 2004). Whether racism is considered an ideological issue, a class issue, or a structural issue may affect the types of analysis and conclusions in the social sciences (Bonilla-Silva, 1997; Harvey, 1973; Massey and Denton, 1993). It does not, however, diminish the impact on the people who must live with the legacies of racism nor does it mitigate the negative effects on the development of many urban centres.

When Jane Jacobs published *The Death and Life* in 1961, cities in the United States faced a provocative set of challenges. *Title I of the Housing Act of 1949* and the *Housing Act of 1954* had initiated a long period during which urban leaders and mayors used 'blight removal' as a strategy to target socio-economic problems and revitalize urban centres in order to retain middle-class residents. The *Federal-Aid Highway Act of 1956* strove to connect cities coast to coast and to facilitate inter-urban movement, but ultimately *undermined* the goals of the 1949 and 1954 *Housing Acts* by opening up areas outside of the urban core to suburbanization. Most city officials during the 1940s and 1950s genuinely thought that highways would encourage commerce, ease congestion, increase mobility and, ultimately, bring wealth to cities (City Plan Commission, 1947). After all, earlier train lines had connected cities and brought business and prosperity into urban areas. But, modern highways created streams that allow vehicles and their passengers to run through or by-pass cities. They also reproduce some of the negative features of the original rail systems when they are elevated (Mumford, 1963, pp. 240–241). In a 1978 interview, Jacobs argued that urban highways do 'enormous damage to a city. And it's the wrong priority for the money. This is a wrong way to treat transportation in the city. And it's an uneconomic way and it's a polluting way, and it's got internal contradictions that cannot be justified. And it is a national problem' (Gratz, 2010, p. 219). Highways introduce space-gobbling off-ramps that consume prime real estate, destroy the urban fabric, congest city streets, and ultimately facilitate suburbanization and sprawl (Gutfreund, 2004; Jackson, 1985; Mumford, 1961, pp. 506–509). They also bring pollution, lower air quality, create inequities, and ultimately perpetuate the legacies of racism.

Highways that could not be driven through low-cost 'natural areas' have been planned instead through low-income and minority neighbourhoods (Dluhy *et al.*, 2002; Mohl, 1989; Mowbray, 1969; Rabin, 1973). The building of highways combined with other Urban Renewal policies that targeted slum areas, adversely affected poorer and minority-dominated communities. For instance, Interstate 95 ploughed through the Overtown neighbourhood in Miami in the 1960s. It is one of the best-known examples of a purposeful destruction of an African-American community in order to give more room for downtown growth (Dluhy *et al.*, 2002; Mohl, 1989). In New Orleans, the I-10 viaduct was built over North Claiborne, an African-American business and cultural street. It also cut through the heart of Tremé, a historically black-Creole district that lost its wide tree-lined public space to this intruder (Crutcher, 2010).

Fewer inner-city minority residents have cars and the allocation of gas-tax funds favours highways over mass transit and suburban roads over urban ones (Bullard, 2004, pp. 3–4). Infrastructural projects leave an enduring mark on a city – even if they are removed at some point. The way a city grows up around the invasive feature is different from what would have happened otherwise. For instance, in the late 1950s in Cincinnati, Fort Washington Way connected I-75 and I-71 and caused the demolition of the West End (a dense African-American community) and the central riverfront neighbourhoods, including Pearl Street and all the buildings on the south side of

Third Street (Davis, 1991; Stradling, 2003, p. 129). In the late 1990s, the roadway was transformed from a six-lane, 680-foot-wide maze of highways to a sunken eight-lane freeway in about half the original width. The city is still disconnected from its waterfront and the multiple neighbourhoods and businesses destroyed have not been rebuilt (Miller and Tucker, 1998; Scheer and Ferdelman, 2001). The highways in Louisville, Kentucky, do not seem at first glance to be purposefully racist in their layout, since blacks and whites lived in zones in close proximity through the first part of the twentieth century. But in analyzing maps of the old Smoketown, an African-American district just east of the downtown core, it becomes clear that the I-65 carefully cut it off from Louisville's Central Business District. Urban Renewal also decimated Walnut Street, the main black business and entertainment area in Louisville (Adams, 2010, pp. 150–152). In Little Rock, I-30 and I-630 largely separate blacks on the east and south and whites on the north and west (Koon, 2011).

Another process that significantly affected urban development was the reaction to the significant in-migration of Southern blacks to Northern and Midwestern cities. This 'Great Migration' occurred in two distinct waves: from the 1910s to the 1940s and post-World War II to the 1970s (Fullilove, 2004, pp. 26–27; Isenberg, 2004, pp. 107–112; Jones, 1993; Trotter, 1993). By law, force, or convention, blacks in cities were forced to live in narrow enclaves and barred from lucrative jobs, which prevented many of them from accumulating the capital needed to improve their material conditions. Areas in which noticeable populations of minorities resided were marginalized and became targets for Urban Renewal and highway construction. The removal of urban blight in the United States in the 1950s and 1960s became so aligned with racial segregation, that it segmented downtown areas and undermined the goal of cities to sustain themselves as economic centres. In African-American communities, Urban Renewal became synonymous with 'Negro Removal'. This contributed to urban unrest in the 1960s and the beginning of the 1970s, which hastened the outflow of middle-income residents, both white and black, leaving behind mostly older and poorer residents of colour (Wiese, 2003). Blight removal tactics were not exclusively levelled against African-American communities – for example, Poles in Detroit (*Poletown*, 1981; Wylie, 1989*)*, Czechs and Ukrainians in Denver (Doeppers, 1967), Italians, Jews, and Irish in Boston (Gans, 1965), and Hispanics and Japanese in Los Angeles (Hayden, 1995), also suffered. Yet, as sociologists Donald Massey and Nancy Denton have argued, the extent of *black segregation* and the associated negative effects have been 'unprecedented' and 'show little sign of change with the passage of time or improvements in socioeconomic status' (Massey and Denton, 1993, pp. 2–3). The policies were clearly intentional (Bonilla-Silva, 1997). The legacy of unequal investment and historic segregation continues to undermine neighbourhoods around city centres today.

Jacobs (1961) describes in detail the impact of various urban policies on particular individuals (Mrs Kostritsky [p. 63]; Mrs Abraham [p. 66]; a young butcher [p. 284]) and neighbourhoods (Boston's North End and West End; Back of the Yards in Chicago, etc.). But she seemingly glosses over the inequities and injustices that are embedded in the economics of development when it comes to race, as evident as they may have been during the period of Urban Renewal. She recognizes that 'Negroes' experience insidious discrimination, that their housing options are very limited, that real estate agents even manipulate the market to their disadvantage (Jacobs, 1961, p. 274). Yet she asserts that this 'racket works only in already stagnated and low-vitality neighborhoods' and the process can turn these areas around when 'colored citizens' who are interested in improving these neighbourhoods replace the fleeing whites (*Ibid.*).

Jacobs's approach set the stage for one of the greatest debates of the mid-twentieth century. What is primary: the physical or the social? In his famous 1962 review of her work, Herbert Gans criticizes Jacobs for missing the larger point. He faults her for a 'physical fallacy' in not recognizing the 'social, cultural, and economic factors that contribute to vitality or dullness' in cities (Gans, 1962, p. 172). Jacobs seems to have been convinced that if the physical attributes of a place align in the ways that she suggests, then it is possible for the appropriate social ones to emerge. For Gans, though, the problem was 'poverty and segregation' not 'the city or city planning'; the crisis was 'national' and had to do 'with economic and social inequality in America' (Gans, 1968, p. 206). In his view, the 'best way of eliminating the slums is to eliminate poverty' and to confront it at the national level (*Ibid.*, p. 205).

Regardless of the disparate directions of their arguments – Jacobs's advocacy of local, physical change and Gans's of national, social change – both authors recognize the *very high human cost* that comes from the construction of large infrastructural projects. The ideals of urbanism should, I believe, be about *both* the physical city (Jacobs's thesis) and economic and social justice (Gans's argument).

By the time the Kennedy administration entered the fray in the early 1960s, after the publication of *The Death and Life*, the ills of the Urban Renewal Program were evident everywhere. President Kennedy's 1961 speech to Congress on Housing and Urban Renewal recognized the failures and the need for metropolitan-scale planning that was more democratic since 'only when the citizens of a community have participated in selecting the goals which will shape their environment, can they be expected to support the actions necessary to accomplish these goals' (Kennedy, 1961). This led to the Model Cities Program (1966–1973) that was a multipronged, neighbourhood-based approach to urban problems. The programme addressed housing, employment, education, and health and welfare issues and mandated user-participation in the decision-making processes, but it was never sufficiently funded to achieve its complex goals in the five-year time frame. Richard Nixon (President, 1969–1974) preferred to reduce the size of the federal government and give funds directly to state and municipal entities that would address urban issues locally. He eliminated funding for the Model Cities Program replacing it with block grants that gave cities more autonomy. He also accepted the counsel of his urban adviser Daniel Patrick Moynihan to refrain from engaging directly issues of race (*New York Times*, 1970). By the mid-1970s urban unrest seemingly ended, and issues of race became less visible (Bonilla-Silva, 2003). Many states extended the use of eminent domain and tax credits to municipalities to support development. Entrepreneurial developers such as John Portman Associates, Victor Gruen, and the Rouse Company, among others created many large-scale mostly inward-focused projects that were 'gate-able'. Race was not explicitly discussed but these projects allowed for the privatization of spaces that previously had been considered 'public' (Davis, 1990).

Today, cities have certainly made some headway in reviving their downtowns. In many older urban centres, the most *effective* development has in fact occurred in the way that Jacobs advocated, through small-scale projects initiated by locals or by urban pioneers looking for a *place/space* in the city – as long as these efforts have not been undermined by city regulations such as zoning laws that restrict the mixing of housing and commercial uses. But, because of global competition, cities have succumbed to the pressure to conform to a type of urbanism that works better for tourist sightseeing than everyday life (a more superficial, transient, and pleasure-consuming type of urbanism, rather than one that nurtures civil society, educates minds, and enables diverse lifestyles) (Birch, 2005; Judd, 1999; Sohmer and Lang, 2001). Urban policies may no longer be overtly racist, but they, nonetheless, appear to prolong embedded racial inequities. For instance, cities often downplay the proximity of revitalized downtowns to concentrated areas of (poor) African Americans in order to attract visitors. Many suburban residents still have prejudicial ideas about downtowns that they characterize as 'dangerous' (aka 'black'). Historically black neighbourhoods must repeatedly mitigate these negative stereotypes that devalue their property and their pride and are a legacy of earlier racist policies (Kelley, 1997).

In the wake of the depopulation of many urban areas of the Midwest and Northeast, city officials have had to devise new strategies to promote development to increase the tax base and promote urban living. David Sawicki, a Professor of Planning and Urban Policy at Georgia Tech, argues, however, that city officials do not consider all costs and benefits of a project before entering into agreements with developers. They often give too much public money and control away at the outset and never test whether these projects achieve their stated goals of creating more jobs and housing or increasing economic activity.

Let us take convention centres for example. In the late 1990s, municipal officials routinely renovated, upgraded, and enlarged their convention centres. According to Heywood T. Sanders, Professor of Public Administration at the University of Texas at San Antonio, between 2000 and 2006, over forty cities expanded or built new convention centres, and this has contributed to the doubling of public sector funding for them, growing to over \$2.4 billion a year by 2000 (Sanders, 2002). In an almost Kafkaesque scenario, cities are told that their convention halls are empty because they are 'too small' and cannot compete for the larger conventions (Alm, 2002). They therefore need to create ever-larger centres and convention hotels with upwards of one thousand rooms nearby to entice these mega-conventions. The convention industry does the research and promotion, but does not revise its statistics, so cities are caught in an endless cycle of competition (Sanders, 2002). Cities are told that the venue is critical, that convention centres need to be in unique and lively areas with upscale shopping, restaurants, and cultural amenities within walking distance. These, in addition to quality urban housing, are also the criteria used to attract the so-called creative class, which reinforces this bias towards cultivating the special *character* of a place (Florida, 2002).

The buzz about cities is very intense and mayors and city councils often visit cities that they consider their 'competition' to learn how to create the perfect storm to succeed, often replicating what they observe. Consequently, there is an increasing homogeneity in the use of large-scale urban infrastructural projects to address city problems. Large projects are popular with mayors: they can be spun as urban regenerators and job creators, since it is extremely difficult to assess their economic impact before the fact and almost equally difficult afterwards. There are too many variables and potential externalities to pinpoint their relative success or failure. Studies have, nonetheless, shown that many of these large-scale projects are ineffective money generators (Gratz and Mintz, 1998; Judd, 2003; Sanders, 2005). They often simply redistribute income and revenue within the same municipality, do not contribute to the city's overall economic health, and do not alleviate the racial legacies of the past. Yet cities have continued to pursue them (Judd, 2003; Sanders, 2005; Sawicki, 1989, p. 349).

Officials in most of the cities I have studied have also changed the way they rationalize these projects to their constituents to address these criticisms. In the 1950s and 1960s, they claimed that urban renewal would halt decay and blight; in the 1970s, the Model Cities Program that engaged local residents fell from favour and 'block grants' that allowed cities more flexibility came to the fore; from the 1980s to the mid 1990s, they presented these developments as job-and-revenue generators; then in the 1990s, the discussion shifted from addressing purely pragmatic aspects of functionality and economy to the symbolic importance of development (especially downtown ball parks, stadia, and arenas) as sources of pride that contribute positively to the status and image of the city (Chapin, 2004). Cities started to recognize that their downtowns often have multiple areas of interest that are in close proximity to each other, but not within the quarter-mile radius for walkability. Over time, the location of new investment relative to these 'special' areas creates either competing areas or uneven development, thus further contributing to inequality.

With these thoughts in mind, I now turn to racism and infrastructure in Kansas City, Missouri.

Protecting Land Values, Expanding Segregation in the Early 1900s

The first major intentional move to create lasting racially segregated neighbourhoods in Kansas City dates to the early twentieth century. Unlike today's developers, real estate mogul Jesse Clyde Nichols (1880–1950) did not have access to government-sponsored programmes or tax credits when he created his well-known Country-Club Plaza development. Before proceeding, he carefully studied the development of two wealthy Kansas City subdivisions, Quality Hill (platted as Coates Addition and Lucas Place in 1857) and Hyde Park (platted in 1886) that had passed their prime (Miller,

1881, p. 71; Whitney, 1908; Worley, 1990, p. 43). Kersey Coates's regulations required that houses be built of brick in his subdivisions; this restricted them to the wealthiest citizens. But eventually the smells of the stockyards wafting up from the West Bottoms (below Quality Hill) and the shanties and shacks creeping up from below undermined the neighbourhood. By the 1880s, wealthy residents had begun to move south to Hyde Park, which was subdivided and designed by the German-American landscape architect George Kessler (1862–1923). During the recession of the late 1890s, landlords were forced to subdivide houses in Hyde Park to make them economically viable, commercial uses proliferated, and billboards sprung up like mushrooms along roadways. This undermined property values in the developments.

When Nichols began his subdivisions in the early twentieth century, he carefully purchased sufficient land to protect the property as much as possible from what he considered undesirable encroachments. He selected land bounded by a country club to the north (located in present-day Loose Park) and Brush Creek to the south, and one block south of Kansas City's official city limits. In 1908, in order to prevent the in-migration of any but the truly well-off, he instituted restrictive covenants on the deeds that specified the type of housing that could be built (single-family homes), the setbacks, and the cost of the home ($5,000 minimum). Sale to and occupancy by blacks was explicitly prohibited (Worley, 1990, pp. 127–28). In his Sunset Hills development, he increased the minimum house price to $10,000. He also created homeowner associations which controlled many aspects of the neighbourhood and were effective at impeding physical and social erosion (*Ibid.*, pp. 166–174). Nichols wanted to prevent the conversion of single-family homes into rooming houses or other uses and to prohibit the erection of billboards and other unsightly elements that had undermined property values in Hyde Park and Quality Hill. He also wanted to prevent the thousands of African Americans who were migrating from the South at that time from moving into these neighbourhoods or their peripheries because he thought this would drive out whites and lower property values.

By the 1910s, restrictive covenants adopted by Nichols and social conventions had made it difficult for African Americans to find adequate housing. In 1915, the bicameral Council passed a Jim Crow law[4] that forbade the siting of a school for children 'of African descent to locate within twenty-four hundred feet of a public or private school for whites', which further restricted the residential options for blacks (Gotham, 2002; Schirmer, 2002, pp. 75–76). Bombings and acts of terrorism against African Americans finally resulted in a *de facto* 'Negro District' bounded by 9th Street on the north to 28th on the south, Troost Avenue on the west to Indiana on the east (Gibson, 1997, p. 114). The four-hundred-square-block district (that this *de facto* Jim Crow delimited area represented) became the centre of African-American residential and business life for the next forty years until the courts loosened segregation's stranglehold.[5] Black-owned businesses, stores, theatres, and restaurants centred on 18th and Vine, while clubs and nightlife thrived along 12th Street. In 1940, the residential density in the District was close to 24 people per net acre (48,000 people on 2,050 acres) (City Plan Commission, 1947, table 4). Although this density was enforced by the practice of racial segregation, it resulted in a vibrant urban environment. News reports and films about the district characterize it as a lively active place where residents could satisfy most of their daily needs from buying shoes to getting legal counsel, from attending a baseball game to listening to jazz, from going to school to participating in social clubs.

The Mid-1900s: Expanding Municipal Control in Development

In 1943, the State of Missouri adopted statutes that gave municipalities the power to condemn and consolidate properties using eminent domain, to implement tax-credit mechanisms, and otherwise to affect development in cities (McBride, 1990) (table 8.1).

Table 8.1. Missouri Laws adopted to facilitate municipal involvement in development.

Law Title	Law No.	Abbreviation	Year Adopted
Urban Redevelopment Corporations Law	Chapter 353	URCL	1943
Land Clearance for Redevelopment Authority Law	99.300	LCRA	1951
The Planned Industrial Expansion Law (Authority)	99.30	PIE/PIEA	1967
Tax Increment Financing (TIF)	99.800	TIF	1982

Source: www.moga.mo.gov/statutes/statutes.htm.

Kansas City adopted its TIF policy in 1982 and the incentive 'typically returns to developers 50 percent to 100 percent of new sales, property, or other taxes generated by the project to help pay for eligible project costs. The money otherwise would go to schools, local fire districts and other public coffers' (Alm, 2007, p. D1). All these funding mechanisms are intended to promote industrial or commercial development that would not otherwise be viable, especially in the centre of cities, but they have often been invested in projects that do not meet the spirit of these criteria. Thus funds have been taken away from other neighbourhoods and city services (Kelsay, 2007).

Each state has its own array of laws to promote and realize major developments (Gordon, 2008, p. 157). Over the years, developers have learned their way around these programmes and have benefited greatly from them. Tax credits have been an innocuous way for leaders at all levels of government to promote particular developments without appearing to increase or lower taxes – and therefore tax credits have not been as controversial an instrument as eminent domain, although they are becoming so. These programmes still reduce available tax resources and are one more mechanism that can exacerbate infrastructural and economic disparities. City officials have tried to enhance Kansas City's tax revenues through these programmes, but as I have learned, no fiscal or programmatic accountability is built into them. Cities do not have to prove that particular TIF or 353 investments actually further economic growth or create jobs in order to continue to mobilize them. Today, practically every development has some kind of PIE, TIF, or 353 enabling it. These programmes are no longer simply 'tools to promote development', but necessary enticements for projects that cities want. If tax breaks or tax credits are not forthcoming to sweeten the deal, developers will threaten to take their projects elsewhere. When a project is granted tax-exempt status for ten years and tax-reduced status for another fifteen, there are long-term implications for other city services. A 2006 study by the *Kansas City Business Journal* shows that 'PIEA approved tax abatements ... cost jurisdictions $1.4 million' in 2005 – almost $800,000 of it lost to public schools alone (Davis, 2006).

1960s and 1970s:
Highways and Urban Renewal in Kansas City

After the Second World War, the creation of the highway system in Kansas City paralleled and reinforced the destructive path of Urban Renewal. Four major highways make up the downtown 'Loop'. They enclose a 1.1 mile x 0.7 mile area (or just over three-quarters of a square mile [about 2 km²]) and contribute to the segmentation of Kansas City's urban landscape (figure 8.1). Aerial photographs from the 1940s show dramatically the dense urban fabric that lay under the path of the proposed highway (City Plan Commission, 1951, pp. 84–101) (figure 8.2).

The south leg, the I-70, cut through the heart of the Vine District between 14th Street and Truman Road and, combined with Urban Renewal clearances, obliterated the nightclub and entertainment venues including the 12th and Vine corner immortalized in the song 'Kansas City' (1952) and the tune 'Twelfth Street Rag' (1914) (figure 8.1). Projects like the nine- and ten-storey Wayne Miner Court housing, erected in 1962, and the low-rise B.T. Watkins Homes, housed only a fraction of those displaced (figure 8.1). Wayne Miner was plagued with problems from the outset, and in 1987, after a history of crime, vandalism, and neglect it was imploded in an event reminiscent of St. Louis's Pruitt Igoe housing demolition.

By the time the South Midtown Freeway, I-71, the last leg of the downtown Loop was started on the east side of the city in the early 1970s, African-American residents organized to fight it. They put together a coalition with help from the NAACP and CORE (Congress of Racial Equality) (Gotham, 1999, p. 339). They could not completely halt its construction, although they delayed it for thirty years. They also insisted on a more attractive design with traffic signals to allow cross-traffic flow (which I-71 commuters decry). The Paseo is another one of George Kessler's City Beautiful boulevards. Tellingly, to create it in the late 1800s, 'cabins and shanties ... occupied mainly by Negroes' were removed (Schott 1905, pp. 7192 and 7204). So one hundred years later, in 2001, the new highway again displaced African Americans. At a total cost of $300 million dollars, the 10 mile (16 km) section of the Bruce R. Watkins Drive, named for one of its staunchest opponents, displaced 10,000 people, mostly African Americans, and saved the average (mostly white) commuter ten to twelve minutes of travel time per trip (Campbell, 2001). It also further isolated the Vine Jazz District from the downtown core and bisected Beacon Hill, Ivanhoe, and other struggling African-American neighbourhoods to the south. As is too often the case with urban infrastructure, those who pay the most comparatively for something, benefit the least.

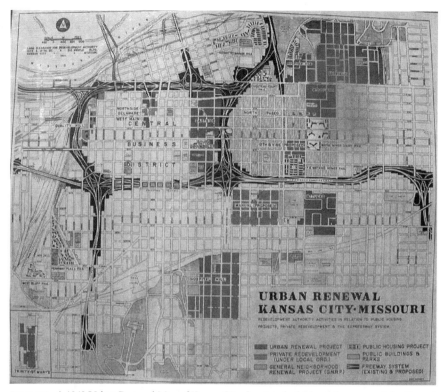

Figure 8.1. A 1960 Urban Renewal Map of Kansas City showing the highway loop around the Central Business District as well as the extent of the Urban Renewal projects in the 18th and Vine District. The nub of I-71 (proposed South Midtown Freeway) is visible on the southeast end of the Loop. The Wayne Miner housing blocks are shown to the east of the Loop (wide V-shaped blocks in a field of white). The T.B. Watkins Homes, a Public Housing Project is to the southwest of the Wayne Miner Project and completed the obliteration of the 12th and Vine corner. Hospital Hill is the shaded area to the south of the rail line (shown white running diagonally from north east to south west). The future Crown Center development is just west of Hospital Hill and south of the rail line. The Crossroads is the area south of the highway Loop and north of the rail line. Quality Hill is noted west of the loop. (*Source*: Missouri Valley Special Collections, Kansas City Public Library, Kansas City, Missouri. Published with permission).

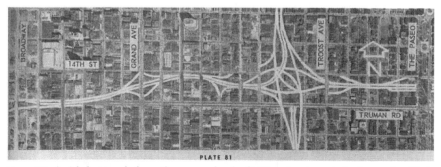

Figure 8.2. Aerial photograph shows the proposed path of I-70 cutting through the dense urban fabric of the segregated neighbourhood to the right of the north-south interchange. (*Source*: City Plan Commission (1951), Plate 81, p. 92)

1970s and 1980s: 'Benign Neglect' of Race

The Crown Center development epitomizes the transition from the Model Cities Program that tried to integrate residents into the decision-making process, to the 1970s top-down style of development that created 'privatized public space' where racial issues were not overtly discussed. In the 1960s Joyce C. Hall, the son of the founder of Hallmark Cards, became concerned about the disintegration of his adopted Kansas City. He wanted to build a completely new environment that would generate 'positive programs for economic and social regeneration' and 'pulsates with life' year round (Kipp, 1995, p. 7). Hall was inspired by President Kennedy and had read Victor Gruen's 1964 work *The Heart of Our Cities*. Jane Jacobs also applauded such physical characteristics and praised Gruen's 1956 plan to remove cars from the centre of Fort Worth, Texas (Jacobs, 1961, pp. 344–346). Hall selected a site adjacent to the 1956 Hallmark headquarters on the blighted 'Signboard Hill' and bought more land than he needed in order to create a buffer, thus taking a page out of J.C. Nichols's earlier development strategy. Crown Center, completed in 1971, is considered a positive out-come of Kansas City's Urban Renewal Program since a steeply sloped, rundown area was turned into a high-end mixed commercial development. In realizing his dream, how-ever, Hall created a 'city within a city', an inward looking complex that observes the centre from a safe distance and does not contribute to its vitality (Garvin, 2002, pp. 134–135; Sobala, 1974, pp. 31–47). Edward Larrabee Barnes, the architect who master-planned Crown Center, describes his first experience of the site: 'I'll never forget it. A great piece of empty land sloping away from the Hallmark headquarters, with down-town Kansas City in the distance. And we were asked what to do with it – to shape a whole new section of the city. This was an architect's dream' (Kipp, 1995, p. 10).

Drivers on Grand Boulevard can travel south under the elevated pedestrian bridges that connect the hotels and office towers, or if they know the secret, take a right and enter into the bowels of the complex (free parking for three hours) and emerge in the centre of another world. I lived in Kansas City for three years before I realized that the cluster of office buildings actually towered over a shopping centre, an outdoor plaza with fountains, a skating rink, theatres, two hotels (with 1,460 rooms), high-end condos, and a lot of other amenities. The artificial environment worked in the 1970s. People could be around other people without having to contend with the urban challenges of congestion, pollution, class, and race. The environment was clean, safe, and *controlled* – a fortress against the city.

The Hall Corporation argues that Crown Center was built with 'private' funds, yet extensive tax credits and property tax abatements have enabled its economic success. Crown Center benefitted from Chapter 353 and when, in the late 1980s, it shifted from paying zero percent to a 50 per cent tax rate, Crown Center officials began to question the yearly tax appraisals. In 1991, they 'successfully argued for a lower assessment and received a $1.2 million refund' and also sold some of their developed properties that no longer benefitted from property tax abatements (Martin, 2009). Nevertheless, despite decades of tax abatements and other incentives, Crown Center struggles to keep its retail and public spaces afloat. It is almost a mile south of the Power and Light District, where the city focused its investments in the 2000s, and three miles north of the Country Club Plaza. Jacobs would have considered such a development a 'border vacuum' because it is inward looking and does not create positive spillover to the adjacent neighbourhoods. The $400 million investment in the 1971 complex is an example of 'cataclysmic money' that accentuated the lack of investment in adjacent areas.

An Alternative Path of Development

Between Crown Plaza and the downtown Loop, in contrast, is exactly the type of urban development that Jane Jacobs admired. It started in the 1980s and represents the beginning of a new urbanity. The Crossroads is an area of late nineteenth- and twentieth-century light industrial buildings and modest storefronts. Kansas City in this area has short (250 foot [76 m]) east-west and north-south blocks, making it very walkable. Until recently, however, there was little to engage a pedestrian. In the 1980s, artists and creative people started renting and buying buildings and making art studio spaces. At the time the neighbourhood had few amenities. Gradually, a restaurant here, a gallery there, and some live-work space opened up. Artists collaborated and began hosting art gallery openings on first Fridays, serving refreshments, playing music, and promoting the Kansas City art scene – all without Urban Renewal, eminent domain, or tax abatements. There were also no local people to displace, so no gentrification occurred. The slow incremental growth took hold and spread east and west between 15th and 21st streets even under the I-71 to the 18th and Vine Jazz District as musicians and artists collaborated in the mid-2000s trying to bridge the racial divide. No cataclysmic money, just sweat equity and a desire to live in a city. The artists and small-scale entrepreneurs, unfortunately, became victims of their own effectiveness. They lacked the business savvy of enterprises like Crown Center to capitalize on their success. They had been paying property taxes fully from the beginning on all the improvements, which started to make it impossible for them to survive economically. The sculptor Jim Leedy, a maverick of the Crossroads, had bought his building in 1985. In 2003 his tax bill jumped from $12,000 to $40,000 (Collison, 2007). After representatives of the artists' community negotiated for three years with city officials and paid several thousand dollars each in fees, the PIEA board finally agreed to fix their property taxes at the 2006 level for the next ten years – a welcome relief, but still a far cry from the great deal that large corporations such as Hallmark have enjoyed. In ten years, the value of taxes not paid by the artists should equal $1.2 million (the same amount by which Hallmark had reduced its 1991 tax bill).

Becoming Visible: Race, Tourist Maps, and City Image

As with most major cities in the United States since the 1990s, Kansas City has tried to encourage growth and urban development using large-scale projects funded through financial instruments such as Chapter 353, PIEAs, and TIFs. Initially the airport, stadiums and auditoriums were built outside the urban centre. But in the 1990s municipal leaders started to recognize that their *own* urban cores were among the most distinctive areas of their cities with the potential for attracting visitors, conventions, and high-income residents. In Kansas City's downtown core, the city expanded the Bartle Hall Convention Center and added a new ballroom. In the mid-2000s to support the conventions, city officials converted half a dozen 'blighted' urban blocks into a $385 million Power and Light Entertainment District – home to dozens of restaurants, bars, theatres, and even an upscale grocery store. The area is anchored on the east end with the Sprint Center, a $231 million multi-purpose (basketball/hockey/concert) arena that is still looking for a permanent tenant. The state-of-the-art $326 million Kauffman Center for the Performing Arts opened in September 2011 south of the new Bartle Hall Ballroom. City boosters are still trying to get the city to support the construction of a one-thousand-room convention hotel nearby since they are convinced that Kansas City loses out on large-scale meetings because of this *one* last deficiency.

What is troubling about the development is alluded to in the murals on the south-facing façades of 14th Street west of Grand Boulevard, the 'back' of the new Power and Light District. A series of images depicts iconic jazz images and musicians such as Count Basie and Charlie Parker and the album cover of the 12th Street Rag with dancing white 1920-era flappers. A second series on the east highlights the Kansas City Monarchs, a 'Negro League' team. The inconvenient fact is that 12th and Vine and 18th and Vine are *eighteen* blocks east of there (Figure 8.3). The historic 12th and Vine corner was obliterated when the area was demolished during Urban Renewal and highway construction. A grassy site in the shape of a grand piano now marks the place. A set of tablets vividly recounts the history that is no longer visible from 12th Street as a 'shimmering street of light and life' following how a 1911 *Kansas City Star* article dubbed it:

The Basie Band held court at the Reno Club, tucked behind the police headquarters at 12th and Cherry. Musicians lined up in the alley behind the Reno Club to challenge Lester Young, Hot Lips Page and other stars of the band during freewheeling all-night jam sessions. A few blocks east, Charlie Parker cut his musical teeth playing at the Green Leaf Gardens and the Bar-Lu-Duc. The Sunset Club at 12th and Woodland featured boogie woogie pianist Pete Johnson and Big Joe Turner, who served thirsty patrons drinks while shouting the blues from behind the bar.

Kansas City under Mayor Emmanuel Cleaver (1991–1999) spent over $26 million renovating the Gem Theater and developing an American Jazz Museum and a new home for the Negro League Baseball Museum in the 18th and Vine Jazz District. His successor Mayor Kay Barnes (1999–2007) spent $385 million on the Power and Light District that capitalizes on Kansas City's Jazz history, thus competing with the historic site, a mile away as the crow flies. Black musicians did play in the clubs in the white part of town but were members of the Colored Musicians Union Local 627 (Mutual Musicians' Foundation, 2006).[6] Financing problems and a lingering negative image compromised housing and business development in the Vine District. Restaurants

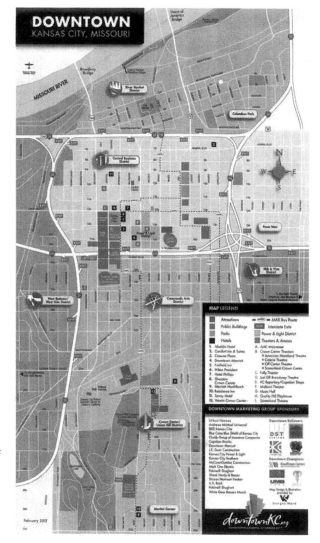

Figure 8.3. Downtown Kansas City Council's map of the Greater Downtown area. The three east side neighbourhoods (north to south) Columbus Park, Paseo West and 18th and Vine District are considered marginal. The 18th and Vine Jazz District is actually to the east of The Paseo, which is just on the east edge of the map and not shown. (*Source*: Kansas City Missouri, Downtown Council. Published with permission)

have struggled to maintain a foothold due to the lack of sufficient traffic. Until 2007, the locations of the Jazz and Negro League museums were not listed on highway signs. The Peachtree soul food restaurant that had struggled for years finally gave up its location at 18th and Vine in 2008 and set up in the Power and Light District that had nine million visitors compared to 236,000 in the Jazz District in 2010.[7] The city needs to promote the area actively to overcome the negative legacy of racial segregation. Instead the city co-opted the history and located it in the downtown Loop, where sixty years earlier African Americans were forced to use segregated facilities.

Tourist maps of Kansas City have also obscured the relationship between the 18th and Vine district and the rest of the city. A 2010 publication defines Greater Downtown

Kansas City as a '6 sq. mile area south of the Missouri River to 31st Street, from State Line east to Troost'. Troost marks the historic colour divide in the city and is eight blocks west of Woodland, the *east* edge of the 18th and Vine Jazz District (Kansas City Greater Downtown Plan, 2010). The Downtown Kansas City Council's newest map (2011) indicates the Vine District but still cuts it off at the Paseo without showing Vine, Highland, and Woodland where the American Jazz and Negro League Baseball Museums and Gem Theater are actually located (figure 8.3). I wonder sometimes at these representational decisions. Is it to save space? Kansas City has generally represented itself in the north–south direction. The city often shows the Kemper Arena located in the West Bottoms; so perhaps showing the 18th and Vine properly in the east would overly extend the east–west orientation? Perhaps it is discomfort over the real history and legacy of Troost? Or is it a calculated move that recognizes that suburbanites still perceive this area as 'dangerous' (i.e. largely African American and poor) and so it would be better not to include it? Representation matters. This distortion hurts the local neighbourhood and does not address the complex history of segregation.

Country Club Plaza, Crown Center, the Crossroads, and the Power and Light District are not overtly racist. Race almost never enters the discussion with the exception of a dress code in the Power and Light. However, these areas are over 90 per cent white with housing values that are appreciating and adjacent to largely African-American neighbourhoods (Ivanhoe, Beacon Hill, and 18th and Vine) where housing values and wealth accumulation have seriously lagged. The housing and retail space in J.C. Nichols's Country Club developments are still some of the most expensive real estate in Kansas City with the *median* home price at over $419,000. Two miles farther east at Troost Avenue in the African-American neighbourhood of Ivanhoe, the median house value is $46,000 (US Census, 2009). The neighbourhoods just east of Troost are largely black (with only a 60–70 per cent high-school graduation rate) and poor (with median incomes in the $20–$30,000 range). These conditions are ubiquitous in the cities I have studied: wealthy enclaves juxtaposed against grinding poverty with just enough hope to keep the formerly called 'ghetto' or 'slum' from exploding.

Race and Infrastructural Legacies

The appearance of city centres evolves and reflects the values of municipal officials and residents over time. Some areas of cities are well served by transportation, housing, employment, and cultural infrastructure while others seem to lack all or most of these. The common real estate mantra of 'location, location, and location' is a distortion when considering some city districts that are adjacent to the central business district and yet are not physically or economically as wealthy as they would be if racial bias were not in play.

Between 2000 and 2010, $5.5 billion was invested in downtown Kansas City (Downtown Council of Kansas City, 2010). It has generated the desired results – people are on the streets, the area has a real grocery store, a new arena, H&R Block's new headquarters, lots of cafés, bars, and restaurants, 11,137 housing units with approximately 18,932 residents, and seven to nine million visitors a year.[8] Margaret May, the head of the Ivanhoe Neighborhood Council who grew up under racial segregation in Kansas City is pragmatic about it. She says that inner-city neighbourhoods need a vibrant downtown and that housing and neighbourhood services will follow.[9] Ivanhoe is part of Representative Emmanuel Cleaver's Green Impact Zone whose main goal is to winterize all the qualified housing in the area and train local residents to do the work. The neighbourhood is trying to renovate properties but funding has been scarce. The Ivanhoe Neighborhood Council (INC) won a very sweet Missouri Supreme Court decision that defeated the PIEA's goal to control the old Horace Mann School building in their neighbourhood (*Planned Industrial Expansion Authority of Kansas City v. Ivanhoe Neighborhood Council and Brown-Caldwell Christian School*, 2010). This suit tested amendments to Missouri's eminent domain laws initiated in 2006 in the wake of the infamous Kelo case (*Kelo et al. v. City of New London et al.*). The neighbourhood has suffered greatly because of recent foreclosures and boarded-up homes, but May and her board are optimistic about the future of Ivanhoe. Neighbourhood residents actively participate in monthly meetings that fill the community hall.

Few people would deny the importance of the physical and material realm in creating lively urban centres that appeal to a range of visitors and residents. Jacobs understood this in *The Death and Life* and emphasized how the built environment should contribute to a city. In the mid-twentieth century urban highways and Urban Renewal isolated minorities from the central business district and segmented many cities. This infrastructural injustice continues to plague these cities yet their current development plans do not adequately mitigate this racial legacy. City mayors have focused on the material aspects of development and neglected the social and racial issues. Thus, they appear to have learned some lessons from Jacobs but not the most important ones.

Notes

1.   This study has been funded in part through a 2005 *New Faculty Research Grant* from the University of Kansas. I also wish to thank Sonia Hirt for her very thoughtful and constructive editorial suggestions.

2.   'Urban Renewal' in the United States refers to a period of time (roughly 1954–1972 or from the Eisenhower to the Nixon Administration) that resulted in the wholesale demolition of large swathes of central-city infrastructure and housing, the construction of mass urban housing, and the domination of the automobile in the planning and layout of highways in urban areas. The goal of the programme was to revitalize urban cores in order that middle-class Americans would continue to live in the city and on this score it failed completely. The term 'Urban Renewal' was first used in association with a 1953 study completed by an Eisenhower Administration committee to remove the federal government from the equation to provide housing for low-income citizens. It became associated with 'slum clearance' and the removal of 'blight' and set the stage for the destruction of whole neighbourhoods and historic buildings. The expression first appeared in print, in quotes, on 16 December 1953 in *The New York Times* (Charles E. Egan, 'Housing program, reducing U.S. aid, goes to President') and in *The Washington Post*, Paul Herron, 'President gets housing plan from advisers'. The term 'Urban Renewal' was incorporated into the 1954 Housing Act and paved the way for large-scale public housing projects that generally

destroyed downtown cores and so targeted largely poor and African-American neighbourhoods that it was referred to as 'Negro removal' by that community.

3.   Specifically, Harvey argues that neither the public nor the private market alone can resolve locational problems, such as why supermarkets are so scarce in 'ghettos' (Harvey, 1973, p. 88); why no low-income housing is accessible to suburban jobs (*Ibid.*, p. 62); and why transportation systems do not facilitate access from the inner city to outlying suburbs for work (*Ibid.*, p. 63). Inequity, not markets, is at work.

4.   Jim Crow Laws were first passed in the South in the aftermath of Reconstruction (1865–1877) after the Civil War (1861–1865) and continued through the passage of the Civil Rights Act (1964) and even beyond (for instance, black and white labour unions such as the Musicians Unions were not fully integrated until 1970). In the South, the Jim Crow Laws ultimately created a *de jure* separation of the races, while in the North, although few formal laws were enacted, *de facto* segregation of the races prevailed through the practices of everyday life. Blacks suffered not only the humiliation of being restricted in where they could eat, sleep, work, go to school, and shop, but also were hindered from developing beneficial social and economic ties. The classic work on Jim Crow is Vann Woodward (1955). Woodward outlines that prior to the early twentieth century blacks and whites in the South occupied overlapping social/geographic realms, and that Jim Crow laws evolved over time to impose and then harden the physical separation between the races.

5.   Today this district comprises about twenty-five square blocks and even these have been mostly rebuilt. Little of the original infrastructure remains – several dozen individual buildings tied together by the stage sets for the Robert Altman's 1996 film *Kansas City*.

6.   Western Historical Manuscript Collection Box 27; Local 627's charter was reinstated in 1933 contingent on the union deferring to the white Local 34.

7.   Pedestrian traffic in the Vine District from an email correspondence from Denise E. Gilmore, President/CEO Jazz District Redevelopment Corporation, 19 August 2011. The Peachtree only survived three years in the Power and Light District before closing in 2010.

8.   Tax revenues are not, however, where the developer promised they would be and the city has to pay up to US$12 million each year to cover the shortfall in the debt service.

9.   From personal conversations 20 May 2011 and 25 August 2011. The Horace Mann School was partially burned by arson in December 2011.

References

Adams, L. (2010) *Way Up North in Louisville: African American Migration in the Urban South, 1930–1970.* Chapel Hill, NC: University of North Carolina Press.

Alm, R. (2002) Conventional wisdom: KC worries that soon it won't be a strong competitor for conventions. *The Kansas City Star*, 26 March, p. D1.

Alm, R. (2007) Little hotels are a big problem for KC. *Kansas City Star*, 17 July, p. D1.

Birch, E.L. (2005) Who Lives Downtown? *Living Cities Census Series.* Washington, DC: Brookings Institution. Available at www.brookings.edu. Accessed 6 February 2011.

Bonilla-Silva, E. (1997) Rethinking racism: toward a structural interpretation. *American Sociological Review*, **62**(3), pp. 465–480.

Bonilla-Silva, E. (2003) *Racism without Racists: Color-Blind Racism and the Persistence of Racial Inequality in the United States.* Lanham, MD: Rowman & Littlefield.

Bullard, R.D. (2004) Introduction, in Bullard, R.D., Johnson, G.S. and Torres, A.O. (eds.) *Highway Robbery: Transportation Racism & New Routes to Equity.* Cambridge, MA: South End Press, pp. 1–12.

Campbell, M. (2001) Bruce R. Watkins Drive nears end of long, bumpy road to completion. *The Kansas City Star*, 21 October.

Castells, M. (1989) *The Informational City: Information Technology, Economic Restructuring, and the Urban Regional Process.* Oxford: Blackwell.

Chapin, TS. (2004) Sports facilities as urban redevelopment catalysts: Baltimore's Camden Yards and Cleveland's Gateway. *Journal of the American Planning Association*, **70**(2), pp. 193–209.

City Plan Commission (1947) *The Kansas City Metropolitan Area.* Kansas City, Missouri.

City Plan Commission (1951) *Expressways: Greater Kansas City: An Engineering Report.* Kansas City, Missouri.

Collison, K. (2007) Tax abatements granted to 31 applicants from Crossroads district. *The Kansas City Star*, 30 October [LexisNexis].

Crutcher, M.E. (2010) *Tremé: Race and Place in a New Orleans Neighborhood*. Athens, GA: University of Georgia Press.

Davis, J. (2006) Tax benefits' cost proves elusive: KC's PIEA doesn't account for number, fiscal effect of abatements. *Kansas City Business Journal*, 15 January. Available at http://www.bizjournals.com/kansascity/stories/2006/01/16/story1.html. Accessed 10 March 2010.

Davis, J.E. (1991) *Contested Ground: Collective Action and the Urban Neighborhood*. Ithaca, NY: Cornell University Press.

Davis, M. (1990) *City of Quartz: Excavating the Future in Los Angeles*. London: Verso.

Dluhy, M., Revell, K. and Wong, S. (2002) Creating a positive future for a minority community: transportation and Urban Renewal politics in Miami. *Journal of Urban Affairs*, **24**(1), pp. 75–95.

Doeppers, D.F. (1967) The Globeville neighborhood in Denver. *The Geographical Review*, **57**(4), pp. 506–522.

Downtown Council of Kansas City (2010) Downtown Kansas City Resident Survey Results 2010. Available at 216.119.82.16/wp.../07/2010_Downtown_Resident_Survey_Results1.pdf. Accessed 19 March 2011.

Florida, R.L. (2002) *The Rise of the Creative Class, and How It's Transforming Work, Leisure, Community and Everyday Life*. New York: Basic Books.

Fullilove, M. (2004) *Root Shock: How Tearing Up City Neighborhoods Hurts America, and What We Can Do about It*. New York: One World/Ballantine Books.

Gans, H.J. (1962) City planning and urban realities. *Commentary*, **33**(2), pp. 170–175.

Gans, H.J. (1965) *The Urban Villagers: Group and Class in the Life of Italian-Americans*. New York: Free Press.

Gans, H.J. (1968) Urban vitality and the fallacy of physical determinism, in *People and Plans: Essays on Urban Problems and Solutions*. New York: Basic Books, pp. 25–33.

Garvin, A. (2002) *The American City: What Works, What Doesn't*. New York: McGraw-Hill.

Gibson, S. (1997) *Kansas City: Mecca of the New Negro*. Kansas City; self published.

Gordon, C.E. (2008) *Mapping Decline: St. Louis and the Fate of the American City*. Philadelphia, PA: University of Pennsylvania Press.

Gotham, K.F. (1999) Political opportunity, community identity, and the emergence of a local anti-expressway movement. *Social Problems*, **46**(3), pp. 332–354.

Gotham, K.F. (2002) *Race, Real Estate, and Uneven Development: the Kansas City Experience, 1900–2000*. Albany, NY: State University of New York Press.

Gratz, R.B. (2010) *The Battle for Gotham: New York in the Shadow of Robert Moses and Jane Jacobs*. New York: National Books.

Gratz, R.B. and Mintz, N. (1998) *Cities Back from the Edge*. New York: Wiley.

Gruen, V. (1964) *The Heart of Our Cities. The Urban Crisis: Diagnosis and Cure*. New York: Simon and Schuster.

Gutfreund, O.D. (2004) *Twentieth-Century Sprawl: Highways and the Reshaping of the American Landscape*. New York: Oxford University Press.

Harvey, D. (1973) *Social Justice and the City*. London: Edward Arnold.

Hayden, D. (1995) *The Power of Place: Urban Landscapes as Public History*. Cambridge, MA: MIT Press.

Isenberg, A. (2004) *Downtown America: A History of the Place and the People Who Made It*. Chicago, IL: University of Chicago Press.

Issel, W. (1999) Land values, human values, and the preservation of the city's treasured appearance: environmentalism, politics, and the San Francisco Freeway Revolt. *Pacific Historical Review*, **68**(4), pp. 611–646.

Jackson, K.T. (1985) *Crabgrass Frontier: The Suburbanization of the United States*. New York: Oxford University Press.

Jacobs, J. (1961) *The Death and Life of Great American Cities*. New York: Random House.

Jones, J. (1993) Southern diaspora: origins of the northern 'underclass', in Katz, M.B. (ed.) *The 'Underclass' Debate: Views from History*. Princeton, NJ: Princeton University Press, pp. 27–54.

Judd, D.R. (1999) Constructing the tourist bubble, in Judd, D.R. and Fainstein, S. (eds.) *The Tourist City*. New Haven, CT: Yale University Press, pp. 35–53.

Judd, D.R. (2003) *The Infrastructure of Play: Building the Tourist City*. Armonk, NY: M.E. Sharpe.

Kansas City Greater Downtown Plan (2010) Available at www.kcmo.org. Accessed 13 February 2011.

Kelley, R.D.G. (1997) *Yo' Mama's Disfunktional! Fighting the Culture Wars in Urban America*. Boston, MA: Beacon Press.

Kelo v. New London (04-108) 545 U.S. 469 (2005). Available through Google Scholar. Accessed 1 November 2010.

Kelsay, M.P. (2007) Uneven Patchwork: Tax Increment Financing in Kansas City. Available at ReclaimDemocracy.org/kc. Kansas City, MO. Accessed 4 May 2010.

Kennedy, J.F. (1961) Special message to the Congress on housing and community development, in Woolley, T. and Peters, G. (eds.) *The American Presidency Project*. Available at http://www.presidency.ucsb.edu/ws/?pid=8529. Accessed 24 January 2011.

Kipp, R.A. (1995) Crown Center: An Emerging Vision for Urban Development. Charles N. Kimball Lecture, Western Historical Manuscript Collection, Kansas City.

Kirsch, S. (1995) The incredible shrinking world? Technology and the production of space. *Environment and Planning D*, **13**(5), pp. 529–555.

Koon, D. (2011) Wilbur's wall I-630, Little Rock and 25 years in a divided city. *Arkansas Times*, 26 January. Available from LexisNexis. Accessed 7 February 2011.

Martin, D. (2009) Greetings from Crown Center at 40: Hallmark's island of misfit ideas. *The Pitch*, 17 December. Available from LexisNexis. Accessed 20 August 2010.

Massey, D. and Denton, N. (1993) *American Apartheid: Segregation and the Making of the Underclass*. Cambridge, MA: Harvard University Press.

McBride, W.S. (1990) The use of eminent domain under Missouri's urban redevelopment corporations law. *Washington University Journal of Urban and Contemporary Law*, **37**, pp. 169–187.

Miller, W.H. (1881) *The History of Kansas City: Together with a Sketch of the Commercial Resources of the Country with which It is Surrounded*. Kansas City, MI: Birdsall & Miller.

Miller, Z.L. and Tucker B. (1998) *Changing Plans for America's Inner Cities, Cincinnati's Over the Rhine and Twentieth Century Urbanism*. Columbus, OH: Ohio State University Press.

Mohl, R.A. (1989) Shadows in the sunshine: race and ethnicity in Miami. *Tequesta*, **49**(4), pp. 63–80.

Mohl, R.A. (2004) Stop the road: freeway revolts in American cities. *Journal of Urban History*, **30**(5), pp. 674–796.

Mollenkopf, J.H. (1983) *The Contested City*. Princeton, NJ: Princeton University Press.

Mowbray, A.Q. (1969) *Road to Ruin*. Philadelphia, PA: Lippincott.

Mumford, L. (1961) *The City in History: Its Origins, Its Transformations, and Its Prospects*. New York: Harcourt, Brace & World.

Mumford, L. (1963) The city and the highway, in Mumford, L. (ed.)*The City and the Highway*. New York: Harcourt, Brace & World, pp. 234–246.

Mutual Musicians' Foundation (2006) *Historic Structures Report and Feasibility Study*. Kansas City, Missouri: National Park Service. Available from Missouri Valley Special Collections, Kansas City Public Library, Kansas City, Missouri.

New York Times (1970) Text of the Moynihan memorandum on the status of Negroes. *New York Times*. 1 March.

New York Times (2009) Interactive census map. Available at http://projects.nytimes.com/census/2010/explorer?ref=censusbureau. Accessed 21 February 2012.

Planned Industrial Expansion Authority of Kansas City, Appellant, V. *Ivanhoe Neighborhood Council and Brown-Caldwell Christian School* No. WD 70655. 27 April 2010.

Poletown Neighborhood Council v. City of Detroit, 410 Mich. 616, Mich: Supreme Court (1981).

Rabin, Y. (1973) Highways as a barrier to equal access. *Annals of the American Academy of Political and Social Science*, **407**(5), pp. 63–77.

Sanders, H.T. (2002) Convention myths and markets: a critical review of convention center feasibility studies. *Economic Development Quarterly*, **16**(3), pp. 195–210.

Sanders, H.T. (2005) *Space Available: The Realities of Convention Centers as Economic Development Strategy*. Washington DC: Brookings Institution. Available at www.brookings.edu. Accessed 18 January 2012.

Sawicki, D.S. (1989) The festival marketplace as public policy: guidelines for future policy decisions. *Journal of the American Planning Association*, **55**(3), pp. 347–361.

Scheer, B.C. and Ferdelman, D. (2001) Inner-city destruction and survival: the case of Over the Rhine, Cincinnati. *Urban Morphology*, **5**(1), pp. 15–27.

Schirmer, S.L. (2002) *A City Divided: The Racial Landscape of Kansas City, 1900–1960*. Columbia, MI: University of Missouri Press.

Schott, H. (1905) A city's fight for beauty, in Page, W.H. and Page, A.W. (eds.) *The World's Work: A History of Our Time*, Volume 11. New York: Doubleday, pp.7191–7205.

Sobala, C.C. (1974) *Kansas City Today* (ULI 1974 Fall Meeting Local Arrangements Committee). Washington DC: Urban Land Institute.

Sohmer, R.R. and Lang, R.E. (2001. *Downtown Rebound*. Washington, DC: The Brookings Institution. Available at www.brookings.edu. Accessed 18 January 2012.

Stradling, D. (2003) *Cincinnati: From River City to Highway Metropolis*. Charleston, SC: Arcadia.

Tarr, J.A. (1984) The evolution of urban infrastructure in the nineteenth and twentieth centuries, in Hanson, R. (ed.) *Perspectives on Urban Infrastructure*. Washington DC: National Academy Press, pp. 143–177.

Trotter, J.W. Jr (1993) Blacks in the urban North, the 'Underclass Question' in historical perspective, in Katz, B. (ed.) *The 'Underclass' Debate: Views from History*. Princeton, NJ: Princeton University Press, pp. 27, 55–81.

United States Census (2009) Available at http://www.census.gov/popest/cities/SUB-EST2009.html. Accessed 30 July 2010.

Vann Woodward, C. (1995) *The Strange Career of Jim Crow*. Oxford: Oxford University Press.

Wiese, A. (2003) *Places of Their Own: African American Suburbanization in the Twentieth Century*. Chicago, IL: University of Chicago Press.

Whitney, C.W. (1908) *Kansas City, Missouri, Its History and Its People 1808–1908*, Volume 1. Chicago, IL: S J Clarke Publishing Co.

Worley, W.S. (1990) *J.C. Nichols and the Shaping of Kansas City: Innovation in Planned Residential Communities*. Columbia, MI: University of Missouri Press.

Wylie, J. (1989) *Poletown: Community Betrayed*. Urbana, IL: University of Illinois Press.

Chapter 9

Jane Jacobs, Jim Crow and the Madness of Borders

Mindy Thompson Fullilove

My field is psychiatry, and it is not a discipline typically linked with studies of space. The great exception would be the spaces of treatment, whether it be the design of hospitals, the organization of day rooms, or the planning of a therapy office. My work has gone far beyond that. I learned in 1989 that the physical destruction of minority neighbourhoods had fuelled the AIDS epidemic. I wanted to understand how the physical upheaval was connected to risk behaviours like intravenous drug use and unprotected sexual encounters.

In a long series of studies, I examined the psychology and psychiatry of place, which taught me how our personal and collective lives are embedded in the physical world. Its structure is our structure. As Winston Churchill, addressing the English Architectural Association in 1924, so aptly put it, 'There is no doubt whatever about the influence of architecture and structure upon human character and action. We make our buildings and afterwards they make us. They regulate the course of our lives' (cited in Brand, 1995). The fundamental truth here is that place is composed of ordered, interconnected and interdependent spatial and social systems.

In my research, I have repeatedly encountered the ways in which the ordering of space affects human behaviour. This occurs in small ways, for example, the 2002 reopening of a series of stores on 145th Street in Harlem restored movement to the area (Fullilove *et al.*, 1999). It also occurs in large ways, for example, the application of redlining in 1937 is linked in a series of steps to urban renewal and massive displacement in the 1950s and 1960s (Fullilove, 2004). At an even larger scale – and arguably as the most important factor ordering the American urban space and affecting our social lives – is racial segregation which sets where people live by race and then distributes resources along the same lines (*Ibid.*).

It was clear that the organization of place could promote health or disease. In *The Death and Life of American Cities*, Jane Jacobs proposes that our city-making goal is 'diversity, intricately intermingled in mutual support' (Jacobs, 1993, p. 240). This ties neatly with concepts which my field, social psychiatry, has proposed for describing environments that are optimal for health. But what we have created in the American city – neighbourhoods sorted by race and class – is both the opposite of what Jacobs proposes we need and the engine for its destruction should we stumble into it. From the perspective of social psychiatry, we have created a spatial system for maximizing illness and disaffection, for creating social madness.

Jane Jacobs notes four forces that destroy diversity:

… the tendency for outstandingly successful diversity in cities to destroy itself; the tendency for massive single elements in cities (many of which are necessary and otherwise desirable) to cast a deadening influence; the tendency for population instability to counter the growth of diversity; and the tendency for both public and private money either to glut or to starve development and change. (1993, p. 241)

In the category of 'massive single elements' we find universities, medical centres, railroad tracks and waterfronts. They act as barriers to easy travel and disrupt the flow of the city because they create impenetrable borders. It is necessary, Jacobs contends, to mend the fracture of borders so that the city may function. She stops at that point, but students of the American city will recognize immediately that the issue of segregation fits neatly under this heading.

In the following sections, I will explore: inequality and its lingering effects on the American landscape; the functional implications of segregation from the perspective of social psychiatry; and the kinds of landscape interventions that can mend our cities.

What is Jim Crow and Why Is It Still Here?

When the Civil War ended in 1865, a programme of reconstruction was instituted. As part of that effort, federal troops were stationed throughout the South to ensure that the freedmen, as the newly liberated slaves were called, would be able to exercise their rights and participate in society. This was an active period of reorganization from slave labour to free labour. Among other necessary transitions were the provision of education to people previously prohibited from having any education, and the engagement in the democratic process for people who had previously had no say over their lives. These dramatic changes took place against the backdrop of the former slave owners, disenfranchised but still wealthy and powerful, searching for ways to reinstitute the lucrative system of inequality.

An opportunity arose in 1876 when the Presidential election was contested. As a result of the Compromise of 1877, the newly elected President Rutherford B. Hayes agreed to withdraw federal troops from the South. Almost immediately, the restored white oligarchy launched a reign of terror on the South, directed at disenfranchising black voters and seizing full control of the machinery of government.

They made some progress, but in the 1890s a new threat to their power arose: a coalition of poor white farmers, black farmers and new industrial workers united in the

Populist Party. They swept into power throughout the South and enacted progressive legislation that sought to give industrial workers and farmers real opportunity.

The Southern oligarchy acted quickly to deter this new challenge. In particular, they found that racism was a key tool. They convinced poor whites that they had more to fear from blacks than from the wealthy. They used the solidarity of whites to institute new laws that separated white and black, institutionalizing black inequality and trapping white working people in substandard living conditions. The laws that created this new system were known as 'Jim Crow'. Segregation in transport and education was accompanied by segregation in occupation and housing.

The Jim Crow system was advertised by blatant signs and enforced with violence. W.E.B. Du Bois's 'Litany for Atlanta', written after the vicious Atlanta race riots cost the lives of twenty-five African Americans, mourned the loss of the city as a place of sanity and interchange (Du Bois, 1903). As life got harder and harder in the South, and industrial employment opened in the urban areas, a massive migration started, known as the Great Migration. Two million people moved from rural to urban areas. Even in the North, Jim Crow was a constant part of life. Department stores would not let black people try on clothes. Schools and recreation facilities were segregated and residential segregation was the norm.

Du Bois started the modern Civil Rights movement when he founded the National Association for Colored People in 1909. Throughout the twentieth century, an intense battle was waged to undo the Jim Crow laws and create a legal and social basis for equality. A series of victories in education (1954), interstate transport (1960), hospitals and medical care (1964) and fair housing (1968) led many to say that Jim Crow had ended.

Two parts of the Jim Crow did not end. The first on-going part of Jim Crow is forced displacement (Fullilove and Wallace, 2011). This policy was used to resettle Native Americans; some tribes were forced to move repeatedly (Jacobs, 1972). Japanese Americans were resettled into internment camps during World War II (Leighton, 1945). Forced displacement of African Americans and other people of colour has been a prominent part of their history during slavery, the Great Migration, and continuing in urban renewal in the 1950s and 1960s. That policy, which followed the fault lines of Jim Crow, uprooted large neighbourhoods of people of colour, destroyed accumulated wealth, undermined psychological, social and political functioning, and set back community life.

The second, and particularly relevant to the problem of borders, is residential segregation, which was not successfully eradicated by the 1960s Civil Rights movement. A prescient observation made in the 1960s by an advocate of open housing was that it was possible for black people to move to white areas, triggering white flight. Once the whites were gone, the area was not integrated; it simply became the new ghetto. He called this 'the ghetto game' and signalled the threat it posed to the fight against residential segregation (Clark, 1962). The 2010 Census has confirmed the continuation of segregation in the American city.

The Madness of Borders

To understand the implications of borders for individuals and communities, I draw on two leading theorists of social psychiatry, Alexander Leighton and Rodrick Wallace. Leighton began his research career studying the displacement of Japanese-Americans during the World War II internment (Leighton, 1945). In the 1950s, he conducted a major study comparing integrated to disintegrated communities (Leighton, 1959). For that study he proposed a model of the manner in which communities affect the individual.

A cornerstone of his model of the way in which community shaped individual mental health was the concept of 'interference with striving'. He posited the existence of ten 'essential striving sentiments', which included: physical security; sexual satisfaction; expression of hostility; expression of love; securing of love; securing of recognition; expression of spontaneity; orientation in terms of one's place in society and the places of others; the securing and maintaining of membership in a definite human group; a sense of belonging to a moral order and being right in what one does, being in and of a system of values (Leighton, 1959, p. 148). Interference in the fulfilment of these strivings could destabilize the individual's basic psychic balance. While acknowledging multiple pathways of interference, he argued, 'Sociocultural situations can be said to *foster* psychiatric illness if they *interfere* with the development and functioning of these sentiments, since the latter in turn affect the essential psychical condition' (Leighton, 1959, p. 158, emphasis in the original).

Leighton stated this as proposition A4: 'Disturbance of essential psychical conditions gives rise to disagreeable feelings' (*Ibid.*, p. 160). Such a challenge to the individual may be managed in many ways, he acknowledged, including some that lead to superior outcomes. He noted that, although in psychiatry one is biased towards seeing people who have suffered from the constraints of society, in the world at large, the smooth functioning of the social system enabled most people to meet their striving sentiments and maintain their psychic balance. But, for most people, the frustration of striving sentiments taxed the individual's mental health.

This frustration of the essential individual striving sentiments could be linked to the sociocultural environment in many ways, including through rapid change and lack of resources. To improve our understanding of this sociocultural environment-person link, Leighton sought to clarify the nature of the sociocultural environment. He identified its parts as: 'family, including extended families; neighborhoods; associations; friendship groups; occupational associations; institutions such as those concerned with industry, religion, government, recreation, and health; cultural systems; socioeconomic classes; and finally societal roles' (*Ibid.*, p. 204).

These subunits communicate and are coordinated with one another. Obviously connections through social networks were important, but Leighton posited that one aspect of culture – 'shared sentiments' – was what kept the whole on track. The shared sentiments acted, he proposed, like governors on a motor, limiting the movement at the extremes and keeping people on track. He wrote, 'The shared feelings of how the world is and how things ought to proceed for self and others make possible the ongoing patterns of family, neighborhood, class, government, and all the other components of the community unit, as well as their coordination into the whole' (*Ibid.*, p. 207).

Rodrick Wallace, a physicist-turned-human-ecologist, advanced Leighton's work by looking more closely at the problem of communication among the subparts of a sociocultural unit (Wallace and Fullilove, 2008). Drawing on findings in many fields during the intervening 50 years since the publication of Leighton's *My Name Is Legion*, Wallace proposed that, in effective social systems, the parts can 'think' together. This collective cognition could recognize patterns of threat and opportunity and plan effective response. This was, he argued, the great advance that made human beings more fearsome than any other species: individuals in groups can pool their knowledge to come up with ideas and solutions many times more effective than those of a single individual. Groups can also share knowledge, making the collection of groups much more powerful than an isolated small group.

Wallace summed this up as:

[Robert] Sampson invokes a vision of community cognition, the ability of a neighborhood to perceive patterns of threat or opportunity, to compare those perceived patterns with an internal, shared, picture of the work, and to choose one or a few collective actions from a much larger repertory of those possible, and to carry them out. Disjunctive or 'strong' social ties define some of the underlying cognitive modules – collective and individual – within the neighborhood. Weak ties, then, are those which link such modules – individual or collective – across the community. Individuals, defined subgroups, or formal organizations, may have multiple roles within that community, permitting the formation of multiple working groups, if the strength of the various weak ties linking them is sufficient. Institutional cognition, in the sense of this work, emerges as a dynamic, collective phenomenon. Cultural constraints and developmental trajectory serve to both stabilize and direct the resulting cognitive process. (2008, p. 18)

Wallace used mathematical tools to work out the concrete processes by which collective cognition operates. He highlighted three processes that interfere with smooth functioning of the collective consciousness. First, he noted, information has to pass among groups, a transfer that takes time. The rate limitation of information transfer is an important factor in the effectiveness of collaboration. Second, it is possible for groups to overlook facts, ideas and events, a process that is called 'inattentional blindness'. Third, groups operate from ideological positions that can exclude information because it does not fit pre-existing models of the world.

There is an important proviso, Wallace noted, to the functioning of collective cognition:

This phenomenon is, however, constrained, not just by shared culture, but the path dependent historic development of the community itself. Recent work ... demonstrates that 'planned shrinkage', 'urban renewal', or other disruptions of weak ties akin to ethnic cleansing, can place neighborhoods onto decades-long irreversible developmental, perhaps evolutionary, trajectories of social disintegration which short-circuit effective community cognition. (*Ibid.*, p. 18)

The 'short circuiting' of effective community cognition by social disintegration interrupts both the recognition of and the response to patterns of threat and opportunity. Communities in this short-circuited state were not, Wallace argued, able to use their collective capacities for their own salvation. This, as Leighton pointed out, leads to 'disagreeable feelings'. As sociocultural disintegration proceeds and groups become more and more impotent, such feelings can become a dominant, dysphoric experience. Anthropologist A.F.C. Wallace has postulated that religious revivals and extremism are the prime solutions groups use to resolve such uncomfortable states (Wallace, 1957).

To underscore the connection with Leighton's views, the parts of the city fractured by segregation lose their shared sentiments. For the white majority, the plight of the oppressed becomes invisible: they can neither see nor sympathize with the actual happenings of ghetto life (Bishop and Harrington, 1997). For the oppressed minority, alienation vies with can-do-in-spite-of-ism for control of the group mood. The fractured parts undergo a social speciation which inhibits effective collection cognition (Héon-Klin *et al.*, 2001).

Mending Our Destiny

Jane Jacobs quoted Kevin Lynch, author of *The Image of the City*, on the solution to borders. 'An edge may be more than simply a dominant barrier if some visual or motion penetration is allowed through it – if it is, as it were, structured to some depth with the regions on either side. It then becomes a seam rather than a barrier, a line of exchange along which two areas are sewn together' (Jacobs, 1993, p. 267).

Transforming the borders of race and class segregation into seams that knit parts together requires great imagination on the part of the planners and urban designers. French urbanist Michel Cantal-Dupart is a master of this art. He had worked on the problem in France, where cities were fractured in the post-war building boom that placed new immigrants and working people in massive apartment blocks at the edges of cities, but disconnected them from the existing urban grid and many urban services. Cantal-Dupart observed that the neighbourhoods disconnected from the grid floundered and became sites of disorder and despair. But, his observations convinced him that the problems were not in the floundering neighbourhoods, but rather in the broken link between the neighbourhoods and the rest of the city. He adopted the position that, to solve the problems of neighbourhoods, one had to act more globally (Cantal-Dupart, 1993). With the authorization of President François Mitterand, he developed a national programme, *Banlieues 89*, to develop ways to repair the connections between the peripheral neighbourhoods and the centre city (Cantal-Dupart, 1994).

In 1998, Cantal-Dupart came to Pittsburgh to consult with community groups in the Hill District neighbourhood. The Hill District was an African-American neighbourhood beset by urban renewal, planned shrinkage, gentrification, and, was facing the demolition of federal housing projects under the HOPE VI Program (Fulliove, 2004; Murphy, 2004).

The problems of the border could be found on both sides. In the Hill, people were suffering from unemployment, the collapse of families, explosive drug use and violence (Simms, 2008). The Hill, weak from too many setbacks, was unable to fend off the latest round of attacks. Around the Hill, people acted as if a neighbourhood considered 'dangerous' must be sequestered from its surroundings. It was assumed that this walling off of a neighbourhood might be carried out without any consequences for the rest of the city. Meanwhile, the divided city was struggling to survive deindustrialization that had cost it almost half of its population. At the time of Cantal-Dupart's consultation, both the Hill and the surrounding neighbourhoods focused on the problems within the Hill District. The border was not seen as an issue.

Cantal-Dupart met with Hill District leaders, toured the area, and noted its assets – its hilltop views, devoted residents and historic buildings – as well as its deficits – its blighted landscape and loss of population. He participated in a mapping exercise, which examined in detail a 12-block area in the neighbourhood designed to focus attention on the depredations caused by disinvestment. He also studied the maps of the area, and attempted to walk on major roads at the periphery of the neighbourhood, nearly getting run over by cars as one apparent thoroughfare turned into a major highway.

He realized that there were rigid borders all around the neighbourhood, disconnecting it from the city and making it nearly invisible to people who did not live or work there. One of the most obvious borders was that at the intersection of the Hill District with downtown Pittsburgh. This border had been created by a massive urban renewal project carried out in the late 1950s. In addition to a massive arena, a large parking lot and a highway were installed, creating multiple barriers between the two areas. The borders around the edge and the disinvestment inside were two faces of segregation. Desegregation – the elimination of the border – he concluded, was the key to revitalization of the neighbourhood itself. 'It is important for this neighborhood to work with other neighborhoods', he told the people with whom he was consulting.

People responded to this proposition by explaining that, in Pittsburgh, the neighbourhoods jealously guarded their independence. They were suspicious of outsiders, which included people from other Pittsburgh neighbourhoods. 'Working with other neighbourhoods is not possible', people informed him.

He passed a sleepless night, searching for ways to express the importance of reconnection. Sometime during that long night, he hit upon a solution. At a meeting the next day, he said, 'The steel mills, where many people were employed, were located on the riverbanks'. He followed that statement with the question, 'How did people get to work from here?'

This provoked a flurry of answers, especially from the elders of the neighbourhood. They remembered the incline – the funicular railroad – that used to connect the Hill District to the Strip District. They described walking down the hill, using the many stairs that dotted the neighbourhood. Some of the pathways people had taken were lost, and others were cut off by highways that had severed the Hill's connections to the rest of the city. Cantal-Dupart nodded with satisfaction as the conversation continued. 'I think you need to find the ways to the river', he urged.

In a memo titled 'Six Priority Issues for a Renaissance of the Hill District', he made a list of recommendations (Robins *et al.*, 1999). Cantal knew the grassroots effort in the Hill District could only win by bringing the weight of the city into the equation, but he also knew that people had to make the right demands. His list focused on making strong public space that served many purposes: increasing ownership; enhancing pride; strengthening the grid; connecting to other parts of the city; and welcoming the world (the drawings below are mine, redrawn from the originals in *Hillscapes*).

1. Creating a Strong Street Façade

First, it is essential to guard the corners of streets and avenues. The houses and stores on these corners have a particularly powerful influence on a community. Strong, well-designed corners protect the intermediate spaces, and create an attractive vista.

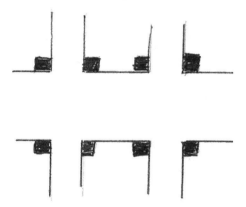

Second, it is important to keep the variety of house façades, as this variety gives depth and appeal to the streetscape. Uniform, unvarying design is visually deadening and detracts from the public space.

2. Personalize the Units in the Housing Projects

Some of the units in the housing project have gardens and this is important because it is a way of creating a sense of belonging, a sense of community, and a sense that one's neighbourhood is worth protecting and maintaining.

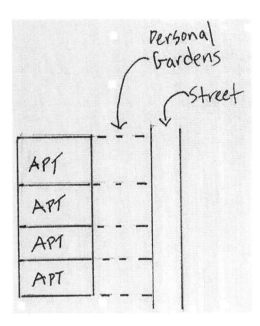

3. Separate the Houses from the Street

Some houses have stairs intruding into the sidewalk without the protection of a front yard. Create the space to enclose the stairs by widening the sidewalks. It is important to understand that there is a need to separate the personal space from the public space of sidewalks, street and avenues.

4. Access to the River

The hillside down from Cliff Street is an ideal site for a park. It is crisscrossed with numerous traces of old stairs and trails. These accessways were obliterated by the highway and have contributed to the isolation of the Hill from much of the city's current growth and development.

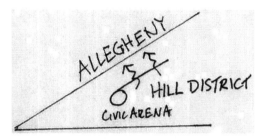

5. Create Market Corners

One feature of urban life that gives neighbourhoods great vitality is the presence of strong market centres. One obvious point of intersection is Centre and Kirkpatrick, while another is a cluster of stores near Hill House. These and others should be developed to serve the community and attract people to visit.

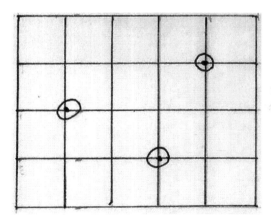

6. Attract People from Around the World

Successful neighbourhoods attract people from all over the world. What is it that would bring people to The Hill District?

Later, as the organizing team was preparing a publication, Cantal-Dupart created a series of maps, examining the linkages that needed to be restored. 'It's not possible to solve the problems of the neighborhood by simply restoring the historic theater. You have to solve the problem of access, which has been obliterated.'

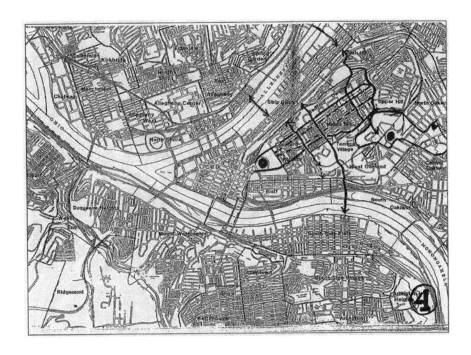

Cantal commented about this map, the fourth map in the series:

Map 4 embodies the essence of what must be done [to revitalize the Hill]. The geography of the Hill complicates things but already the restitution of the traces of what once existed on these slopes is there in the form of a park which needs only the building of a few foot bridges [*passerelles*] and the creation of a garden. At present this undeveloped space is open to all sorts of mischief [*delinquances*]. Thus I propose first and foremost a path which would go down Kirkpatrick Road as it is the southward connection to the southside flats. (Robins *et al.*, 1999)

Cantal-Dupart's ideas became a substrate for many years of work by the people of the Hill District. The organization 'Find the Rivers!' was launched in 2002, with the goal of reconnecting the Hill to the riverbanks. Early on in their organizational efforts, co-founders Terri Baltimore and Denys Candy travelled to France to get advice from Cantal-Dupart. In an undated report, Denys Candy documented the activities they engaged in and the lessons they learned (Candy, nd). He noted, 'Michel Cantal-Dupart walked down a spillway at the edge of the Seine and rolled up his sleeves. "It is vital," he said, "for people to touch the water. We must be able to put our hands in the water. There are 8 million people in Paris. How many of them actually touch the water?"'

In visits to the Seine in Paris and the Loire in Nantes, Cantal-Dupart demonstrated the need for development of the relationship to water in three domains: on the water, on the banks of the rivers, and on the streets that access the rivers. On the water, there should be houseboats, tourist boats and transit, all offering opportunities to experience the river as fish and birds might, as well as in all the ways people can. On the banks, there should be place for walking, sunning, fishing, and visiting. On the streets that have access to the river there should be places to look over the river, enjoying the ever-changing scenery.

Candy (nd), after describing the careful dialogue that Cantal-Dupart advocated for the linking elements of bridges, stairs and vistas, noted that a parallel dialogue needed to occur among the citizens of Pittsburgh. He argued:

Planning for the rivers and creating increased access to them must, by definition, be a process that builds new bridges among the diverse people of Pittsburgh. A bridge to the future depends on remembering community history and honoring the multiple perspectives and stories of that history. It's easy to say. The question for us in Pittsburgh is, are we ready to do so?

This perspective guided the work of Find the Rivers! (FTR!). One of the projects FTR! undertook was the development of the greenway along Kirkpatrick Street. Another was the development of a park along Cliff Street, a location with spectacular views of the Allegheny River and the North of Pittsburgh. Both were guided by community participation, and hands-in-the-water experiences with rivers.

Many other efforts to revitalize the neighbourhood, overcome isolation and begin reinvestment were also undertaken. One of the highlights was an effort to attract a new supermarket to the area. The work of Find the Rivers!, as well as other groups, was coordinated by the Hill District Consensus Group, an organization formed in 1991 to provide a common table for exchange of ideas about the Hill.

While these efforts were going on, the Pittsburgh Penguins began to demand a new arena. As the arena would be built with public money, the Hill District organized to fight for a community benefits agreement. This effort recognized the harm that had been done to the neighbourhood as a result of the urban renewal in the 1950s, as well as the strains a vibrant new arena would place on the area. Over 100 organizations joined together to create the 'One Hill Coalition'. After using a collective process to define key demands, the One Hill Coalition advocated for an arena that would provide: support for a master planning process; first-source hiring of people from the Hill District; 'family- supporting' jobs with decent wages and benefits; money for a grocery store; and on-going communications with the neighbourhood about the progress of all development. After an intense year of struggle, these demands were accepted by the Penguins and the City and County of Pittsburgh, and ratified in an agreement in August 2008.

The Master Planning process started shortly afterwards, and was finalized in June 2011.

Find the Rivers! proposal for the Kirkpatrick Greenway was incorporated into the Greater Hill District Master Plan (Sasaki Associates, 2011). Other ideas that Cantal-Dupart put forward in 1998 were also mirrored in the Master Plan, including the strengthening of connections between the Hill and the rest of the city, the development of a set of market corners, and preserving strong street façades.

In the context of unvanquished Jim Crow, the Hill faced the challenge that, throughout the US, re investment has been strongly coupled with displacement. This relationship has operated through a variety of mechanisms, generally lumped under the heading of 'gentrification'. These include rising rents and taxes, which the poor cannot afford; code enforcement directed at older dwellings, which often belong to the poor; harassment; suppression of the history and culture of a place; and loss of supporting services, such as dollar stores and check cashing places. Over time, gentrifying neighbourhoods become unaffordable and inhospitable to the old-timers, who leave or are driven out.

These problems were anticipated in the Greater Hill Master Plan. 'Displacement prevention' was directly addressed, through job creation, rent supports, and other interventions to protect the African American residents. In addition, the Master Plan was framed as celebrating the history and culture of the African-American neighbourhood. These protections mean that the evolution of the neighbourhood has a strong chance of being inclusive of African Americans and their contributions to the area.

Perhaps most important was the evolution of the Hill District Consensus Group (HDCG) as a forum for clarifying ideas and sharing information. Although in 1998 HDCG meetings were attended by ten to fifteen people mostly from the Hill, in 2011 the HDCG could regularly count on fifty to seventy-five people showing up, including people from all over the city and even the region.

From the perspective of social psychiatry, the acknowledgement of the problem of the border opened a critical new perspective on the problems facing the Hill. This perspective was translated into a development agenda that engaged all sectors of the community. The work of FTR! and the One Hill Coalition are two examples of neighbourhood organizations reaching out to learn from people in the area, to promote broad, action-oriented dialogue. This social process reactivated the collective consciousness, and mobilized collective wisdom to guide the unfolding story of the Hill.

Conclusion

Jane Jacobs recognized that the effective city arises from the fine mesh of an intricately interwoven physical plant. Streets, plazas, homes, factories, schools and hospitals must be tightly connected with a strong flow among them. Segregation, by imposing impenetrable borders, wrecks the function of the city and leads to a loss of the city's critical functioning: the city's ability to recognize and respond to patterns of threat and opportunity. These problems are not simply unfortunate and they are not simply an issue facing only the oppressed. The malfunction of our cities is a problem for the nation. Most importantly, by undermining the functioning of the city, it weakens the nation's competitive position. By creating 'disagreeable feelings', it invites fanatics to come forward with ideas that will ease the discomfort.

Michel Cantal-Dupart, by convincing the leaders of the Hill District to attend to the border issues, unleashed a much-needed period of creativity and problem-solving. This has been a source of energy and inspiration for the whole city of Pittsburgh. It points the way to undoing the historic harm of segregation and achieving the state Jane Jacobs proposed: diversity, intricately intermingled in mutual support.

References

Bishop, M. and Harrington, S.D. (1997) The Invisible Inner City: Poverty, Crime and Decay in Roanoke's Oldest Neighborhoods. *The Roanoke Times and World News*.

Brand, S. 1995 *How Buildings Learn: What Happens After They're Built*. New York: Viking.

Candy, D. (nd) *Connecting Pittsburgh's Neighborhoods to our Rivers: Lessons from France*. Pittsburgh: Find the Rivers!

Cantal-Dupart, M. (1993) La crise des villes. *Les Temps Modernes*, **49**(567), pp. 261–263.

Cantal-Dupart, M. (1994) *Merci la Ville!* Bordeaux: Investigations Le Castor Astral.

Clark, D. (1962) *The Ghetto Game: Racial Conflicts in the City*. New York: Sheed and Ward.

Du Bois, W.E.B. (1903) *The Souls of Black Folk*. Chicago, IL: A.C. McClurg & Co.

Fullilove, M. (2004) *Root Shock: How Tearing Up City Neighborhoods Hurts America and What We Can Do About It*. New York: Ballantine/One World.

Fullilove, M.T., Green, L.L. and Fullilove, R.E. (1999). Building momentum: an ethnographic study of inner-city redevelopment. *American Journal of Public Health*, **89**, pp. 840–844.

Fullilove. M.T. and Wallace, R. (2011) Serial forced displacement in American cities, 1916–2010. *Journal of Urban Health*, **88**(3), pp. 381–389.

Héon-Klin, V., Sieber, E., Huebner, J. and Fullilove, M.T. (2001).The influence of geopolitical change on the well-being of a population: the Berlin Wall. *American Journal of Public Health*, **91**(3), pp. 369–374.

Jacobs, J. (1993) *The Death and Life of Great American Cities*. New York: Random House.

Jacobs, W.R. (1972) *Dispossessing the American Indian*. New York: Charles Scribner's Sons.

Leighton, A.H. (1945) *The Governing of Men*. Princeton, NJ: Princeton University Press.

Leighton, A.H. (1959) *My Name is Legion: Foundations for a Theory of Man in Relation to Culture*, Volume I. New York: Basic Books.

Murphy, P. (2004) The housing that community built. *Shelterforce Online*. Available at http://www.nhi.org/online/issues/138/bedford.html. Accessed 2 December 2008.

Robins, A.F.M., Fullilove R.E., Myers, T., and Baltimore, T. (1999) *Hillscapes: Envisioning a Healthy Urban Habitat*. Pittsburgh: University of Pittsburgh Graduate School of Public Health.

Sasaki Associates (2011) *Greater Hill District Master Plan, Final Report*. Pittsburgh: City of Pittsburgh.

Simms, E.-M. (2008) Children's lived spaces in the inner city: historical and political aspects of the psychology of place. *The Humanistic Psychologist*, **36**(1), pp. 72–89.

Wallace, A. (1957) Mazeway disintegration: the individual's perception of socio-cultural disorganization. *Human Organization*, **16**, pp. 23–27.

Wallace, R. and Fullilove, M. (2008) *Collective Consciousness and Its Discontents: Institutional Distributed Cognition, Racial Policy and Public Health in the United States*. New York: Springer.

Part IV

Jane Jacobs, Urban Designer

Chapter 10

Jane Jacobs and the Diversity Ideal

Emily Talen

For Jane Jacobs, diversity was 'by far' the most important condition of a healthy urban place. This was not an academic observation. Jacobs translated this view into a normative ideal about what this meant for the physical context of socially diverse neighbourhoods. As cities expanded in the twentieth century, design ideology and technological 'progress', along with other social and economic factors, fuelled a built environment that worked against diversity. Jacobs was a keen observer of this problem, and sought to reverse it.

This chapter narrows in on Jacobs's diversity ideal and the challenges it created. I am particularly interested in what the elevation of diversity has meant for urban design. Was Jacobs right to argue that diversity can be promoted through the presence of generative conditions? What are the internal contradictions and debates associated with trying to promote diversity and is there any hope of a resolution? Beyond the notion that diversity is good for cities, many are sceptical about the wisdom of using design or public intervention to support diversity. Partly this is a matter of the divorce between social goals and urban design that has been brewing since the demise of modernist urbanism, with its emphasis on functionalism, automobile accommodation and land-use separation. Can the wisdom of Jane Jacobs be used to reignite the role urban design plays in the support of diversity?

Recapping the Main Idea: Jacobs's Diversity Ideal

Urban diversity, the 'size, density, and congestion' of cities, was considered by Jacobs to be 'among our most precious economic assets' (Jacobs, 1961, p. 219), a topic she explored at length in many of her writings. Social benefits included the promotion of trust between people as well as unscripted forms of community surveillance. An overriding interest was the role of diversity in promoting economic opportunity (see especially Jacobs (1961) and Jacobs (1970)). In Jacobs's words, cities, if they are diverse, 'offer fertile ground for the plans of thousands of people' (1961, p. 14). Non-diversity offers little hope for future growth, either in the form of personal or economic development. What counted for Jacobs was the 'everyday, ordinary performance in mixing people', forming complex 'pools of use' that would be capable of producing something greater than the sum of their parts (*Ibid.*, pp. 164–165).

This basic idea has been taken up by many urban reformers, each casting a slightly revised version of Jacobs's argument that the maximizing of 'exchange possibilities', both economic and social, is the key factor of urban quality of life (Greenberg, 1995). Feminists might speak in terms of an 'infrastructure of everyday life' whereby urban spaces are given multiple roles, not categorized as satisfying either the 'reproductive or productive arena' (Gilroy and Booth, 1999, p. 308). The mixture of land uses – especially housing, schools and shopping – is regularly employed as the basic definition of 'a good pedestrian neighborhood' (Hayden, 2003, p. 121).

More specifically, diversity is seen as the primary generator of urban vitality because it increases interactions among multiple urban elements. A 'close-grained' diversity of uses provides 'constant mutual support', and planning must, Jacobs argued, 'become the science and art of catalyzing and nourishing these close-grained working relationships' (1961, p. 14). Thus the separation of urbanism into categories, like land use, miles of highways, square footage of office space, park acreage per capita – all of these abstracted calculations lead to, as Mumford termed it, the 'anti-city' (1968, p. 128). Jacobs similarly objected to planners who tried to treat the city as a series of calculations and measurable abstractions that rendered it a problem of 'disorganized complexity', and made planners falsely believe that they could effectively manipulate its individualized parts.

Diversity was not to be seen as chaotic or random. For Jacobs, social, economic and physical diversity effectively co-existed within an underlying system of order, which she termed 'organized complexity'. Modernists, according to Jacobs, lacked this understanding. Neither Le Corbusier's towers in the park nor Eliel Saarinen's 'organic decentralization' constituted the right approach. Their mistake was in treating the city as if it were a two-dimensional problem of simplicity rather than treating every issue as a multi-sided aspect of complexity that was, in fundamental ways, organized. Cities, as heterogeneous settlements, should not be treated as relationships between two variables, like the ratio of open space to population. Further, diversity must be substantive, not superficial: 'it is the richness of human variation that gives vitality and color to the human setting' (Raskin, quoted in Jacobs, 1961, p. 229). In this sense, a commercial street that looks garish and chaotic is most likely not diverse but homogenous. Venturi et al. (1977) showed how architecture attempts to present a sense of variety by being exhibitionist in the midst of an underlying homogeneity. Extreme variations in colour, form and texture are buildings crying out to be recognized amidst an underlying pattern of sameness.

The real task of urbanism, Jacobs argued, is to maximize interaction, promote interchange at all levels, stimulate both social and economic contact, and look for ways to promote diversity wherever feasible. Jacobs further contended that this diversity should be 'grown' in place, not produced through some form of intra-urban social migration resulting in gentrification and displacement. She called this grown-in-place approach 'unslumming', which 'hinges on whether a considerable number of the residents and businesses of a slum find it both desirable and practical to make and carry out their own plans right there, or whether they must … move elsewhere'.

Translating the Diversity Ideal into Urban Design Principles

In *The Death and Life*, Jacobs articulated the fundamental connection between place – physical urban form – and diversity. This was unusual because, while planning and design of the built environment are believed to have played a strong role in fostering the patterns of segregation that characterize American cities, urban redesign was not looked to as a way to reverse the situation. In discussions about how to address the antithesis of diversity – segregation – American city planning, in its capacity as a profession that plans and designs cities, has been relatively withdrawn. Peter Hall (2002) observed that the problems of inner-city disinvestment, white flight and segregation – the most potent manifestations of non-diversity – are problems that, 'almost unbelievably', city planning has not been called upon to answer. Unlike in other countries, 'Americans are capable of separating problems of social pathology from any discussion of design solutions', focusing instead on 'a bundle of policies' (Hall, 2002, p. 461) – often only weakly related to city planning.

This was not always the case. The need to support social mix through the mechanisms of planning and design had long been a concept embedded in city planning idealism (Talen, 2008). The twentieth century began with demands that city reformers do something about the 'monotony' of the slums, and the earliest proposals – those of Ebenezer Howard, for example – called for settlements that were internally focused but complete in their provision of the diverse and essential needs of life. Lewis Mumford, Kevin Lynch, William Whyte, and Eliel Saarinen are only a few of the urbanists who thought deeply about the physical context of diversity.

But it was Jacobs who articulated the design parameters of diversity in a more sophisticated way than previous generations. She pronounced that diversity corresponds to physical forms and patterns that maintain human interactions – relationships and patterns of relationships. Her definition of diversity consisted of a mix of uses, including variety in 'cultural opportunities', the inclusion of a 'variety of scenes', and 'a great variety [in] population and other users' (Jacobs, 1961, pp. 143–151). On the effect of the physical environment on human diversity she was not ambiguous: there are physical qualities that create diversity in uses and users, and this would be the basis of a well-functioning, vital and healthy city. Her propositions – mixed primary uses, mixed ages, short blocks, concentration – have been the guiding principles for planners who came of age after modernist urbanism and urban renewal had inflicted irrefutable damage.

Jacobs's ideas about the physical context of diversity were different from what previous generations had been advocating. For example, Lewis Mumford (1968) believed that a healthy diversity required limits on size, density and area, an idea that Jacobs rejected. Instead, Jacobs argued that a sufficient concentration of population – perhaps at least 100 dwellings per acre, but this was not absolute – was necessary for a lively city and for healthy urban diversity.

Jacobs stressed the importance of use rather than size as a key ingredient of diversity. Offices, factories, dwellings, and other types of primary uses were essential for bringing people to a place, and secondary uses were essential for serving the people that came. Above all, Jacobs argued, there was a logic to the particular mix of uses that would be most likely to succeed and produce a healthy, diverse urbanism. Mixed building age was essential for this, too, by insuring there would be places for new enterprises and entrepreneurs (in old buildings) alongside larger business and chain stores (who can afford new buildings).

Jacobs proposed a number of more specific ideas about urban form and how it supports diversity. Short blocks were considered necessary for diversity 'because of the fabric of intricate cross-use that they permit among the users of a city neighborhood'. Long blocks blocked this cross-fertilization because they funnelled people onto only a few streets, which tended to then be overdeveloped commercially. Sidewalks were important for maintaining diversity because they helped the city 'handle' strangers and, if they were well used, induced people to watch over them. Then there were the many tactics of 'emphasis and suggestion', (Jacobs, 1961, p. 377) that planners could use to help people make order out of the diversity around them (diversity that might otherwise be interpreted as chaos). Small changes that accomplish this include the provision of visual interruptions in long city streets, or the placing of limits on the maximum street frontage permitted for a single building. Tactics for illuminating an underlying order to promote a more vital and intense city could, Jacobs argued, be relatively small. She wrote, 'emphasis on bits and pieces is of the essence: this is what a city is, bits and pieces that supplement each other and support each other'.

Complications

While these principles have resonated with several generations of urbanists, the implementation of Jacobs's ideas presents certain complexities for planners. One issue is the degree to which her principles can be employed in the vast number of places that do not have the kind of concentration she advocated. Manhattan density is unique in the US. If diversity depends on a given level of urban concentration, as Jacobs prescribed, diversity may be confined to a relatively small part of a metropolitan area.

In this sense, it is difficult to reconcile Jacobs's views connecting diversity and concentration with proposals for community-oriented, small-scale, traditional neighbourhood development. New Urbanism – the contemporary urban design movement that aspires to many of Jacobs's principles – makes the argument for smaller-scale community building today, but Lewis Mumford made it back in the 1930s: 'limitations on size, density, and area are absolutely necessary to effective social intercourse'. Jacobs relished the diversity of cities with 'so many people' living 'so close together' in places of 'exuberant variety', but critics have likened the approach to 'home remedies for urban cancer' (Mumford, 1968).

The empirical record does not always support Jacobs's observations on the link between diversity and concentration. Demographic analyses show that places outside large, dense metropolitan cores are often the most diverse. My research on Chicago, for example, showed that neighbourhoods (measured by census block group) that were diverse by income, race, and ethnicity tended to be in older, formerly industrialized neighbourhoods close to downtown, but not in the densest areas (Talen, 2008). How is it possible, then, to deploy Jacobsian conditions for generating diversity in places that could never hope to satisfy her condition of concentration? There is a need to come to terms with the fact that building diversity may not rest on the densest urban core alone, and that there may be a need to engage with the 'semi-suburbs', as Jacobs disdainfully called them.

In short, the relationship between density and diversity may be more complicated than Jacobs allowed. Jacobs preferred densities in the range of 100 dwellings to the acre, and anything significantly lower, she argued, was in danger of producing 'gray areas'. High density and high ground coverage were to be relieved by frequent streets (created by small block size), and variation in building type would have the effect of increasing the diversity of both population and business enterprise. Jacobs argued, further, that this variation would be difficult to achieve wherever land coverage was low and density was high – factors characterizing modern public housing projects.

And yet, despite these calculations, diversity and density do not seem to be correlated in a direct, linear way. As Pendall (2001) explains, density may exacerbate segregation by housing type and class because gentrification is more likely to occur in high-density neighbourhoods where 'proximity-related benefits' increasingly enter 'people's utility functions' (Pendall and Caruthers, 2003, p. 547). While density is required for a corner grocery store – the ubiquity of the corner market in Manhattan is evidence enough of that – density might not be necessarily diverse. Eventually, incremental improvements may have the collective effect of raising property values, taxes and rents. Promoting an urban appreciation of the kind advocated by Jane Jacobs can trigger a back-to-the-city movement, and Jacobs was critiqued early on for stimulating, however inadvertently, the replacement of the corner grocery store with 'Bonjour, Croissant' (Muschamp, cited in Hall, 1996, p. 295).

Increasing density holds a real danger of increasing social segregation (Huie and Frisbie, 2000) and, as a result, suburbanization is sometimes viewed as a mediator of segregation (Logan et al., 2004). As higher-income groups attempt to move back to the city, valuing walking and access to amenities (Hughes and Seneca, 2004), enclaves may be formed, as opposed to places with income mix. Some studies have shown that low-density development increases choices for a wider range of socioeconomic groups (Glaeser and Vigdor, 2003). Low-density areas have even been shown to be more diverse than the compact city in some cases (Pendall and Carruthers, 2003). If this is the case, environmental goals and social diversity goals may conflict wherever the former is defined as reducing land consumption and increasing density.

Another issue is that Jacobs might have underestimated the difficulty of mixing uses to support diversity. Different types of users have different types of needs, and, since it is unlikely that all needs will be satisfied in one neighbourhood, some residents will have better access than others. While many agree that mixed uses – including public and quasi-public facilities and neighbourhood-level commercial enterprises – are essential for sustaining socially mixed communities (Myerson, 2001), finding the appropriate mix to support diversity – especially income diversity – can be problematic. As Goetz (1996) cautioned, 'the poor relate to [neighborhood] amenities in ways fundamentally different from more affluent families'. For example, public transportation and affordable day care are likely to be much more important to poor families than rich ones (see also Bayer, 2000).

The question of whether it is possible – or even desirable – to plan for diversity constitutes a fundamental divide in urban planning theory. The question that critics pose is: how can diversity, which is the byproduct of many individuals working in myriad, individual ways constantly to alter urbanism, be conceived of on a level that is not individually scaled, but is the product of one planner's or one group of planners' decisions? This was the theme explored by Jane Jacobs, Christopher Alexander, Richard Sennett, and countless other sceptics of the viability of the urban planning profession (Jacobs, 1961; Alexander, 1965; Sennett, 1970). Jacobs believed it was politically untenable to support pre-determined definitions and parameters about urbanism – she wrote 'we are too adventurous, inquisitive, egoistic and competitive to be a harmonious society of artists by consensus' (1961, p. 374).

In line with Jacobs's critique of planning, other urban scholars have argued that planning is essentially a quest for ruralized social order imposed on the assumed unnaturalness of urban disharmony. Boyer (1983) equates civic improvements of the 1890s with the 'self-righteous superiority and economic militarism' of American imperialism in Cuba, Puerto Rico, and the Philippines around the same time. Urban improvements are exercises in social control, impositions of a façade of ceremonial harmony. Even surveys of urban residents have been interpreted as unhealthy sur-veillance, as the detailed collection of data on the city could be used to 'carve up the field of urban disorders' into specialized concerns (Boyer, 1983, p. 32). Whether concerned with worker exploitation or damage to the urban physical environment, the critique is based on a perception that these concerns essentially involved 'fear of the urban crowd and a belief that the city was an unnatural abode for humanity' (*Ibid.*, p. 9).

Urban planners, in defence, argue that maintaining urban liveability requires intervention, and that the 'freedom' of the random, chaotic, unregulated urbanism of individual choice creates an inhumane, sometimes anti-urban settlement form. Daphne Spain points out in her book *How Women Saved the City* (2001) that women's groups in the Municipal Housekeeping Movement of the early twentieth century were trying to establish order where there was none in existence – and this was out of necessity. They were trying to establish a meaningful pattern of urban places, one that could help urban newcomers cope with urban disorder.

The argument against diversity of the kind advocated by Jacobs was made most cogently by Lewis Mumford (see for example Mumford (1968)). Mumford pointed out with sarcasm that Jacobs was apparently never hurt by 'ugliness, disorder, confusion', and that, requiring only a 'haphazard mixture' of urban activities, is not a further basis for beauty (Mumford, 1968, p. 197). This position he called 'esthetic philistinism with a vengeance'. He argued that Jacobs's approach did not lead to a healthy 'organized complexity' of urban life, but instead resulted in an 'aimless dynamism', that used confusion as something essential in life, dismissing 'the accompanying increase in nervous tensions, violence, crime, and health-depleting sedatives, tranquillizers, and atmospheric conditions'.

There is tangible evidence that urban design proposals – in their ordered coherency, in the strength and conviction of their vision, and in their 'clarity of standards'– have tended to have the greatest and most immediate impact on urban reform (see, for example, Altshuler's 1983 discussion of the intercity freeway). Accommodating difference and diversity may mean that there is a need to put forth a material expression – a plan – that rests on some sense of order, however nuanced and subordinated. In other words, there may be legitimate ways of nurturing diversity that involve pre-conceived designs and coerced urban forms.

Jacobs rejected this view, and might have seen the approach as indistinguishable from large-scale master planning. Fishman (1977) compares Jacobs's critique of large-scale planning to the ideas of Joseph de Maistre and other counter-Enlightenment theorists from the early nineteenth century who opposed the French and American revolutions, and who thought the writing of a constitution for government was too complex a task for the human mind. Jacobs is sometimes aligned with anti-government ideology, and conservatives like William F. Buckley, Jr and Steven Hayward (2000) have latched on to Jacobs's views as part of the 'pedigree of conservative urban thought'.

Without government control, Jacobs expressed 'great wonder' (1961, p. 391) at the intricate order that cities exhibited because of the countless freedoms available to urban dwellers. Others have similarly extolled the virtues of such 'freedoms'. Richard Sennett, in *The Uses of Disorder*, promoted an urban social life that is 'disordered' and 'unstable', because it causes residents to become more directly involved with the mitigation of neighbourhood problems (Sennett, 1970, p. 144). Without land use laws, Sennett reasoned, residents would not rely on government or plans to solve problems, but would take it upon themselves to initiate change. To some extent, this view appears unrealistic in light of Rosen's (1986) study in which shared neighbourhood power was largely negative. Individuals and small groups – not business elites – thwarted each other's attempts at urban improvement. It also contrasts with notions of justice and equity. Jacob Riis (1901) thought of the tenement slum as the antithesis of freedom: 'Life, liberty, pursuit of happiness? Wind! says the slum'.

The argument against planning meant that the provision of services and facilities – even if constructed for the purpose of stabilizing a fragile neighbourhood diversity – was often thought of as being too contrived. For example, Jacobs saw playground development as an attempt to 'incarcerate incidental play' (1961, p. 85). She would have similarly disliked the idea of creating separate venues for youth, such as dancing halls, on the grounds that they not only segregate young from old, but they require an unnatural surveillance. Such venues are by definition isolated from the rest of the urban system, constituting a fine-scale segregation that would ultimately lead to the destruction of the city. If systems of activity – whether for children or for the elderly – did not overlap, there would be anarchy (in the sense of a loss of caring), and sterility, Jacobs argued. She was more concerned with the underlying processes that could be instilled to generate connectivity and complexity, not the need for static goals like playground development.

A century ago, the idea of purposefully avoiding planned elements like playgrounds using the argument that they are too disruptive of urban inter-relatedness and true diversity would have seemed a strange way to put things. Early planners believed that if the city did not provide places for organized play – public places where all members of society congregate – then the population would be forced to find segregated venues. Jane Addams (1909), for example, wrote that if the city fails in its civic duty to provide public venues for play, 'then we, the middle aged, grow quite distracted and resort to all sorts of restrictive measures'. She regretted the loss of the village green as a venue for youthful frivolity because there 'all of the older people of the village participated. Chaperonage was not then a social duty but natural and inevitable'. Ironically, the idea of natural chaperonage is not far removed from Jacobs's notion of 'eyes on the street'.

Ultimately, the inhumane designs endorsed by planners – i.e. modernist urbanism – did the most to change societal impressions of the benefit and need for government-backed master planning. The experience legitimized Jacobs's views on diversity. Jacobs was able to romanticize city streets as the ultimate playground for children, 'teaming with life and adventure', because they contrasted so profoundly with the sterility of the modernist plaza (1961, p. 85).

And yet, dichotomizing cities as controlled (via plans) versus spontaneous (via freedom) may be somewhat misleading. One is viewed as a product of order and control, while the other is associated with being eventful and responsive, but as Kostof points out, the duality has to be strongly qualified. Even the most seemingly random, meandering path can be the product of order having to do with established conventions and social contracts, 'a string of compromises between individual rights and the common will' (Kostof, 1993, p. 85).

Conclusion

One stark reality sustains the debate about the best approach to sustaining diversity – there are too few neighbourhoods that are simultaneously diverse and have a high degree of place quality. Neighbourhoods that possess the kind of physical design that supports diversity – good connectivity, mix of uses, a diversity of housing types and styles, dignified public buildings, what Fishman (2005, p. 363) described as 'precious legacies of long-lost civic idealism' – tend to have a highly desirable kind of character, vitality and location. Since supply does not match demand, such places become unaffordable, and many residents and businesses are displaced. Jane Jacobs's

Greenwich Village is but one example. It bears repeating, then, that diversity requires a supporting physical urban framework *as well as* a progressive, anti-displacement policy that helps to 'unslum' and stabilize.

In the realm of urban design, there is a need to reconcile both the Jacobsian view of diversity-generating factors, as well as the more traditional view about the legitimacy of plan-making. To return to the playground example, public places, especially playgrounds, might need to be 'contrived' where alternatives for play are lacking, but in addition, children should be able to play within the interstices of urban complexity, as Jacobs advocated. Children need freedom, but it is conceivable that plans play a role in ensuring that cities are kept alive and vibrant. It may require some degree of foresight and control – or at least, faith in the legitimacy of a collective response, one that does not necessarily inhibit the freedom to explore.

It is important to emphasize that order is not the enemy of diversity – a point Jane Jacobs cogently made. Jacobs would have agreed that some recognizable sense of order is needed to be able to identify the 'collective' aspects of urban life. It allows us to grasp a shared construct, a collective expression that counterbalances the individualism of diversity. Order is what allows diverse urban elements to relate to each other in some way. This implies the need for at least some control, a point even Jane Jacobs admitted. Left unplanned, profitable uses can start to take over, housing of one kind can begin to dominate, sorting into one primary use can occur, or the scale of a building can start to undermine a successful street. Diversity, Jacobs knew, is perfectly capable of self-destructing.

Jane Jacobs should be especially appreciated for her lack of ambiguity on the subject of physical urban form and its role in promoting – or undermining – diversity. In the hands of others, the idea of diversity, translated to principles of urban form, has been susceptible to an interpretation so broad that it becomes meaningless. In one recent interpretation, for example, urbanism was defined on the basis of 'indeterminacy', where the legitimate need for urban adaptation was said to be a matter of exploiting 'discontinuities and inconsistencies' (Durack, 2001). This kind of definition, ambiguous about what diversity in urbanism requires, may just as readily condone haphazard growth and chaotic urban form. It can entail, on the one hand, an elevation of the importance of the 'mythic aspect of the ordinary and ugly' (Kelbaugh, 2002, p. 287), and on the other, a promotion of the view that strip malls merely represent a new, as yet underappreciated, aesthetic ideal (Kolb, 2000). In architecture, mass consumer culture or the speed of an automobile can – and have – become fetishized.

Outside of architectural discourse, there has been a sense of idealism about diversity that has been reverberating throughout planning scholarship, albeit from different angles. Dowell Myers (2007), for example, wrote about the need to recognize interdependencies and mutual self-interest among the growing 'immigrants and boomers' that will define metropolitan society in the coming decades. Robert Fishman (2005) hoped for the 'reurbanism' of our cities into diverse, mixed-income neighbourhoods through a combination of 'unslumming' and, if need be, a softer form of gentrification. Nan Ellin's (2006) *Integral Urbanism* is defined by networks, relationships, connections and interdependencies that counteract separation and retreat. These are part of an emergent, sophisticated understanding of diversity that draws from the essential writing of Jane Jacobs, developing it further and in a way that she would have appreciated.

References

Addams, J. (1909) *The Spirit of Youth and the City Streets*. New York: Macmillan, 1909; BoondocksNet Edition, 2001. Available at http://www.boondocksnet.com/editions/youth/. Accessed 21 January 2012.

Alexander, C. (1965) A city is not a tree. *Architectural Forum*, **122**, April, pp. 58–62; May, 58–61.

Altshuler, A.A. (1983) The intercity freeway, in Krueckeberg, D.A. (ed.) *Introduction to Planning History in the United States*. New Brunswick, NJ: The Center for Urban Policy Research, pp. 190–234.

Bayer, P. (2000) Tiebout Sorting and Discrete Choices: A New Explanation for Socioeconomic Differences in the Consumption of School Quality. Working paper. Available at http://aida.econ.yale.edu/~pjb37/papers.htm.

Boyer, M.C. (1983) *Dreaming the Rational City: the Myth of American City Planning*. Cambridge, MA: MIT Press.

Durack, R. (2001) Village vices: the contradiction of New Urbanism and sustainability. *Places*, **14**(2), pp. 64–69.

Ellin, N. (2006) *Integral Urbanism*. London: Routledge.

Fishman, R. (1977) *Urban Utopias in the Twentieth Century: Ebenezer Howard, Frank Lloyd Wright, and Le Corbusier*. New York: Basic Books.

Fishman, R. (2005) The fifth migration. *Journal of the American Planning Association*, **71**(4), pp. 357–366.

Gilroy, R. and Booth, C. (1999) Building an infrastructure of everyday lives. *European Planning Studies*, **7**(3), pp. 307–325.

Glaeser, E.L. and Vigdor, J. (2003) Racial segregation: promising news, in Katz, B. and Lang, R.E. (eds.) *Redefining Urban and Suburban America, Evidence from Census 2000*. Washington DC: Brookings Institution Press.

Goetz, E.G. (1996) *Clearing the Way: Deconcentrating the Poor in Urban America*. Washington DC: Urban Institute Press.

Greenberg, M. (1995) *The Poetics of Cities: Designing Neighborhoods that Work*. Columbus, OH: Ohio State University Press.

Hall, P. (1996) 1946–1996: from new town to sustainable social city. *Town & Country Planning*, **65**(11), pp. 295–297.

Hall, P. (2002) *Cities of Tomorrow: An Intellectual History of Urban Planning and Design in the Twentieth Century*, 3rd ed. Oxford: Blackwell.

Hayden, D. (2003) *Building Suburbia: Green Fields and Urban Growth, 1820–2000*. New York: Pantheon.

Hayward, S. (2000) The Irony of Smart Growth. Speech to the Center of the American Experiment Luncheon Debate with Ted Mondale, Chairman, Twin Cities Met Council, 18 January 2000. Available at http://www.pacificresearch.org/pub/sab/enviro/irony.html#Steven Hayward.

Hughes, J.W. and Seneca, J.J. (2004) The Beginning of the End of Sprawl? Rutgers Regional Report, Issue Paper No. 21. New Brunswick, NJ: Edward J. Bloustein School of Planning and Public Policy.

Huie, S.B. and Parker Frisbie, W. (2000) The components of density and the dimensions of residential segregation. *Population Research and Policy Review*, **19**, pp. 505–524.

Jacobs, J. (1961) *The Death and Life of Great American Cities*. New York: Vintage.

Jacobs, J. (1970) *The Economy of Cities*. New York: Vintage.

Kelbaugh, D.S. (2002) *Repairing the American Metropolis*. Seattle, WA: University of Washington Press.

Kolb, D. (2000) The age of the list, in Algreen-Ussing, G. *et al.* (eds.) *Urban Space and Urban Conservation as an Aesthetic Problem*. Rome: L'Erma di Bretschneider, pp. 27–35.

Kostof, S. (1993) The design of cities. *Places*, **5**(4), pp.85–88.

Logan, J.R., Stults, B.J. and Farley, R. (2004) Segregation of minorities in the metropolis: two decades of change. *Demography*, **41**(1), pp. 1–22.

Mumford, L. (1968) *The Urban Prospect*. New York: Harcourt Brace Jovanovich.

Myers, D. (2007) *Immigrants and Boomers: Forging a New Social Contract for the Future of America*. New York: Russell Sage Foundation.

Myerson, D.L. (2001) Sustaining Urban Mixed-Income Communities: the Role of Community Facilities. A Land Use Policy Report prepared for The Urban Land Institute, Charles H. Shaw Annual Forum on Urban Community Issues, Chicago, 18–19 October.

Pendall, R. (2001) Exploring Connections between Density, Sprawl, and Segregation by Race and Income in the U.S. Metropolitan Areas, 1980–1990. Paper presented at the 'International Seminar on Segregation in the City', Lincoln Institute of Land Policy, Cambridge, MA.

Pendall, R., and Caruthers, J.I. (2003) Does density exacerbate income segregation? Evidence from U.S. metropolitan areas, 1980 to 2000. *Housing Policy Debate*, **14**(4), pp. 541–589.

Riis, J. (1901) *Making of An American*. New York: Harper and Row.

Rosen, C.M. (1986) *The Limits of Power: Great Fires and the Process of City Growth in America*. Cambridge: Cambridge University Press.

Sennett, R. (1970) *The Uses of Disorder: Personal Identity and City Life*. New York: Knopf.

Spain, D. (2001) *How Women Saved the City*. Minneapolis, MN: University of Minnesota Press.

Talen, E. (2008) *Design for Diversity: Exploring Socially Mixed Neighborhoods*. Oxford: Elsevier.

Venturi, R., Izenour, S. and Scott Brown, D. (1977) *Learning from Las Vegas: The Forgotten Symbolism of Architectural Form*. Cambridge, MA: MIT Press.

Chapter 11

Diversity and Mixed Use: Lessons from Medieval China

Jing Xie

Mixed-use urban patterns – patterns which combine living, working and leisure – have been widely advocated since the mid-twentieth century. They were very much the norm in pre-industrial cities around the world but were consistently eroded throughout the 1900s as a result of increasing economic and functional specialization in cities and urban planning interventions that aimed to outlaw mixed use and create segregated land-use patterns. There is little doubt that Jane Jacobs was among the first to recognize the many flaws of land-use separation in cities. She was also one of the most passionate and eloquent advocates of mixed use. In *The Death and Life of Great American Cities* (1969 [1961]), Jacobs argued that a mixed-use urban fabric is a vital precondition for creating socially diverse and healthy communities – communities that allow their residents opportunities for personal growth and social interaction. Her call for mixed use has since been echoed by a long line of scholars and practitioners. Among them are well-known contemporary proponents of returning to the design tenets of traditional, pre-industrial cities as a solution to the problems of modern urban development such as Lèon Krier (1984) and Andrés Duany *et al.* (2000). Influenced by the works of such urban activists, many planners today take for granted that mixed-use development is a panacea for reviving decaying urban neighbourhoods and creating vibrant, diverse and sustainable urban environments.

Regardless of the popularity of the terms 'mixed use' and 'diversity', however, neither has a precise definition. Further, there is no clear consensus on what their benefits are or how the two are connected. It is commonly claimed that mixed use and social diversity contribute to the richness and completeness of the human experience in cities. For example, Gloria Levitas points out that people in mixed-use and diverse settings experience a variety of roles and will have many opportunities for self-redefinition (Levitas, 1986, p. 235). Jacobs famously proposed four generators of urban diversity: mixed use, short city blocks, a variety of buildings (in age, condition and style), and a concentration of people. In her interpretation, mixed use, notably, comes first, perhaps suggesting that she saw it as the most crucial of the diversity generators.

Fascination with urban diversity is not new. One can find it in the works of scholars and travellers writing hundreds of years ago. Take for instance Pietro Aretino, a poet and playwright who came to Venice in 1527. In a letter to his landlord, he depicted his pleasure when looking out of his window:

Never do I lean out but I see at market time a thousand persons and as many gondolas. In my field of vision to the right are the Fish Market and the Meat Market. To the left are the bridge and the Fondaco dei Tedeschi. Where both views meet I see the Rialto packed with merchants. I see grapes in the barges and game birds in the shops, vegetables on the pavement … it is all so fascinating … as the atmosphere varied from clear to leaden. (Cited in Hibbert, 1998, pp. 90–91)

Similarly, Mary Ward, a philanthropist and novelist living in London, recounted an ecstatic moment of viewing street life from her carriage in 1885:

I can recall one summer afternoon, in particular, when as I was in a hansom driving idly westward towards Hyde Park Gate, thinking of a hundred things at once, this consciousness of intensification, of a heightened meaning in everything – the broad street, the crowd of moving figures and carriages, the houses looking down upon it – seized upon me with a rush. 'Yes, it is good – the mere living!' Joy in the infinite variety of the great city as compared with the 'cloistered virtue' of Oxford; the sheer pleasure of novelty, of the kind new faces, and the social discoveries one felt opening on many sides; the delight of new perceptions, new powers in oneself; all this seemed to flower for me in those few minutes of reverie – if one can apply such a word to an experience so vivid. (Ward, 1919, p. 197)

If such an urban bustle defined by diversity of experiences is fascinating and desirable, as these travellers felt and as Jacobs assumed, how can it be achieved? Does such diversity require specific physical, planning and/or architectural configuration? Many scholars (e.g. Foucault, 1977; Evans, 1997; Lynch, 1960) have reflected on the important role that architectural settings play in shaping social relations and behaviours. Jacobs herself, quoting Eugene Raskin, asserted that architecture can (and should) set the stage for social experiences, including for diversity; or in her words, for:

… the interweaving of human patterns. They [the urban settings] are full of people doing different things, with different reasons and different ends in view, and the architecture reflects and expresses this difference – which is one of content rather than form alone. (Jacobs, 1969, p. 229)

In his theory of the 'imageability' of the city, Kevin Lynch reinforced Jacobs's assertion by claiming that places of 'vitality need to have their remarkable functional order clarified' (Lynch, 1960; Jacobs, 1969, p. 377). Jacobs also argued that planners should employ 'zoning for diversity' (Jacobs, 1969, pp. 252–253) – a proposition which has been strongly advanced by those working in the New Urbanist tradition such as Andrés Duany and Emily Talen (2002).

The question posed in this chapter is whether physical, land-use diversity is inherently connected to a broader pattern of diversity, understood here as the diversity of human interactions and experiences. Is there a particular architectural configuration that is conducive to a diversity of interactions and experiences? Does such diversity happen in environments that have certain physical, functional or architectural configurations? Can diversity be architecturally codified? For regardless of the popularity of Jacobs's ideas, some of her fiercest critics such as Herbert Gans have argued that the physical environment cannot directly influence human behaviour (Gans, 1968, p. 19).

In this chapter, I offer ways of addressing these questions through an historical inquiry: examining the urban fabric of Chinese communities and the everyday experiences of people living in them during the Tang and Song dynasties (*c.* 800– 1200 AD). I believe that this historical case offers fruitful ground for exploring the connection between mixed use and diversity. Tang-Song China was doubtlessly the most advanced civilization of its time. The Song dynasty especially, even though it centralized imperial power, permitted an unparalleled degree of economic freedom. Its subjects were allowed to practice business relatively freely, which in turn led to striking economic growth and created the foundation of the exceptionally vibrant traditional Chinese mixed-use urban fabric. This fabric was typical of Chinese cities until the First Opium War in the mid nineteenth century (Ma, 1971, p. 3; Heng, 1999, p. 202). In fact, traces of Song era urban living patterns are still visible today.

I present an analysis of the experiences of two classes which emerged in Tang-Song China, *merchants* and *scholar-officials*, whose lifestyles integrated work and living in different ways.[1] Specifically, I discuss how these two classes lived in relation to their physical environments, and use this to investigate the relationship between physical and social diversity, which is commonly assumed by Jacobs's followers. My sources come from literature, such as poetry, prose and travellers' accounts, and from paintings from the Tang-Song era.

The chapter represents a partial critique of Jacobs's (or at least her followers') theory that social and functional diversity can be architecturally codified. At the same time, however, I believe it represents a celebration of her legacy. What has been 'most refreshing, provocative, stimulating and exciting' in Jacobs's thought is precisely her humanistic approach to city life, which fundamentally challenged and altered the orthodox planning methodologies of her time.[2] Like Raskin, Jacobs subscribed to the philosophy that 'human beings are what interest us most' (cited in Jacobs, 1969, p. 229). In this study, the everyday experiences of people in relation to their physical environment are a key feature. I hope that in line with Jacobs's legacy this chapter too can serve, in some modest way, as a challenge to today's planning orthodoxies.

Tang-Song's China: A Brief History

During the mid-Tang to the Song period, the urban fabric of major Chinese cities underwent a dramatic transformation as a result of political reforms and significant population and economic growth. The system of separating residential wards and market wards – a predominant urban configuration that had existed since the Xizhou dynasty (*c.* 1000 BC) – was gradually eroded. From the mid-Tang period onwards, business premises started to emerge in many residential wards. Subsequently, various shops spread throughout cities and replaced the previously tightly controlled market wards. Song era cities began to exhibit a vibrant mixed-use fabric. We can perhaps imagine how this fabric looked from famous paintings such as Zhang Zeduan's (1085–1145 AD) *Qing Ming Shang He Tu*[3] (*Along the River During the Qingming Festival*), which reveals an exuberant urban landscape in the Kaifeng, the capital city, during the reign of the Northern Song dynasty (960–1227 AD)[4] (figure 11.1).

Figure 11.1. Detail from *Qing Ming Shnag He Tu* 清明上河图, by Zhang Zeduan 张择端, in Northern Song era. (*Source*: The Palace Museum, Beijing)

The emergence of new urban forms during the Song dynasty was undoubtedly brought about by the changing social context. One notable characteristic of the Song political system was the trend towards centralization (see Liu, 1959; Kuhn, 2009). Many attempts at organizational reform were carried out; for example, the national examination system for recruiting government officers was perfected. This reform diminished the power of hereditary feudal lords and distributed power more widely among aspiring intellectuals from a range of backgrounds. The centralization of political power broke the dichotomy of social classes (i.e. between the aristocracy and the rest of the population) and encouraged the growth of new social groups, such as merchants and scholar-officials. Further, many court officials sought commercial opportunities to offset their lost political privileges and accumulate new fortunes. The growing urban economy constantly attracted new populations, as people abandoned their farms to become artisans and merchants or to acquire sufficient education to become scholar-officials (Wu, 2005). In short, large numbers of people flooded into cities to take advantage of the new job opportunities and alluring urban lifestyles.

As James T.C. Liu states, by promoting family businesses and a 'free market', the Song government 'saw in strengthened kinship groups a stable local organization that could serve as the crucial link between the people and the always thinly-spread local administration' (Liu and Golas, 1969, pp. xii–xiii). As a result, countering the dynasty's centralization reforms, economic growth in fact loosened and decentralized political control over urban space.

Song-era urban society began openly to celebrate the new opportunities and lifestyles. Architecture reflected this trend. The merchants' houses began to flank the main urban streets. This represented a clear break with tradition: during the earlier Tang dynasty, upper- and middle-strata dwellings were typically hidden inside walled compounds and gated wards (Ebrey, 1999, p. 144). But during the Song period, residents began increasingly to extend their homes and shops right onto the public thoroughfares, thereby mixing public and private, and bringing a new vibrancy to cities.

In the following sections, I focus on the lifestyles and the built environments that housed Song-era merchants and scholar-officials. Their living and building habits have been relatively well recorded in Chinese historical documents.[5]

Living Mixed with Work:
The Experiences of Song-Era Merchants

As in medieval Europe, many members of the urban merchant/artisan classes in China lived in houses where residential and commercial quarters intermingled; the latter, of course, typically faced the street. For example, the writer Meng Yuanlao described a major thoroughfare in Kaifeng in 1147 as follows:

The Imperial Way continues towards the south across the Zhou Bridge, thrust into the residential areas. There is a coal shop of the Chen family and a tavern of the Zhang family on the eastern side of the street. Next to these premises, there is a food shop selling stuffed buns, a perfume shop of the Li family, a meat pancake shop of the grandmother Chao, and a teahouse of the Lee family. (Meng, 1982, p. 13) (figure 11.1)

Translated from Chinese, these shop names comprise the family name and the type of business: 'Chen Family Coal Shop', 'Zhang Family Tavern', 'Li Family Perfume Shop' and 'Lee Family Teahouse'. This pattern reveals the strong, intensely personal bonds that people felt to the places where their family life was interlaced with the family business. At the time, the Chinese family was the basic unit of socioeconomic organization.[6] Under the influence of Confucianism, the Chinese were particularly loyal to their families. Although a degree of individualism existed in the intellectuals' circle (Tuan, 1982, pp. 146–149), most individuals belonged strictly to their families and clans. Indeed, there was an obligation for family businesses and estates to be inherited and developed (if possible) by the descendants of the household head. The fact that living areas were mixed with workplaces created dual bonds uniting the family: one of blood and kinship, and the other of business. The new mixed-use urban forms expressed an advanced economic organization. In the countryside, the economic system still depended on slaves and serfs; there, people were restricted to the land by legal bondage. But the numbers of farmers and their servants diminished during the Song period (Ma, 1971, p. 21). In cities, the mixed-use living pattern emancipated families from financial and personal constraints and hardship, at least to an extent. Even those who were employees (rather than blood-related members of the household that owned the business) often had harmonious and intimate (rather than antagonistic) relationships with their employers because their jobs and lives were so deeply involved with the family affairs. Jacques Gernet observed that these economic ties in fact enhanced social bonds:

The number of people employed in the workshops, pork-butchers' shops, restaurants, tea-houses and luxury-trade shops was confined to as few hands as possible. But the relationship between all these people and their masters or employers was everywhere the same: a paternalistic attitude on the part of the master, and one of respect and submission on the part of the servants or employees. The latter formed part of the family, and sometimes served from father to son in the same house. Their complete economic dependence together with the persistence of the old family system provides an explanation for the strength of this bond. (Gernet, 1962, p. 93)

It should be noted that the built environment of Song era merchants and artisans – living mixed with work – was pre-dated by environments inherited from the Tang period. During that time, most commerce was conducted in central markets (called wards) – places where merchants and artisans lived and worked (Kuhn, 2009, p. 191). Literature from the period recorded that many Tang era shops located in the market place had the same naming scheme as those in the later Song era (family name plus business type), thus denoting that the merchant's living area was mixed with work (Xue, 2006).

Although the centrally located market place gradually disappeared during the transition from the Tang to the Song dynasty, the typical housing form of the Tang merchants in the market place was adopted by their successors, the Song merchants. The difference was that Song era shops were not confined to a few central locations, but became more dispersed throughout the built fabric and often flanked the main streets. Shops in Tang era marketplaces were built in identical style and arranged in rows, so that all the dealers in a particular commodity were grouped together. These rows (*hang* in Chinese) were the basis for the organization of traders (Twitchett, 1966). Most of the shop-fronts were 6 metres wide and contained two bays/rooms (*jian* in Chinese). Small ones had only one bay, with a shop frontage of 4 metres. The largest ones were 10 metres wide and contained three bays/rooms. In general, the shop depths were roughly 3 metres (Ma, 1982).

An idea of how these shops looked can be obtained from a relief tile from the earlier Eastern Han period (25–220 AD). The tile (figure 11.2) clearly indicates that shops were arranged as row houses and were divided into bays/rooms of different size. Zhang Zeduan's painting (*Qing Ming Shang He Tu*), produced during the Song period, seems to confirm this: the majority of buildings are in multi-housing forms arranged in rows, built either alongside the river or along the street (figure 11.3). Although the shops adopted different façade principles from those of the courtyard houses that were typical in imperial China (i.e. the shops had to have larger openings to the street and had to allow better access for goods and people), they were still built with the same construction methods and had the same physical form as a typical residence. In order to articulate some difference between a house and a house with a shop, the term 'gallery house' (*lang fang* in Chinese) was introduced in the literature. It was also used in the taxation laws of the Song dynasty (for details see Ma, 1986, p. 186). Thus, the difference between a purely residential place and one that combined living with work was not architectural but only legal and linguistic, and the word denoting a shop (i.e. 'gallery house') was itself derived from the word used for a dwelling.

A long-scroll painting, *Can Zhi Tu (Silk Making)*, from the period of the Southern Song dynasty (1227–1279 AD) also illustrates the pattern of living mixed with work on a rather magnificent scale. The painting, consisting of twenty-four different scenes, vividly depicts the process of silk production in a domestic workplace (from domesticating silkworms to the final fabrication of the silk). As background, it shows a

Figure 11.2. Relief of a marketplace in Chengdu, Eastern Han period (25–220 AD). (*Source*: Reproduced by author from Shatzman Steinhardt, 1990, p. 90, with the permission of Chinese Cultural Center, San Francisco)

Figure 11.3. Detail from *Qing Ming Shnag He Tu* 清明上河图, by Zhang Zeduan 张择端, from the Northern Song era. (*Source*: The Palace Museum, Beijing)

long house divided into a series of rooms that link various working and living activities. Seventy-four figures, from babies to seniors, are portrayed altogether. Most seem satisfied with their lives and labour; some are obviously chatting and working with smiles on their faces (figure 11.4). There is no clear division between purely domestic and work-related activities. For example, in one room, a lady is resting on a couch and breastfeeding her baby; nearby is her chaperone doing needlework. In an adjacent room, two ladies are playing with a little baby; nearby, other men and women are working hard (figure 11.5). People seem able to navigate freely between activities; the boundary between their working and domestic lives barely exists. The space appears to have provided a stage for mixing people of different ages and gender, although this mixing tended to occur between people of similar social status.

As the painting illustrates, the free switching of activities and the transparency of the work-living boundary is underscored by the fact that the architecture of each room is identical to that of the others. There was no differentiation between the different functional areas, no physical codification of expected human behaviour, no clear division between the public and private sphere. On the contrary, certain freedoms of

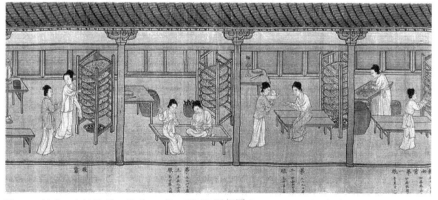

Figures 11.4 and 11.5. Details from *Can Zhi Tu* 蚕织图, by anonymous artist from the Southern Song period. (*Source*: Museum of Hei Long Jiang Province)

movement and mixing of activities seem to follow precisely from the lack of specialized architecture.

The theme of family silk-making and other family businesses such as farming was portrayed in many other Song era paintings. Such paintings were highly praised by the Song government and were imitated by some court painters during succeeding dynasties. The artist Lou Chou who lived during the Southern Song period, for example, produced twenty-one paintings of farming families and twenty-four paintings of silk-making families. He also accompanied each painting with a poem. Another artist, Liu Songnian, was rewarded by the Emperor for his paintings on a similar theme. Unfortunately, the original paintings of these artists are lost and only copies produced during the Yuan, Ming and Qing dynasties have been preserved, but all show the same pattern of home as a place of production. While we may doubt the 'objectivity' of the late court painters, the subjects they painted were derived from real life. The paintings invariably present peaceful, content and self-sufficient family lives in which working activities seem to integrate seamlessly with everything else (figure 11.6).

Figure 11.6. Silk fabrication in a domestic house, reproduced by author from *Geng Zhi Tu* 耕织图, 1696, by the court painter of the Qing dynasty.

A similar picture of family life emerges from biographies written during the same period. Economic activities were interwoven with domestic life and with community interaction. In fact, helping neighbours (and sometimes newcomers) in both settling and setting-up business appears to have been a social norm. In a chapter titled 'folk-custom', Meng Yuanlao described life in Kaifeng in the following positive terms:

When people from outside moved into the neighbourhood, neighbours would lend them [utensils or tools] to assist their settlement and living, present them with soup and tea, and guide them in business… The owners of big wine shops would lend silver utensils worth three to five hundred cash to small shop owners if they had bought wine from their stores several times. For poor families, if they were buying food and drink, the wine shop then would use silver utensils to deliver service. For some families who wanted to drink over night, a pick up [for silver utensils] would be arranged the next day. This service was even extended to the brothels on a regular basis. (Meng, 1982, p. 31)

This paragraph illustrates that the benefits of social interaction (partially following from spatial propinquity) and those of economic advancement were perceived not merely as complementary but as virtually indistinguishable from each other. The 'natural' goal of business – to provide service and make a profit – seems to have coincided with an impulse to maintain good relationships among neighbours. The boundary between the two goals was in fact hard to discern; emotional and economic gains were considered virtually coincidental. The built forms of the merchants of the Song era seem to have both reflected and reinforced this amalgamated lifestyle.

Itinerant Diversity: The Experiences of Scholar-Officials

Unlike merchants, Tang-Song era scholars searched for semi-solitary living in order to cultivate their selfhood and intellect. Like the merchants, most lived in the busy city. However, their dwellings exhibited a clearer demarcation between private and public. The homes were modest with small gardens, which were enclosed from the street in order to accommodate privacy. The scholars have valued both vibrant community life and quiet solitude. In fact, they saw the porosity of the public-private border, the constant switching between serenity and boisterousness, as the ideal form of living. Luo Ye, a Tang poet, described this ideal in the opening couplet of *On the Canglang Gorge*:

Facing the red dust (mundane life), the gate opens every day;
Entering the gate, one's mind becomes distant from the realm of dust.

(Cited and translated in Yang, 2003, p. 54)

The house sheltered scholars from the urban hustle and bustle, and allowed them a reflective existence, but without eliminating the possibility of merging with city life. Liu Yuxi (772–842 AD), a Tang litterateur and philosopher, depicted the two opposite landscapes (and states of mind) that his house allowed him to experience:

In front of the gate, there is the road to Luoyang;
Inside the gate, there is the path to Peach Blossom Spring.
Between the dusty ground and the misty rosy clouds,
There are only a dozen paces

(Cited and translated in Yang, 2003, p. 53)

Scholar-officials typically supported themselves through their writing or painting (in addition to receiving a moderate government stipend). Their working activities, understood largely as mental labour, could be naturally integrated into private living.

A house and a garden with a variety of plants yielded serene delight and allowed the occupant to practice his craft. Sima Guang (1019–1086 AD), a pre-eminent historian and writer during the Northern Song dynasty, expressed some reluctance to go outside his home to meet a close friend in the poem *In Reply to Shao Yaofu's 'Chanting of My Business in the Nest of Peace and Joy'*:

Your carefree mind idles at ease day in and day out;
The whence of your peace and joy is not to be sought from without.
Gentle drizzle and chilly wind call for sitting alone;
Warm weather and fine scenery invite sauntering in leisure.
Pine trees and bamboos are enough to win your favourable look;
Peach and plum flowers may well be put on your white head.
Although I take the writing of the book as my business,
For you I will steal a moment to climb the tower.

(Cited and translated in Yang, 2003, pp. 216–217)

According to Stephen Owen, the intellectual's plea for privacy, in literature at least, was ultimately a form of social display. Through public declarations, the scholar-officials attempted to legitimize their private domain as independent from the omnipresent monarchy (Owen, 1996, pp. 101–102). Unlike the merchant classes, whose experiences were defined by intertwining living and working and by active social engagement, many Song scholars, like Sima Guang, claimed to prefer more secluded, private lives. However, they did not shy away from social experiences. Economically, as earlier noted, they depended on a government stipend and/or income from intellectual production, which enabled them to detach themselves partially from a fixed workplace and to have freedom to participate in various social activities. But the imperial monarchy often deemed their careers futile. A dilemma thus arose for scholar-officials: their disappointment pushed them to withdraw from society, but their emotional impulse to serve their communities brought them back to the city. Further, their intellectual inspiration did not come only from serene private reflection but also from engaging with the public world outside. Thus, their ideal lifestyles were perhaps best defined by the notion of 'middling hermit' – a term coined by Bai Juyi (772–846 AD), a renowned Tang poet. In his poem *Middling Hermit*, written in 829 AD, Bai Juyi vividly illustrated the scholar-officials' attitude towards urban living. Indeed, 'great' scholars could only reside in the busy cities, he claimed; only 'petty' ones would choose to disengage themselves from an active social life:

Great hermits reside in the capital;
Petty hermits go into the mountains.
In the mountains it is too desolate;
In the capital it is too boisterous.
It would be better to be a middling hermit:
Hiding in the Regency in the Eastern Capital.

As if in office, as if in seclusion,
Neither busy, nor idle.

…

It is only this middle hermit
Who can live in both prosperity and peace.

(Cited and translated in Yang, 2003, pp. 38–39)

The 'enjoyable' way of life, illustrated by the poem, consisted of serenity, boisterousness, work, retirement, recreation, sociability and so on; life was meant to be experienced in many different places. Scholar-officials had no financial need to confine themselves to a single workplace as merchants did. They were more flexible and could engage with various aspects of urban life by integrating them into their daily itineraries. In this sense, the scholar-officials' diversity of experiences had little to do with particular architectural structures; it was a matter of deliberate movement from place to place.

This trait was especially pronounced in the lives of those intellectuals who dedicated themselves to serving their communities. Shao Yong (1011–1077 AD), a Northern Song philosopher, refused to be an official and led a hermit's life. In 1049 AD, he moved to Luoyang (the second capital city in the Tang dynasty) and lived on an income from teaching. Admiring Shao Yong for being so erudite and righteous, members of many social groups were honoured to become his acquaintance. He named his house, which was given to him by other scholar-officials who were his friends, the 'lotus land'. Shao set his agenda for participating in local community life according to the changing seasons. 'Go out in February for spring and return home in April because of the hot summer. Go out in August and back in November because of the cold winter' (Shao, 1997, p. 222). 'Every time he went outside he would receive warm welcomes from various people, even children and slaves. Every household he visited he would be greeted by people with cordiality and drink… Even for the most private affairs, people would consult him if they had some unsettling concern to resolve. Indeed, there are more than ten families who built their houses exactly the same to Shao Yong's *lotus land*, in order to make him feel comfortable when visiting' (*Ibid.*, p. 223). Shao Yong's popularity and his engagement with the local community were perhaps unparalleled. However, many other Song scholars, who did not hold political posts nor lived as hermits, chose a life of service (see Huang, 2006, chapter 9).

The scholars also craved diverse leisure experiences. Huang Tingjian (1045–1105 AD), a scholar-official and a renowned poet and calligrapher during the Northern Song period, was expelled from the court by a new political party in 1094 AD and demoted to the Prefect of Yizhou in Guangxi Province in his later years. He wrote a diary called *Yizhou Jia Cheng* which recorded many details of his daily life in Yizhou. Take, for example, his bathing activity as described in 1105 AD:

On 17th January (lunar calendar), I accompanied Yuan Min (a guest) having a bath in a domicile near the stone bridge at Southern Gate.
On 19th February, in fine weather, I took a bath at Shi Qing Zhi Fu (the name of the bath place).

On 24th April, a sunny day, I had a bath at a domicile in the city south.

On 30th May, rainy, I took a bath at Chong Ning (a Taoist temple). (Huang, 1983, pp. 73–75)

Clearly, Huang Tingjian did not always bath in the same place; he consciously sought a diversity of places and people. Yizhou, a small town remote from the capital, apparently provided him with these options. Undoubtedly, for scholar-officials who lived in the capital, the choices were much richer.

As a unique social group, scholar-officials aimed to transcend social hierarchy, and engage with both the court and local communities. Their economic standing and social attitudes (driven by the pursuit neither of money nor of power) enabled them to enjoy lifestyles that were both solitary and social. For them, individuality and sociality were equally important and could be experienced both sequentially and simultaneously. Scholars switched freely between private and public space; this constant switching gave them the ultimate delight. Their private dwelling was separated from the public domain but the richness of their lives came from their conscientious pursuit of diverse living trajectories. Thus, their preferred lifestyles were a mixture of experiences arranged in a dynamic spatio-temporal sequence.

Discussion and Conclusion: Mixed Use and Diversity

What do we learn about mixed use and diversity of social experiences from medieval China? Does it help us better understand the connection between diversity and spatial forms? Can diversity, functional and social, be strengthened through particular architectural actions?

Before addressing these questions, let us summarize the findings. Tang-Song-era merchants focused on their business; they enjoyed gregarious communal lives and had no taste for solitude. They lived in houses where living was mixed with work. The architecture of their homes did not reflect functional specialization and they saw the street as a place where they could extend their everyday living and business practices (figure 11.3). For the merchants, then, there was little physical demarcation between private lives and public domain. Scholar-officials, on the other hand, as a prestigious social group following Confucian tradition, were not expected to engage in labour production. Instead, they were responsible for teaching social virtues through their intellectual prowess (Ch'ü, 1967, pp. 235–250). They balanced social responsibility with individualism, which strengthened during the Tang-Song period. The scholar-official's life was constantly oscillating between the private and public spheres. A modest house with a garden in the city allowed for private reflection without eliminating the possibility of rich social experiences. In fact the scholar-official purposefully sought diverse social engagements as integral to his intellectual nature and mission.

These findings suggest that the spatial organization of people's activities was linked to their social and economic position. In other words, it was the larger social forces that structured individuals' lifestyles and spatial experiences. It is incontrovertible that individuals are not rigidly held to any single living pattern. Indeed, the patterns discussed above are only general. In reality, people's daily lives crossed patterns due to their individual preferences and social mobility. To a certain extent, living patterns are resistant to change through physical intervention alone (Winkel, 1986, p. 243). The changing urban fabric during the Tang-Song period, notably the transformation of market place to street market, for instance, did not lead to significant modification in merchants' lives. At the same time, as people's social positions changed, so did their spatial preferences, at least to an extent.

From the historic evidence it is not clear that spatial, functional or architectural diversity will necessarily lead individuals to live more socially active lives. There may be some connection: merchants lived closest to the public sphere and experienced it most intensely. But scholar-officials lived in private dwellings yet purposefully sought diverse experiences because they perceived them necessary to fulfil their social responsibility. Because of the ambiguous connection between spatial diversity and diversity of social experiences, Yi-Fu Tuan remains unconvinced by the four conditions of diversity proposed by Jacobs. He argues: 'To live in a neighborhood of exuberant diversity may not be to everyone's taste, even if it were generally considered desirable' (Tuan, 1982, pp. 195–196). Indeed, introverts may keep themselves isolated even if they live in an exuberant community.

In terms of the relationship between architectural configuration and living diversity, our historical case study also shows an obscure connection. Traditional Chinese architecture, as Xu Yinong (2009) states, is markedly different from its European counterpart which exhibits the different social institutions by building type. Construction methods in pre-modern China, including building materials, styles of architecture, structural frames and joinery details, followed a universal norm. Different social institutions were not manifested by 'self-assertive structures', but rather by people's activities in and around these premises (Xu, 2009). Li Jie (1035–1110 AD), a Song scholar-official in charge of the imperial building department, faithfully recorded all the construction methods and details in his *Ying Zao Fa Shi* – the first official book on architecture and construction preserved to date in Chinese history. The building forms for palace halls, great temples, and the halls of official houses, illustrated in this book, though varied in scale, were identical in principle (Li, 1954). For domestic housing, there was indeed a rigid hierarchy, legitimized by sumptuary laws, which codified the scale and decoration of buildings according to the owner's social position (Wang, 1955, p. 575). These articulations were achieved through multiplying standard modules and formulated patterns of decoration. The architectural forms of commoners' and officials' houses were not much different in essence. Xu (2009) also observes that 'the basic cleavages in building form [of traditional Chinese society] in a certain sub-cultural region were those of social hierarchy, not those between diverse social institutions'.

It was during the Song dynasty that commercial buildings became widespread. Yet their architectural treatment was the same as that of domestic houses. A sumptuary law enacted in 1036 AD, seemed to grant commercial buildings the same significance as officials' residences:

For scholars and commoners houses, if they were not shops or lofty pavilions facing the street, could neither apply flying-roof on four sides of the building, nor use *dou ba* [a particular ceiling treatment] inside. (Li, 1995, p. 2798)

Features like the 'flying-roof' and 'dou ba' were previously only allowed in officials' houses (Yuan, 1977, p. 3600). Then, these physical treatments were applied to commercial buildings. In other words, there was no particular architectural treatment specific to commercial buildings. Even the timber barriers used to block the traffic at the front gate of official buildings were widely used in commercial premises for creating a sense of privilege for their customers. Indeed, private houses and business premises took on a similar architectural appearance during the Song era. This is also evidenced in Zhang Zeduan's *Qing Ming Shang He Tu*, where the physical forms of private houses and commercial premises were presented as almost identical. Different business premises were advertised through their signs either attached to or erected at the front of the buildings (figure 11.1).

Furthermore, even in the early Tang period, as Victor (Cunrui) Xiong has pointed out, different religious places were haphazardly developed throughout the residential areas, and many domestic houses were converted to religious premises without any alteration (Xiong, 2000, pp. 235–276). This adaptive reuse of house as monastery (or school, or government compound) and *vice versa* was widely practiced across the country, and it was recorded in many biographies of cities from the Tang to the Qing dynasties.[7] In that sense, traditional Chinese architecture did not specifically convey the variety of underlying urban institutions through physical form (much like the dwelling's variety of uses was not reflected in the architecture of Tang-Song merchants' houses). However, through a ubiquitous wood frame structure, the architecture offered flexibility for both internal division and external fenestration. 'A single structure or a building complex in traditional China rarely altered its form when its use was changed' Xu Yinong (2009) states; 'it was not designed for a single function in the first place, but rather built as a generic, enabling setup that intrinsically was meant to accommodate multifarious and alternating uses'. Different ways to appropriate a building were a matter of individual needs and preferences. The mixed-use urban fabric was an incidental success which allowed for the clustering of individual actions. Mixed use was neither designed nor anticipated; in fact it was forged under a rather loose regulatory environment. Certainly, nobody planned or 'zoned' for diversity in medieval China. No architectural codification was in play; rather, it was the uniformity of architecture that allowed for fluidity of uses.

The connection between mixed use and diversity thus seems to have at least two different interpretations. The first is Jacobs's: that the physical configuration of buildings encourages a variety of uses and demographics and provides for richer social experiences (Jacobs, 1969, pp. 252–253). The second is that the diversity of people's everyday lives may occur in various places and that no architectural codification of diversity is possible. It seems that the first interpretation does not quite work in practice (even though many architects and planners expect it to), in part because a community is always shaped by larger forces (e.g. social, political and economic) rather than design. 'No individual or group' as Tuan argues, 'has the power to call these large diffuse forces into being and direct their paths toward the re-creation of a richly textured society' (Tuan, 1982, pp. 195–196). Gans similarly criticized Jacobs's ideas as 'the physical fallacy', because 'it leads her to ignore the social, cultural, and economic factors that contribute to vitality or dullness' (Gans, 1968, p. 28). He points out that 'Visibility is not the only measure of vitality', and continues, 'areas that are uninteresting to the visitor may be quite vital to the people who live in them' (*Ibid.*, p. 29).

Today, most mixed-use developments take the form of vertical 'zoning' which formulaically designates the lower podium for commercial uses and the upper floors for housing. But often, each component has its own entry and independent circulation. There is little interaction between the two components, let alone free switching of activities. Without inquiry into individual living patterns, the argument that 'suburban development is monotonous' seems dubious, as the person who lives in a suburban house may have a lifestyle much richer spatially than a person who lives in a mixed-use apartment building. The theory that architecture acquires its meaning largely through daily habitation, rather than through physical treatment, has been well elucidated by Xing Ruan in his seminal book *Allegorical Architecture* (2006). Urban diversity is a series of living trajectories drawn by different individuals through their daily experiences. It cannot be well understood from a fragmented scene (local area or street), nor can it be reproduced by planning at a certain physical site. In most modern mixed-use buildings, for example, those who live on the upper floors do not normally work at the lower floors. In fact, the retail spaces are usually used by people who live elsewhere, often far away.

Through this historical inquiry, I have demonstrated that diversity in China during the Tang-Song era was produced by interwoven daily human practices. It was certainly not produced by any conscious planning or design. Mixed-use space was thus a result and an expression of living diversity. It was a legible text produced by life. However, it is doubtful that the text itself can create urban diversity.

Notes

1. In another article, I contrast the lifestyles of merchants and scholar-officials with those of the aristocracy.
2. Harrison Salisbury, comments on *The Death and Life of Great American Cities*, on the back cover of the book.
3. The system of Romanization of Chinese in this chapter is pinyin. Unless noted, all translation from Chinese is by the author.
4. The Song dynasty is divided into two distinct periods: the Northern Song (960–1127 AD) and the Southern Song (1127–1279 AD). During the Northern Song dynasty, the capital was in the northern city of Bianjing (now Kaifeng). The Southern Song dynasty refers to the period after the Song lost control of northern China to the Jin dynasty. During this period, the Song court retreated to the south of the Yangtze River and established their capital at Lin'an (now Hangzhou).
5. Evidence of how the people from the lower classes lived is much scarcer. Most of the poor had little freedom and many were basically homeless.
6. Household size varied during the Song dynasty. According to Song literature, the average family

had ten members: say, six adults and four children. Most families had two or three generations living together (Tan, 2008, pp. 251–252).

7. Chinese literature for example, Song Minqiu宋敏求 (Song) *Chang'an Zhi*长安志 (Zhong Hua Shu Ju, 1991), for the city of Chang'an (the Tang Capital); Li Lian李濂 (Ming) *Bianjing Yi Ji Zhi* 汴京遗迹志 (Zhong Hua Shu Ju, 1999), for the city of Kaifeng (the Northern Song Capital); Lu Guangwei陆广微 (Tang) *Wudi Ji*吴地记 (Jiangsu Ancient Literature Press, 1999), for the city of Suzhou.

References

Ch'ü, T'ung-Tsu (1967) Chinese class structure and its ideology, in Fairbank, J.K. (ed.) *Chinese Thought and Institutions*. Chicago, IL: University of Chicago Press.

Duany, A., Plater-Zyberk, E. and Speck, J. (2000) *Suburban Nation: The Rise of Sprawl and the Decline of the American Dream*. New York: North Point Press.

Duany, A. and Talen, E. (2002) Making the good easy: the smart code alternative. *Fordham Urban Law Journal*, **29**(4), pp. 1445–1468.

Ebrey, P.B. (1999) *Cambridge Illustrated History of China*. Cambridge: Cambridge University Press.

Evans, R. (1997) *Translations from Drawing to Building and Other Essays*. Cambridge, MA: MIT Press.

Foucault, M. (1977) *Discipline and Punish, the Birth of the Prison*. New York: Penguin Books.

Gans, H.J. (1968) *People and Plans: Essays on Urban Problems and Solutions*. New York: Basic Books.

Gernet, J. (1962) *Daily Life in China, on the Eve of the Mongol Invasion 1250–1276*. Translated by H.M. Wright. Stanford, CA: Stanford University Press.

Heng, C.K. (1999) *Cities of Aristocrats and Bureaucrats: The Development of Medieval Chinese Cityscapes*. Honolulu, HI: University of Hawaii Press.

Hibbert, C. (1988) *Venice, the Biography of A City*. New York: Grafton Books.

Huang Tingjian 黄庭坚 (1983) (*Song*) Yizhou Jia Cheng 宜州家乘, in *Bi Ji Xiao Shuo Da Guan*, 笔记小 说大观 第十册. Yangzhou: Jiangsu Guangling Ancient Literature Press, chapter 10.

Huang Yunhe 黄云鹤 (2006) *Research of the Tang-Song Lower Scholar-Officials* 唐宋下层士人研究. Shijiazhuang: Hebei People's Press.

Jacobs, J. (1969) *The Death and Life of Great American Cities*. New York: The Modern Library.

Krier, L. (1984) House, palaces, cities. *Architectural Design*, **54**(7/8).

Kuhn, D. (2009) *The Age of Confucian Rule: The Song Transformation of China*. Cambridge, MA: Belknap/ Harvard University Press.

Levitas, G. (1986) Anthropology and sociology of streets, in Anderson, S. (ed.) *On Streets*. Cambridge, MA: MIT Press, pp. 225–240.

Li Jie 李诫 (1954) (Song) *Ying Zao Fa Shi* 营造法式. Shang Wu Ying Shu Guan.

Li Tao李焘 (1995) (Song) *Xu Zi Zhi Tong Jian Chang Pian* 续资治通鉴长篇. Shanghai: Zhong Hua Shu Ju.

Liu, J.T.C. (1959) *Reform in Sung China*. Cambridge, MA: Harvard University Press.

Liu, J.T.C. and Golas, P.J. (eds.) (1969) *Change in Sung China: Innovation or Renovation*. Washington DC: Heath.

Lynch, K. (1960) *The Image of the City*. Cambridge, MA: MIT Press.

Ma Dezhi 马德志 (1982) Chang'an and Luoyang in the Tang Dynasty 唐代长安与洛阳. *Archeology*考 古. **6**, pp. 642–645.

Ma Duanlin马端临 (1986) (Yuan) *Wen Xian Tong Kao* 文献通考. Zhong Hua Shu Ju.

Ma, L.J.C. (1971) *Commercial Development and Urban Change in Sung China 960–1279*. Ann Arbor, MI: Department of Geography, University of Michigan.

Meng Yuanlao 孟元老 (1982) (Song) *Dong Jing Meng Hua Lu* 东京梦华录. Shanghai: China Commercial Press.

Owen, S. (1996) *The End of The Chinese 'Middle Ages': Essays in Mid-Tang Literary Culture*. Stanford, CA: Stanford University Press.

Ruan, X. (2006) *Allegorical Architecture: Living Myth and Architectonics in Southern China*. Honolulu, HI: University of Hawaii Press.

Shao Bowen 邵伯温 (1997) (Song) *Shao Shi Wen Jian Lu* 邵氏闻见录. Shanghai: Zhong Hua Shu Ju.

Shatzman Steinhardt, N. (1990) *Chinese Imperial City Planning*. Honolulu, HI: University of Hawaii Press.

Tan Gangyi 谭刚毅 (2008) *Chinese Housing and Morphology in Northern and Southern Song Periods* 两宋时期的中国民居与居住形态. Nanjing: Southeast University Press.

Tuan, Y.F. (1982) *Segmented Worlds and Self, Group Life and Individual Consciousness*. Minneapolis, MN: University of Minnesota Press.

Twitchett, D. (1966) The Tang market system. *Asian Major*, **12**(2), pp. 202–248.

Wang Pu 王溥 (1955) (Song) *Tang Hui Yao* 唐会要. Shanghai: Zhong Hua Shu Ju.

Ward, H. (1919) *A Writer's Recollections*. London: W. Collins Sons.

Winkel, G.H. (1986) Some human dimensions of urban design, in Anderson, S. (ed.) *On Streets*. Cambridge, MA: MIT Press, pp. 241–248..

Wu Xiaoliang 吴晓亮 (2005) Changing urban life and consumption in the Tang-Song societies. 从城市生活变化看唐宋社会的消费变迁. *China Economic History Research*, **5**, pp. 83–87.

Xiong, V.C. (2000) *Sui-Tang Chang'an: A Study in the Urban History of Medieval China*. Ann Arbor, MI: University of Michigan.

Xu Yinong (2009) Legacy from the past, impetus for the future: notes on architectural adaptive reuse. *World Architecture*, No. 230, pp. 115–121.

Xue Pingshuan 薛平拴 (2006) The prosperity and the cause of commerce in the Sui-Tang Chang'an. 隋唐长安商业市场的繁荣及其原因. *Journal of Shanxi Normal University* (*Philosophy and Social Sciences Edition*), **35**(3), pp. 89–95.

Yang Xiaoshan (2003) *Metamorphosis of the Private Sphere, Gardens and Objects in Tang-Song Poetry*. Cambridge, MA: Harvard University Asia Center.

Yuan Tuotuo 元脱脱 (*et al.*) (1977) (Yuan) *Song Shi* 宋史. Shanghai: Zhong Hua Shu Ju.

Acknowledgement

This topic is part of my PhD thesis. I would like to thank my mentor Professor Xing Ruan for his constant support and guidance. I am highly indebted to the editors, particularly Professor Sonia Hirt, for her constructive comments and tremendous help in reshaping and polishing my writing. I am also grateful to Professor David B. Brownlee (the first reader of the draft chapter) for his critique and encouragement and Dr John Blair for his editorial assistance.

Chapter 12

Jane Jacobs's Relevance in Beirut

Ibrahim Maarouf and Hassan Abdel-Salam

This chapter considers Jane Jacobs's book *The Death and Life of Great American Cities* and whether the ideas presented there are still relevant. Specifically, the chapter is an attempt to correlate the general principles in Jacobs's writings with the current state of revitalization in the Beirut Central District (BCD).

Lebanon has come under foreign rule on many occasions in its history, and the physical and social environment of Beirut reflects this multicultural past as well as the city's proximity to the other cultures of the Mediterranean region. Both city and nation have experienced periods of political, civil and military conflict, followed by periods of rebuilding, evolution and change.

By 1832, during the Egyptian occupation, Beirut's political and economic significance was on the rise. A map of the city from that era reveals the irregularity of both street patterns and general development (figure 12.1).

The Ottomans introduced modern urbanism to Beirut in 1878, reorganizing the city following the model of Turkish ports such as Istanbul. Two perpendicular axes intersected the old town, linking the port to the roads to Damascus and Sidon, and reaffirming a strong relationship between the city centre and the seaport. These elements were retained in future plans for the city.

During the late nineteenth and early twentieth centuries, major changes in the urban morphology and building types of Beirut's centre were introduced. Khans or caravansaries, the traditional inns for travelling merchants and traders (Hillenbrand, 1994, pp. 331, 598), were converted into office buildings, and land lots reshaped into different parcels and sizes (Saliba, 2004). These changes brought some positive transformations, new functions and urban infill, and thus added numerous assets to the physical fabric. But some changes were problematic as they did not respect the local built heritage and instead chose to remodel it following erroneously (as Jane Jacobs would have likely argued) various foreign urban utopian ideas, from the Garden City to the Radiant City.

Beirut became a secondary trading port in the 1910s, as economic activities shifted from inland caravan towns to coastal cities. The city centre was subjected to several dramatic transformations affecting the sizes of both buildings and parcels of land. From the early twentieth century onwards, and until the new BCD project, the ideas of the utopian movements became the dominant paradigms of restructuring in Beirut, as they did elsewhere. Take, for example, the remodelling of the district carried out in the 1930s. The Danger brothers' plan[1] imposed a clear separation between public uses and private housing – something which was not part of the local built heritage. This kind of rigid separation creates conditions unfavourable both to diversity and to safety, which are two prerequisites for any liveable city. Ebenezer Howard's ideas

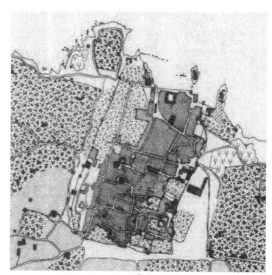

Figure 12.1. Planning of Beirut according to British army maps, 1841. (*Source*: Saliba, 2004, p. 66)

Figure 12.2. The 1932 plan of central Beirut prepared by the Danger brothers. (*Source*: Saliba, 2004, p. 77)

appear to have been the Dangers' main inspiration. The influence of the City Beautiful and Le Corbusier's Radiant City can be seen in the Grand Axis that was formed by the positioning of various towers within the BCD zone. More recent development activity, such as the Beirut International Exhibition and Leisure Complex (BIEL) (opened in 2001) also hark back to the ideas of these utopian movements.

By the French Mandate Period of the 1920s, the city's medieval fabric had been lost. It was reorganized on a radial-grid layout, with orthogonal and star-shaped geometry (in Foch-Allenby and Etoile respectively). These produced a large diversity of block and parcel configurations and sizes (Saliba, 2004, pp. 65–122; figures 12.2 and 12.3). The French army engineer, Camille Duraffourd presented a proposal for the layout of new streets in the city in 1926, which the Dangers used as the basis for their 1932 plan for Beirut (see figure 12.2). The Armenian architect, Mardiros Altounian won the competition for the 'Etoile Clock Tower' in that same year. According to Saliba (2004):

The present Etoile sector corresponds to the upper town, which extended to the southern city walls. It grouped local markets and crafts, as well as the city's main administrative and communal activities. Characterized by narrow and winding alleyways, the upper town was marked by a set of squares. Some of these squares were equipped with fountains, or bordered with cafes. In contrast with the works undertaken to enlarge and modernize the port, the old town was increasingly perceived as a barrier to the flow of people and goods. Hence the idea emerged of cutting through the urban fabric to connect harbour to periphery, using straight arteries to improve linkage to the regional trade route.

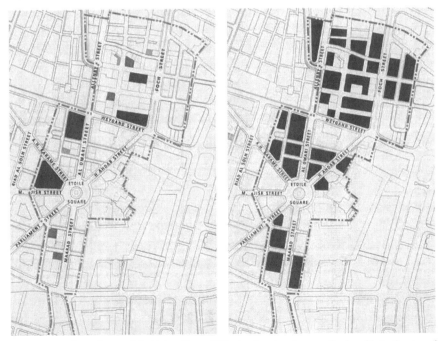

Figure 12.3. Plans of parts of the Beirut Central District showing the overall urban fabric, the size of blocks and parcels (*left*), and building footprints (*right*). (*Source*: Saliba, 2004, p. 88)

By the 1930s, the increasing popularity of movies, and the opening of the 'Grand Theatre', paved the way for new types of buildings in different areas of the city. Multi-use commercial centres – for example, the landmark Lazariya and Starco commercial complexes – soon followed (1940s to 1960s). Saliba (2004) asserts that 'along with the modernization of the urban fabric, the buildings themselves underwent an accelerated process of structural, spatial and stylistic change. Commercial, administrative and public structures took the lead over residential structures in terms of technological and stylistic innovation'.

Beirut's diverse history and character is most visible in the BCD, which is a source of pride for the local community. In a description of the historic centre, Solidere, the Lebanese Company for the Development and Reconstruction of Beirut Central District, explains that the area has been continuously inhabited for more than 5,000 years, with civilizations from the Canaanite to the Ottoman leaving their mark on an ever growing, culturally rich and sophisticated city. Beirut's centre was traditionally the focus of activity in a major regional capital and has long included a rich variety of functions: banking, business and commerce; government and parliament; education and culture; and leisure. The city centre also contains charming residential neighbourhoods and was home to a hotel district, which in the early 1900s was considered exceptionally modern for its time.

Today, the BCD is a hub for investment, trade, tourism and culture. The District contains a high concentration of historic buildings, with a blend of local and European architectural styles.

Following the widespread destruction and damage caused by the civil war (figure 12.4), the BCD has, since the early 1990s, been undergoing extensive renovation and rapid transformation. Solidere has been entrusted with revitalizing a 191 hectare (472 acre) area in the BCD.[2] The company's scheme aims to restore the District's physical character and its historic buildings, and to re-establish a sense of place.

Figure 12.4. Destruction in Beirut Central District in the aftermath of the devastating civil war which lasted from 1975 to 1990. (*Source:* Trawi, 2003, p.114)

The current rebuilding of central Beirut will bring about significant changes to the city's physical and social structure. Thus, we argue that there is an urgent need to examine this process, because it could ultimately threaten the BCD's rich cultural and architectural heritage, its complex urban morphology, and its diverse socioeconomic characteristics. We therefore propose a systematic review of Solidere's revitalization plans based on the values and beliefs outlined by Jane Jacobs in *The Death and Life of Great American Cities*.

Our evaluation is in three sections. The first briefly summarizes the relevant ideas of Jane Jacobs and their application to the BCD revitalization project. The next examines the BCD revitalization project in detail, and the lessons learned from that experience. The final section offers recommendations that should guide future development in Beirut's City Centre, and considers whether the Beirut example supports the applicability of Jacobs's ideas in other contexts worldwide. We conclude that the problems of cities that Jacobs discussed in her book can, and do, exist today, in a variety of locations and settings – and the Beirut Central District is a pertinent example.

Revisiting Jacobs:
Key Ideas for the Beirut Central District Revitalization Plan

When *The Death and Life* was first published in 1961, it generated widespread debate. Jacobs dared to suggest that the newly rebuilt neighbourhoods she observed around her were not safe, interesting or lively, nor were they economically good for cities. Jacobs emphasized the need for planners and designers to understand how cities work in real life. She drew attention to the flaws of urban renewal, and the negative impacts renewal was having on the lives and opportunities of urban dwellers.

Fifty years later, Jacobs's ideas still attract attention, not only in America but worldwide, and Beirut is a good example. Because it can be argued that the BCD is now undergoing the same sort of revitalization and renewal that Jacobs criticized in her book, it is essential that we understand Jacobs's claims and then consider the degree to which her views are applicable to the project in today's Beirut Central District.

According to Jacobs's philosophy on successful city revitalization, multiple tactics are available for converting cities from a near-death situation to a vibrant and liveable one. These tactics may also be applicable to the Beirut Central District's redevelopment. Below is a concise review of the key ideas in *The Death and Life* that are relevant to the revitalization of the BCD.

1. *Revitalize, but retain*: Jacobs understood the need to 'un-slum the slums'. She supported the renewal and revitalization of decaying neighbourhoods when this included residential and business opportunities for existing residents and property owners so that they could remain in the neighbourhood. Jacobs believed that long-term engagement and investment were critical to the on-going success of a neighbourhood. Thus, residents need access to public and/or private financing, housing subsidies, etc.

2. *Support diversity*: According to Jacobs, a 'great' city is comprised of multiple districts or neighbourhoods. Each of these neighbourhoods must provide for the needs of a broad array of property owners, businesses, residents, and visitors; and this necessarily requires a mix of land uses throughout the neighbourhood.

3. *Create connectivity*: Sidewalks and streets are key elements of public space. They carry people in, around, and through the neighbourhood. The goal is to provide for and encourage pedestrian activity throughout the neighbourhood, and at all times of the day and into the evening. Therefore, residents and visitors walking in the neighbourhood must feel welcome and safe, and safety is an outcome of lively use of the sidewalks, enhanced by people watching from nearby buildings. Pedestrian movement is enhanced by using a design that includes short blocks and through streets. Motor vehicles detract from the overall character of – and pedestrian opportunities in – a neighbourhood.

4. *Offer variety and improve clarity*: The physical design of the neighbourhood is a critical aspect of both neighbourhood vitality and public safety. Jacobs recognized the qualities that arise out of urban neighbourhoods with 'organized complexity'. She supported variety, a mix of building types/styles/ages/sizes. According to Jacobs, seeming chaos and congestion can enrich and support, rather than inhibit, the life of a neighbourhood; however, visual cues and physical organization are important as well.

The question we will address is whether Solidere's plan for the Beirut Central District, taken within the context of the many changes that the District has experienced over time, incorporates the concepts Jacobs outlines in her book.

In *The Death and Life of Great American Cities*, Jacobs is critical of the utopian urbanisms. She says that Ebenezer Howard, for example, set in motion city-destroying ideas (1961, pp. 18–19). According to Jacobs, Howard believed that the city's functions could be sorted into a set of simple uses and arranged in relative self-containment. Howard focused on the provision of 'wholesome' housing, defined in terms of suburban physical qualities and small-town social qualities. He was not interested in issues such as how cities police themselves, exchange ideas, operate politically, or invent new economic arrangements. Jacobs also noted that followers of Le Corbusier and the Radiant City favoured institutionalization, mechanization, and depersonalization (*Ibid.*, pp. 22–23). At the time, their attempts to make planning for the automobile an integral part of urban redevelopment may have seemed an exciting idea that conceptualized the city as a wonderful mechanical toy.

Looking at some of the recently added building complexes, Beirut seems to be infected with the same problems that Jacobs identified elsewhere, since both Howard and Le Corbusier have influenced its remodelling. Beirut's history corroborates Jacobs's criticism of both the Garden City and the Radiant City (*Ibid.*, p. 24). In many parts of the city, the negative impacts of importing foreign utopian notions could be seen. Current problems include the loss of the original mix of functions, and the shrinking of visible activities into limited places and times of day. Also to be noted are the over-emphasis on vehicular accessibility/mobility through the urban centre, the shift in local residents' socioeconomic character, the heavy infiltration by offices and business uses (at the expense of residential uses), and the widespread gentrification and mounting speculation in real-estate prices (Abdel-Salam and Maarouf, 2011).

The current BCD revival scheme centres on rehabilitation by the public sector boosted by private sector investment. Solidere works as a public-private partnership. The public sector oversees implementation of the project's objectives, and deals with overcoming bureaucratic obstacles. Solidere, as a private firm, is working on property consolidation, by grouping landlords and others into one integral body of shareholders. The company's operations and management techniques are ostensibly aimed at creating a sustainable business environment that will attract commercial and corporate enterprises. Solidere hopes that businesses will be drawn by the quality development it offers, as well as by its skilful property management.

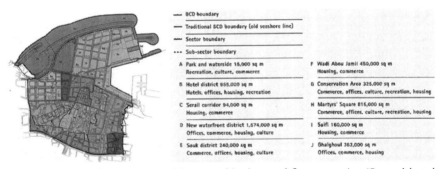

Figure 12.5. BCD planning sectors with proposed land use and floor area ratios. (*Source*: Adapted from Saliba, 2004, p. 188)

Solidere's master plan (figure 12.5) attempts to restore and enhance the existing physical fabric of the BCD. Of the 191 hectares the project occupies, around 98 ha will be public spaces, with 59 ha allocated to roads and 39 ha to landscaped open space. Approximately 93 ha are designated for development, including about 22 ha retained for public or religious property. The master plan provides an urban design framework and prescribes a mix of land uses within a total development target of 4.69 million square metres of floor space. The guidelines for the various end-uses (e.g. residential, commercial, or cultural projects) are modifiable depending on market conditions (Solidere, 2011).

The plan retains the surviving street patterns and 265 existing buildings, and carefully restores twenty-six public and religious buildings. It conserves important archaeological sites that were identified under the UNESCO protocol, and reintegrates them into the townscape. In addition, the plan calls for strict design requirements for infill development, as a way to preserve the contextual urban character and scale.

Solidere argues that the new city centre capitalizes on the area's assets and provides a functional and attractive environment. A new clientele, the company believes, will join former residents in occupying restored or modern residential space. Public and private housing come in the form of projects such as Beirut Terraces, District//S, Landmark, Beirut Gardens, Beirut Village, and Al Wadi Grand Residence (figure 12.6). Indeed, several residential projects are currently underway in the city centre. Since most of them are still under construction, their ultimate impact has yet to be revealed.

Figure 12.6. From the left: Beirut Terraces, District//S, and Al Wadi Grand Residence as examples of public and private housing projects in BCD. (*Source*: Order of Engineers and Architects of Beirut, 2010, pp. 20, 21, 61)

Shopping facilities, leisure and cultural activities are to keep the city centre bustling with residents, daily visitors and tourists, well beyond normal business hours (Solidere, 2011). One aim has been to create genuine 'settings' for public contact, recreation, and children's play, supported by a mix of uses. A good example is the Beirut Souks project (figure 12.7). As described by Solidere, this is a modern commercial district located within archeologically rich surroundings. Since the French Mandate period in the 1930s and until the civil unrest in 1975, this location has continually accommodated prosperous and vibrant markets. Solidere ensured the integration of historical aspects

Figure 12.7. Beirut Souks, the new shopping complex – a large-scale development project designed to regenerate commercial activities on the site of the old markets. (*Photos*: the Authors)

into the project's design, in order to reflect its primary role as a portal between the past and the future. An elite group of international and Lebanese architects worked on the design, including award-winning Spanish innovator Rafael Moneo. The project combines aspects of the old Beirut markets by conserving the trail of the historical streets while providing a contemporary architectural vocabulary. This mix between historical features and modern design turned Beirut Souks into an 'open area' offering a distinctive journey that ostensibly goes far beyond the generic shopping-mall experience.

Beirut Souks involves a complex design, with a variety of pedestrian areas, multi-faceted shops, and open spaces. Large numbers of citizens and tourists frequent the Souks, drawn by entertainment activities and cultural events (for example, the many shows that take place at the ends of the Souks' corridors), as well as the shops and cafés. The cafés add an element of mixed activity that includes both entertainment and business.

In addition to the physical changes, new policies and techniques for urban management are being adopted, including joint coordination and scheduling of events and sponsored activities. This is boosting people's sense of safety and the level of outdoor activity by the redesign of open spaces and the re-introduction of amenities and support facilities for outdoor social life.

But, what would Jacobs say about the revitalization project?

What would Jane Jacobs Say?

Revitalize, but retain: Revitalization activity in the Beirut Central District has been significant, but with mixed results. The area has seen an increase in private offices and businesses; however, the BCD real estate market is now subject to gentrification and speculation. Soaring real estate values have, on occasions, led to a reduction in both the sale and renting of properties. Only a small number of families, mostly affluent, can start moving into the newly developed housing units in the area, while local residents and users are being replaced by a wealthier clientele (BAU, 2010). Furthermore, the process of regeneration remains vulnerable, and its implementation is frequently affected by continuing political instability and unrest in Lebanon.

Support diversity: In her discussion about urban variety and vitality, Jacobs stresses the importance of population density and diversity, mixed building uses, short block sizes and buildings of varied age. The land-use plan for BCD shows that approximately 80 per cent of the area is for public and commercial uses and the other 20 per cent of the area is dedicated to residential uses. This means that the area does qualify as mixed-use; however, the original mix of functions is lost. Also, the plan does not encourage, or make enough room for, residential projects.

The new residential projects are randomly distributed within the historic area. On one hand, this hinders the continuity of sidewalk observation, which may translate into less safety. But on the other hand, it creates a much-needed variety of building types and styles. We should ask, though, what kind of variety is generated by this situation? Do the new buildings work with the old? The old buildings are restored and preserved but, we argue, deprived of vitality. Often, the only used spaces within the old buildings are those directly accessible from outdoor entrances at street level. The prices and regulations together impede the use of the upper floors within these older buildings. So, in this case conservation has in some way reduced the building variety and consequently the sense of safety and vitality that may have otherwise been generated by a better mix of new and old construction.

A primary issue in the case of Beirut is that a single private-sector company is operating and managing the redevelopment process and supervising all renovation and new construction. This poses a threat to the ongoing diversity of the district, since all major decisions and day-to-day activities are, in essence, centrally managed. Solidere's primary focus is on the relationship of new projects to older buildings, and on the opportunities for investment, rather than on the mix of uses and the interactions among them. Building codes determine the new buildings' heights, configuration, and relationship with the planned sidewalks. Some stakeholders, especially developers, argue that Solidere is imposing over-stringent planning rules for new projects, which might potentially reduce the district's diversity (Abdel-Salam and Maarouf, 2011).

Our conclusion is that the BCD is not very 'liveable'. Liveable mixed-use districts are areas which people can inhabit, work and play in, in which the various uses are located closely and conveniently (Barr, 2002). Recent academic studies and field surveys of the BCD (BAU, 2010) indicate a perception of dwindling activity and a decreased use of open spaces by residents and visitors alike, at certain times of day, on some specific days and at certain times of year. The key reasons revealed by these surveys include a reduced sense of safety caused by the very few residential projects, the low density and the low numbers of residents; the perception of public functions as fragmented or uncoordinated; and concerns about the absence of public transport and activity-supporting amenities.

To counteract these problems, to enhance the vibrancy of the city centre and create a sustainable level of activities and services, Solidere (2011) has decided to implement temporary activities in the District and to engage in hospitality management as a revenue-generating activity. It is too early to tell whether this approach will work.

Create connectivity: As a result of the infusion of new and revived land uses, some social activity has returned to the BCD. The observable result is a renewed interest in investment and an increase in the number of visitors. Tactics such as the pedestrianization of the built environment, area-wide patrolling, conservation of visual character and well-conceived infill projects could potentially further contribute to the overall rebirth of this promising district. However, alternative plans for vehicles and rerouting of circulation within the district remain limited. This causes problems in terms of accessibility and increased traffic congestion along the peripheral arteries.

Offer variety and improve clarity: Because of the historical references in the design of the Beirut Souks, for example, we see a series of arcades, interconnected open spaces, and alleys, with many access points. There the shops and cafeterias need a high degree of security twenty-four hours a day, seven days a week. But the result has been the installation of a formal protection and security system, making these spaces feel restricted and over-protected. This would not have been necessary, had there been a greater number of residents with their 'eyes on the street'. But, as already stated, because of the limited number of occupied dwelling units in this district, the population density is low. Thus, the development process could be seen as unsuccessful in its inability to create naturally secure places. More residential projects are necessary in order to increase the population density and induce a sense of ownership and territoriality among residents and other users. This would in turn create well-managed urban settings, constantly kept under control by residents, thus deterring crime and violence (Flink, 2009).

Given the discussion above, we would like to add a point with respect to the potential of residential schemes to produce a defensible environment. This can be derived from Jacobs's work as well as Oscar Newman's who was also interested in improving safety, especially in large public housing projects, through territoriality and natural surveillance (Flink, 2009; Newman, 1973). Jacobs addresses safety in her discussion of 'street neighbourhoods'. One of her points relevant in the case of the BCD is related to the importance of maintaining a good balance of public and private uses in new residential blocks.

Jacobs's idea of 'natural' surveillance or 'eyes on the street' can be used as an instrument to improve safety (see also Newman, 1973), including that of the BCD. According to both Jacobs and Newman, housing blocks with a good balance of connected public and private spaces increase the residents' sense of ownership and territoriality and enhance the degree of mutual observation, thus minimizing both crime and fear of crime. But the land-use pattern of central Beirut reveals that housing projects are situated in segmented or disconnected parcels, resulting in a reduced sense of safety.

So, one solution for this kind of problem can be derived from Jacobs's advice to stimulate and catalyze diversity among uses and users. Jacobs would also certainly suggest that the BCD process becomes far more inclusive than it is currently.

Recommendations for the Beirut Central District: Ongoing Lessons from Jacobs

This chapter argued that many key issues presented by Jane Jacobs are still relevant in the case of the BCD. Based on Jane Jacobs's ideas and our own observations, we recommend the following strategies for improving the liveability of the BCD:

◆   Establish a planning committee assigned with the task of studying the land uses of the BCD and their relationship to sidewalks and other infrastructure.

- Establish a local organization which would comprise representatives of different stakeholders, including residents and users of the BCD. This organization should take part in the overall management process, and help develop mechanisms for balancing land prices and housing projects, so that the area can indeed attract a more diverse population.

- Reconsider the uses of old buildings and study the recent regulations, especially those which obstruct the redevelopment process.

- Channel a larger part of investment funds into redeveloping low-income areas and unused buildings within the BCD as well as its vicinity.

- Review the density of the BCD, in terms of population and buildings, and find strategies which can be used to optimize both.

We believe that Jacobs's *The Death and Life of Great American Cities* still presents valuable lessons for the different actors involved in the revitalization and management of cities. Jane Jacobs continues to inspire the debate on the strategies needed to upgrade, revitalize and maintain the quality of urban life far beyond that of 1960s American cities. Studying the development of Beirut's Central District, from its inception into the twenty-first century, illustrates the perennial applicability of Jacobs's ideas. Beirut's current redevelopment led by Solidere seems nominally to reflect some of Jacobs's ideas: mixed uses, preservation of historic buildings, and respect of the local architectural heritage. But the fact that the project is led by a single, large development firm with little participation from local residents goes contrary to Jacobs's core philosophy. Furthermore, the BCD's physical improvements – such as its spectacular new projects sited without relation to one another or the surroundings – seem to have resulted in a built fabric that lacks the true diversity and vitality from which Beirut's citizens would benefit.

Notes

1. The Danger brothers' firm, La Société des plans régulateurs de villes, was active elsewhere in the Near East during the 1930s. See http://archiwebture.citechaillot.fr/awt/fonds.html?base=fa&id=FRAPN02_DANGE_fonds-358. Accessed 10 January 2012. See also Hastaoglou-Martinidis (2011).
2. Solidere was incorporated as a Lebanese joint-stock company in 1994. According to the company's promotional literature, it offers a broad range of land and real estate development services. Solidere (2011) describes itself as combining 'the business independence and acumen of a private company with a global vision and a strong sense of public service'.

References

Abdel-Salam, H. and Maarouf, I. (2011) Local Identity and Cultural Appropriateness: The Rebuilding of Central Beirut. Paper presented at the IX International Forum, Le Vie Dei Mercanti, S.A.V.E. Heritage, Napoli, 9–11 June.

Barr, A. (2002) SoHo, New York: mixed use, density and the power of the myth. *Urban Design Studies*, **8**, pp. 29–48.

BAU (Beirut Arab University) (2010) Field Survey and Case Study of Adaptive Re-Use Potentials in Beirut Central District. Unpublished research conducted by students from Faculty of Architectural Engineering, Beirut Arab University, Spring 2010

Flink, S. (2009) *Million Dollar Blocks*. Montana, MT: Montana State University. Available at http://etd. lib.montana.edu/etd/2009/flink/FlinkS0509.pdf. Accessed 10 February 2012.

Hastaoglou-Martinidis, V. (2011) Urban aesthetics and national identity: the refashioning of the Eastern Mediterranean. *Planning Perspectives*, **26**(2), pp. 153–182.

Hillenbrand, R. (1994) *Islamic Architecture: Form, Function and Meaning*. Edinburgh: Edinburgh University Press.

Jacobs, J. (1961) *The Death and Life of Great American Cities*. New York: Random House.

Newman, O. (1973) *Defensible Space: Crime Prevention Through Urban Design*. New York: Macmillan.

Order of Engineers and Architects of Beirut (2010) International architects in Beirut, special report. *Al Mouhandess*, **25**, November, pp. 15–65.

Saliba, R. (1998) *Beirut 1920–1940: Domestic Architecture between Tradition and Modernity*. Beirut: The Order of Engineers and Architects.

Saliba, R. (2004) *Beirut City Center Recovery: The Foch-Allenby and Etoile Conservation Area*. Gottingen: Steidl.

Shayya, F. (2010) *At the Edge of the City: Reinhabiting Public Space Toward the Recovery of Beirut's Horsh Al-Sanawbar*. Beirut: Discursive Formations.

Solidere (2011) *Beirut City Center*. Available at http://www.solidere.com/solidere.html. Accessed 25 July 2011.

Trawi, A. (2003) *Beirut: The Wars of Destruction and the Perspectives of Reconstruction*. Beirut: Anis Commercial Printing Press.

Chapter 13

Jane Jacobs and Diversity of Use of Public Open Spaces in Thailand

Kan Nathiwutthikun

Public open spaces (POS) in a city are very important to both residents and visitors. They can support the local economy, attract investment and tourism, create cultural opportunities, increase safety for pedestrians, and help improve public health. In her 1961 book *The Death and Life of Great American Cities*, Jane Jacobs emphasized both the social aspects of urbanization and the importance of the physical features of a city. She advocated the social benefits of streets, paths and parks as places for social interaction (1961, pp. 36–85). Unfortunately, her ideas on what makes successful public spaces have not been fully tested.

The importance of POS for social interaction can be seen in many traditional cities in Southeast Asia. For example, the old quarter in Hanoi, where people make full use of streets and paths, is very vibrant. Street vendors sell food to buyers and occasional passersby along the sidewalks. This activity creates rich interaction among sellers and customers, thus bringing together business and social life. The same happens in Bangkok and Chiang Mai in Thailand. One can find many pedestrian sidewalks crowded with wheeled cart-shops, sidewalk shops, and hawkers. The trade brings money to the vendors and the space becomes a site of spontaneous public interactions. However, municipal authorities often consider these types of trading activity illegal. The streets where they take place do not conform to official images of 'ideal' public spaces. Thus, municipalities invest in public parks but these tend to be dead, empty spaces lacking the bustling activity found in traditional streets.

This chapter has two goals: to test empirically some of Jane Jacobs's ideas and to provide insights for municipal authorities interested in creating better public spaces. Specifically, the chapter examines the relationship between urban morphology and the pattern of uses in POS. It asks whether certain types of urban morphologies are linked to the diverse use of space. For the purposes of this chapter, diverse use of space is defined as space used by different people, at different times, and for different types of activity. The hypothesis is that urban morphology influences the level of pedestrian use of POS and the use patterns. The study relates level and patterns of use to the four key spatial characteristics that promote diversity according to Jacobs: mixed uses, small blocks, mixed aged buildings, and concentration.

The study's site is the city of Chiang Mai, Thailand. Chiang Mai is over 700 years old and is located in the northern part of Thailand often referred to as the Lanna Kingdom. It has a rich tradition in the arts and architecture. Chiang Mai has retained its historic structure despite recent expansions to the north, south and east. The city's economy is very dynamic with tourism being a major source of income. Chiang Mai has dozens of POS; in this study, we counted forty-two major sites. These include the town square, the old city, plazas, leftover spaces, pedestrian streets, walking streets (or streets where vehicular access is restricted at certain times), waterfront public places, public parks and a sports complex. Most of the POS are actively used. This pertains especially to the pedestrian streets, the spaces between landmark buildings, and the lanes around the markets in the local neighbourhoods and around the tourist sites. These spaces are used by many groups of people at different times and for different purposes. In contrast, the public parks are only rarely used. For the purpose of this study, three sites were analyzed in depth: the streets of the Warorot market in the old commercial district; the Rajadamnern walking street in the heritage district; and the Suthep path in the university district. The study's methods include analysis of figure-ground maps and of maps revealing population density and the sites and types of urban land uses. Data were collected on the users' profiles, their routes and their activities.

Conceptual Framework of the Diverse Use of Public Open Spaces

What is Diverse Use of Public Open Spaces?

The concept of the diverse spatial use of POS and its benefits has a long history through the twentieth and twenty-first centuries, but Jacobs (1961) was one of the first authors to explore it. She discussed the behaviour of local people at various times around street corners every day of the week, and argued that the mixed uses of buildings lead to diverse activities and that those activities differ at different times of day. Lynch (1960, p. 452) stated that the timing of activities is as important as their location. Chapin (1972, pp. 221–253) explained that activities can be conceptualized as including the behaviour of people, families and institutions. He classified them in three groups: firm activities (production and service activities); institutional activities (activities resulting from the actions of people organized in various groups and institutions), and individual and household activities (daily activities, socialization and recreation activities). Gehl (1998, pp. 17–31) focused on three types of outdoor activity: necessary, optional and social. He argued that optional and social activities relate to higher and better use of POS. Crawford (1999) discussed the use of street space and leftover space for the operation of the informal economy, which can potentially contribute to the formal economy.

From all these studies, we can infer that POS, if designed right, can offer high-quality environments that allow for rich uses of space: uses by different people, at different times and for different purposes.

Factors Creating Diversity of Use in Successful POS

Jacobs (1961) emphasized the importance of pedestrian streets as connecting spaces for lively neighbourhood interaction. She identified four spatial factors as generators of diversity. First, an urban district should include buildings that serve at least two primary functions (e.g. residential and business). Second, most urban blocks should be short in order to afford pedestrian opportunities to turn corners frequently. Corners, Jacobs argued, are important interaction sites. Third, a district must mingle buildings of varying ages and condition and in close grain. Old buildings must comprise a large share of the building stock because they yield important economic opportunities (e.g. low rents), especially for small businesses that provide goods and services to local residents. (Without old buildings, large investors will gear towards chain businesses whose operation discourages community interaction and may cause POS to fail.) Finally, a district must include a high concentration of people and buildings.

Other scholars have discovered additional factors that may help the diverse use of POS, many of them having to do with the connectivity of the urban tissue. Carmona *et al.* (2003, pp. 169–172) posited that movement through POS is in fact the heart of the urban experience. Gehl (1998) argued that people rarely conduct journeys with a single purpose in mind; they often stop for alternative activities, which could be very important to the overall success of POS. Hiller (1996) termed such optional activities the 'by-product' of movement. The pattern and scale of POS networks and the activities they invite are major components of the 'urban web' concept. According to this concept, the primary POS and the street network connecting them are very important to the lives of cities. Sitte (1889, cited in Carmona *et al.*, 2003, p. 67) as well as Pushkarev and Zupan (1975, pp. 26, 64, 173) emphasized that POS must be well integrated within the town and its street network. They must also provide access to the wider vicinity. Thus, in order to create successful POS, several factors related to urban morphological structure should be taken into account.

Urban Morphological Structure and the Use of POS

The study of urban morphological structure typically entails a large-scale analysis of the basic physical characteristics of urban form. Conzen (1960) concentrated on four major components of urban morphology: land use, the relationship of building mass to open areas, the land plot pattern, and the street pattern.

The present study made use of Conzen's conceptual framework, while its specific tools were those used by Trancik (1986) who, using the figure-ground technique, found that the significance of POS tends to relate to certain morphological features. These tools, however, could be employed to explain only two physical dimensions:

building density and street network. For this reason, the study also applied the overlay mapping technique, which can be used to explore the concentration of economic, social and cultural activities, as well as the quantity of pedestrian traffic.

Summary of Methods and Citywide Results

Focusing on the morphology of the selected sites and the level and patterns of their use, the study used figure-ground and mapping techniques to measure the following:

Diversity of Uses

As earlier said, the study defines diversity of use as consisting of three elements: people diversity, time diversity, and activity diversity.

To measure people diversity, the study used:

1.   Age diversity: young children (1–11 years old), teenagers (12–19), young adults (20–30), adults (31–60), and elderly people (60 years old and older);

2.   Gender diversity: male and female;

3.   Purpose-of-visit diversity which divided the population into passersby, buyers, sellers and other service providers, and strollers;

4.   Status diversity which classified people as local residents, outsiders or workers, and Thai and foreign tourists.

To measure time diversity, the study took into account:

1.   Time range diversity: morning, noon, evening, and night;

2.   Day diversity: workday, weekend, annual holiday or festival;

3.   Duration diversity: long period (> 30 minutes) and short period (<30 minutes).

To measure activity diversity, the study used Gehl's typology (1998) and recorded:

1.   Necessary activities: overlapping activities, separate activities, activities involving changing mode of transit, activities using the area as main destination, and 'transitional' activities – those that lead to other locations;

2.   Optional activities: street performances, shopping, eating and drinking, sports and recreation, and reading and hobbies;

3.   Social activities: people watching, resting and chatting, group conversations, or group gathering to watch street performances.

There is a total of thirty-seven categories (made up of: fourteen people-diversity elements, of which five are age-related, two gender-related, four related to purpose of visit, and four related to local (or not) status; nine time-diversity categories, of which four are related to time of day, three to workday (or not), and two to duration of activity; and fourteen activity-diversity elements, of which five are necessary activities, five optional activities, and four social activities). Thus, if a POS showed diversity in all elements, it would receive a score of thirty-seven. In the study, the highest score was thirty-three at the Three Kings Monument Square in the heritage district, whereas the 'official' public parks received very low scores, from 0 to about ten.

Altogether, the research team recorded data on thousands of subjects in all of Chiang Mai's forty-two major POS (figure 13.1) over a six-month observation period. Observations were recorded at peak times of use. Certain limitations to this method are obvious: for example, whereas it was easy to record a subject's gender by simply looking at him or her, age had to be estimated and errors may have occurred. Now, how do these data relate to urban morphology?

Public Open Space

- ■ Square and Urban Element
- ⊕ Walking Street
- ☻ Path
- ◖ Waterfront Public Place
- △ Plaza
- ☒ Leftover Space
- ⊙ Pocket Park
- ◎ Public Park

Figure 13.1. POS in Chiang Mai.

To record additional information on the physical characteristics of Chiang Mai (population density, land use, and location of economic and cultural sites), the study used the overlay mapping technique (figures 13.2 to 13.7).

The figures illustrate several relationships. Higher population density seems to bring greater opportunities for diverse POS use (figure 13.2). Mixed primary uses, especially residential and commercial, were also conducive to diverse use of POS (figure 13.3). The old commercial and the heritage district have the highest mix of uses and the most actively used POS. An area with a good street network meant better access

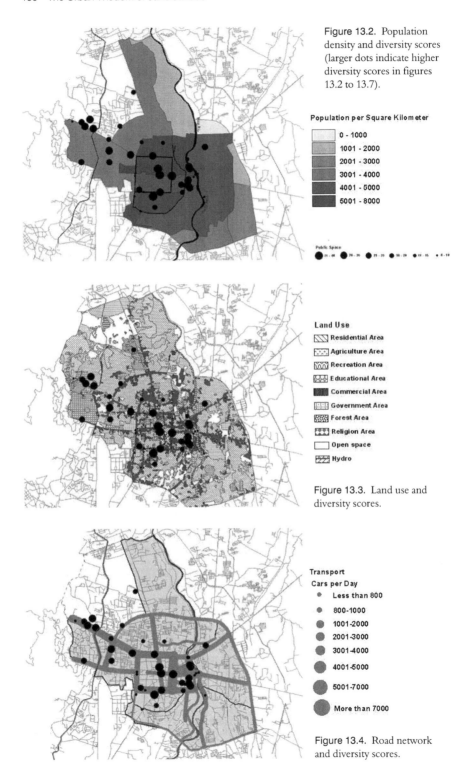

Figure 13.2. Population density and diversity scores (larger dots indicate higher diversity scores in figures 13.2 to 13.7).

Population per Square Kilometer

	0 - 1000
	1001 - 2000
	2001 - 3000
	3001 - 4000
	4001 - 5000
	5001 - 8000

Public Space

Land Use

- Residential Area
- Agriculture Area
- Recreation Area
- Educational Area
- Commercial Area
- Government Area
- Forest Area
- Religion Area
- Open space
- Hydro

Figure 13.3. Land use and diversity scores.

Transport
Cars per Day

- Less than 800
- 800-1000
- 1001-2000
- 2001-3000
- 3001-4000
- 4001-5000
- 5001-7000
- More than 7000

Figure 13.4. Road network and diversity scores.

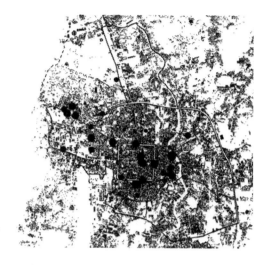

Figure 13.5. Figure-ground and diversity scores.

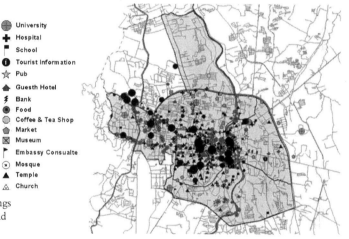

Figure 13.6. Buildings by economic type and diversity scores.

⊕	University
✚	Hospital
▛	School
❶	Tourist Information
☆	Pub
⛰	Guesth Hotel
⚡	Bank
◉	Food
◯	Coffee & Tea Shop
⬠	Market
⊠	Museum
▐	Embassy Consualte
⊙	Mosque
▲	Temple
△	Church

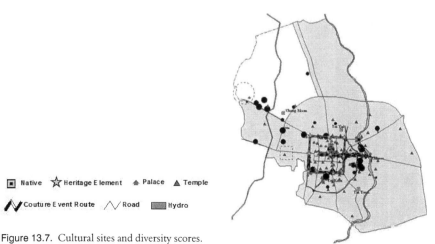

▣ Native   ☆ Heritage Element   ⬥ Palace   ▲ Temple

⋀ Couture Event Route   ⋀ Road   ▬ Hydro

Figure 13.7. Cultural sites and diversity scores.

Table 13.1. Comparison of the three sites. Nathiwutthikun, 2007: 294).

District	Area 1: Rajadamnern Historical district	Area 2: Warorot Old commercial district	Area 3: CMU University district
Background	The route connects to other parts of the city between the Thapae Gate and the Klang Wiang intersections and the Three Kings Monument. The commercial path links to the Klang Wiang market and the Central Court open space area as well as the Tha Pae Gate area. In 2002, a walking street was set up for commercial, handicraft and cultural production.	The commercial district in the inner city has existed since ancient times. It is connected to the market by a boat pier for unloading goods shipped via the Ping River. It has also been a node for the exchange of agricultural products. Later, the area developed into a modern commercial district. Today it is a pedestrian shopping area, which takes over the entire street after 7 pm.	At first, this area was vacant space. Even though a university (CMU) was established in 1964, the area remained mostly a scrub forest and was sparsely inhabited. More recently, rapid residential development has increased the density on both sides of the Suthep Road, followed by stores and other commercial buildings. Since 1997, the increase of businesses targeting pedestrians has grown so much that traffic congestion is a nuisance.
Land uses	Religious, educational, government office, and old residential uses	Commercial and old residential uses	Educational, new residential and commercial uses
Density: persons/km²	5,001–8,000 persons/km²	5,001–8,000 persons/km²	3,001–4,000 persons/km²
Building mass to area	6.58:10	5.63:10	2:10
Network system	Grid	Mixed grid, semi-organic lane and alley	Mixed grid and semi-organic
Block size	Short	Medium	Large
Traffic flow	Closed to vehicle traffic	One-way traffic	Two-way traffic
Amount of traffic	20,000 vehicles per day	20,001–30,000 vehicles per day	50,000–60,000 vehicles per day
Amount of public transportation	2,001–3,000 vehicles per day	>7,000 vehicles per day	4,001–5,000 vehicles per day
Pedestrians	68,480 persons/day (7 hours) 9,783 persons/hour Recorded only on Sundays	47,040 persons/day (17 hours) 2,767 persons/hour Every day	10,212 persons/day (7 hours) 1,458 persons/hour Every day Recorded only in the evenings
Profile of main users	Tourists, young residents of Chiang Mai	Chiang Mai local residents and residents of other districts and cities	CMU students, staff and workers

Source: Nathiwutthikun, 2007, p. 294.

and thus greater diversity of POS use (figure 13.4). Dense morphology was another factor (figure 13.5). Concentration of economic and cultural sites had a similar effect (figures 13.6 and 13.7). In short, the study results suggest that urban morphological structure and the use of POS in Chiang Mai are related as Jacobs would have expected (Nathiwutthukun, 2007, p. 62). To achieve a better understanding of these factors, the study focused on three sites in greater depth.

Three Cases

The three sites were: the Rajadamnern walking street in the heritage district; the streets of the Warorot market in the old commercial district; and the Suthep path in the university district (figure 13.8). These were selected as sites of most intense activity. The Rajadamnern walking street is notable as it is located in a historically and architecturally significant district with fifty-four temples and other heritage attractions. On the east side, there are numerous tourist sites and guesthouses. In 2002, the municipality of Chiang Mai set up a pedestrian path in the area in order to promote tourism. The second site, the area around the Warorot market, is in the city centre and has been a commercial node since ancient times. It has expanded significantly over the past 100 years and serves as a wholesale and retail market for city residents and those from nearby areas. Chiang Mai University (CMU) was established in 1964. The area around it attracts mostly workers and local residents. When the economic crisis hit Thailand in 1994, flea markets spread all over the city and especially in this university area. The flea market there has now become one of the most popular attractions for the younger generation. The area hosts many pubs and bars. While all three sites are intensely used, they also have different functional and morphological characteristics, thus making them good comparative case studies.

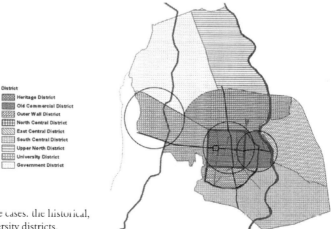

Figure 13.8. The three cases: the historical, commercial, and university districts.

Figure-Ground Analysis of the Three Sites

Figures 13.9–13.11 show the building density; i.e. the proportion of building mass to open space in each of the three sites:

The Rajadamnern Walking Street has the highest ratio of building mass to open space among the three districts: 6.58:10 (figure 13.9). Its index of POS use diversity is also the highest: 31–33.

The Warorot Market street path has a ratio of building mass to open space of 5.63:10 (figure 13.10) and a POS use diversity score of 26–30.

The CMU District has the lowest ratio of building mass to open space of the three districts: 2:10 (figure 13.11) and its POS use diversity score is also lowest: 21–25.

Figure 13.9. Figure-ground of the Rajadamnern heritage district. Building-mass-to-open-space ratio is 6.58:10. The high density and the small city blocks are evident in the illustration. The district had the highest POS use diversity value: 30–33.

Figure 13.10. Figure-ground of the Warorot market in the old commercial district. The building-mass-to-open-space ratio is 5.63:10. The district has semi-organic paths and slightly larger blocks than the heritage district and a slightly lower POS use diversity score: 26–30.

Figure 13.11. Figure-ground of the university district. The building-mass-to-open-space ratio is 2:10. The city blocks are much larger, density is lower, and the POS use diversity value of 20–26 is lower as well.

This suggests a relationship between the ratio of building mass to open space and POS use: the greater the building density (and the shorter city blocks), the higher the use diversity of POS. This result provides some empirical support to Jacobs's ideas on the importance of building-mass density and short blocks as generators of diverse activity.

Furthermore, there seems also to be a relationship between concentration of economic activities and the use of POS. Both the concentration of economic activities and the use diversity scores are high in the old commercial and heritage areas. It appears that specific types of land use have something to do with use diversity as well. Areas with markets, hotels, guesthouses, restaurants, pubs and coffee shops attract more diverse use of POS than areas with schools, government offices or banks (figure 13.6). Cultural functions also appear to be conducive to a greater diversity of POS use (figure 13.7).

Table 13.2 compares the three sites. It seems that the areas which conform to Jacobs's prescriptions for mixed primary uses, short blocks, old buildings and high density, are more likely to have greater diversity of uses in POS. This is especially the case in the heritage district which has the highest POS use diversity score. On the contrary, in areas like the university district where blocks are large and most buildings are new, the POS use diversity score is much lower.

Table 13.2. Factors affecting diversity according to Jacobs applied to the three study sites.

	Factors	Rajadamnern in the Heritage District	Warorot in the Commercial District	Suthep in the University District
Jacobs's generators of diversity	Mixed primary uses	High score	High score	Medium score
	Short blocks	High score	High score	Low score
	Aged buildings	High score	High score	Low score
	Concentration	Medium score	High score	Medium score
Building mass to area	Density of buildings	6.58:10	5.63:10	02:10
POS diversity use value		31-33	26–30	21–25

Further Study of Users' Behaviour

The behaviour of POS users is of course very complex and depends on a much larger variety of factors that can be investigated in this study. Users' behaviour can be further studied using additional tools such as photography and expanded observation. Whyte (1980, p. 16), for instance, studied a plaza using a movie camera. The main limitation was that the camera had to follow the subjects. Once the subjects went outside of the camera frame, their behaviour could not be examined. Therefore, the technique could work only in small areas. Paksukcharern Thammaruangsri (2003, p. 97) discovered people's routes and the attractions they visited by following them for three minutes until they left the area or turned to other activities that took longer than five minutes. He covered short routes of about 200 metres. But the walking streets were as long as 1,000 metres and thus it was difficult to follow the subjects. However, the data overlay mapping he used revealed the points where subjects stopped for activities and provided a clear picture of the routes that pedestrians took in the POS. This approach allowed the researcher to explain users' routes and the reasons they choose them. Earlier, Lynch (1960) used another technique – users' mental pictures of the routes they took and the attractions they visited. Lynch's method had the benefit of covering entire cities, but the drawback was that it relied on people's memories, which could be inaccurate.

For the three selected sites, this study used the following method: questionnaires were distributed among 289 subjects. They were randomly approached when entering the three sites. The subjects were followed for 200 metres to record their activities and the sites they visited (Paksukcharern Thammaruangsri's method). The questionnaires asked subjects for basic demographic data, and for their activities and the sites they visited outside the 200-metre range, based on their memories (Lynch's method).

Figures 13.12–13.14 show the use patterns of the study areas. Static activities are represented by dots and the routes of movement by lines. Figure 13.12, the heritage district on Sunday evening, indicates that the users are mostly tourists, often coming

Static Activities

○ In Municipal Area

◉ Outter Municipal Area

◕ Other District

● Other Provinces or Abroad

Route of Pedestrians

╱╲ In Municipal Area

╱╲ Outter Municipal Area

╱╲ Other District

╱╲ Other Provinces or Abroad

Figure 13.12. Sunday use patterns of the walking street in the heritage district.

from other provinces. Figure 13.13, on the other hand, shows that the old commercial district is used for everyday activities. Its users are the most diverse, including both local residents and people coming from outside areas. Figure 13.14, the university district, suggests that the POS are used every day, mostly in the evenings and during the school semesters. Most users are university students.

Regarding the dynamic activities, figure 13.12 shows that people walking on Sunday in the heritage district are concentrated around corners and intersections. The open spaces around the temples are used for food and for their public restrooms. Figure 13.13 shows a web-route pattern in the old commercial district, which is shaped by

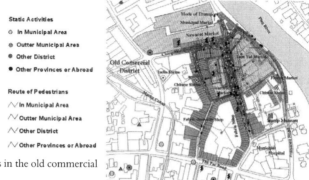

Figure 13.13. Use patterns in the old commercial district.

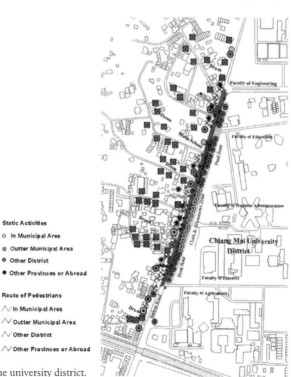

Figure 13.14. Use patterns in the university district.

the intersection of two main streets interwoven with some secondary lanes. An organic POS use pattern seems to have developed in this hustle-and-bustle area, especially around the fresh-food and the wholesale markets. Figure 13.14 indicates that the university area serves as a spontaneous POS with linear movement patterns. Most users visit it daily for food and other services.

Conclusion

This study suggests that urban morphological structure and the patterns of use of POS are related, thus empirically supporting Jacobs's proposition for the four generators of diversity – in this case, diversity of POS use.

Mixed Primary Uses

Chiang Mai is characterized by the co-location of commercial and residential functions. The study found that the open spaces of the old commercial district are used at dawn, during the day, in the evening and at night by different groups of people. The heritage district is used most intensely and by the most diverse group of people but primarily on Sunday. Its users are mostly tourists visiting the main attraction places, purchasing various goods and strolling along the commercial paths. They tend to cluster at corners and intersections. The much newer university district accommodates young, university-age people who like to hang out in the evening. Different primary uses, thus, attract different users, and cause different behaviours.

Small blocks

Block characteristics also affect the use of POS. Small blocks seem to give more frequent chances of turning at corners and allow interaction along pedestrian paths, much as Jacobs suggested. The heritage and the old commercial districts have grid street networks and small blocks, which appear to invite greater and more diverse use of POS. In contrast, the university district has large blocks and lower density. The use of its POS is much lower.

Old Buildings

The heritage and the old commercial districts are historic areas. Nowadays, these areas include many old buildings scattered throughout their fabric. These attract many users. In contrast, the university district is a new development area with modern-style buildings, which do not serve as attractions.

Concentration

Both the old commercial and the historic districts are locations with high concentration of economic and cultural activities. They also include a dense urban fabric. The users of their POS came from various settlements and many were tourists. The heritage district attracted the greatest number of tourists. The crowd in the old commercial district flowed along the commercial paths and gathered at intersections mostly around shops. The university district, in contrast, had use patterns related to food vending and grocery stores – functions attractive to local residents. It also provided the types of functions that attract young people at night and facilitated mostly linear movement.

In summary then, POS in Chiang Mai are used in many different ways. Their success depends on social, economic and physical factors, as argued by Jane Jacobs.

Municipal authorities should understand that the diverse use of POS could be beneficial to urban development in many ways. Diversification should occur in terms of types of users, and the timing and types of their activities. More diverse use of POS results in urban renewal, infrastructure improvements, economic development and subsequent new property development. In Chiang Mai, many old buildings have recently been renovated to include new functions as a result of the increasing vibrancy of some of the city's POS. In the heritage district, especially, there are many new restaurants, pubs and other entertainment places that attract both tourists and local people. Greater POS use is partially dependent on the informal economy, which can in turn strengthen the formal economy. The most heavily used POS have many temporary shops, vendors and kiosks that benefit both their owners and their users, most of whom are lower- and lower-middle class people. In fact, spontaneity, informality and diversity of POS use all seem to be related. Municipal authorities should take these lessons into account. Not only should they invest in the existing POS but if they decide to build new ones, they should take cues from the social and physical generators of diversity that the traditional POS offer.

References

Carmona, M., Heath, T., Oc, T. and Tiesdell, S. (2003) *Public Space: The Dimensions of Urban Design*. Oxford: Architectural Press.

Chapin, F.S. (1972) *Human Activity Patterns in the City*. London: Pion.

Conzen, M.P. (1960) Alnwick: a study in town plan analysis. *Transactions of the Institute of British Geographers*, **27**, pp. 1–122.

Crawford, M. (1999) Blurring the boundaries: public space and private life, in Chase, J., Crawford, M. and Kaliski, J. (eds.) *Everyday Urbanism*. New York: Monacelli, pp. 22–35.

Gehl, J. (1998, 1971) *Life between Buildings: Using Public Space*. Washington, DC: Island Press.

Hillier, B. (1996) *Space is the Machine*. Cambridge: Cambridge University Press. Available at *discovery.ucl.ac.uk/1403/1/hillier-96-citiesmovementeconomies.pdf. Accessed 12 February 2012.*

Jacobs, J. (1961) *The Death and Life of Great American Cities*. New York: Random House.

Lynch, K. (1960). *The Image of the City*. Cambridge: MIT Press.

Nathiwutthikun, K. (2007) The Logic of Multi-use of Public Open Spaces in Chiang Mai City. Doctoral Dissertation. Faculty of Architecture, Chulalongkorn University, Bangkok.

Paksukcharern Thammaruangsri, K. (2003) Node and Place: A Study of the Spatial Process of Railway Terminus Area Redevelopment in Central London. Doctoral Dissertation. Faculty of Architecture, University College London.

Pushkarev, B. and Zupan, J. (1975) *Urban Space for Pedestrians*. Cambridge: MIT Press.

Trancik, R. (1986) *Finding Lost Space: Theory of Urban Design*. New York: Wiley.

Whyte, W. (1980) *The Social Life of Small Urban Spaces*. Washington DC: Conservation Foundation.

Chapter 14

Revisiting Jane Jacobs's 'Eyes on the Street' for the Twenty-First Century: Evidence from Environmental Criminology

Paul Cozens and David Hillier

This chapter explores the writings of Jane Jacobs as they relate to safety and the reduction of crime. *The Death and Life of Great American Cities* (1961) is commonly accredited with highlighting a new perspective on the role of the urban designer, planner and architect in influencing the level of crime. The chapter discusses the context within which Jacobs's ideas were written and their subsequent influence on Oscar Newman's *Defensible Space* (1973) and on contemporary ideas commonly referred to as Crime Prevention Through Environmental Design (CPTED).

We discuss briefly how Jacobs's views on safety have influenced planning policy in the UK, USA and Australia and examine the safety claims of one of the most popular planning paradigms of our time, New Urbanism, which is based largely on her ideas. These ideas relate to the promotion of permeable, high-density and mixed-use developments. It is argued that since Jacobs's work, built environment professionals have failed to refine their ideas and policies about crime and urban space in the light of ongoing evidence and theories emerging from environmental criminology. These are briefly discussed as useful frameworks for developing further understanding of crime risks in local contexts.

Significantly, Jacobs explicitly warned against transplanting her ideas to all cities, smaller cities, towns and suburbs. Clearly, planners, urban designers and architects have not heeded her warnings. This chapter does not assert that the safety assumptions of Jacobs were wrong. Rather, the issue is that transplanting her ideas to smaller towns and cities has continued at an international scale, in spite of her warnings to the contrary. The promotion of 'natural surveillance' and 'eyes on the street' as the 'cure all' crime prevention strategy in planning has therefore occurred in locations with insufficient pedestrian densities, such as small cities, towns and suburbs. Sufficient numbers of people are simply not there to use or watch the streets, and public safety may be compromised in certain situations.

Some have argued that Jacobs's ideas were operationalized in Newman's *Defensible Space* in 1973 (Jeffrey and Zahm, 1993). The Defensible Space concept was based on observations of select locations in two large American cities in the 1960s. Society, lifestyles, routine activities and research about crime and urban spaces have developed significantly since then. It is argued that the application of Crime Prevention Through Environmental Design 'solutions' need to be grounded in the systematic evaluation of crime risks, before solutions are generated and evaluated. Fifty years on, a re-evaluation of Jacobs's groundbreaking works on planning and safety is pertinent, both temporally and in terms of those current British, American and Australian planning policies that are often collectively referred to as New Urbanism.

This chapter begins by summarizing the key literature and findings on crime and safety, which were discussed by Jacobs, and then examines the context within which they were written.

Jacobs, Crime and Safety

The Death and Life of Great American Cities begins with a declaration of war on the major contemporary schools of urban planning: 'This book is an attack on current city planning and rebuilding. It is also, and mostly, an attempt to introduce new principles of city planning and rebuilding, different and even opposite from those now taught in everything from schools of architecture and planning to the Sunday supplements and women's magazines' (1961, p. 3). The book was a reaction to the high-rise public housing inspired by Le Corbusier, and other inner-city attempts at regeneration and renewal of the times. For Jenkins (2006, p. 1), 'Jacobs stepped out of her New York front door sometime in the late-1950s and became the Charles Darwin of the city. She observed. She watched her street, her neighbourhood, her city, how they moved, breathed, changed over time. Like Darwin she tore up the rule book'.

Early in her book Jacobs (1961, p. 30) identified safety and security as the key elements of a well-functioning city: 'the bedrock attribute of a successful city district is that a person must feel personally safe and secure on the street'. She also observed that a few incidents of violence can create fear among residents which can discourage use and make the streets feel more unsafe. She observed that crime is not a problem of the slums, rather 'the problem is most serious, in fact, in genteel-looking quiet residential areas' (*Ibid.*, p. 31).

Jane Jacobs is commonly accredited with focusing attention on the fundamental elements of safety which may (or may not) be facilitated by the design, management and use of the urban environment. Specifically, she wrote that: 'A city street equipped to handle strangers, and to make a safety asset, in itself, out of the presence of strangers, as the streets of successful city neighborhoods always do, must have three main qualities:

1. There must be a clear demarcation between what is public space and what is private space.

2. There must be eyes upon the street, eyes belonging to those we might call the natural proprietors of the street. The buildings on a street equipped to handle strangers … must be oriented to the street…

3. The sidewalk must have users on it fairly continuously, both to add to the number of effective eyes on the street and to induce the people in buildings along the street to watch the sidewalks in sufficient numbers' (*Ibid.*, p. 35).

Jacobs also observed how 'large numbers of people entertain themselves, off and on, by watching street activity' (*Ibid.*). These ideas are often collectively known as the concept of 'eyes on the street'. Importantly, they would later be operationalized in Oscar Newman's *Defensible Space* (1973) as territoriality, natural surveillance, and milieu (see below).

'Eyes on the street' could therefore be promoted through mixed land uses, where 'a substantial quantity of stores and other public places [are] sprinkled along the sidewalks of a district … [and] are used evening and night (*Ibid.*, p. 36). These flourish alongside residences, and ensure that there are always both people watching and people being watched. For Jacobs, strangers, therefore, inadvertently keep one another safe. Land uses such as retail stores, bars and restaurants 'work in different and complex ways to abet sidewalk safety' (*Ibid.*):

♦   they provide reasons for using the sidewalk;

♦   they attract people along the sidewalk and near to places which basically lack public attraction, but become travelled as routes to somewhere else;

♦   storekeepers and business people are great 'street-watchers' and sidewalk guardians when they are present in sufficient numbers, and;

♦   activity generated by users on errands or looking for food/drink attracts other users.

Essentially, for Jacobs, the promotion of 'eyes on the street' via diverse and well-used vibrant city streets is the principal method underpinning public safety. However, she notes that this is not necessarily an easy task as you cannot 'make people use streets they have no reason to use' … nor 'make people watch streets they don't want to watch' (*Ibid.*). Later, she argues that the process of watching itself is more fundamental than the act of intervention (*Ibid.*, p. 38). Jacobs also recognized that increases in commercial and residential densities in one location may lead to a thinning out of activity on and around peripheral streets. This is associated with reduced levels of eyes on the street and potentially, increased crime risks. Beyond this threshold, extended residential/commercial density and street activity are associated with reduced crime risks.

Angel's (1968) concept of crime as a function of land-use intensity has refined Jacobs's ideas (figure 14.1). Angel argued that reduced levels of crime occur in areas with low land-use intensity since there are limited opportunities for offending (zone 1). As land-use intensity increases, so does the number of potential victims/targets, thereby attracting offenders to the area, where there are insufficient 'eyes on the street' to act as guardians to potentially discourage crime. Angel called this scenario the 'critical intensity zone' (zone 2) where most crime occurs. As land-use intensity increases beyond this critical threshold, there are sufficient numbers of guardians present potentially to deter offenders (zone 3). Furthermore, as Sorensen (2003, p. 34) argues, 'pedestrian traffic thus seems to increase risk (from the standpoint of target selection) and decrease risk (from the standpoint of natural surveillance) depending on whether that traffic is through traffic or local traffic'.

Significantly, Jacobs asserts that the streets of the North End of Boston, 'are probably as safe as any place on earth' (Jacobs, 1961, p. 33) and compares this context with an allegedly crime-ridden suburban locality. However, many of her assertions about crime and the city were based on anecdotal observations and Jacobs did not provide much detail in the way of systematically recorded crime data to support her assertions. She compares crime rates (for rape, assault and 'major crimes') per 100,000 of the population for large cities such as St. Louis, New York, Los Angeles, Baltimore, Philadelphia, Chicago and Houston. Jacobs also cites increased crime rates in ostensibly low-density cities such as Los Angeles. Although she acknowledges that

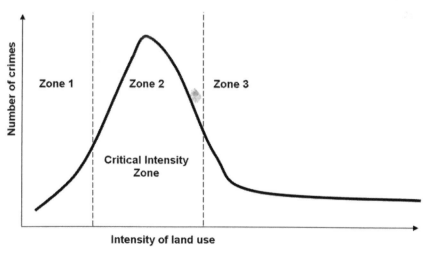

Figure 14.1. 'Eyes on the street' and crime as a function of land-use intensity. (*Source*: Angel, 1968, p. 16)

there are complex reasons underpinning such differences, she asserts that we can be sure that 'thinning out a city does not ensure safety from crime and fear of crime' (*Ibid.*, pp. 32–33). However, when she studied the streets of New York and Boston, she did not observe (or collect any systematic data) on incidents of crime when concluding that they were safe. At a time of economic decline for many central cities, Jacobs (*Ibid.*, p. 32) observed how 'the problem of insecurity cannot be solved by spreading people out more thinly, trading the characteristics of cities for the characteristics of suburbs'. For Jacobs, busy city streets can handle the presence of strangers whom she saw as an asset capable of enhancing self-policing. Simply speaking, for Jacobs more 'eyes on the street' equates to safer spaces.

The Context of Jacobs's Observations on Crime and Safety

Jane Jacobs wrote at a time when social science research was in its infancy and certain observation techniques were considered cutting-edge. Her approach was situated in an era when the analysis of city spaces was also in its infancy. Indeed, the science of empirical enquiry was more or less simply about collecting data, often unsystematically, rather than discerning patterns or stories within the data. One might label her approach 'radical' or 'ground-breaking'. Jacobs takes us on a journey of which CPTED research subsequently became a very important development.

Jacobs focused on the crimes her society acknowledged and publicized. Given how fragile and idiosyncratic her data were, she clearly made more of it than would be acceptable today by our higher standards of empirical evidence. Car crime, for example, was less important as car ownership and usage levels were yet to increase dramatically. Jacobs, thus, effectively lived and breathed a different menu of crime from urbanites today. However, her work was pioneering and hindsight should not reduce our sense of its importance in underpinning the developments of later, more radical ideas, such as Defensible Space and CPTED.

'Eyes on the street' was a different phenomenon in the 1950s. The usage of interior (domestic) and exterior (public) space was markedly different from what it is today (Felson, 1987; Moores, 2000). Adults used public transport much more often, went to the cinema, worked in their garden spaces, shopped on foot locally, walked routinely and frequently to visit relatives (these then lived nearby) and simply chatted and interacted at street level. Children walked to school, played in the streets, walked to town and went to their friends' houses. Today, interior spaces are much more heavily used, filled with a plethora of new technologies and means of entertainment (Moores, 2000). Indeed, interior space is now defined as the 'leisure action space' for both adults and children. This has led to declining use of exterior public spaces (*Ibid.*). This withdrawal has undoubtedly contributed to the re-labelling and redefinition of such spaces as 'dangerous' or 'risky'. In the UK, Australia and the USA, many children are now driven to school because walking is perceived as unsafe.

One of the most obvious changes we have witnessed since the Jacobs's era relates to car ownership and use. With increased levels of disposable income and diversified home entertainment options, with new technologies, and negative images of city centres in the media (e.g. as places of binge drinking, drugs, and violence after dark, etc.), avoidance of urban spaces has increased (Schneider and Kitchen, 2007; Graham and Homel, 2008). Public spaces have to some degree been reconstructed as 'their' responsibility to manage, not 'ours' (Roberts, 2004; Thomas and Bromley, 2000; Graham and Homel, 2008). The streets are often viewed as 'belonging' to some abstract entity, rather than to the community itself. Furthermore, in the USA, new subdivisions often include private streets such that there is some confusion about exactly what is public space and what is private space.

Social responsibility and community cohesion are often seen as increasingly outdated and outmoded values to the point that private affluence, rather than public improvement, is considered the primary goal of public policies (e.g. Gilbert, 2002; Marquand, 2004). These and other issues combine to make the care, maintenance and routine community control of public spaces less likely (Wilson and Kelling, 1982; Kelling and Coles, 1996) and can leave a vacuum for other users to occupy and exploit (Atlas, 1991; Ross and Mirowsky, 1999).

Given the empirical shortcomings of her initial enquiry, all the comparisons Jacobs proceeds to make must be treated with some scepticism. Her variables are not narrowly and scientifically defined and therefore the replication of her work, a basic scientific requirement, is not possible. Furthermore, the observed safety of the streets of Greenwich Village in New York and the North End of Boston in the 1950s may well be partially explained by other variables that were not considered at the time. Speculatively, one element of the social context, which is rarely discussed, concerns the presence (perceived and real) of local gang/street networks. For example, the mafia may well have 'contributed' towards the safety of the streets observed by Jacobs. Indeed, the urban narratives of William Whyte's *Street Corner Society* (1943) and Herbert Gans's *The Urban Villagers* (1962) both highlight the persistence and relevance of Italian culture in American cities. In relation to the bohemian streets of Greenwich Village and the famous White Horse bar (frequented by Dylan Thomas among others), Jacobs (1961, pp. 40–41) observes 'the comings and goings from this bar do much to keep our streets reasonably populated until three in the morning and it is always safe to come home to'. She cites a violent assault which was noticed by a resident, who intervened. She claims that (*Ibid.*, p. 41) he knew 'he was part of a web of strong street law and order'.

Crucially, whether Jacobs was right about her observations about the crime reduction effectiveness of 'eyes on the street' in the 1950s is not the point. Rather, the issues raised indicate that hers were times very different from ours. Thus, revisiting her work is timely, appropriate and potentially rewarding.

Fundamentally, Jane Jacobs participates in a debate that has a lengthy pedigree stretching back to the very first cities and the enactment of the first formal laws and associated punishments for legal infraction. What she unambiguously offers is a re-focusing of the debate. In the spotlight, which was previously dominated by the 'actors' (criminals), she firmly places the 'stage' (city spaces). This shift changes the very character of the questions to be posed and the character and content of the possible answers. Jacobs's contribution is so profound that the analysis of crime in the city has simply never been the same following the publication of *The Death and Life*. Like all 'good' scholarship, her book raises new questions to be asked and in seeking to answer these, discovers new knowledge and insights, which raise yet new and additional questions. Consequently, theory, understanding, and policy evolve. The next section briefly discusses how Jacobs's ideas have evolved in the last half century.

Jacobs's 'Eyes on the Street', Defensible Space and CPTED

As the operationalization of Jacobs's ideas (Jeffery and Zahm, 1993), Defensible Space requires a brief introduction. There are four elements of Defensible Space (Newman, 1973) which act individually and in combination to assist in the creation of a safer urban environment:

◆   the capacity of the physical environment to create perceived zones of territorial influence;

◆   the capacity of physical design to provide surveillance opportunities for residents and their agents;

◆   the capacity of design to influence the perception of a project's uniqueness, isolation, and stigma; and

◆   the influence of geographical juxtaposition with 'safe zones' on the security of adjacent areas (*Ibid.*, p. 50).

Clearly, Defensible Space focuses on increasing 'eyes on the street' and on clear delineation between private and public space (figure 14.2). These are two of Jacobs's three qualities for a successful city neighbourhood, discussed earlier.

Since attracting both support and criticism in the 1970s, Defensible Space diminished in popularity from the beginning of the 1980s and into the mid-1990s, both in the UK and in America. Cisneros (1995, p. 1) states that 'for a time, in important policy circles, strategies stressing physical change simply became unfashionable'. He suggests that by the mid 1990s, Defensible Space was once again gaining popularity, as a policy instrument, primarily under the banner of CPTED in Europe, America and Australia, and as Secured By Design (SBD) in the UK.

The Defensible Space ideas have been investigated, refined and expanded by the work of numerous researchers. Arguably, they represent the foundations of the concept known as CPTED, which can be divided into seven inter-related areas (figure 14.3). Indeed, Moffat (1983, p. 23) observed CPTED can be divided into seven aspects where 'defensible space' is at the 'root of the concept'.

Defensible Space and CPTED both seek to manipulate the design of urban places in order to reduce opportunities for crime and there are many connections between these

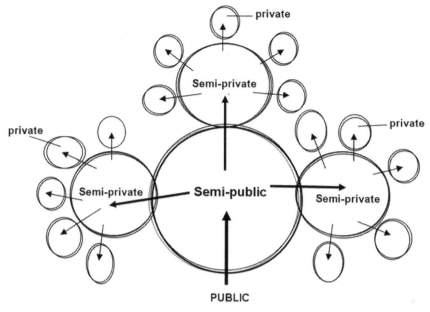

Figure 14.2. levels of the hierarchy. (*Source*: Newman, 1973, p. 9)

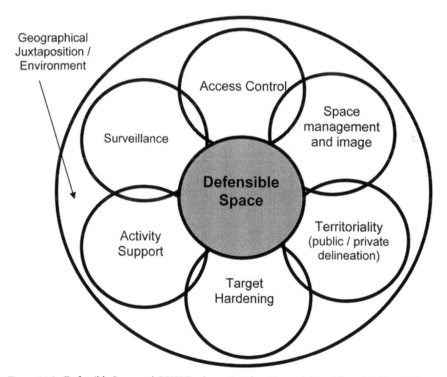

Figure 14.3. Defensible Space and CPTED – key principles. (*Source:* Adapted from Moffatt, 1983, p 23 and Newman, 1973)

two approaches (see Schneider and Kitchen, 2002, p. 12). Jacobs's three main qualities discussed earlier are clearly central to these CPTED ideas. Globally, a multitude of urban design, planning and CPTED guidelines and policies have been produced, all of which seek to promote 'eyes on the street' and Jacobs's three qualities of a safe and successful city (see Cozens *et al.*, 2005; Schneider and Kitchen, 2007; Cozens, 2008*a*, 2008*b*).

Browning *et al.* (2010, p. 333) note the influence of Jacobs's (1961) work on highlighting the importance of mutual trust and shared expectations in the control of public space, arguing that 'it can be seen as a forerunner of Sampson's concept of collective efficacy (Sampson and Raudenbush, 1999; Sampson *et al.*, 1997)'. This resonates today as part of second generation CPTED thinking which focuses on fostering a sense of community (see Saville and Cleveland, 1997). As Saville and Cleveland (*Ibid.*, p. 1) observe: 'what is significant about Jacobs's "eyes on the street" are not the sightlines or even the streets, but the eyes'. The 'eyes on the street' are of course inevitably attached to citizens who must be capable and motivated to respond, individually or collectively. Second generation CPTED ideas thus promote the design and maintenance of functioning communities in order to develop a sense of community pride and wellbeing. This dynamic can then potentially work to encourage residents to act routinely as 'eyes on the street'. This chapter next discusses how such ideas have influenced international planning policy and particularly the ideas and policies associated with New Urbanism.

Jacobs, CPTED and International Planning Policies such as New Urbanism

Government policy in the UK, USA and Australia has increasingly advocated the development of high-density, mixed-use residential developments in 'walkable', permeable neighbourhoods, close to public transport, employment and amenities (Commonwealth of Australia, 1995; DETR, 1998; ODPM, 2004; American Planning Association, 2007). Such policies are often associated with New Urbanism. It is argued that such designs reduce opportunities for crime by increasing opportunities for surveillance of public spaces, by encouraging walking and social interaction, and by promoting a sense of community and social control (CNU, 2001). Plater-Zyberk (1993, p. 12) comments that 'we believe that the physical structure of our environment can be managed and that controlling it is the key to solving numerous problems confronting government today – traffic congestion, pollution, financial depletion, social isolation, and yes, even crime'.

Jane Jacobs's (1961) observations underpin much of New Urbanist thinking and current planning policy in Australia, the UK and America, particularly in relation to safety from crime. The concept of 'eyes on the street' is the foundation of a number of safety assumptions in planning, which are associated with increasing permeability, mixed uses and higher densities (Cozens and Hillier, 2008; Cozens, 2008*c*, 2011). The theoretical basis for supporting permeability, mixed use and higher densities as crime reduction strategies rest upon the promotion of activity; i.e. it is assumed that crime can be decreased by increasing the number of 'eyes on the street'. Arguably, however, while this concept may (or may not) work in large vibrant cities, certain crimes flourish under the cover and anonymity provided by crowded spaces (e.g. pick-pocketing).

Recently, reviews have identified over forty studies conducted since 1975 which suggest that increased permeability is in fact linked to increased levels of crime (see for example Cozens, 2008c, 2009, 2010; Cozens and Love, 2009; Johnson and Bowers, 2010). Furthermore, mixed-used development and higher densities may also not be universally benign in criminogenic terms (Schneider and Kitchen, 2007).

Jacobs (1961) argued that different densities were appropriate for different settings: for instance, low densities (say, six dwellings per acre) can function successfully in the suburbs. Significantly, she noted 'we ought to look at densities in much the same way as we look at calories and vitamins. Right amounts are right amounts because of how they perform. And what is right differs in specific instances' (Jacobs, 1961, p. 209). Since Jacobs's observations, there have been some significant changes in family structure (such as the breakdown of the extended family), in the character and content of domestic lifestyles, and in the role of women in the workplace (Putnam, 1995). Consequently, there are now fewer residents in urban buildings available to watch the streets. And here is another point of caution: Jacobs's interest was in personal attacks (Poyner, 2006) but the crime prevention concept of 'eyes on the street' has since been applied to all types of crime.

Along with Jacobs (1961), Newman (2003) and others have also observed that the presence of 'eyes on the street' does not guarantee intervention. Indeed, studies that have investigated bystander apathy have found that as the number of bystanders increases, the likelihood for intervention decreases (Darley and Latane, 1968; Morgan, 1978; Hart and Miethe, 2008; Barnyard, 2008).

Crucially, few planners or other built environment professionals are aware of the criminological evidence associated with favoured planning strategies such as permeability, high densities and mixed-use developments (see Cozens, 2011). Indeed, evidence and insights from environmental criminology (and other disciplines) indicate that certain crimes may concentrate around certain socio-spatial configurations and these are not necessarily the configurations expected by Jacobs (table 14.1).

Environmental Criminology and the Need to Progress beyond Jacobs and Current CPTED

One of the objectives in revisiting Jacobs (1961) is to highlight those contributions from her initial ideas, which have arguably failed to be disseminated into the planning profession or which have been ignored. They relate to the scale of analysis, which extends beyond the micro-level application of 'eyes on the street'. Both Jacobs (1961) and Newman (1973) were aware of the potential influence of surrounding land uses and activities on street-level crime and the effectiveness of 'eyes on the street'.

In relation to certain land uses, Jacobs (1961, p. 41) laments that 'bars, and indeed

Table 14.1. Some insights from environmental criminology and other disciplines.

Permeability	High Densities	Mixed-Use Development
Isolated culs-de-sac are least accessible to crime and grid-like inter-sections are most accessible to crime (Beavon et al., 1994).	High densities nurture a sense of 'anomie', which can destabilize the individual and the community (Durkheim, 1893; Wirth, 1938).	Routine activities theory (Cohen and Felson, 1979) suggests higher levels of crime in high-activity, mixed-use developments.
Corner houses are significantly more vulnerable to burglary (Taylor and Nee, 1988; Hakim et al., 2001) and burglaries are more frequent in grid layouts.	Calhoun's 'crowding theory' (1962) argues that as densities increase, so do violence and aggression.	There are multiple studies, which revealed that mixed-use development in residential areas is 'not totally benign' (Schneider and Kitchen, 2007).
Reported crime is five times higher in permeable New Urbanist layouts (Town and O'Toole 2005; Town et al., 2003).	Very dense urban areas generally experience higher crime levels than less densely populated areas (Bottoms and Wiles, 1997; Ellen and O'Reagan, 2009).	Homogenous residential environments exhibit lower rates of crime than areas with mixed uses (Greenberg et al., 1982; Greenberg and Rohe, 1984).
The UK's SBD scheme promotes the building of non-permeable culs-de-sac layouts and reduced levels of both crime and fear of crime (Cozens et al., 2004).	Heavy pedestrian and vehicular traffic flows are associated with higher victimization rates and the shape of traffic intersections also influences crime (Beavon et al., 1994).	Increased vehicular and pedestrian flows reduce the potential for interaction and for recognition of strangers (Baum and Valins, 1977; Appleyard, 1980, Taylor and Harrell, 1996).
Converting grids into culs-de-sac using road closures reduces crime (Matthews, 1992; Newman, 1995; Lasley, 1998; Zavoski et al., 1999).	Large numbers of people sharing common entrances in social housing contribute to higher rates of crime (Newman, 1973).	Proximity to a range of different land uses 'generates' crime (Luedtke and Associates, 1970; Buck et al., 1993).
Newly introduced pedestrian pathways connecting the ends of culs-de-sac lead to higher crime (Sheard, 1991).	Crime is concentrated where people congregate and along the routes linking activity nodes (Kinney et al., 2008).	Residential burglary is more frequent in residential properties close to commercial areas (Dietrick, 1977).
Reducing connectivity reduces crime (Bevis and Nutter, 1978; Beavon et al., 1994; Wagner, 1997; White, 1990; Bowers et al., 2005; Yang, 2006; Armitage 2007).	Urban population density is associated with various physical, psychological and behavioural problems, including increased levels of crime (Gove et al., 1977).	Research by Wilcox et al. (2004) revealed that businesses in residential areas exhibit an increased risk of burglary.
A dense permeable housing estate reported higher levels of crime compared to a lower-density estate dominated by culs-de-sac (Schneider and Kitchen, 2007).	Rubenstein et al. (1980) reported that heavy pedestrian and vehicular traffic flows are associated with higher victimization rates.	Yang's research (2006), which investigated some three thousand burglaries, found that burglaries are more likely to occur in properties located in mixed-use sites.
Crime is more frequent in accessible areas with commercial land uses (Davison and Smith, 2003).	Crime is associated with high densities in prisons (Paulus, 1988), nightclubs (Macintyre and Homel, 1997) and naval ships (Dean et al., 1978).	Mixed land uses increase activity in some nodes and produce a clustering of crime (Kinney et al., 2008; Browning et al., 2010).
Johnson and Bowers (2010) reviewed the literature and found that connectivity increases crime.	Most types of crime occur more frequently when population density increases (Harries, 2006).	Research by Taylor et al. (1985) and Taylor et al. (1995) suggested that as business activity increases in residential areas, the prevalence of crime increases too.
Armitage et al. (2010) found pure culs-de-sac are safer than through routes.		

Source: Cozens, 2012.

all commerce, have a bad name in many city districts precisely because they do draw strangers, and the strangers do not work out as an asset at all'. Arguably, Newman's (1973) Defensible Space component of geographical juxtaposition attempts to build on Jacobs's somewhat limited perspective. Crucially, Newman's (1973, p. 112) ideas on the potential crime risks associated with locating commercial and institutional facilities within a housing project (geographical juxtaposition) challenged Jacobs's assertions as being 'unsupported hypotheses'. He argued that increasing activity in order to provide safety in numbers 'needs to be critically evaluated in terms of the nature of business, their periods of activity [and] the nature and frequency of the presence of concerned authorities' (*Ibid.*).

It is helpful here to reflect on Brantingham *et al.* (1976, p. 264) in their discussion of crime, seen through the 'cone of resolution'. They analyze crime data from national to city-block level to highlight how limitations associated with the aggregation of data 'changes our perception of the where and when of the crime problem' and 'the questions that can be reasonably asked of the data'. It is argued here that the wider geographical environment requires consideration as well and that several theories from environmental criminology can assist our understanding of crime and 'eyes on the street' beyond the micro-level of Jacobs's sidewalks.

Environmental criminology focuses on the spatial and temporal location of crime and the fear of crime and how individual behaviour is influenced by place-based factors. It is underpinned by three related crime opportunity theories, which provide an alternative perspective from which to consider the potential performance of 'eyes on the street' and the issues of permeable urban configurations, mixed-use developments and higher population densities. Jacobs (1961, p. 33) was cognizant of wider opportunities for crime. Indeed, she suggests that the all-important question about any street is 'how much easy opportunity does it offer to crime?'. However, her analysis was largely focused on the sidewalk itself.

An alternative perspective is offered by routine activities theory (RAT) which was proposed by Cohen and Felson (1979). This theory argues that for a crime to occur there must be a motivated offender, a suitable target and the absence of capable guardians (see also Felson, 1987). Like most citizens, offenders have routine daily activities (work/school, visiting friends, shopping and entertainment) during which they passively discover or actively search for potential targets (e.g. Maguire, 1982). Such activities and travel routes form the 'awareness space' (Brantingham and Brantingham, 1984, 1993) of the offender (figure 14.4). Simply put, crime is an activity, which concentrates in and around where other, legal activities are located.

This theory is linked to Brantingham and Brantingham's (1981, 1984) Crime Pattern Theory (CPT), which seeks to understand the search and selection processes that criminals use. Crimes against the person obviously occur in and around locations where people are to be found. Such locations include the home, places in and around drinking establishments (Fattah, 1991), hospitals, public transit nodes and retail settings (Clarke and Eck, 2007). Property crimes such as robbery are concentrated at or near activity nodes and attractors, where people congregate; while burglaries predominate

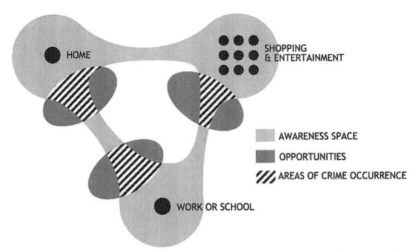

Figure 14.4. Awareness spaces – routine activities theory. (*Source*: Adeane, 2007, adapted from Brantingham and Brantingham, 1981)

in locations where people reside or where they might visit or work (Brantingham and Brantingham, 1993, 1998, 2008; Kinney *et al.*, 2008). The routine activities of the users of urban spaces therefore contribute to the crime patterns found in such locations. Clearly, these two theories fundamentally challenge the assumption that increased levels of 'eyes on the street' are, always, necessarily and automatically associated with lower crime rates. Understanding routine activities is therefore crucial if designers and planners are to contribute towards the creation and maintenance of safer cities.

Finally, Cornish and Clarke's (1986) 'rational choice theory' (RCT) argues that most opportunistic criminals are rational in their decision-making and recognize, evaluate and respond to a variety of environmental stimuli, opportunities and cues. These include environmental factors and signals within the built environment, which relate to the perceived risk, reward and effort associated with an offence, and are central to the offender's decision-making process. This theory and its refinements largely underpin Clarke's (1992, 1997) situational crime prevention (SCP) approach. Briefly, this approach is concerned with the role of design and the management of specific situations in the facilitation of crime. SCP analyses specific situations and seeks to increase the risks and the effort associated with committing a crime while also reducing the rewards, provocations and excuses related to offending.

Specific land uses (and the routine activities that they influence) can therefore represent crime generators, crime attractors or crime detractors (Brantingham and Brantingham, 1993, 1998, 2008; Kinney *et al.*, 2008). Activity nodes, which attract large numbers of people and potentially provide increased opportunities for crime, are known as 'crime attractors' (e.g. railway stations and shopping centres). Activity nodes, which provide well-publicized criminal opportunities and obvious motivations to offend are 'crime generators' (e.g. night clubs, bars). Finally, activity nodes, which lack popular and attractive activities and discourage use by legitimate citizens are 'crime detractors' (Brantingham and Brantingham, 1998, 2008; Kinney et al., 2008). For example, poorly designed and unmanaged and neglected open spaces and parks with few attractions can facilitate use by potential offenders.

Crime concentrates at specific places and at specific times. It is not random. In *Crime and Everyday Life*, Felson and Boba (2010) observe how daily life is divided into different types of settings, which can generate significant levels of crime. Settings with significant crime risks are:

- public routes (especially footpaths, parking facilities and unsupervised transit areas);
- recreational settings (especially bars and some parks);
- public transport (especially transit stations and their vicinities);
- retail stores (especially for shoplifting);
- educational settings (especially at their edges);
- offices (especially when entered for theft);
- human support services (especially hospitals with 24 hour activities);
- industrial locations (especially warehouses with 'attractive' goods).

Within each setting, however, a small number of locations (typically 20 per cent) are commonly found to be accountable for the majority of the crime (commonly 80 per cent), while most locations exhibit relatively low levels of crime (Clarke and Eck, 2007). In short, different settings and land uses will provide different opportunities for crime, which may or may not be associated with levels of 'eyes on the street'. This does not mean that we should not design diverse and vibrant urban spaces, as Jacobs (1961) advised. Rather, it means that all urban areas should be assessed with a critical understanding of their potential crime risks in order to employ the appropriate mitigation strategies against such risks.

Conclusions

In a rapidly urbanizing world, where over half of the population now lives in cities, urban sustainability has tremendous significance. Indeed, crime can adversely affect both urban sustainability and public health (Du Plessis, 1999; Cozens, 2002, 2007a, 2007b). In *The Death and Life* (1961, p. 26) Jacobs states: 'I hope no reader will try to transfer my observations into guides as to what goes on in towns, or little cities, or in suburbs which are still suburban'. Few planners, however, seem to be familiar with this passage and planning policies (including those associated with New Urbanism) appear to ignore Jacobs's warnings. More importantly, the profession has not engaged with the theories and evidence on crime and the city since Jacobs's first attracted attention to this topic in 1961.

Jacobs (*Ibid.*, p. 31) commented: 'To build city districts that are custom made for easy crime is idiotic. Yet that is what we do'. Failing to refine Jacobs's ideas in the light of subsequent developments in criminological theory and in data collection and analysis may mean that we continue to design urban spaces, which are inevitably criminogenic. Fifty years ago, Jacobs (*Ibid.*, p. 16) wrote 'I hope any reader of this book will constantly and skeptically test what I say against his own knowledge of cities and their behavior'. By ignoring both Jacobs and her successors, and treating the issue of urban crime in a marginal manner at best, the opportunity for planners and other professionals to create truly sustainable cities for tomorrow is at the very least jeopardized, if not denied. This chapter has attempted to revisit Jacobs (1961) as well as those who have followed in her footsteps and to test their ideas within a twenty-first century context. Crime is as much a barrier to the future wellbeing of urban society as is unemployment, the physical deterioration of the fabric of cities, or economic decline. Jacobs (1961) initiated and built the very foundations of the discussion that focuses on how this task may be achieved.

If the nature of knowledge is to build on the contributions of previous analysts (acknowledging both the strengths and weaknesses of their research), then Jane Jacobs has undoubtedly earned her place on the list of significant contributors in planning and all associated built environment professions, including those charged with the responsibility for policing our cities. However, it is argued that the disciplines of planning, architecture and urban design have failed to keep pace with the development of key theories and evidence from the field of environmental criminology ever since Jacobs highlighted the importance of the urban stage in the complex understanding of crime. On the positive side, it should be noted that all forty-three police forces in England and Wales have now appointed dedicated architectural liaison officers who are responsible for advising developers, planners and local authorities on issues concerning the relationship between the design of the urban fabric and crime. This clearly underpins the operational impact of Jacobs's ideas. Jane Jacobs (*Ibid.*, p. 50) identified the city as 'a complex order' where she astutely observed the 'heart-of-the-day ballet' and the 'deep-night ballet'. A half a century later, it is likely that she would have encouraged planners and other built environment professionals to engage routinely and tirelessly with the complexity of crime, considering both the stage and the 'balletic drama' that is the city of the twenty-first century.

References

Adeane, M. (2007) Personal communication via email 17 February. Drawings produced by Design Design, Perth, Western Australia.

American Planning Association (2007) *Legislation and Policy*. Available at http://www.planning.org/policyguides/smartgrowth.htm. Accessed 15 February 2012.

Angel, S. (1968) Discouraging Crime through City Planning. Working paper No. 75. University of California, Berkeley.

Appleyard, D. (1980) *Livable Streets, Protected Neighborhoods*. Berkeley, CA: University of California Press.

Armitage, R. (2007) Sustainability versus safety: confusion, conflict and contradiction in designing out crime, in Farrell, G., Bowers, K., Johnson, S. and Townsley, M. (eds.) *Imagination for Crime Prevention, Prevention Studies*, 21. New York: Criminal Justice Press, pp 81–110.

Armitage, R., Monchuk, L. and Rogerson, M. (2010) It looks good, but what is it like to live there? Exploring the impact of innovative housing design on crime. *European Journal on Criminal Policy Research*, **16**(4), pp. 1–26.

Atlas, R. (1991) The other side of defensible space. *Security Management*, March, pp. 63–66.

Barnyard, V. (2008) Measurement and correlates of pro-social bystander behaviour: the case of interpersonal violence. *Violence and Victims*, **23**(1), pp. 83–97.

Baum, A. and Valins, S. (1977) *Architecture and Social Behavior: Psychological Studies of Social Density*. Hillsdale, NJ: Erlbaum.

Beavon, D., Brantingham, P. and Brantingham, P. (1994) The influence of street networks on the patterning of property offenses, in Clarke, R. (ed.) *Crime Prevention Studies*, Volume 2. Monsey, NY: Criminal Justice Press.

Bevis, C. and Nutter, J. (1978) *Changing Street Layouts to Reduce Residential Burglary*. Minneapolis, MN: Minnesota Crime Prevention Center.

Bottoms, A. and Wiles, P. (1997) Environmental criminology, in Maguire, M., Moran, R. and Reiner, R. (eds.) *The Oxford Handbook of Criminology*. Oxford: Clarendon Press.

Bowers, K., Johnson, S. and Hirschfield, A. (2005) Closing-off opportunities for crime: an evaluation of alley-gating. *European Journal on Criminal Policy and Research*, **10**(4), pp. 285–308.

Brantingham, P.J. and Brantingham, P.L. (1981) *Environmental Criminology*. Beverly Hills, CA: Sage.

Brantingham, P.J. and Brantingham, P.L. (1984) *Patterns in Crime*. New York: Macmillan.

Brantingham, P.J. and Brantingham, P.L. (1993) Nodes, paths and edges: considerations on the complexity of crime and the physical environment. *Journal of Environmental Psychology*, **13**, pp. 3–28.

Brantingham, P.J. and Brantingham, P.L. (1998) Environmental criminology: from theory to urban planning practice. *Studies on Crime and Crime Prevention*, **7**(1), pp. 31–60.

Brantingham, P.J. and Brantingham, P.L. (2008) Crime pattern theory, in Wortley, R. and Mazerolle, L. (eds.) *Environmental Criminology and Crime Analysis*. Cullompton, Devon: Willan.

Brantingham, P., Dyreson, A. and Brantingham, P. (1976) Crime seen through a cone of resolution. *American Behavioral Scientist*, **20**(2), pp. 261–273.

Browning, C., Byron, R., Calder, C., Krivo, L., Kwan, M., Lee, J. and Peterson, R. (2010) Commercial density, residential concentration, and crime: land use patterns and violence in neighborhood context. *Journal of Research in Crime and Delinquency*, **47**(3), pp. 329–357.

Buck, A., Hakim, S. and Rengert, G. (1993) Burglar alarms and the choice behavior of burglars: a suburban phenomenon. *Journal of Criminal Justice*, **21**, pp. 497–507.

Calhoun, J.B. (1962) Population density and social pathology. *Scientific American*, **206**, pp. 139–148.

Cisneros, H.G. (1995) *Defensible Space: Deterring Crime and Building Community*. Washington, DC: Department of Housing and Urban Development,

Clarke, R. (1992) *Situational Crime Prevention: Successful Case Studies*, 1st ed. New York: Harrow and Heston.

Clarke, R. (1997) *Situational Crime Prevention: Successful Case Studies*, 2nd ed. New York: Harrow and Heston.

Clarke, R. and Eck, J. (2007) *Understanding Risky Facilities*, Problem-Oriented Guides for Police Series, Problem-Solving Tools No. 6. Washington DC: U.S. Department of Justice.

CNU (Congress for the New Urbanism) (2001) *Charter of the New Urbanism*. Available at http://cnu.org/sites/files/charter_english.pdf. Accessed 15 February 2012.

Cohen, L. and Felson, M. (1979) Social change and crime rate trends: a routine activity approach. *American Sociological Review*, **44**, pp. 588–608.

Commonwealth of Australia (1995) *AMCORD: A National Resource Document for Residential Development*. Canberra: Commonwealth of Australia, Department of Housing and Regional Development.

Cornish, D. and Clarke, R. (1986) *The Reasoning Criminal*. New York: Springer.

Cozens, P. (2002) Sustainable urban development and crime prevention through environmental design for the British city; towards an effective urban environmentalism for the 21st century. *Cities*, **19**(2), pp. 129–137.

Cozens, P. (2007a) Planning, crime and urban sustainability, in Kungolas, A., Brebbia, C. and Beriatos, E. (eds.) *Sustainable Development and Planning III*. Southampton: WIT Press, pp. 187–196.

Cozens, P. (2007b) Public health and the potential benefits of crime prevention through environmental design. *The NSW Public Health Bulletin*, **18**(11/12), pp. 232–237. Available online at http://www.publish.csiro.au/nid/226/issue/4094.htm.

Cozens, P. (2008a) Crime prevention through environmental design (CPTED) in Western Australia: planning for sustainable urban futures. *International Journal of Sustainable Development and Planning*, **3**(3), pp. 272–292.

Cozens, P. (2008b) Crime prevention through environmental design (CPTED); origins, concepts, current status and future directions, in Wortley, R. (ed.) *Environmental Criminology and Crime Analysis*. Cullompton, Devon: Willan, Chapter 9, pp. 153–177.

Cozens, P. (2008c) New Urbanism, crime and the suburbs: a review of the evidence. *Urban Policy and Research*, **26**(3), pp. 1–16.

Cozens, P. (2009) Environmental Criminology and Planning: Dialogue for a New Perspective on Safer Cities, paper presented at the 5th International Conference on Planning and Design, College of Planning and Design, National Cheng Kung University, Taiwan, 25–29th May.

Cozens, P. (2010) Planning policy and designing out crime in Western Australia – the issue of permeability, in Alexander, I., Hedgcock, D. and Grieve, S. (eds.) *Planning Perspectives from Western Australia: A Reader in Theory and Practice*. Fremantle: Fremantle Press, Chapter 17, pp. 307–323.

Cozens, P. (2012) *Crime Prevention for Planners, Designers and Communities: Beyond the CPTED Approach*. Western Australia: Praxis Education.

Cozens, P. (2011) Urban planning and environmental criminology: towards a new perspective for safer cities. *Planning Practice and Research*, **26**(4), pp. 481–508.

Cozens, P. and Hillier, D. (2008) The shape of things to come: new urbanism, the grid and the cul-de-sac. *International Planning Studies*, **13**(1), pp. 51–73.

Cozens, P. and Love, T. (2009) Permeability as a process for controlling crime: a view from Western Australia. *Built Environment*, **35**(3), pp. 346–365.

Cozens, P., Pascoe, T. and Hillier, D. (2004) Critically reviewing the theory and practice of secured-by-design for residential new-build housing in Britain. *Crime Prevention and Community Safety*, **6**(1), pp.13–29.

Cozens, P., Saville, G. and Hillier D. (2005) Crime prevention through environmental design (CPTED): a review and modern bibliography. *Journal of Property Management*, **23**(5), pp. 328–356.

Darley, J.M. and Latane, B. (1968) Bystander intervention in emergencies: diffusion of responsibility. *Journal of Personality and Social Psychology*, **8**, pp. 377–383.

Davison, E. and Smith, W. (2003) Exploring accessibility versus opportunity crime factors. *Sociation Today. The Journal of The North Carolina Sociological Association*, **1**(1). Available at http://www.ncsociology.org/sociationtoday/raleigh.htm.

Dean, L.M., Pugh, W.M. and Gunderson, E.K. (1978) The behavioral effects of crowding: definitions and methods. *Environment and Behavior*, **10**, pp. 413–31.

DETR (1998) *Places, Streets and Movement. A Companion Guide to Design Bulletin 32: Residential Roads and Footpaths*. London: HMSO.

Dietrick, B. (1977) The Environment and Burglary Victimization in a Metropolitan Suburb. Paper presented at the Annual Meeting of the American Society of Criminology, Atlanta, Georgia.

Du Plessis, C. (1999) The links between crime prevention and sustainable development. *Open House International*, **24**(1), pp. 33–40.

Durkheim, E. (1893) *The Division of Labour in Society*. New York: Free Press.

Ellen, I. and O'Reagan, K. (2009) Crime and U.S. cities: recent patterns and implications. *The Annals of the American Academy of Political and Social Science*, **626**(1), pp. 22–38.

Fattah, E.A. (1991) *Understanding Criminal Victimization: An Introduction to Theoretical Victimology*. Scarborough, NJ: Prentice-Hall.

Felson, M. (1987) Routine activities and crime prevention in the developing metropolis. *Criminology*, **25**, pp. 911–931.

Felson, M. and Boba, R. (2010) *Crime and Everyday Life*, 4th ed. Thousand Oaks, CA: Sage.

Gans, H. (1962) *The Urban Villagers*. New York: Free Press.

Gilbert, N. (2002) *Transformation of the Welfare State. The Silent Surrender of Public Responsibility*. Oxford: Oxford University Press.

Gove, W.R., Hughs, M. and Galle, O.R. (1977) Over-crowding in the home: an empirical investigation of its possible pathological consequences. *American Sociological Review*, **44**, pp. 59–80.

Graham, K. and Homel, R. (2008) *Raising the Bar: Preventing Aggression in and around Bars, Pubs and Clubs*. Cullompton, Devon: Willan.

Greenberg, S. and Rohe, W. (1984) Neighborhood design and crime: a test of two perspectives. *Journal of the American Planning Association*, **50**, pp. 48–60.

Greenberg. S., Rohe, W. and Williams, J. (1982) Safety in urban neighborhoods: a comparison of physical characteristics and informal territorial control in high and low crime neighborhoods. *Population and Environment*, **5**(3), pp. 141–165.

Hakim, S., Rengert, G. and Shachamurove, Y. (2001) Target search of burglars: a revisited economic model. *Papers in Regional Science*, **80**, pp. 121–137.

Harries, K. (2006) Property crimes and violence in United States: an analysis of the influence of population density, *International Journal of Criminal Justice Sciences*, **1**(2). Available at http://cjsjournal. brinkster.net/harries.html.

Hart, T. and Miethe, T. (2008) Exploring bystander presence and intervention in nonfatal violent victimization: when does helping really help? *Violence and Victims*, **23**(5), pp. 637–651.

Jacobs, J. (1961) *The Death and Life of Great American Cities*. New York: Random House.

Jeffery, C. and Zahm, D. (1993) Crime prevention through environmental design, opportunity theory, and rational choice models, in Clarke, R. and Felson, M. (eds.) *Routine Activity and Rational Choice*. Piscataway, NJ: Transaction Publishers, pp. 323–350.

Jenkins, S. (2006) Jane Jacobs: adapt, don't destroy: Leeds is the template to revive our scarred cities. *The Guardian*, 5 May. Available at http://www.guardian.co.uk/commentisfree/2006/may/05/ comment.communities. Accessed 17 February 2012.

Johnson, S. and Bowers, K.J. (2010) Permeability and burglary risk: are cul-de-sacs safer? *Quantitative Journal of Criminology*, **26**(1), pp. 89–111.

Kelling, G.L. and Coles, C. (1996) *Fixing Broken Windows. Restoring Order and Reducing Crime in Our Communities*. New York: Touchstone, Simon and Schuster.

Kinney, J.B., Brantingham, P.L., Wuschke, K., Kirk, M.G. and Brantingham, P.J. (2008) Crime attractors, generators and detractors: land use and urban crime opportunities. *Built Environment*, **34**(1), pp. 62–74.

Lasley, J. (1998) *Designing Out Gang Homicides and Street Assaults*. Washington DC: U.S. National Institute of Justice.

Luedtke, G. & Associates (1970) *Crime and the Physical City: Neighborhood Design Techniques for Crime Reduction*. Washington DC: U.S. Department of Justice.

Macintyre, S. and Homel, R. (1997) Danger on the dance floor: a study on interior design, crowding and aggression in nightclubs, in Homel. R. (ed.) *Policing for Prevention: Reducing Crime, Public Intoxication and Injury*. Monsey, NY: Criminal Justice Press, pp. 91–113.

Maguire, M. (1982) *Burglary in a Dwelling*. London: Heinemann.

Marquand, D. (2004) *Decline of the Public*. Cambridge: Polity.

Matthews, R. (1992) Developing more effective strategies for curbing prostitution, in Clarke, R. (ed.) *Situational Crime Prevention: Successful Case Studies*. New York: Harrow and Heston.

Moffat, R. (1983) Crime prevention through environmental design – a management perspective. *Canadian Journal of Criminology*, **25**, pp. 19–31.

Moores, S. (2000) *Media and Everyday Life in Modern Society*. Edinburgh: Edinburgh University Press.

Morgan, C.J. (1978) Bystander intervention: experimental test of a formal model. *Journal of Personality and Social Psychology*, **36**, pp. 43–55.

Newman, O. (1973) *Defensible Space: People and Design in the Violent City*. London: Architectural Press.

Newman, O. (1995) Defensible space: a new physical planning tool for urban revitalization/ *Journal of the American Planning Association*, **61**, pp. 2149–2155.

Newman, O. (2003) Personal email to Stephen Town, Police Architectural Liaison Officer, Bradford District. Received 1 December.

ODPM (Office of the Deputy Prime Minister) (2004) *Places: The Planning System and Crime Prevention*. London: ODPM.

Paulus, P. (1988) *Prison Crowding: A Psychological Perspective*. New York: Springer.

Plater-Zyberk, E. (1993) Five qualities of good design. *ANY*, No. 1, July/August, p. 12.

Poyner, B. (2006). *Crime Free Housing in the 21st Century*. London: Jill Dando Institute of Crime Science.

Putnam, R. (1995) Bowling alone: America's declining social capital. *Journal of Democracy*, **6**(1), pp. 65–78.

Roberts, M. (2004) *Good Practice in Managing the Evening and Late Night Economy: A Literature Review from an Environmental Perspective*. London: ODPM.

Ross, C. and Mirowsky, J. (1999) Disorder and decay: the concept and measurement of perceived neighborhood disorder. *Urban Affairs Review*, **34**(3), pp. 412–432.

Rubenstein, H., Murray, C., Motoyama, T. and Rouse, W. (1980) *The Link between Crime and the Built Environment. The Current State of Knowledge*. Washington DC: National Institute of Justice.

Sampson, R. and Raudenbush, S. (1999) Systematic social observation of public spaces: A new look at disorder in urban neighborhoods *American Journal of Sociology*, **105**, pp. 603–651.

Sampson, R., Raudenbush, S. and Felton, E. (1997) Neighborhoods and violent crime: a multilevel study of collective efficacy. *Science*, **227**, pp. 918–923.

Saville, G. and Cleveland, G. (1997) 2nd Generation CPTED: An Antidote to the Social Y2K Virus of Urban Design. Paper presented at the 2nd Annual International CPTED Conference, Orlando, FL, 3–5 December. Available at www.cpted.net.

Schneider, R. and Kitchen, T. (2002) *Planning for Crime Prevention: A Transatlantic Perspective*. London: Routledge.

Schneider, R. and Kitchen, T. (2007) *Crime Prevention and the Built Environment*. London: Routledge.

Sheard, M. (1991) *Report on Burglary Patterns: The Impact of Cul-de-Sacs*. Delta, British Columbia: Delta Police Department.

Sorensen, D. (2003) *The Nature and Prevention of Residential Burglary: A Review of the International Literature with an Eye towards Prevention in Denmark*. Copenhagen: Ministry of Justice.

Taylor, M. and Nee, C. (1988) The role of cues in simulated residential burglary. *British Journal of Criminology*, **28**, pp. 396–401.

Taylor, R. (1988) *Human Territorial Functioning*. Cambridge: Cambridge University Press.

Taylor, R. and Harrell, A. (1996) *Physical Environment and Crime*. Washington, DC: U.S. Department of Justice.

Taylor, R., Koons, B., Kurtz, E., Greene, J. and Perkins, D. (1995) Street blocks with more nonresidential land use have more physical deterioration: evidence from Baltimore and Philadelphia. *Urban Affairs Review*, **31**, pp. 120–136.

Taylor, R.B., Shumaker, S.A. and Gottfredson, S.D. (1985) Neighborhood-level links between physical features and local sentiments: deterioration, fear of crime, and confidence. *Journal of Architectural Planning and Research*, **2**, pp. 261–275.

Thomas, C. and Bromley, R. (2000) City-center revitalisation: problems of fragmentation and fear in the evening and night-time city. *Urban Studies*, **37**(8), pp.1403–1429.

Town, S. and O'Toole, R. (2005) Crime-friendly neighborhoods: how 'New Urbanist' planners sacrifice safety in the name of 'openness' and 'accessibility'. *Reason*, February. Available at http://www.reason.com/news/show/36489.html. Accessed 17 February 2012.

Town, S., Davey, C. and Wooton, A. (2003) *Design Against Crime: Secure Urban Environments by Design*. Salford: The University of Salford.

Wagner, A. (1997) A study of traffic pattern modifications in an urban crime prevention program. *Journal of Criminal Justice*, **25**(1), pp. 19–30.

White, G. (1990) Neighborhood permeability and burglary rates. *Justice Quarterly* **7**(1), pp. 57–67.

Whyte, W. (1943) *Street Corner Society: The Social Structure of an Italian Slum*. Chicago, IL: University of Chicago Press.

Wilcox, P., Quinsenberry, N., Cabrera, D. and Jones, S. (2004) Busy places and broken windows? Towards defining the role of physical structure and process in community crime models. *Sociological Quarterly*, **45**(2), pp. 185–207.

Wilson, J. and Kelling, G. (1982) The police and neighborhood safety. 'Broken windows'. *The Atlantic Monthly*, No. 3, pp. 29–38.

Wirth, L. (1938) *Urbanism as a Way of Life*. New York: Irvington Publishing.

Yang, X. (2006) Exploring the Influence of Environmental Features on Residential Burglary using Spatial-Temporal Pattern Analysis. Unpublished PhD thesis, University of Florida. Available at www://etd.fcla.edu/UF/UFE0013390/yang_x.pdf.

Zavoski, R., Lapidus, G., Lerer, T., Burke, G. and Banco, L. (1999) Evaluating the impact of a street barriers on urban crime. *Injury Prevention*, **5**, pp. 65–68.

Chapter 15

Jane Jacobs and the Theory of Placemaking in Debates of Sustainable Urbanism

Anirban Adhya

In 2011 Alan Berger, founder of P-REX and Professor of Urban Design and Landscape Architecture at Massachusetts Institute of Technology presented a keynote lecture to the Architecture Research Centers Consortium Conference hosted by the Lawrence Technological University College of Architecture and Design. Berger's lecture explored 'Exterior Landscapes', large-scale unintended environmental consequences produced by distant politico-economic activities, as sites of research, analysis, and 'systemic design'[1] intervention (Berger, 2009). Throughout his lecture, he showed examples of ill-planned decisions of the past and called for creative research-based design approaches today. During the question-and-answer session, I brought up Jane Jacobs's thoughts from *Dark Age Ahead* (2008) about the failure of the five fundamental pillars of life in the United States and Canada – family, education, government, science, and culture – in relation to Berger's position on the role of the professional in today's society. In response, Berger argued for making changes in the system by being a part of the system itself, rather than criticizing the system from outside as Jacobs did. Although he conceded the relevance of the issues Jacobs raises, he concluded by saying, 'I will not quote Jane Jacobs in a research conference as she is not an urban planner' (Berger, 2011).

Like *Dark Age Ahead*, but many years earlier, Jane Jacobs's best-known book, *The Death and Life of Great American Cities*, elicited strong reactions from the disciplines of architecture and planning. Like Professor Berger, most of Jacobs's 1960s critics asserted that her lack of formal education in urban planning disqualified her as a relevant critic of the discipline. They dismissed her work as mere narrative and the reflections of a naïve woman who lacked scientific knowledge and training in urban research methods. For example, after Jacobs published *The Death and Life*, the Pittsburgh Housing Commissioner said that she has 'seemingly limited experience in her chosen field' and the *Pittsburgh Post-Gazette* described her as 'a housewife who likes her neighborhood as it is, diverse' (Alexiou, 2006, p. 86). From a scientific research perspective, her work seems conversational and atheoretical because her observations are grounded in common sense and human experience. I argue, however, that Jacobs's narrative in *The Death and Life* is grounded in the theory and practice of placemaking. In her book, she speaks of people and places, how people come to love the places they live in, and how people continuously appropriate the environments they find themselves in.

In this chapter, my goal is to expand Jacobs's seminal thinking from 50 years ago by (1) uncovering Jacobs's model of scepticism, (2) underlining Jacobs's relevance to debates of sustainable urbanism and (3) theorizing her work through the framework of placemaking. To that end, I simultaneously analyze Jacobs's work and the theory of placemaking. First, through a critical review of *The Death and Life*, I outline Jacobs's model of scepticism, discussing her critique of orthodox architecture and planning practices. I then acknowledge the importance of Jacobs's call for a critical planning practice that recognizes the perpetual gap between abstract theoretical planning practices (i.e. the production of space) and the lived experiences of people in places (i.e. the consumption of space). Second, I apply Jacobs's critical planning approach to the discussion of sustainable urbanism and explain how Jacobs's vision of the city as a system of organized complexity, as well as her focus on human relationships, helps us to develop an ecological perspective on sustainability in cities. Finally, I analyze Jacobs's work – which addresses the gap between production and consumption of space as a question of sustainability – through the lens of placemaking theory, outlining the intellectual origins of placemaking and their connection to Jacobs's narrative. This theoretical analysis demonstrates that key components of Jacobs's model of scepticism (empirical understanding, critical questions, and everyday human action) can also be seen as components of the theory of placemaking, specifically 'confirmation, interrogation, and action framing'[2] (Schneekloth and Shibley, 1995, p. 7).

Jacobs's Model of Scepticism

The Death and Life of Great American Cities (1961) was Jane Jacobs's call for radical reform of the architecture and planning practices of her time. Taking a highly critical stance and underscoring the value of a humanistic understanding of cities, Jacobs presented a 'model of skepticism' (Goldberger, 2006). She questioned the reductionist philosophy of classical planning practices and challenged the seemingly complex statistical justifications for planning theories and interventions prevalent during the 1960s. This chapter extends the model of scepticism presented in *The Death and Life* and argues for its relevance in today's urban context. In her book, Jacobs highlights the role of diverse human values, everyday human actions, and common everyday spaces in sustaining the vitality of urban environments.

Questions of difference and diversity in the 'post-modern' city have dominated recent architecture and planning practice discourses. In developing their ideas in *The Intercultural City*, Wood and Landry (2007) have underscored the value of variety as 'a driving force for long-term urban prosperity' and have credited Jane Jacobs as the 'first writer' to think about social, economic, and environmental diversity as essential components of a vibrant urban life (*Ibid.*, pp. 46, 183). In a similar vein, Sandercock's (1998, 2000) call for planners to learn to acknowledge and work with emotions within the long-term project of intercultural co-existence also highlights the reality of working in today's multidimensional and complex urban environments. This need for architects and planners to learn to become comfortable with acknowledging differences and accommodating shifting possibilities of development has also been argued in recent debates about *Planning in Divided Cities* (Gaffikin and Morrissey, 2011) and *The Uncertain City* (Rahder and Milgrom, 2004). Jacobs's model of scepticism thus remains relevant as we attempt to understand the city and to address urban problems in the face of evolving social, economic, and environmental crises. Jacobs's model of scepticism is invaluable for its unrelenting critique of prevalent planning processes and for its unceasing search for creative, human-oriented planning.

Jacobs's Critique of Architecture and Urban Planning

The Death and Life was an 'attack' on the practices of 'city planning and rebuilding' adopted by the dominant individuals and establishments of the modernist planning profession in the 1950s and 60s (Jacobs, 1961, p. 3). Traditional planning approaches were based on normative rationalization reflecting professional knowledge created by the institutions of learning and practice. Jacobs proposed a new and radical lens through which to view the urban world: the lens of empirical observation and community intuition. Writing about 'common, ordinary things', Jacobs draws conclusions based on an understanding of 'how cities work in real life' (*Ibid.*, p. 4), and she applies this understanding to the planning and rebuilding of cities. Empirical observation is thus an important strategy in her work, which provides a counterbalance to the normative values of education, practice, and power.

Jacobs argues that architects, planners, politicians, and bureaucrats accept modernist urban planning theories such as the City Beautiful (Daniel Burnham, 1893), the Garden City (Ebenezer Howard, 1898), and the Radiant City (Le Corbusier, 1935) at their face value. The proponents of these planning and design theories, through their revolutionary visions and strong imagery, created a utopian ideal symbolizing progress and modernism. These ideals, however, failed to address questions of appropriateness and applicability and were often used to generate abstract forms of urban planning and design. At the same time, architects, planners, politicians, and bureaucrats who embraced the modernist vision dismissed their own intuitive knowledge of cities – knowledge based on common sense, observation of everyday urban life, and social statistics – simply because it was not part of their traditional physical planning and policy education. Jacobs's critique of the planning establishment in the United States of the 1960s is often specifically studied in the context of Robert Moses's urban renewal in New York City. However, Jacobs's critique of the stagnation of urban design and planning as a profession and as a discipline remains relevant to recent urban conversations within the United States and beyond (Klemek, 2007; Ouroussoff, 2006; Sancton, 2000; Wekerle, 2000).

Jacobs demonstrated that traditional planning is driven by a political-economic 'growth machine' (Molotch, 1976, p. 310) shaped by the norms, institutions, and power structures of exclusive decision-making processes. *The Death and Life* is a fundamental critique of this traditional top-down planning methodology and the modernist architecture and planning approach prevalent during the 1960s. Jacobs's contributions to everyday urbanism, civic activism, historic preservation, and community-based planning have long been acknowledged. The philosophy of accommodating grassroots-level efforts has led to a proliferation of community-based bottom-up planning approaches, often opposed to traditional planning policies based on economic development and political interests (Jacobs, 1961, p. 3). Inspired by Jacobs's participatory planning ideology, subsequent works like *Mongrel Cities* (Sandercock, 2003) and *Cities: Reimagining the Urban* (Amin and Thrift, 2002) have further developed new inclusive models of urban planning. These inclusive models are characterized by grassroots-level functions, neighbourhood and community institutions, people-driven decision-making processes, and place-specific design processes (table 15.1).

Table 15.1. Jacobs's critique of orthodox urban planning and key contributions of *The Death and Life*.

Issue	Traditional Urban Planning	Jane Jacobs's The Death and Life
Philosophy	Normative and rationalistic	Empirical and humanistic
Framework	Positivism – scientific and rational search for a single truth	Emancipatory and post-structural – pluralistic possibilities
Premise	Planning as reaction to socio-political-environmental contexts	Planning as intrinsic understanding of places and creative placemaking
Methodology	Imposition of orthodox modern design principles	Design recommendations based on resident experience and direct naturalistic observation
Boundaries	Exclusive and profession-based	Inclusive and people-oriented
Knowledge	Professional or expert knowledge	Situated knowledge – expert knowledge merged with local knowledge

Jacobs's Call for a Critical Planning Practice

The urban planning discipline has continually encountered questions of formal intervention and its social implications. Jane Jacobs underlines the debate between a modernist morphological understanding of the urban environment (Lofland, 1998; Mumford, 1937; Project for Public Spaces, nd) and a post-modern notion of the public sphere in cities (Sandercock, 2003, Amin, 1995). This urban debate is evident in the polarization of contemporary urban design theory and practice regarding understanding of the 'city'. Some planning scholars and practitioners are committed to social processes of diversity and equity in cities, but they often neglect questions of form, material, and spatial order. Others are devoted to technology, computation, and morphology, but they tend to disregard social and cultural concerns (Hatuka and

D'Hooghe, 2007). Bernard Tschumi (1998) asserts that architects and designers have been unable to reconcile their need to address everyday life with their desire to engage abstract concepts. In a critical urban design article, Aseem Inam proposes a 'meaningful approach to urban design' that is 'teleological' (process-oriented and driven by environmental purpose and role), 'catalytic' (empowering and helpful in improving quality of life) and 'relevant' (grounded in interdisciplinary principles and fundamental human values) (Inam, 2002, pp. 38, 39, 48).

The gap between the spatial understanding of the city (abstract imagined space) and the social experience of the city (lived experience) highlights a problem that has long plagued classical architecture and planning: the difficulty of balancing abstract professional knowledge with specific local knowledge. The ongoing search for a meaningful framework for urban design highlights the incapacity of current urban design philosophies and approaches to bridge that spatial-social divide. The orthodox design and planning approaches consider cities as objects and address urban problems in terms of spatial form and aesthetic values. In contrast, Jacobs's work underscores the importance of understanding cities from the perspective of people's experience of places. In other words, Jacobs's critical practice reveals a need for a humane and process-oriented understanding of the city. Jacobs's approach, built on ongoing attempts to understand the urban context through strategies of empirical analysis, questioning and inclusive decision-making, can be seen as a creative process of placemaking. Through the theory of placemaking, her critical approach also questions the *status quo* and empowers communities and individuals at the grassroots level, making them relevant in the planning and sustenance of a city.

Jane Jacobs's Relevance in Debates of Sustainable Urbanism

Renewed interest in urbanism in the last ten to fifteen years has led to a timely exploration of the roles of urban planning and urban design. Sustainable urbanism in particular is a critical topic now playing out in several current urban debates such as those on metropolitan growth vs. intercity decline (Berger, 2006; Lerup, 2000), urban desirability vs. suburban liveability (Farr, 2007; Neuman, 2005), and defining sustainability vs. practicing sustainability (Neuman, 2005; Fisher, 2010; Sandercock, 2003; Amin and Thrift, 2002). As cities and metropolitan regions face social, economic, and environmental problems associated with the post-industrial economy, these discussions reflect a reinvigorated interest in cities and underscore the need for reflection on the increasingly contested terrain of urban resources and environments.

Despite the richness of debates on the topic, there is no universally accepted definition of sustainable urbanism (Neuman, 2005, pp. 13–14). Farr defines it as 'walkable and transit-served urbanism integrated with high-performance buildings and high-performance infrastructure' (2007, p. 42). This definition emphasizes compactness (density) and biophilia (the intricate bond between humans and nature). Sloan (2008) identifies sustainable urbanism as the recent convergence of complementary philosophies of sustainability and urbanism: 'density, walkability, and integration of mass transit are key to housing large numbers of people with the least impact on the environment' (2008, p. 29). Such an emerging urban-environment alliance is prominent in the development of Leadership in Energy and Environmental Design for Neighborhood Development (LEED ND). In the LEED ND 2009 rating system, sustainable urbanism is defined as a combination of the principles of Sustainable Development, New Urbanism, and Smart Growth movements (USGBC *et al.*, 2009). In LEED ND, building location and community design are considered important to environmental issues of energy conservation and zero-carbon emissions. According to Farr (2007) and Sloan (2008), and LEED ND, common design elements in all sustainable urban projects are the presence of narrow streets, small urban lots, parks and open space, mixed-use buildings, flat green roofs, and public transit system. These design elements highlight an expert knowledge-based approach to sustainable urbanism defined by compactness, density, and green architecture (Neuman, 2005, p. 11). Within these form-based definitions of sustainable urbanism, however, important elements of urban processes such as social diversity, economic equity, and environmental justice are ignored. Jane Jacobs's work is critical in addressing this gap of understanding sustainable urbanism as a process. Jacobs envisioned the city as 'a system of organized complexity' – a notion that allows critical examination of sustainability in cities as a systematic process encompassing social, economic, political, and environmental issues.

The question of sustenance of quality urban environments, posed by Jacobs as a reaction to modernist planning approaches, remains valid: how do urban design and planning practitioners nurture a practice amidst the evolving challenges presented by urban complexity? Our attempts to define sustainability will be more fruitful if we begin from Jacobs's premise that cities are systems of organized complexity (Jacobs 1961, p. 14). Her systematic approach to urban problems also supports a relatively new model of sustainability – the ecological model (Williams *et al.*, 2007, pp. 2–5). Ecology is the scientific study of the distribution and abundance of life and the interactions between organisms and their natural environments (Begon *et al.*, 2006). An ecological point of view recognizes that everything is related to everything. Within this relational framework, the focus shifts from understanding sustainability in terms of a 'green', product-based approach to valuing sustainability as a system of dynamic connective processes – biological interchanges, efficient use and storage of energy, and effective management of natural resources. Inspired by classic works such as *Fundamentals of Ecology* (Odums, 1953) and *Design with Nature* (McHarg, 1992), the ecological model bases its notion of sustainability on systems of relationships within natural systems. Jacobs's notion of cities as organized complex systems adds another dimension to this natural and biological idea of sustainability. Sustainable urbanism or sustainability in an urban system, as interpreted by Jacobs, expands the notion of ecology to relationships among natural systems (soil, climate, hydrology), human systems (social ethics and values), and economic systems (allocation, distribution, and management of resources). In *The Death and Life*, Jacobs describes cities as sites of human ecosystems comprised of human actions, reactions, and interactions. Jacobs reinforces this human-oriented notion of urban sustainability by advocating natural-social-economic diversity. She argues for lively neighbourhoods, heterogeneous demographics, a mix of uses, and pedestrian-friendly design, all of which facilitate human interaction in the urban environment.

In sum, this ecological model of sustainability has three important implications: (1) the ecological systems approach emphasizes a process-oriented notion of sustainability; (2) Jacobs's human-oriented understanding of sustainable urbanism highlights local knowledge and place-specific socio-spatial processes; and (3) this place-specific approach emphasizes connections among environmental, social and economic systems.

Theorizing Jacobs's Model in Relation to the Theory of Placemaking

In *The Death and Life*, Jacobs challenges the orthodox premises of modern planning and the related dogmatic practice of the 1960s profession. She questions the normative values of the profession and sceptically tests them using empathetic observation of everyday human activities. Examining Jacobs's model of scepticism in relation to the two predominant themes discussed in this chapter – critical practice in urban planning and the sustainable-urbanism debate – reveals two common elements. First is the notion of place specificity – place knowledge based on local experience. Second is the process of placemaking – human interaction with and appropriation of a specific environment. Jacobs describes placemaking as an ordinary but fundamental human activity that sustains communities. Her emphasis on place and placemaking suggests a human-oriented understanding of urban sustainability. In this vision, people define, construct, and control the quality of their own environments.

Jacobs's sceptical approach critiques oversimplified constructions of reality (i.e. cities are simple, and urban problems have uniform solutions) as well as overcomplicated scientific analyses (i.e. cities are complex systems with infinite variables, and urban problems cannot be addressed within existing frameworks). Instead, working from her premise that cities are problems of organized complexity, Jacobs argues for a systemic approach to understanding cities by documenting patterns of urban life, observing specific human behaviour in places, and analyzing relationships among important social, economic and environmental variables within an urban system. Jacobs notes that 'cities have the capability of providing something for everybody, only because, and only when, they are created by everybody' (1961, p. 13). She envisions a multifaceted urban ecology in which a place and its publics are fundamental to each other's existence, a view that celebrates interaction as much as it values the shared construction of spaces. Jacobs poses a critical question: how can a place be transformed by everyone living in that place? This question is fundamental to the theory and practice of placemaking.

The Art and Practice of Placemaking

Placemaking is defined as 'the creation, renovation, and maintenance of the shared physical world through the integration of expert professional knowledges with knowledges of place'[3] (Schneekloth and Shibley, 1995, pp. 1, 191). The distinction between professional knowledge and local knowledge has been sharpened since the advent of the Modern Movement in architecture and planning, marked by Congrès International d'Architecture Moderne (CIAM). For sustainable urbanism, this disjunction has had particularly negative consequences, since it provides no appropriate framework for comprehending the heterogeneous complexities of current urban environments. In *The Death and Life*, Jacobs criticizes orthodox professional practitioners for remaining ignorant of local cultures and community contexts (i.e. for lacking place knowledge). In architecture and planning practice, professionals used orthodox modern design models[4] – such as Ebenezer Howard's Garden City and Le Corbusier's Radiant City – irrespective of the urban context and cultural situations (Jacobs, 1961, pp. 17–23). Challenging the indiscriminate implementation of urban renewal projects in the 1960s, Jacobs argues for a systematic, creative process that builds relationships between people and places and among people (Shibley *et al.*, 2003, p. 28).

Placemaking can be understood as the ways in which all human beings transform the places in which they live through diverse creative processes (Schneekloth and Shibley, 1995, p. 1). When planners and architects focus on political processes, social ideologies, and formal typologies, they lose sight of people's everyday actions and experiences. In contrast, Jacobs argues for an alternate understanding of the city based on everyday human experience of urban spaces (e.g. appropriation, micro-public behaviour, and cultural heterogeneity). Thus, Jacobs's emphasis on people and their experiences offers an informal counterpoint to hegemonic planning practices. This alternate approach pushes the boundary of planning and offers challenging yet exciting opportunities to create sustainable places and to incorporate placemaking as an integral part of the planning process.

Components of Placemaking

The theory of placemaking dovetails with Jacobs's view of an ecological system of urban living in which residents and professionals continually strive to understand place ecology and to develop a collaborative approach to decision-making. Jacobs's model of scepticism involves continuous questioning and testing of traditional professional knowledge and intervention practices. In *The Death and Life*, Jacobs not only critiques the traditional planning process, but also outlines different tactics for urban planning and redevelopment (1961, pp. 321–427). Part Four elaborates on specific tactics for housing subsidies (*Ibid.*, p. 321), pedestrian-oriented development (*Ibid.*, p. 338), historic preservation (*Ibid.*, p. 372), economic viability (*Ibid.*, p. 392), and management of urban projects of critical mass (*Ibid.*, p. 405). Jacobs's method of critical inquiry and the strategies she recommends are similar to those of the theory of placemaking, which employs three intellectual processes: (1) confirmation, (2) interrogation, and (3) action framing. Though Jacobs did not discuss the critical components common to her tactics, we can analyze them in relation to these three specific components of placemaking.

Jacobs considers the dialectic of 'confirmation and interrogation' (Freire, 1973) essential to create a space for dialogue for any decision-making process in a place. Through this dialogic process people can discuss diverse ideas, consider opposing interests, and engage conflicting power structures in their communities and neighbourhoods. In the process, they can confirm existing local knowledge. At the same time, the dialogic space also allows people to challenge their own sense of certainty and the *status quo* in their environment. This participatory process empowers residents to question the underlying political and economic forces in the community. The process of interrogation uncovers the basic values and assumptions of human intentions and institutions. Jacobs argued that planning and design insights into the urban environment should be constructed within a dialogic space shared by all participants, including both experts and local residents. The placemaking conversation, according to Jacobs, should situate abstract expert knowledge into specific circumstances without privileging either the experts or the citizens. The confirmation-interrogation process of placemaking, which is also integral to the Jacobs's model of scepticism and her approach to radical intervention, is based on a worldview that recognizes the legitimacy of every person's life experience. Thus Jacobs's approach to planning as critical practice can be conceptualized as applying a thoughtful process of confirmation and interrogation to existing urban conditions and proposed interventions.

Action framing involves examining decisions and interventions in terms of inclusion and exclusion. Those implementing action framing ask who should be involved, what the boundaries of the intervention are, and what methods should be used both in the inquiry and in the project. Answers to these questions help determine the conditions for a participatory process and collaborative action. Proponents of placemaking realize that decisions must be taken during interventions, and that not everybody can be always involved in every decision. But these decisions should be made consciously and sensitively with an awareness of the ethical implications of including and excluding others from the process. Thus, action is framed by a dialogue kept open through the process of confirmation and interrogation. Collective action involves dialogues, debates, and discussions that facilitate an inclusive and emancipating practice of creative placemaking. Jacobs's work thus acknowledges and celebrates a process of action, reaction, and interaction allowing appropriation, transformation, and the development of diverse human interests into a collective framework for placemaking (table 15.2).

Table 15.2. Jacobs's model of scepticism in relation to the process of placemaking.

Features	Jacobs's Model of Scepticism	Process of Placemaking
Confirmation	Bases understanding on empirical observations of the city	Recognizes and acknowledges different sources of knowledge and insight when framing an intervention
Interrogation	Questions *status quo* and conventional planning practices	Constructs knowledge through questions exploring the underlying value structure
Action framing	Bases decisions and interventions on an understanding of the city as a problem of organized complexity	Constructs rules of action in which all knowledges are shared, valued, and evaluated for possible implementation

Conclusions

Twentieth-century discussions of the sustainable city have evolved into a debate about choices between competing interests (e.g. the environment versus the economy). In her understanding of the 'post-modern' city as characterized by heterogeneous agencies with competing interests, Jacobs calls for an ecological approach based on an understanding of the relationships among these agencies. This systemic approach integrates human values in planning decisions that affect choice and accessibility of people to urban resources. Jacobs's call for placemaking, the creation of places for everyday human activities, portrays sustainable urbanism as a catalytic process – a dynamic motivating condition that all strive to reach for the wellbeing of human life. When viewed through the lens of placemaking theory, her work illustrates the powerful role of human construction and of people's engagement in places through spontaneous everyday actions. This human-oriented view encourages us to pursue sustainability within a shared 'dialogic space' (Schneekloth and Shibley, 1995, p. 6), where diverse constituencies are empowered (confirmation), various critical agencies from multiple disciplines are questioned (interrogation), and interventions are implemented (action framing) in a system of organized complexity.

Sustainable Urbanism as an Everyday Human Action

Dolores Hayden (1995) points out that the power of a place is embedded in the everyday actions of people who continuously work to create place. In the same vein, in *The Death and Life*, Jacobs questions the motives behind engineered public policies and utopian public spaces imposed on city life. Jacobs's 'shout on the streets' has inspired post-modern creative planning in which the public realm recognizes the 'right to differences' and 'right to the city' (Sandercock, 2003; Lefebvre, 1991). In her embrace of heterogeneity in cities and 'micro-publics' in the public sphere, Jacobs values the differences that coexist in the everyday urban experience and in analyses of the city. An understanding of the city, which emerges from both Jacobs's model of scepticism and the theory of placemaking, underscores the value of a human-oriented approach to urban problems and a human-oriented creative planning process.

The disciplines of architecture and planning have long struggled to understand the problem of the sustainable city. Current practices often ignore everyday human experience and disregard the importance of everyday human actions in sustainable development. There is a gap between the production and consumption of sustainable design. First, the design profession focusing on iconic green architecture and the planning profession focusing on top-down normative policy-making have struggled to define sustainability in the framework of a city. Sustainability has often been reduced to a 'glistening vision' of green aesthetics and 'branding strategies' of specific interest groups such as political power groups and economic investors (Ventiroso, 2010). Second, the everyday spaces produced for use by people suffer either from over-design and control or from poor planning.

This post-modern crisis in the architectural and planning profession has been summarized by Nan Ellin as a 'postwar development accused of destroying urban heritage; disrupting communities and displacing people; increasing social segregation, accentuating gender role distinctions; diminishing the public realm; and of environmental insensitivity, aesthetic monotony, and downright ugliness' (Ellin, 1996, p. 236). Ellin further explains these transformations not just as results of 'demographic trends, economic policies, and new technologies', but also as those of utopian visions combining incompatible utopian design theories and powerful economic-political influences (*Ibid.*, pp. 236–237). The disconcerting fact is that these normative theories and misplaced priorities of the profession have been producing places that are non-humanistic and unsustainable, and have been diminishing the role of architecture and planning in sustainable placemaking. Jacobs, on the other hand, emphasizes the human connection to place and a process-oriented understanding of sustainability: this is her key contribution to the theory of placemaking. This process-oriented approach is critical to restoring the role of urban planning and design in addressing evolving questions regarding the future of cities and sustainable urbanism. Through the philosophical framework of placemaking, *The Death and Life* and its sceptical approach offer a model of sustainable placemaking through everyday human actions.

Planning as a Creative Process of Placemaking

According to my analysis of *The Death and Life* and the theory of placemaking, Jacobs's work portrays planning as a creative process of placemaking. Jacobs's model of scepticism – pragmatic, anti-essential, and non-deterministic[5] (Plowright, 2010) – is crucial to architecture and urban planning's redefinition as people-oriented and place-specific professions.

Jacobs's conceptual positions and practical tools for understanding cities – the structure of the ordinary, everyday urbanism, naturalistic observation – have strong connections to the theory and practice of placemaking. First, she values the local knowledge people gain from their everyday urban experiences. This form of knowledge, which is based on human actions, reactions, and interactions in places, is as important as professional knowledge. By relying on diverse sources of knowledge rather than one dominant form, Jacobs engages in a complex form of confirmation, the first component of the placemaking process. Second, she demonstrates a new way of understanding cities and developing verifiable positions through ethnographic embedded participation (in communities and places), anthropological empathetic observation (of people and their everyday activities), and objective empiricism (facts and statistics regarding the city and how it really works). Jacobs's reliance on empirical tools for documentation and analysis suggests specific ways to engage in collective interrogation, the second component of the placemaking process. Finally, Jacobs saw the city as 'a problem of organized complexity' (Jacobs, 1961, p. 433) and envisioned urban planning as a systematic search for knowledge to better understand the evolving organized complexity of the city. This view requires a systematic process-oriented understanding of urban life that allows planners and designers to move away from an orthodox framework based on normative 'behavior and appearance' (*Ibid.,* p. 16). It also discourages the tendency to address urban problems using predetermined formal solutions adapted from inappropriate contexts. Jacobs argued that planners and designers should continuously question the *status quo*, address evolving issues through trial and error in cities, and learn from the successes and failures of different tactics. This is the creative process of implementing actions, the third component of the placemaking process. This tripartite system of query-analysis-application (or, to use placemaking terminology, confirmation-interrogation-action framing) represents an attempt to 'constantly and skeptically test' urban knowledge (*Ibid.,* p. 16), and it is central to Jacobs's notion of critical planning. In other words, Jacobs's tools for a query-based critical planning approach support the continuous construction, validation, and application of situated knowledge through the placemaking process.

Notes

1. Alan Berger (2009) coined the term 'systemic design' to describe interventions to reintegrate disvalued landscapes into urbanized territories and regional ecologies.
2. In *Placemaking: The Art and Practice of Building Communities* (1995, p. 7), Lynda Schneekloth and Robert Shibley identify 'confirmation, interrogation, and action framing' as three important components of collective placemaking in which professionals and local residents are engaged in 'sustained conversation about making places'.
3. Schneekloth and Shibley (1995) describe the conceptual framework of placemaking as a fundamental, ordinary activity and as a process of human labour that 'makes, transforms, and cares for places'.
4. Orthodox modern city planning and architectural design ideas and interventions like the Garden City (Ebenezer Howard), La Ville Radieuse (Le Corbusier), and Broadacre City (Frank Lloyd Wright) are based on the premise that the contemporary city is an unhealthy, dying place. The same premise is at the root of modern urban programmes in United States such as the Urban Renewal programme and the suburban movement after World War II. Recent urban paradigms such as New Urbanism and Post-Urbanism try to act as counterpoints to contemporary urban trends such as suburban sprawl, inner-city decline and the formation of edge cities.
5. Plowright, in his oral presentation 'Use of Philosophy' (2010), outlines three core philosophical characteristics necessary for the relevance of theory to architectural application. These three qualities are integral to Jacobs's model of scepticism, and they reinforce Jacobs's model as a continuous process of testing and validation rather than one that offers deterministic physical models.

References

Alexiou, A. (2006) *Jane Jacobs: Urban Visionary*. New Brunswick, NJ: Rutgers University Press.

Amin, A. (1995) *Behind the Myth of European Union: Prospects for Cohesion*. London: Psychology Press.

Amin, A. and Thrift, N. (2002) *Cities: Reimagining the Urban*. Cambridge: Polity Press.

Begon, M., Townsend, C.R. and Harper, J.L. (2006) *Ecology: From Individuals to Ecosystems*. Malden, MA: Wiley-Blackwell.

Berger, A. (2006) *Drosscape: Wasting Land in Urban America*. New York: Princeton Architectural Press.

Berger, A. (2009) *SYSTEMIC DESIGN: Wetland Machines*. P-REX. Available at http://www.theprex.net/#!__pontine-machine. Accessed 2 January 2011.

Berger, A. (2011) Exterial Landscapes. Keynote lecture presented to CONSIDERING RESEARCH:

Reflecting upon current themes in Architectural Research, Architecture Research Centers Consortium Conference, Lawrence Technological University, Michigan, 21 April 2011.

Ellin, N. (1996) *Postmodern Urbanism*. New York: Princeton Architectural Press.

Farr, D. (2007) *Sustainable Urbanism: Urban Design with Nature*. New York: Wiley.

Fisher, T. (2010) Viral cities. *Places* [online]. Available at http:// http://places.designobserver.com/feature/viral-cities/13948/. Accessed 17 February 2012.

Freire, P. (1973) *Education for Critical Consciousness*. New York: Continuum.

Gaffikin, F. and Morrissey, M. (2011) *Planning in Divided Cities: Collaborative Shaping of Contested Space*. Chichester: Wiley-Blackwell.

Goldberger, P. (2006) Uncommon sense: remembering Jane Jacobs. *The American Scholar* [online], Autumn Issue. Available at http://www.theamericanscholar.org/uncommon-sense/. Accessed 23 March 2011.

Hatuka, T. and D'Hooghe, A. (2007) After postmodernism: readdressing the role of utopia in urban design and planning. *Places*, **19**(2), pp. 20–27.

Hayden, D. (1995) *The Power of Place: Urban Landscapes as Public History*. Cambridge, MA: MIT Press.

Inam, A. (2002) Meaningful urban design: teleologic/catalytic/relevant. *Journal of Urban Design*, **7**(1), pp. 35–58.

Jacobs, J. (1961) *The Death and Life of Great American Cities*. New York: Random House.

Jacobs, J. (2008) *Dark Age Ahead*. New York: Random House.

Klemek, C. (2007) Placing Jane Jacobs within the transatlantic urban conversation. *Journal of American Planning Association*, **73**(1), pp. 49–67.

Lefebvre, H. (1991) *The Production of Space*. Translated from French by D. Nicholson-Smith. Oxford: Blackwell.

Lerup, L. (2000) *After the City*. Cambridge, MA: MIT Press.

Lofland, L.H. (1998) *The Public Realm: Exploring the City's Quintessential Social Territory*. New York: Hawthorne.

McHarg, I.L. (1992) *Design with Nature*. New York: John Wiley.

Molotch, H. (1976) The city as a growth machine: toward a political economy of place. *American Journal of Sociology*, **82**(2), pp. 309–332.

Mumford, L. (1937) What is a city? *Architectural Record*, **82**, November, pp. 59–62.

Neuman, M. (2005) The compact city fallacy. *Journal of Planning Education and Research*, **25**, pp. 11–26.

Odums, E.P. (1953) *Fundamentals of Ecology*. Philadelphia, PA: Saunders.

Ouroussoff, N. (2006) Outgrowing Jane Jacobs and her New York. *New York Times,* 30 April. Available at http://www.nytimes.com/2006/04/30/weekinreview/30jacobs.html. Accessed on 17 February 2012.

Plowright, P. (2010) The Use of Philosophy. Paper presented to Straining Pulp Theory from Architecture Discourse symposium. University of Newcastle and the International Society for the Philosophy of Architecture,14 June 2010.

Project for Public Spaces (nd) [online] Available at http://www.pps.org. Accessed on 17 February 2012.

Rahder, B and Milgrom, R. (2004) The uncertain city: making space for difference. *Canadian Planning and Policy – Amenagement et politique le Canada*, **13**(1), pp. 27–45.

Sancton, A. (2000) Jane Jacobs on the organization of municipal government. *Journal of Urban Affairs*, **22**(4), pp. 463–471.

Sandercock, L. (1998) *Towards Cosmopolis: Planning for Multicultural Cities*. Chichester: Wiley.

Sandercock, L. (2000) Negotiating fear and desire, the future of urban planning in multicultural societies. *Urban Forum*, **11**(2), pp. 201–210.

Sandercock, L. (2003) *Cosmopolis II: Mongrel Cities of the 21st Century*. New York: Continuum.

Schneekloth, L. and Shibley, R. (1995) *Placemaking: The Art and Practice of Building Communities*. New York: Wiley.

Shibley, R., Schneekloth, L. and Hovey, B. (2003) Constituting the public realm of a region: placemaking in the bi-national Niagaras. *Journal of Architectural Education*, **23**(2), pp. 28–32.

Sloan, D. (2008) Sustinable urbanism, in Sloan, D., Goldstein, D. and Gowder, W. (eds.) *A Legal Guide to Urban and Sustainable Development for Planners, Developers, and Architects*. New York: Wiley, pp. 29 60.

Tschumi, B. (1998) The architectural paradox, in Hayes, M. (ed.) *Oppositions.* New York: Princeton Architectural Press, pp. 224–227.

U.S. Green Building Council (USGBC), Congress for the New Urbanism (CNU), and Natural Resources Defense Council (NRDC). 2009. *Leadership in Energy and Environmental Design (LEED) 2009 for Neighborhood Development Rating System*. Washington, DC: USGBC.

Ventiroso, O. (2010) New Towns and Politics Conference, International New Town Institute, Almere, The Netherlands, 11–12 November. Available at http://m.bdonline.co.uk/culture/new-towns-and-politics/5009474.article. Accessed on 30 September 2011.

Wekerle, G. (2000) From eyes on the street to safe cities. *Places*, **13**(1), pp. 44–49.

Williams, D., Orr, D.W, and Watson, D. (2007) *Sustainable Design: Ecology, Architecture, and Planning*. New York: Wiley.

Wood, P. and Landry, C. (2007) *The Intercultural City: Planning for Diversity Advantage*. London: Earthscan.

Chapter 16

Making the Familiar Strange: Understanding Design Practice as Cultural Practice

B.D. Wortham-Galvin

Traditionally anthropology (aka ethnology) has been the academic arena most attentive to everyday life; it is the empirical registering of ways of life. This recording of the quotidian is a means to the end of what anthropologist Clifford Geertz would call a thick description. An ethnographically thick description is the way in which Jane Jacobs's methods of the writing *The Death and Life of Great American Cities* (1961) is most often characterized. Although it makes up a small portion of the corpus, Jacobs's observations about the people and activities on Hudson Street (her home) are what resonate for most readers. Like anthropologist Bronislaw Malinowski, Jacobs was inextricably immersed in the daily lives of the people and place she was studying. In making visible the 'street ballet' of Greenwich Village, by recording the mundane and highly specific actions of daily life, she made the familiar strange. She made visible and significant 'where the what' happens and, most noteworthy, by whom.

But it is also this approach to an anthropology of urbanism that leaves Jacobs under attack and her methodology in question. Often characterized as a housewife without a college degree, Jacobs was in fact an experienced journalist – including a stint at *Architectural Forum* in the 1950s – well versed in the design and socio-economic issues surrounding cities in mid-twentieth-century America (Laurence, 2011). That she eschewed the research methodologies of the university (she attended Columbia University for two years) was purposeful, as it stifled her ability to collect and observe the lived city on her own terms. Her approach was neither scientifically empirical, nor subjectively anecdotal. Incorporating a (for some, uncomfortable) mix of both, the approach clearly rang true for several generations of readers.

Nevertheless, the legitimacy of Jacobs's methods has been called into question (her lack of footnotes and citations being one of the problems noted). She borrows from ethnology, but does not truly replicate it. Why is her version of research so problematic and what does it mean for the design of the built environment – a discipline that is often characterized as creative, mysterious, and anything but scientific? If Jacobs uses ethnographic values rather than strict methodologies, does this render her techniques and observations worthless? Does it mean they are not applicable to design?

This chapter will assert that an anthropology of urbanism is a critical design methodology to be embraced in the making of places in the twenty-first century. This is because place should be more than a simulation of identity or the destruction of existing neighbourhoods in order to make way for new ones with a real 'sense of place'. If place offers a realm of conflicting simultaneity between ideal forms and performative tactics, then an anthropological approach to design offers the ability to understand how people enact places to reveal the politics of context, both to instil and destabilize beliefs and values, and to perpetuate and rebel against tradition (Wortham-Galvin, 2008). Using an anthropology of urbanism as a core design methodology allows places that appear permanent also to embrace the ephemeral nature of dwelling and being. It allows people to become equal partners with form and space in the making of place, instead of being subservient or non-existent to them.

With its emphasis on people, Jacobs's *The Death and Life of Great American Cities* marks an early break from the continuing formalism of modernism and the emerging physicality of postmodern contextualism. In establishing an anthropology of urbanism, Jacobs acknowledges architecture's role beyond that of object and as a place people inhabit. She puts the designer inside of (rather than removed from) the place and inverts the customary primacy of product over process. Her methodology is to make the familiar strange. She allows us to see ourselves, our ways of life, our conflicts and our traditions by rendering them legible, not hidden, or even more often assumed and generalized. Making the familiar strange means immersing oneself in the banalities of the quotidian as a means to the simultaneous stewardship and transformation of place.

In asserting an anthropology of urbanism as a way of broadening good design practice into good cultural practice, this chapter will first discuss anthropological definitions of culture and introduce their relevance to Jacobs and how she constructed her research methods. Then the transformational nature of Jacobs's research and what it means for contemporary design as cultural practice will be examined. This general discussion will lead to one that focuses on a contemporary example of anthropological design practice in Bayview, Virginia. The counter-practice of contemporary New Urbanism – which seeks to remake the familiar while pointing to Jacobs as cultural mentor – will follow, along with a critique of Jacobs. The chapter ends with a critical query into how cultural practice can transform twenty-first century urban design practice into a significant component in the making of place.

Building Culture

The idea of architecture borrowing from other disciplines in the pursuit of design practice is not new. Certainly a whole generation of postmodernists borrowed from the study of linguistics and semiotics to further their design agendas. While the postmodernists were looking at signs and symbols, Jacobs looked at people as a means with which cultural specificity in placemaking could be achieved. In other words, while not self-stated, her disciplinary lens was anthropology and her subject was culture.

What needs to be discussed first is the protean nature of the term culture (Wortham-Galvin, 2009). The distinction between Culture and culture becomes possible when the definition itself expands from something that is a standard of excellence to something that is a 'whole way of life' (Hebdige, 1979). The first definition derives from an appreciation of 'high' aesthetic form (opera, ballet, drama, literature, art, and architecture). Thus the initial conception of culture is one reified, bound in formalism, and held static in the site of the material object. The counter anthropological concept of culture sites itself in the social. For anthropologist Clifford Geertz (1973), '… man is an animal suspended in webs of significance he himself has spun, I take culture to be one of those webs, and the analysis of it to be therefore not an experimental science in search of law but an interpretive one in search of meaning'. While the former definition of culture remains a product tightly bound to an elitist realm, one of excellence and therefore exclusion; the anthropological definition is more populist and all-embracing, it is both the product and process of dynamic social interaction in all its forms.

An understanding of culture as a bottom-up process (as opposed to a top-down imposition) – one which makes the ordinary visible – begins in part in the early twentieth century with the work of anthropologist Bronislaw Malinowski. The corpus of his work and writing focused on his ethnological study of the people living on the Trobriand Islands, an archipelago to the northeast of Papau New Guinea. Malinowski took a radical stance against the ethnological orthodoxy of the time; he believed that anthropologists needed to immerse themselves in the daily life of the people they are studying.

As I went on my morning walk through the village, I could see intimate details of family life, of toilet, cooking, taking of meals; I could see the arrangements of the day's work, people starting on their errands, or groups of men and women busy at some manufacturing tasks. Quarrels, jokes, family scenes, events usually trivial, sometimes dramatic but always significant, formed the atmosphere of my daily life, as well as theirs. (Malinowski, 1922)

It is these contingencies of everyday life that Malinowski believed were only revealed when one pitched a tent in the village. And it is these contingencies that he believed would reveal not only the ephemeral and quotidian practices of the people, but also an interpretation more 'permanent and unconscious' (Augé, 1999). In other words, Malinowski's radical methodology was to move from the particular to the general based not on the exceptional ritual or limited contact, but on the banalities of everyday life. The result was an understanding of culture enriched by the dialogue between the qualitative and quotidian experience and the more stable and fixed cultural structures.

Geertz (1973) expanded Malinowski's revolution of ethnographic practices with his assertion that 'ethnography is thick description'. But what does Geertz mean by thick description? Thick description is set opposite to thin description. Thin description would be satisfied with the ontological status of an action (i.e. winking as an eyelid contraction) or with the mimesis of an action without understanding its fullest and subtlest meanings and nuances. If culture is not a power or a causation but a context, then thick description is the means by which one gets at an understanding of that context. Thick description as a methodology is useful only in a discipline that does not search for universals and laws, but for particulars and meaning. It is, thus, useful when one conceives not of *a* culture but of many cultures. In order for Jacobs to pursue the particular and potentially disjunctive aspects of lived places, she needed to embrace a trans-disciplinary and transformative notion of research.

Constructing Research

Throughout the twentieth century, in the United States design has been seen as removed from or antithetical to research. In part, this was because research was deemed the primary mission of the academy (something in which Jacobs was not a member). Research was circumscribed within a scientific paradigm which values gathering observable, empirical, measurable evidence, subject to principles of quantification and objective rationality with the intent of reducing biased interpretation (Wortham, 2007).

The *Oxford English Dictionary*'s (*OED*) definition of research, while incorporating some notions of creative work, ultimately demarcates its description within a scientific rubric. This is not surprising since it is a culturally situated document arising out of a rapidly industrializing mid- to late-nineteenth century Great Britain. When historian Raymond Williams (1985) critiques the *OED* as a socio-cultural invention and reminds us that words are not just defined by their philological and etymological past but also by their cultural history, he makes transparent the notion that research is a construct. Research practices, likewise, are culturally conditioned. In the university system of the twentieth and twenty-first centuries, it is the cultural memory of the Enlightenment that still holds fast in describing what the work of the scholar should be.

Because research is artifice, it can be reconstructed. The argument is not to abandon scientific methods of research, but to make them one of many ways of pursuing knowledge so that intervention in the built environment does not sacrifice connection and interaction at the altar of rationality. This appears to be Jane Jacobs's agenda. In order to save the city from urban renewal, and the concomitant methodologies of the urban planning profession, Jacobs sought to inquire about the nature of the city, to gain knowledge about how it worked, so that future interventions would build it up, not deteriorate and destroy it.

Jacobs (1961) was very clear that her book 'is an attack … on the principles and aims that have shaped modern, orthodox city planning'. In order to launch that attack, she wanted to write 'about how cities work in real life, because this is the only way to learn what principles of planning and what practices in rebuilding can promote social and economic vitality…' (*Ibid.*). This was not research about the current state of the city, but an agenda of transformation of a discipline (or several of them) and of policies towards the city. Jacobs's values came first and she sought knowledge to back them up. As Peter Laurence (2011) notes, 'She achieved what she set out to achieve: to present a "new system of thought about the great city" – the foundation for an idealized field of city planning, architecture, and urban design that would recognize the complexity and fragile intricacy of the great city'. And she did so with 'synthetic interdisciplinarity' (*Ibid.*).

For Jacobs, knowledge should not be confined to a narrow dictionary or scientific definition that delimits the province of knowing to what is known in a particular field. Clifford Geertz (1980) would later affirm her notion of loosening the tight disciplinary circumscriptions by noting:

Something is happening to the way we think about the way we think... [P]hilosophical inquiries looking like literary criticism (think of Stanely Cavell on Beckett or Thoreau, Sartre on Flaubert) ... baroque fantasies presented as deadpan empirical observations (Borges, Barthelme) ... documentaries that read like true confessions (Mailer), parables posing as ethnographies (Castanesda), theoretical treatises set out as travelogues (Levi-Strauss), ideological arguments cast as historiographical inquiries (Edward Said)...

Jacobs's approach in all of her works implicitly acknowledges the unnecessary nature of this disciplinary knowledge as the reason why boundary crossing should be deemed necessary and not subsidiary. Knowledge production depends on the trans-disciplinary, on identifying larger patterns, and on hermeneutics as much as it does on facts, hypothesis and reproducible results. This means moving speculative and inventive inquiry from the margins to the centre of what is deemed significant work.

Design Practice as Cultural Practice

Jacobs's trans-disciplinary discourses, perhaps, began with her relationship with social worker Ellen Lurie (Laurence, 2011). Lurie worked in East Harlem, which served as New York's testing laboratory for ideas regarding urban renewal in the 1950s. As Laurence (*Ibid.*) notes:

By January 1956, when Jacobs first visited East Harlem, 10 housing projects had consumed 57 blocks, more than two-thirds of East Harlem... Laurie had detailed documentation of every neighborhood store and social club that was destroyed, along with the old storefront buildings that were razed for the new monolithic housing projects, and it was these studies that formed the basis of Jacobs's Harvard conference paper and marked the end of her belief in the 'city planner approach'.

Lurie's documentation of the destruction of East Harlem can be seen as the implicit influence on Jacobs's ethnographic approach, which would be interwoven with economics, geography, sociology, biology, and planning. Ethnographers are in the business of looking at culture as 'texts', whether those texts are spoken, gestured, performed or written. Jacobs's work asserts that texts can also be, or result in, built form. For designers, grounding a trans-disciplinary approach in the ethnographic, as Jacobs's did (whether rigorously or transformatively), allows for places to be designed around the living experiences of real people in real places.

Ethnography deployed in an architectural schema means that it is not just the product that is of consequence. The process itself, the search, the inquiry, can be as substantial, if not more so, than the rendering of conclusions. What is revelatory about Walter Hood's work in the mini-parks in Oakland, California is not necessarily a final design scheme, but the methodology employed in his search for the revitalization of these public spaces. Hood's *Urban Diaries* (1997) are illuminating as an inquiry into how to acquire knowledge about the relationship between people and space before one (re)makes it into another place. His diaries record textually and visually how both individuals and groups enact space. He particularly focuses on those at the margins of society and, thus, rendered invisible in places, like children, the homeless, the drug addicted, and prostitutes. His transformation of an ethnographic approach advocates that lived space should not be the outcome of design but should, in fact, inform design decisions.

If Jacobs's methods are characterized as the go-and-see method, then Walter Hood's might be deemed the go-and-live method. A believer in experience, Hood urges designers to leave their expert-driven separation behind and become a member of the community in order to understand its webs of significance. He, thus, puts himself in the community of West Oakland, California to see who the people are and his own connections to them, what they are doing, what their needs are, and 'what the flow of change discloses' (Hood, 1997). As Jacobs, he believes the demolition of blighted, mixed-use neighbourhoods in the name of urban renewal should no longer be an acceptable solution, and points out that over the past twenty-five years many sites of previous urban renewal efforts have become public nuisances sponsoring illicit activity and attracting repeated vandalism. Hood believes the illicit behaviour present in these forgotten spaces occurs because people have been marginalized and left out of a system which designs public spaces for only certain members of the community, but not all. He reminds us that those who set foot in community meetings are not a fully representative public. The people who need to be heard most are those who are either not invited or do not feel welcome. He encourages designers and planners to become witnesses to the daily activities and circumstances of all members of the public, to legitimize all constituencies and find a place for all in the making of place.

Hood believes the inadequacies of the contemporary policy responses are directly linked to the fact that designers and planners look at the problem from the outside, without a connection to the place, the people, or the problem. His *Urban Diaries* are daily journal entries about his experience as an insider, a resident, which 'allow social and cultural patterns to be transformed into physical form'. Clearly his methods for acquiring design knowledge are inextricably tied to human action. And while Hood seeks a thick description of the patterns of culture before placemaking, his work asserts that design should remain focused on the particular and not move to generalized principles.

Hood's work is not an isolated example. The design work produced by the firm RBGC, Architecture, Research and Urbanism under the leadership of Maurice Cox in Bayview, Virginia is another such model of architectural design practice as cultural practice (Wortham-Galvin, 2009). What is significant about this example is that it asserts that placemaking can be initiated outside the design professions by the residents themselves.

The Ethnography of Bayview

On a sun-kissed afternoon, Victoria Cummings fetches her 5-year-old daughter, Kadijah, from the Head Start bus stop up on the asphalt road. Together they walk home, ambling through mud and skirting huge rain-filled holes that scar the half-mile dirt road. They stroll past rickety outhouses, the privy seats and floors encrusted with dried sewage that seeped up through the ground during spring's heavy rains… Once home, Kadijah exerts her tiny biceps by pumping a dishpan full of off-color rust-flavored water from the outdoor hand pump that her mother will use for her 'bath'. Cummings plans a trip to the store to buy bottled water for drinking and cooking with her food stamps. Her 12-year-old, Latoya, gets home about 3:30 p.m., and Cummings leaves shortly after that for her night-shift job cutting fat off plucked chickens. Cumming's dream is simple: 'Water – running water – inside the house', she says. (Moreno 1998a)

Abject poverty defined the daily lives of the residents of Bayview at the close of the twentieth century. Isolated on a peninsula across the Chesapeake Bay on Virginia's eastern shore, freed slaves settled this community during the Emancipation of the mid-nineteenth century. Many of its residents trace their family heritage as slaves back to the founding of the Commonwealth in the seventeenth century. Their living conditions in the late twentieth century belied 350 years of progress and change, as more than 100 residents were among Virginia's most impoverished in one of its poorest counties, Northampton. With no community centre or retail stores, dirt roads 'paved' with crushed oyster and clamshells, the chapel in near ruins, the demise of the local economy dependent on fishing and potato farming, and no running water to service the one-room shacks, Bayview's residents simply wanted to improve their quality of life. Their immediate goals: affordable housing and running water.

The feasibility of attaining these aims seemed bleak, particularly when employing conventional wisdom and methods to such a problem. The then governor, James Gilmore, echoed the sentiments of many who presumed such problems unsolvable and such communities destined to extinction. Gilmore 'questioned whether enough local capital [would be] available to install running water and central heating in homes in Bayview and nearby hamlets, where there is little industry and unemployment rates are high' (Melton, 1998). Instead of waiting for a solution from the top or for the demise of their community and its replacement with an upscale vacation enclave, the residents sought to solve their own problems.

Bayview's community activism got its jump start in 1994 when a group of black and white residents teamed up to defeat the location of a large maximum security state prison in their community. The grassroots organization, Bayview Citizens for Social Justice (BCSJ), rallied against the demolition of homes, despite the promise of nearly

500 jobs that the prison would create in this economically depressed area. 'We were brought here to be slaves, and now they were going to demolish these little African American towns', Alice Coles, head of BCSJ, said. 'I opposed it' (Moreno, 1998a).

After successfully defeating the state's prison plans during a three year battle, the newly formed BCSJ partnered with the Nature Conservancy (the Conservancy runs a 45,000acre (18,220 ha) preserve along the peninsula's shore) and applied for a $20,000 grant from the Environmental Protection Agency to create a plan for eradicating the near-Third-World living conditions in Bayview. The BCSJ saw their collaboration with the influential land conservation organization as a statement of political defiance – that the improving of the quality of life was really an issue of environmental urgency. The grant allowed the BCSJ to bring in an interdisciplinary coalition of experts, led by Maurice Cox and his firm RBGC, Architecture, Research and Urbanism. This team worked with the citizens of Bayview to provide more than just a band-aid on their housing and water dilemmas, but collectively produced a long-term plan to rebuild Bayview both physically and socially. The resurrection of Bayview – under the official nomenclature Bayview Rural Village Plan – would include retail stores, churches, a post office, privately owned homes, rental units, cottage industries, affordable housing, and three deep-water community wells to provide drinking water. Also included were forty new sanitary pits to deal with the immediate severe sewage problems until the new homes were built. The partnership with the Nature Conservancy was not ephemeral, but an ongoing relationship, in which the Conservancy provides the community with technical, fundraising and organizing assistance.

The Viability of an Anthropological Approach

'We want to preserve open space. We want to remember the fields our people worked. Here people are tied to the land. We want to teach our children their history and to protect the environment, the air, and the water.' Alice Coles. (Flint, 1999)

What exactly was the design process at Bayview and how does it differ from the public charrettes heralded by New Urbanists such as the famous Duany Plater-Zyberk (DPZ)? And, is it really anthropologically driven?

As Alice Coles recalled,

Our approach was that we had ... the architect to come in as a facilitator and they really began to listen to what the community was like ... what was the vision and ... how did we want to proceed in living? (Hamma, 2003)

One of the first things Cox did was to organize a community-wide clean-up campaign and demolish the burned-out shacks.

'They were not trying to run away from their roots. They actually were trying to embed them deeper. And it was a wonderful moment when they decided that the new Bayview will be erected right across the street from the old', says Cox. (Leung, 2004)

Cox and the 'experts' met with Bayview residents in both formal design workshops *and* informal community events such as picnics, concerts, and fish fries. At Bayview an integration of storytelling, oral history, design workshops, community events, and other low-tech approaches helped the residents collaborate on their environmental and housing problems, not only with each other but with the professional team. In other words, the education process was not linear and from the top down, but cyclical: it engaged both sides (residents and professionals) for their expertise. In addition, the process began with the residents themselves, not as a speculative development. While certainly the members of the Nature Conservancy or RBGC did not go and live in Bayview for a year *à la* Malinowski, their equal partnership with the residents and their consistent and long-term contact began to reveal the particulars of life in Bayview, which illuminated what anthropologist Ruth Benedict (1989) called the 'patterns of culture'.

For instance, in recognizing the need to provide a physical form for the social life of the community, Cox did not merely import the European precedents of the *place* or piazza. Instead, he observed that public gathering happened organically around personal grooming activities such as haircutting, styling and shaving. A beauty/barber shop became part of the local economic plan. It received specific design consideration in recognition of its crucial contributions to sustain public life.

When working on the design of the houses, for the BCSJ 'living like people' meant designing houses with front porches. But since this was government-funded public housing, Coles says they had to justify why they were necessary:

'Because that's where our family life was spent, on the porch. And so, if you take the porch, just like taking your farm, you take a part of our past. That's where old stories were told. And songs were taught. And our poems and the scriptures of the Bible were all taught on the front porch... We rehearse everything from the Gettysburg Address to the Creation ... on the front porch. We held the books for others, and others held the books until we learned together. So, a part of this village concept was the porch.' (*Ibid.*)

The porch was not a nostalgic add-on, but a form deeply embedded in their historical and contemporary way of life that the residents sought to maintain.

Remaking the Familiar

The work of Cox, Hood and many others (Teddy Cruz, Bryan Bell, Sergio Pallerioni, to name a few) has begun to coalesce in the early twenty-first century around a term currently called Public Interest Architecture. While they clearly fall within the exhortations of Jacobs's call to cultural practice, their work remains at the margins within the design discipline instead of central to its mission. Rather, the urban design field in the United States has been dominated by another design practice that lays claim to being Jacobs's heirs: the New Urbanism.

Founded almost thirty years ago, New Urbanism is arguably the most significant urban design and planning movement to have emerged in the late twentieth century in response to the mid-twentieth century's perceived loss of place. As the website newurbanism.org notes, 'Currently there are over 4,000 New Urbanist projects planned or under construction in the United States alone, half of which are in historic urban centers'. New Urbanism's principles address issues as diverse as transportation, health, urban morphology, building typology, and socioeconomics. However, it is not the specifics of any of these that most provoke critics, but the sense that the image of these places and their built forms and spaces replaces reality with neo-traditional idyllic fantasies (Wortham-Galvin, 2010).

The New Urbanist vision that dominates the discourse is that proffered by the husband-wife team, Andrés Duany and Elizabeth Plater-Zyberk and symbolized in their design for Seaside, Florida. In their New Urbanist schema, a revitalized sense of place is made in villagescapes that promote small-town values (Wortham-Galvin, 2009). The designers achieve this reinvention of small-town America by creating building types that conform to strict codes. In fact, Vincent Scully (1994) asserts that in DPZ's designs, 'the important place-maker is the code'. Part of the New Urbanist rhetoric (more appealing and persuasive to the public than the endless charts of codes) is the application of local typological precedents to each project (and certainly the white and pastel frame motifs of Windsor, Florida contrast with the staid Georgian brick of Kentlands, Maryland). Nevertheless, the movement asserts the myth of a nationally and culturally coherent urbanism; an urbanism which combines the ideals of the nineteenth-century Main Street and the twentieth-century Garden City; an urbanism which appeals to middle- and upper-class consumers seeking cultural stability and nostalgia in the face of an increasingly cacophonous and pluralized United States. As John Kaliski (1999) notes, 'The so-called neotraditional town tugs at emotions and speaks to a mythologized memory of socially homogenous innocence, of golden ages conveniently distant'.

Despite all their claims to urbanism, even supporter Scully (1994) suggests 'the New Suburbanism might be a truer label'. Frequently lambasted for the greenfields application of their principles (where there is no extant community), New Urbanists have recently begun to add abandoned downtowns and brownfields sites to their foci of study. Nevertheless, despite claims to the contrary, their approach yields results that are still dismissive of that which falls outside a nostalgic American vision. In their application of a singular ideal to all existing conditions, their design approach is as problematic as the modernist *tabula rasa* approach to the city. While their designs are careful studies in the morphology of the public realm, the New Urbanists have chosen the historical typologies that suit their vision and then have their vision guide their designs. While they engage in public charrettes, these charrettes are venues used to educate the community on the principles of good design instead of opportunities to record local residents' understanding of their own history and values (particularly if they are in conflict with the expert view).

The New Urbanists employ a tautological approach – that architecture should be based on architecture. In contrast, Jacobs's seminal tract, *The Death and Life of Great American Cities*, makes the argument that architecture should start with culture in order to make place in the city. Nevertheless, the New Urbanists lay claim to Jane Jacobs as one of their seminal predecessors. Certainly their approaches that focus on pedestrian friendly environments, denser urban morphologies, mixed uses and their use of the charrette would affirm their allegiance to some of Jacobs's tenets. In addition, Jill Grant (2011) notes that Jacobsian insights are interwoven into both New Urbanists' founder Andrés Duany's rhetoric and into New Urbanist theorist Emily Talen's writings in a purposeful way. But the New Urbanists are not the only ones who cite Jacobs as inspiration for their urban design principles. Harrison Fraker (2007) notes that New Urbanism, Everyday Urbanism, and Empirical Urban Morphology all cite her work as their 'theoretical roots' but retain outwardly opposing positions on what is 'essential for a "good" city'.

New Urbanism diverges from Jacobs's ideas about the city when it comes to how 'time, scale, and control affect urban outcomes in significant ways' (Grant, 2011). As Grant notes, the quickness with which these developments are built, most often in greenfields sites, belies Jacobs's criticisms of master planning and working at the totalizing scale of the neighbourhood. She adds, 'Jacobs conceived of scale as creating a matrix for social, political, and economic action, while new urbanism accepts scale as a spatial constraint fixed by development economics and planning conditions' (*Ibid.*).

It is hard for New Urbanism to foster Jacobs's beloved notions of diversity and vitality of uses, people, economies and ecologies when implementing the unifying vision of a comprehensive plan, instead of infilling tactically in an extant culture. When culture is, therefore, rendered homogenous and applied from the top down, organic transformation and the potential for democratic action are slighted and made invisible, if not impossible.

In an interview with James Howard Kunstler (2000), Jacobs stated:

I do not think that we are to be saved by new developments done to New Urbanist principles… I think that when this takes hold and when enough of the old regulations can be gotten out of the way – which is what is holding things up – that there is going to be some great period of infilling. And a lot of that will be make-shift and messy and it won't measure up to New Urbanist ideas of design – but it will measure up to a lot of their other philosophy.

What is messy and makeshift is culture. And Jacobs's philosophies beg the question: shouldn't architecture start with culture, instead of generalized typologies, in order to achieve the making of place?

Patterns of Culture

Achieving a simultaneous and diverse urbanity, rather than one that is singular and homogenous, is not as simple as moving from New Urbanist morphology to Everyday Ethnography. Making conclusions from the observation of everyday life can be problematic at best, as is revealed in Jacobs's seminal tract. Jacobs begins by making observations of the daily life of the city – mainly her neighbourhood of Greenwich Village – that are detailed to the point of tedium, in the tradition of Malinowski's ethnographic research.

But despite her anthropological approach, Jacobs quickly associates specific forms with good urbanism and defines those forms as good… The absolutism of her observations … results in a non-inclusive theory of place-making that cannot encompass, observe, value, incorporate, or utilize a full urban spectrum. (Kaliski, 1999)

In other words, her culturally specific observations of a built environment lead to a pattern of culture that is reified into *the* Pattern of the built environment, as opposed to a pattern of culture embraced by a specific taste, as Herbert Gans would put it, namely that of 1950s Greenwich Village (Wortham-Galvin, 2009). In a discussion of a 1950s New York that also includes a community very different than that of Jacobs's Hudson Street, namely the community surrounding Andy Warhol, Timothy Mennel (2011) penetrates the problematic of Jacobs's ethnographic observations of the street ballet:

The deeper question here is what participating in a dance actually entails … knowing codes and expectations is a critical part of participating successfully in the 'ballet'… At some point individual behavior will cross a line beyond which a person can be said to be 'not dancing' or not functioning as part of a certain kind of community. That judgment itself is the product of social expectations and codes – and it is here that we can see the most critical divergence between Warhol's conception of urban life and community and Jacobs's. Where Warhol is in effect asking why society has created particular forms for physical and social interaction when there are so many other possibilities, Jacobs seems not to have seriously questioned the validity or socially constructed nature of the ballet of the sidewalks that she depicted. Rather, she posits it as an ideal, and perhaps even a norm.

So even though her investigation of architecture is broader than that of the New Urbanist typological foundation, Jacobs appears to fall into the same trap. Once the investigation reveals a result, it is taken as the primer to be applied to all situations; and, thus, replaces the heterogeneous diversity of the city with a homogeneous idyll.

When Jacobs moves from the particular to the general, there is not an explicit acknowledgement that these universal urban principles are being situated in a specific time and place with an implicit value system leading the way. While she observes the dancers of the street ballet, she does not explicate the 'for whom and by whom' of Hudson Street, nor does she acknowledge that their performance may exclude other urban dancers.

As Jacobs moved beyond this work, her actions and her voice usually affirmed the pluralism of the particularities of people and place that her initial tract invisibly belied. While her legacy of diversity and vitality is not a false one, it still emanates from a culturally conditioned set of values that informed her observations. This is the legacy of Jane Jacobs to which the New Urbanists have stayed true. Another legacy connection between Jacobs and the New Urbanists is that which elevates 'the where' over 'the what' and 'the for whom' (i.e. the human action). For Jacobs and the New Urbanists, it is still the physical presence of the city that situates the socio-cultural rather than the other way around – the way advocated by Hood and Cox. Jacobs is, perhaps, so popular in architectural curricula precisely for this problematic of the text, precisely because while she is both spatially and socially aware of the city, she still places primacy on the first. As Richard Harris (2011) notes:

Although here, as in later books, Jacobs insists on the importance of process, she always views it in relation to the forms that, in her view, shape and enable it… Herbert Gans was perhaps the first to challenge her inclination in this direction, flagging it in the very title of his review of Death and Life, 'Urban Vitality in the Fallacy of Physical Determinism'. But Jacobs's physical determinism … persisted.

Gans's (1968) critique of Jacobs, which appeared seven years after the initial publication, accused her of the same trap as the modernists to whom she was responding: overestimating the capacity of physical interventions in the city to influence the life of the people. Gans argues that it is not so much the physical form of the city that determines behaviour; rather, it is the cultural codes of each social group. He asserts that the way people use urban spaces depends on the social or ethnic group to which they belong. The reason why people in a certain neighbourhood have an intensive street life (like Jacobs's Greenwich Village or the North End of Boston) and others do not, could have been caused by how they understood and used their houses (e.g. for family life, for privacy). This shaped the kind of social life that they participated in on the street. Thus, for Gans, what determines the use of space is in itself not physical but sociological. He argues that Jacobs's view of the primacy of the street and the sidewalk allows her to fall into the same trap of physical determinism that plagued the modernists, albeit leaping from a different value system and albeit achieving a desired morphological result.

Making the Familiar Strange

Advocating the study of the ordinary in architectural discourse did not wait until the end of the twentieth century for the Everyday Urbanists, but happened on the heels of Jacobs's publication. Its most prominent articulation was made by another husband-and-wife team, Robert Venturi and Denise Scott Brown. Their work in the 1960s and 1970s – through studios and exhibitions – created a taxonomy of the everyday built environment. A prime example is the exhibition they designed in 1976 as part of the American Bicentennial, *Signs of Life, Symbols in the American City*. Exhibited in the Renwick Gallery for seven months, *Signs of Life* presented the ordinary landscapes of mid-twentieth century America – the traditional city street, the highway, the commercial strip, and the suburb – in 7,000 photographs with little text or analysis (Fausch, 1997). This 'visual anthropology of American settlement forms' achieved a thin description of American places because it was not inclusive of all people and how they enacted these settlements.

In advocating the methodology of the thick description, Geertz (1973) believes, 'The thing to ask about a burlesqued wink or a mock sheep raid is not what their ontological status is… The thing to ask is what their import is: what it is … that, in their occurrence and through their agency, is getting said'. Venturi and Scott Brown are more concerned that we notice and value the burlesqued wink, but do not want to get at what the wink means. Also focused on where the what happens, their observations of the 'ugly and the ordinary' remain a collection of visual culture, not of human actions and their significances. In reference to their work on the Las Vegas strip, they declare, 'Las Vegas is analyzed here only as a phenomenon of architectural communication; its values are not questioned' (Venturi [1968] 1996). Even though Venturi and Scott Brown advocate designing based on an understanding of the existing built environment and are not offering up a mythic ideal of what that environment should be, in making those familiar landscapes strange they ultimately offer up only a thin description. And it is a description based more on the visual than the social side of semiotics.

Conclusion

Action is with the scholar … essential… Without it, thought can never ripen into truth… The preamble of thought, the transition through which it passes from the unconscious to the conscious, is action… But the final value of action, like that of books, and better than books, is, that it is a resource. (Ralph Waldo Emerson, 1837)

Certainly Jacobs's body of work follows Emerson's exhortation. The experience of the city is at the core of both her values and her research that stemmed from a moral proposition: that the city should benefit from good design – design Jacobs defined by the morphology of a street that fosters diverse and vital environments. A value-laden approach to design work still exists today. For example, Bryan Bell's direction of Design Corps could be considered a practice that begins with a moral proposition: that the underserved should benefit from good design. From that proposition, Design Corps' then engages a myriad of social, aesthetic and scientific disciplines (often simultaneously) as the group's members make cultural inquiries and surveys, conferences, texts, designs, and as they construct buildings. While both Jacobs's and Bell's agendas are laudable, they still put the moral agenda first (as did the modernists). The difference, however, is in how that agenda is implemented. Bell, like Hood and Cox, is interested in how specific cultural practices can inform and define design practice. Physical form does not determine cultural practice; rather design practice follows cultural practice.

In some ways the difference between a New Urbanist approach and the beginnings of an anthropological design approach could be what anthropologist and historian Michel de Certeau terms strategies and tactics (Highmore, 2002). In design terms, Barbara Kirschenblatt-Gimblett (1999) deems it the difference between planning and the vernacular. Strategy results from the practices of the powerful who compose and manage place, whereas the tactical comes from below and relies on seized opportunities and adaptation to the particular.

In the application of an anthropological model to urban and architectural design, is it possible to design forms valid for social groups other than the designer's own? In other words, can one educated in a certain culture (often Culture) design for another?

In the case of Bayview, Virginia, how viable is it to replicate the unique partnership where all partners – the Nature Conservancy, a politically active citizenry, and the designers – were on equal footing, while providing different contributions? In the case of the parks in Oakland, how feasible is it to get policy-makers and neighbourhood stakeholders to give a voice to prostitutes, drug addicts, and the homeless? How thick was the description achieved at Bayview or in Oakland? Is everyone really being included? Is culture being stewarded in a manner that includes change or that tries to keep a neighbourhood fixed like a museum object under glass? If Bayview is deemed successful, how much of it was the result of the grassroots activism of the citizens? Can the same results be achieved without the process beginning from residents who live in such a dire situation? And what process should design follow when the marginalized constituencies actively dismiss the relevancy of participating in the process?

The object of Geertz's study is human beings. Therefore, his definition of culture and his employment of thick description in method and analysis fit his object of study. Jacobs's loci of observation are usually categorized as the city and economics; and, yet, at their foundation, her studies too focused on people in order to localize meaning. In architecture, the objects of study are things (most often buildings and/or the physical aspects of places), not people. While these things can be 'read' as signifiers – what do these buildings and/or places signify? To whom do they convey what meaning? How does the meaning change with time, place, people, prevailing ideologies, and/or with the ones inscribing the meaning? Are these objects as dynamic as our social rituals? Geertz (1973) says, 'Anthropologists don't study villages … they study in villages'. His turn of phrase is both clever as well as true to his theory. By contrast, Jacobs (1961) declares that 'Cities have the capability of providing something for everybody, only because, and only when, they are created by everybody'. Geertz's disciplinary formulations still puts the power in the hands of the expert scholar, whereas Jacobs transfers the agency to impact place into the hands of the people. How apt an anthropological approach is in its application to architectural design is being tested and explored by designers like Hood, Cox, Bell and others who are creating design practices that really are trans-disciplinary cultural practices.

References

Augé, M. (1999) *An Anthropology for Contemporaneous Worlds*. Translated by Amy Jacobs. Stanford, CA: Stanford University Press.

Bayview Rural Village Plan. Available at http://www.virginiacoastreserve.org/major_projects/bayview.html. Accessed 30 September 2005.

Bell, B. (ed.) (2004) *Good Deeds. Good Design: Community Service Through Architecture*. New York: Princeton Architectural Press.

Benedict, R., (1989) *Patterns of Culture*. First published in 1934. Boston, MA: Houghton Mifflin.

Chase, J., Crawford, M. and Kalisky, J (eds.) (1999) *Everyday Urbanism*. New York: Monacelli Press.

Cox, M. (1999) Rebuilding Bayview: Community Design as Catalyst for Social Change (Abstract). Symposium: Sites of Memory: Landscapes of Race and Ideology, University of Virginia, Charlottesville, VA, 25–27 March.

Cox, M. (2002) A View from the Grass Roots, Public lecture, University of Maryland, College Park, MD, 15 April 2002.

Emerson, R.W. (1837) The American Scholar. Originally a speech given to Phi Beta Kappa Society at

Harvard University, in Irev, E.F. (ed.) (1981) *A Concordance to Five Essays of Ralph Waldo Emerson*. New York: Garland.

Fausch, D. (1997) Ugly and ordinary: the presentation of the everyday, Harris, S. and Berke, D. (eds.) *Architecture of the Everyday*. New York: Princeton Architectural Press.

Flint, W. (1999) A sustainability miracle for the holidays. *Sustainability Review*, No. 9, 27 December.

Fraker, H. (2007) Where is the urban design discourse? *Places*, **19**(3), pp. 61–63.

Gans, H.J. (1968) Urban vitality and the fallacy of physical determinism, in *People and Plans: Essays on Urban Problems and Solutions*. New York: Penguin Books.

Geertz, C. (1973) *The Interpretation of Cultures*. New York: Basic Books.

Geertz, C. (1980) Blurred genres: the refiguration of social thought. *The American Scholar*, **49**, 165–166.

Grant, J. (2011) Time, scale, and control: how New Urbanism (mis)uses Jane Jacobs, in Page, M. and Mennel, T. (eds.) *Reconsidering Jane Jacobs*. Washington DC: American Planning Association Press.

Hamma, D. (2003) Interview with Alice Coles. Bayview, Virginia. 1 April.

Harris, R. (2011) The magpie and the bee: Jane Jacobs's magnificent obsession, in Page, M. and Mennel, T. (eds.) *Reconsidering Jane Jacobs*. Washington DC: American Planning Association Press.

Harris, S. and Berke, D. (eds.) (1997) *Architecture of the Everyday*. New York: Princeton Architectural Press.

Hebdige, D. (1979) *Subculture*. London: Methuen.

Highmore, B. (ed.) (2002) *The Everyday Life Reader*. London: Routledge.

Hood, W. (1997) *Urban Diaries*. Washington DC: Spacemaker Press.

Jacobs, J. (1961) *The Death and Life of Great American Cities*. New York: Random House.

Kaliski, J. (1999) The present city and the practice of city design, in Chase, J., Crawford, M. and Kalisky, J (eds.) *Everyday Urbanism*. New York: Monacelli Press.

Katz, P. (1994) *The New Urbanism. Toward an Architecture of Community*. New York: McGraw-Hill.

Kirshenblatt-Gimblett, B. (1999) Performing the city: reflections on the urban vernacular, in Chase, J., Crawford, M. and Kalisky, J (eds.) *Everyday Urbanism*. New York: Monacelli Press.

Kunstler, J.H. (2000) Interview with Jane Jacobs for Metropolis Magazine, March 2001. Interviewed September 6, 2000 in Toronto, Canada. Available at http://www.kunstler.com/mags_jacobs1.htm and http://www.kunstler.com/mags_jacobs2.htm. Accessed 18 February 2012.

Laurence, P.L. (2011) The unknown Jane Jacobs: geographer, propagandist, city planning idealist, in Page, M. and Mennel, T. (eds.) *Reconsidering Jane Jacobs*. Washington, DC: American Planning Association Press.

Leung, R. (2004) Alice Coles of Bayview. Model Resident Transformed Poor Village into Modern Community. *60 Minutes, CBS News*. Available at: http://www.cbsnews.com/stories/2003/11/26/60minutes/main585793.shtml. Accessed 18 February 2012.

Malinowski, B. (1922) *Argonauts of the Western Pacific*. London: Routledge.

Melton, R.H. (1998) Gilmore seeks to aid destitute Va. town. *Washington Post*, 20 May, p. B1.

Mennel, T. (2011) Jane Jacobs, Andy Warhol, and the kind of problem a community is, in Page, M. and Mennel, T. (eds.) *Reconsidering Jane Jacobs*. Washington, DC: American Planning Association Press.

Moreno, S. (1998a) In the spotlight, a community's poverty, despair: Bayview, VA. cries out for decent housing and running water. *Washington Post*, 10 May, p. A1.

Moreno, S. (1998b) Gilmore Pledges to Help Bayview. *Washington Post*, 12 August, p. B1.

Page, M. (2011) Introduction: more than meets the eye, in Page, M. and Mennel, T. (eds.) *Reconsidering Jane Jacobs*. Washington, DC: American Planning Association Press.

Scully, V. (1994) The architecture of community, in Katz, P. (ed.) *The New Urbanism*. New York: McGraw-Hill.

Venturi, R. and Scott Brown, D. (1996) *A Significance for A&P Parking Lots or Learning from Las Vegas*. First published 1968. Reprinted in Nesbitt, K. (ed.) *Theorizing A New Agenda for Architecture*. New York: Princeton Architectural Press.

Williams, R. (1985) *Keywords: A Vocabulary of Culture and Society*. First published 1976. New York: Oxford University Press.

Wortham, B.D. (2007) The way we think about the way we think: architecture is a paradigm for reconsidering research. *Journal of Architectural Education*, **61**(1), pp. 44–53.

Wortham-Galvin, B.D. (2008) Mythologies of placemaking. *Places*, **20**(1), pp. 32–39.

Wortham-Galvin, B.D. (2009) Place: The Socio-Cultural Context of Making Spaces. Proceedings of ACSA 97th Annual Conference, Portland, OR.

Wortham-Galvin, B.D. (2010) The fabrication of place in America: the fictions and traditions of the New England village. *Traditional Dwellings and Settlements Review*, **21**(2), pp. 21–34.

Chapter 17

Jane Jacobs and Designing Cities as Organized Complexity

Jonathan Barnett

Warren Weaver was an executive at the Rockefeller Foundation from 1932 to 1958, where he was an important figure in funding scientific research, particularly in the natural sciences. In 1948 he published an article entitled 'Science and complexity' in the *American Scientist*. This article, based on a book chapter published the year before, is still considered a foundational statement about the study of complexity. Weaver defined three categories of scientific problem. Physical science before 1900, he said, was largely concerned with understanding problems that, at their root, had only two variables, such as the motion of a billiard ball across a table. Weaver called them Problems of Simplicity. More recently science had learned to deal with problems which had enormous numbers of variables and which could be studied statistically. Weaver's category for this area of investigation is Problems of Disorganized Complexity. In between are what Weaver called Problems of Organized Complexity: 'problems which deal simultaneously with a *sizable number of factors which are interrelated into an organic whole*' (Weaver's italics).

The Kind of Problem the City Is

Jane Jacobs received grants from the Rockefeller Foundation in the late 1950s while she was writing *The Death and Life of Great American Cities*, and she became familiar with Weaver's formulation from its publication in the Rockefeller Foundation's 1958 annual report. Weaver himself had just retired from Rockefeller and become a vice president and board member of the Sloan Foundation, and it is not clear whether Weaver and Jacobs ever had a discussion about the subject.[1] In her concluding chapter, 'The kind of problem a city is', Jacobs cites Weaver to assert that cities can only be understood as problems of organized complexity, and many urban failures were traceable to planners thinking about cities as if they were problems of simplicity or of disorganized complexity. Studying housing was to abstract only one element from the complexity of the city. To then study housing statistically leads to simplistic conclusions, when any reasonable person could see that people and their living conditions were part of a complicated, constantly changing set of conditions and could not be fitted into 'file drawers' labelled by family income.

Jacobs in her introduction and in her concluding chapter delivers a sweeping criticism of city planning and design based on an assumption that its practitioners had been trying to reduce cities to problems of simplicity or had assumed that cities presented problems of disorganized complexity. Many of her specific criticisms were justified, but are partly explained by the difficulty of both recognizing and creating organized complexity, and not just the obtuseness and misplaced self-confidence of planning and design professionals.

Jacobs made two foresighted observations in her concluding chapter. The first is that cities are part of nature and can never be separated from it, and that nature is itself one vast system of organized complexity. Ian McHarg's *Design with Nature*, first published in 1969, formulated this observation more definitively and was more effective in getting it across to planners and designers, but Jacobs was there first. The second foresighted observation was her description of the systems of behaviour in city streets and neighbourhoods. Jacobs concluded that the aggregate effect of these behaviour patterns created cities, thus anticipating many current studies on the emergence of complex patterns from the interaction of individual actors or smaller sub-groups.

Initiatives by Jacobs's Contemporaries

In the fifty plus years since *The Death and Life of Great American Cities* was published, there has been substantial progress, although nowhere near enough, towards solving problems of organized complexity in cities. Looking back, Jane Jacobs's book is the first of several important works that appeared within a few years of each other, and which all recognized that the planning and design of cities required a deep understanding of complex organizational systems. These landmark studies include Herbert Gans's *The Urban Villagers* (1962), *Silent Spring* by Rachel Carson (1962),[2] Christopher Alexander's 'A city is not a tree' (1965),[3] Paul Davidoff's 'Advocacy and pluralism in planning' (1965), Robert Venturi's *Complexity and Contradiction in Architecture* (1966), and, as mentioned before, Ian McHarg's *Design with Nature* (1969).

The 1960s were also the years of major federal legislation intended to correct the mishandling of urban problems by identifying and dealing with complex interactions. The federal Departments of Transportation, and Housing and Urban Development were established, recognizing that transportation was more than just highways and urban development was more than housing. The National Historic Preservation Act and the Demonstration Cities and Metropolitan Development Act were both passed in 1966. The historic preservation movement was largely a reaction against the demolition of well-loved landmark buildings, and the popular belief that what was replacing them was nowhere near as good. Historic preservation meant safeguarding both individual buildings and the character and variety that historic buildings and districts bring to cities. Demonstration Cities, later known as Model Cities, were an attempt to recognize the complexity of improving inner-city neighbourhoods by integrating social and physical planning. An example: in theory money given to people by social welfare programmes should not be used to pay for substandard and deteriorated housing. Most notable of all, the National Environmental Policy Act of 1969 begins: 'The Congress, recognizing the profound impact of man's activity on the interrelations of all components of the natural environment…' and goes on to mandate that all agencies of the federal government shall '…insure the integrated use of the natural and social sciences and the environmental design arts in planning and decision making which may have an impact on man's environment'.[4]

Jane Jacobs may have had some influence on other landmark studies published during the 1960s, and even on federal legislation, but it is more appropriate to situate her book as part of an ongoing effort to improve society, which was being carried out by many people who recognized that urban problems were complex and were searching for better ways to solve them.

The Complexity of Urban Society

The Urban Villagers describes the intricate networks of people and activities in Boston's West End – soon to be demolished as a 'slum'. By living in the West End and interviewing the residents, Herbert Gans was able to understand its complicated social networks, some brought to Boston from villages in Italy. He concludes that the neighbourhood worked very well for many of its residents. The reason for tearing it down was primarily the underlying value of its real estate for other uses, and not an attempt at social improvement. Jacobs cites an earlier version of Gans's research (1959) to support her own discussion of slumming and un-slumming in urban neighbourhoods.

Silent Spring

Rachel Carson's opening chapter in *Silent Spring* (1962) begins 'Once there was a town…'. In an ideal American town with a charming natural setting the vegetation begins to sicken and die, the sound of birds disappears, and eventually the people themselves become ill. The town had brought this calamity on itself by the indiscriminate use of DDT and other pesticides. Carson goes on to say that, while she does not know a single place where all of these tragedies had taken place at once, they had all happened somewhere. *Silent Spring* was a powerful force in getting people to understand that all living things are part of a single complex system with many inter-connections, and that major interventions in nature required care if the unintended consequences were not to be as bad, or worse, than the original problem.

A City is Not A Tree

Christopher Alexander's original title for his article was 'A City is a Semi-Lattice and Not a Tree'.[5] An architect, he also brought a background in mathematics to his discussion of the kind of problem a city is not. 'The tree and the semi-lattice are ways of thinking about how a large collection of many small systems goes to make up a large and complex system. More generally, they are both names for structures of sets.' A hierarchical organization chart is an example of a tree: a branching system of self-contained boxes. A semi-lattice is composed of sub-components that overlap, as in the familiar Venn diagram. Alexander goes on to say that a tree based on twenty elements can contain at most nineteen further subsets of the twenty, while a semi-lattice based on the same twenty elements can contain more than 1,000,000 different subsets. Alexander illustrated his article with diagrams of nine well-known modern plans for cities, all of which he shows to be trees, because their sub-components are arranged as self-contained elements. Alexander contrasts these plans with what he calls 'natural cities'; that is, cities not organized by planners and designers, which he characterizes as semi-lattices. Alexander is rephrasing in mathematical form the observation that cities are systems of organized complexity, not a simple hierarchy of discrete elements. He backs up his assertions by citing a book by British sociologist Ruth Glass (1948) on the overlapping of social groups in the Yorkshire town of Middlesbrough. Alexander was not able to show how to design a city as a semi-lattice, but he makes it clear that this is the city-design problem that needs to be solved.

Community Participation in Planning Decisions

Paul Davidoff was a planner who was also a lawyer. He was incensed by situations, like the West End of Boston, where slum clearance or highway construction were carried out without concern for the needs of the people who lived in the way of the new development. In his article, 'Advocacy and pluralism in planning' (1965), he proposed that neighbourhoods should have planners of their own to serve as their advocates. He helped define the need for citizen participation in planning, which was incorporated in the Demonstration Cities legislation the following year and has now become standard planning practice. Responding to the complexity of cities by giving citizens a voice was an important step.

Architecture as Organized Complexity

The complexity and contradiction that Robert Venturi (1966) advocates in what he called a gentle manifesto about architectural design was not complexity of organization but complexity of thinking. The simplified and formulaic designs for public housing are rightly characterized by Jane Jacobs as derived from Le Corbusier's *Radiant City* (see discussion in Barnett, 2011). Venturi also criticizes orthodox modernist architecture derived from the work of Le Corbusier and his colleagues in the Congrès Internationaux d'Architecture Moderne. Venturi proposes opening up architecture to wider influences. He uses 350 illustrations, itself a powerful statement at a time when many architects thought there were only a few definitive prototypes. One of Venturi's examples is the inner courtyard of a palace in Mantua designed by Giulio Romano in 1524 where elements of the frieze, the sculptured band at the top of the building, are carved to look as if they are slipping out of place. What was iconoclastic about Venturi's book was first to suggest that historical examples might still be relevant for architects in the modern world, and, second, that modern architects should design buildings with richness and idiosyncrasy of expression, and not repeat simple, formulaic prototypes. *Complexity and Contradiction* was as influential within the architectural profession as *The Death and Life* has been to the practice of planning. Both Jacobs and Venturi were able to put into closely-argued words what a great many other people had been vaguely thinking. Venturi reminded his readers that the kinds of problems that architects needed to solve were complicated, and important aspects of architecture could not be resolved into a single, simple result.

Nature as Organized Complexity

The central theme of Ian McHarg's *Design with Nature* (1969) is that the natural environment is a system of organized complexity: many potentially conflicting elements such as varied vegetation patterns, seasonal rainfall, land contours, soil conditions, rivers, and sub-surface water flows resolve themselves over time into a natural equilibrium. This natural organization can be destabilized by building construction and engineering projects. Eventually a new natural equilibrium will be established, but it can be far less suitable for human habitation.

In an initial chapter entitled 'Sea and survival', McHarg contrasts the way that the Dutch have learned to use natural dune systems to safeguard their land from encroachment by the sea, while, along the New Jersey shore, property owners heedlessly bulldoze the dunes or destroy the grasses that hold the sand in place and rely on concrete pile-foundations and sea walls. The engineering only makes storm damage worse, undermining the sea walls and leaving houses on tottering supports high above the new sand level. The engineering fails because it is in conflict with the powerful natural systems that govern the interface between land and sea, which McHarg meticulously diagrams. Understanding how the dune systems work is, in the Netherlands, 'the stuff of kindergarten classes'; but in the United States 'has made no impact on engineering manuals'. McHarg suggests designing with nature, instead of in opposition. He shows examples of his mapping system, where transparent overlays document the sensitivity of various parts of the ecological system to development. The areas that are most appropriate for development show up as the places where there are the fewest overlays. McHarg's philosophy and his mapping systems have been influential in explaining the complexity of the natural environment, but are only just now finding their way into engineering manuals.

Replacing housing projects and subdivisions with neighbourhood design concepts, preserving historic buildings and districts, protecting the environment, letting the public participate in planning decisions, recognizing and planning for the relationship of transportation to development patterns, and designing the interaction of the built and the natural environment are all initiatives that began in the 1960s. Each has gone some way towards making interventions in cities more sensitive to the kind of problem the city is. More recently there has been some progress in synthesizing sub-elements of city design into a larger design process through the use of codes and advanced computer simulation techniques.

Steps Toward Designing Cities

Christopher Alexander explicitly defined cities not just as organized complexity, but as problems that are susceptible to being solved by design. Unlike the work of prominent Philadelphia City Planner, Edmund Bacon, who in his 1967 book, *Design of Cities*, claimed that city design is 'an act of will', the modern practice of urban design grew up in the 1960s as a problem-solving technique. The city-designer seeks to resolve conflicting aspects of public policies, community interests, and economic objectives much as an architect resolves functions, spaces, structure, and costs in designing a building.

Urban designs based on community participation, preserving historic buildings, and de-emphasizing the open spaces required by a new zoning code, took place in New York City at a time when Jane Jacobs was living there and spending much of her time as a community activist. While I was still a student, I was on a picket line with Jane Jacobs to protest the demolition of Pennsylvania Station, although the media focus at this August 1962 event was not on Jacobs but on celebrity architect Philip Johnson. The same year, Jane Jacobs spoke out vehemently from the audience at a Museum of Modern Art panel discussion where Robert Moses and well-known renewal administrator Edward Logue both said that Jacobs's West Village neighbourhood was suitable for urban redevelopment. The story, widely believed, is that she also hit Edward Logue with her handbag, although I have not been able to find any written account that would substantiate this. In 1968, Jane Jacobs was arrested on charges of second-degree riot and criminal mischief for disrupting a public meeting on the construction of the proposed Lower Manhattan expressway (Martin, 2006). These theatrical tactics were arguably necessary, given the complacency of those in power, but a new kind of urban design was already emerging.

John Lindsay became mayor of New York City in January 1966. His election platform had included Little City Halls, a programme to decentralize some of the executive functions of the city to neighbourhoods like the West Village. This proposal was blocked in the City Council, but the Lindsay administration instituted community participation in all planning studies, and put teams of planners and other administrators into field offices to make better connections with local citizens. Subsidized housing proposals made by New York City after 1966 were based on interpolating new construction into existing neighbourhoods. The old policy of widespread demolition followed by the construction of towers surrounded by green space, rightly opposed by Jane Jacobs, was replaced by 'vest-pocket' buildings within the existing neighbourhoods. One such project was the small-scale West Village Houses, strongly influenced by community leaders including Jane Jacobs.

The City's Landmarks Preservation Commission, created the year before Lindsay took office, was staffed by the new administration and strongly supported. The need to integrate highways into their surrounding neighbourhoods was also well understood at City Hall. The Lower Manhattan Expressway had originally been proposed as part of the Regional Plan Association's 1929 *Plan for New York City* and already had full federal funding. The Lindsay administration's first take on the Lower Manhattan Expressway was that perhaps it could be contained within a huge series of linear residential buildings, proposed by architect Paul Rudolph. The high costs of this design, plus an understanding that it would destroy the buildings of an old manufacturing district with historically important cast iron façades, led to the highway's cancellation in 1972, during Lindsay's second administration, followed by the designation of the Cast Iron Historic District by the Landmarks Preservation Commission the following year. Zoning changes by the Planning Commission permitted the transition of this old industrial area into the Soho loft district with its mix of shops and residences.

A new zoning code had become effective just before Lindsay was elected. This code embodied exactly the principle that Jacobs had rightly likened to the archaic medical practice of bleeding patients: it incentivized public open space over street frontages and separating buildings over urban continuity. The Lindsay administration was able to walk the new code back from the brink by using special zoning districts, such as those that saved the midtown theatres, shopping on Fifth Avenue, and low-rise buildings in Brooklyn Heights. A planned unit development chapter was also added to the code, which made it easier to preserve important elements of the natural environment in those parts of the city which were not yet fully developed. By the time Jane Jacobs left New York City for Toronto in 1968, some of the causes she had championed were succeeding, not just because of her influence but because of the larger general conversation about the kind of problem a city is.[6]

First Steps Toward the Designed City

A comparable story about neighbourhood planning, smaller-scale public interventions, development regulations that recognize existing context and historic buildings, plus more reliance on transit and less on highways can be told about most other US cities. Cities have remade themselves in ways that have made them more walkable and more hospitable to individual choices, notably Boston, San Francisco, Charleston, South Carolina, and Portland, Oregon.

A later phase of city design began with the recognition that the bulk of urban development had shifted to what had once been suburbs. The New Urbanist movement, beginning in the early 1990s, denounced the common development practice of designing large chunks of suburbia as residential subdivisions, often with hundreds of houses all the same size on the same size lots, while commercial development sprawled out in narrowly-zoned strips along highways. Instead the New Urbanists advocated following the design principles of traditional towns, with offices and shopping grouped in walkable centres, surrounded by compact neighbourhoods

– also designed to be walkable – made up of a mix of different housing types. I was on the board of the Congress for the New Urbanism, and took part in a meeting with Jane Jacobs in Toronto in 1998 where board members explained these approaches. My recollection was that Jane Jacobs was friendly but non-committal. She saw that New Urbanist projects were often carried out by large development companies, which would have made her sceptical about the ultimate results.

Many New Urbanist projects have turned out to be good settings for communities and business. The problem has been that these projects are only a tiny fraction of current development. Their locations have been dictated by the real-estate holdings of developers who found New Urbanist principles convincing; they have seldom been places selected as part of a larger city-design or regional plan.

Every city-design problem has been well-solved somewhere, but most urban development continues to be badly managed and now poses huge systemic problems for the whole of US society. Reliance on automobiles and trucks for most transportation has made the economy over-dependent on oil, while over-use of artificial lighting, heating, and cooling in buildings has made them inefficient consumers of energy. Adapting to a changing climate and taking steps to reduce future climate change both make understanding and shaping cities as systems of organized complexity more important than ever.

Computers and Urban Complexity

Advances in computer technology are making it more likely that cities can be understood and managed as complex systems. Geographic Information Systems (GIS) are now available in most US cities and towns, providing both far more detailed information than was available before, and a new ability to search for correlations and relationships. In studying the natural environment, GIS replaces the kind of analysis that Ian McHarg had to map with markers on tracing paper, using overlays that are a direct outgrowth of McHarg's methods. GIS layers are not just maps; they can contain complicated mathematical information, which can be synthesized using today's computer power, providing techniques far in advance of those available to McHarg. It is possible to assign different weights to the information on different layers, and seek optimal relationships that balance one kind of environmental sensitivity against another. Traditional transportation models to predict the use of highways or transit systems have often failed because they do not incorporate predictions about future population and land use. GIS makes it possible to relate a new highway or transit line to its potential land-use consequences. The Spatial Analyst Program in ArcGIS can relate predictions about future population to future land use along a highway or transit route, producing alternative conceptual maps that can display the potential land-use outcomes from a new transportation proposal, and then feed back these predicted results to the design of the transit system. Standard transportation modelling techniques had long ignored the potential of new access patterns to stimulate future growth, leading to the well-known result that by the time a new highway has been completed it may be operating at the capacity that designers thought would not be reached for decades into the future (see Putman, 2001).

At the level of individual urban projects, GIS makes it possible to learn immediately how many residents might be displaced by a proposed development, what the property values are, whether any properties are tax-delinquent or have building violations, as well as the age of the buildings involved and their precise shape and location on a map. In the 1960s, decision-makers often had only a sketchy idea what the effect of a development proposal might be on a site and its surroundings, as more detail required laborious building-by-building surveys. In the 1960s, maps based on aerial surveys were expensive and hard to keep up to date. Generally only governments had access to them. Today, CommunityViz[7] is an example of a GIS-based programme that allows planners to discuss complex problems with communities. Alternative concepts can be mapped and displayed in three-dimensional representations and the environmental impacts and cost implications of each alternative can also be modelled. Google Maps, and other competing services, provide detailed maps and aerial photographs for most places, and this information is available to everyone.

Planners and city designers are now much more likely to recognize the complexity of making interventions in cities. They are guided by community participation, which has become standard procedure, and, for large projects, plans have to include an environmental assessment – difficult to do well, but the requirement force-feeds consideration of a long list of complexities. Design sensibilities have also changed. A tower in a park is no longer a standard choice. Recognizing communities and the importance of preserving old buildings has made city design much more sensitive to the surrounding built environment. New energy efficiency standards like LEED[8] have made urban development more responsive to the natural environment as well.

Towards Self-Organizing Cities

In chapter 15 on 'Unslumming and slumming' in *The Death and Life*, Jane Jacobs not only looks at urban neighbourhoods as systems of organized complexity but proposes a dynamic of change that can be described as a self-organizing system. Slum communities can evolve and diversify until people will choose to stay there, as opposed to having no alternative. Jacobs says this is the ultimate test of whether a neighbourhood is successful or not and she illustrates her point by describing the evolution of a particular neighbourhood, Boston's North End. She deduces that there must be general principles governing the emergence of a stable neighbourhood from a slum and is clearly sympathetic to this idea.

Self-organizing complex systems are of growing interest in many disciplines (see, for example, Johnson, 2001). A flock of birds, despite appearances, has no leader, but navigates according to principles that mathematicians can simulate. Individual ants going about their specific, genetically programmed tasks together make up a self-sufficient colony with its own complete physical structure. Cellular automata are rules systems for adding individual cells together. Some rule systems produce distinct patterns. Stephen Wolfram has catalogued many of them in his book, *A New Kind of Science* (2002), and believes that these mathematical formulations are likely to correspond to underlying principles of physical reality. More informally, in everyday life, Wikipedia is a good example of social self-organization.

Being able to write a rule system that would produce good cities through a process of self-organization would clearly make city planning and design more responsive to the kind of problem a city is. There are people currently working on discovering self-organizing principles for cities, using advanced computation techniques made possible by computers. Michael Batty, at University College London, proposes that there are mathematical algorithms that generate patterns comparable to systems of organization to be found in cities (Batty, 2009; see also Batty, 2005). He is looking at systems of proximity and efficiency that could represent clusters of population and activities generated by people with similar needs and interests, plus the connections created by streets.

Self-organizing systems and the complex forms that can be generated by computers are of great interest in architecture schools right now, and some architecture teachers are making claims that these concepts can also be applied to cities. This is a very promising line of research and should eventually prove productive. The danger is that complexity theory can produce analogies as misleading as the statistical analogies applied to housing conditions so correctly criticized by Jane Jacobs. Recognizing the kind of problem a city is does not necessarily mean that all solutions to this class of problem will apply to cities. It is worth remembering Jane Jacobs's scepticism about theories that do not include observable realities.

However, there are self-organizing urban systems in plain view in cities; property ownership is one. Individual properties each have owners, who develop and operate their properties for their self-interest. They obviously do not operate as blindly as ants in an ant colony, but, like the ants, their actions have a collective effect, interacting with other properties and ultimately shaping the whole city. There have always had to be rules to protect the rights of individual owners from the activities of other owners. Early examples are regulations to prevent the encroachment of buildings into streets, and codes requiring fire-resistant walls between properties. Modern building, zoning and subdivision codes have grown up to manage property development. The computer game SimCity[9] uses typical urban zoning and street mapping as the basis for its rules. Although choices made playing the game are much simpler than real urban decision-making, SimCity's rapid timeframe illustrates that development regulations are a system that can generate a variety of urban forms, depending on how critical decisions are made.

If development regulations are shaping private property into the current city, improvements in city design could follow from improvements in regulations. Jacobs criticized regulation in the 1960s as simplistic, enforcing too much separation of uses and not recognizing the importance of different scales of development. Form-based codes, which provide for a mix of uses and a diversity of scales, are an advance from these earlier methods. More improvement will come as computer technology is incorporated within development regulations. Zoning maps are still much as they were in the 1920s, two-dimensional representations of streets and property lines, overlaid by rectangular boxes that correspond to categories of permitted uses. When zoning maps are merged with today's Geographic Information Systems, the maps will embody information about the existing natural environment and buildings already on the ground. Such improvements can help regulatory decisions become far more sensitive to larger principles of city organization.

City Systems as Part of Larger Systems

In 1961, when *The Death and Life of Great American Cities* appeared, it was still possible to think of cities as autonomous units, although urban geographer Jean Gottmann published *Megalopolis: The Urbanized Northeastern Seaboard of the United States* the same year. Cities which Jacobs used as examples, such as New York City, Boston, and Philadelphia, are shown by Gottmann to be part of a much larger urban system extending from south of Washington to north of Boston. Jacobs herself expanded her theories to include city regions in her 1984 book, *Cities and the Wealth of Nations*. City regions are also examples of organized complexity; but the level of complexity is obviously much greater than for a city considered individually. City regions include many sub-systems, and many of these systems overlap. Tracing the process which creates a product, one of Jacobs's primary methods, can today take one through several city regions and several nation-states. The environment, the complex system that is the setting for cities, city regions, and nations, is proving to be far more dynamic than was understood in the 1960s. Rising sea levels, more extreme storms, droughts, and changes in local climate are all taking place at an accelerated pace, requiring society to understand the causes and devise measures for managing them. Many people now understand the kind of problem a city is, but solving the problem is more challenging than ever.

Notes

1.   Jacobs cites the 1958 Annual Report of the Rockefeller Foundation as her source for Warren Weaver's '… splendid summary and interpretation…'. Warren Weaver is not listed in the acknowledgements at the front of *The Death and Life of Great American Cities* where there is a long list of people Jacobs interviewed or who reviewed part of the manuscript. For a biography of Warren Weaver, see Rees (1987).

2.   *Silent Spring* was initially serialized in three parts in the 16, 23 and 30 June 1962 issues of *The New Yorker* magazine.

3.   This article carries on work begun by Alexander as a doctoral thesis at Harvard, published in 1964 by the Harvard University Press as *Notes on the Synthesis of Form*.

4.   These words are from Title 1 of the *National Environmental Policy Act*.

5.   I know about the original title because Alexander's article was first submitted to me at *Architectural Record*, where I was an editor. The chief editor decided to turn it down as Record had recently published two other pieces by Alexander. The editors at *Architectural Forum* made the title more effective, but less descriptive.

6.   I was part of the Urban Design Group of the New York City Planning Department, and then

director of urban design for the Planning Department, during the Lindsay administration and have described some of the lessons learned in two books (Barnett, 1974 and 1982).

7.   CommunityViz is a GIS programme developed by the Orton Family Foundation to help communities make good decisions about their future by including as many people in the process as possible.

8.   Leadership in Energy Efficiency and Design, a certification programme established in 1998 by the US Green Building Council, a private organization.

9.   SimCity was first released by its creator, Will Wright, in 1989.

References

Alexander, C. (1965) A city is not a tree. *Architectural Forum*, **122**(1), pp. 58–61 and **122**(2), pp. 58–62.

Bacon, E. (1967) *Design of Cities*. London: Penguin Books.

Barnett, J. (1974) *Urban Design as Public Policy*. New York: Architectural Record Books/McGraw Hill.

Barnett, J. (1982) *Introduction to Urban Design*. New York: Harper & Row.

Barnett, J. (2011) Modernist city design, in *City Design, Modernist, Traditional, Green and Systems Perspectives*. London: Routledge, pp. 13–55.

Batty, M. (2005) *Cities and Complexity: Understanding Cities with Cellular Automata, Agent-Based Models, and Fractals*. Cambridge, MA: MIT Press.

Batty, M. (2009) Generating cities from the bottom up: using complexity theory for effective design, in Alexiou, K., Johnson, J. and Zamenopoulos, T. (eds.) *Embracing Complexity in Design*. London: Routledge.

Carson, R. (1962) *Silent Spring*. Boston, MA: Houghton Mifflin.

Davidoff, P. (1965) Advocacy and pluralism in planning. *Journal of the American Institute of Planners*, **31**, pp. 186–197.

Gans, H.J. (1959) The human implications of current redevelopment and relocation planning. *Journal of the American Institute of Planners*, **25**(1), pp. 15–25.

Gans, H.J. (1962) *The Urban Villagers; Group and Class in the Life of Italian-Americans*. New York: Free Press of Glencoe.

Glass, R. (1948) *The Social Background of a Plan: A Study of Middlesbrough*. London: Routledge and Kegan Paul.

Gottmann, J. (1961) *Megalopolis: The Urbanized Northeastern Seaboard of the United States*. Cambridge, MA: MIT Press.

Jacobs, J. (1961) *The Death and Life of Great American Cities*. New York: Random House.

Jacobs, J. (1984) *Cities and the Wealth of Nations*. New York: Random House.

Johnson, S. (2001) *Emergence: The Connected Lives of Ants, Brains, Cities, and Software*. New York: Scribner.

Martin, D. (2006) Jane Jacobs, urban activist, is dead at 89. *New York Times*, 25 April. Available at http://www.nytimes.com/2006/04/25/books/25cnd-jacobs.html?pagewanted=all. Accessed 20 February 2012.

McHarg, I. (1969 [1995]) *Design with Nature*. New York: Wiley.

Putman, S.H. (2001) Highway planning and land use: theory and practice, in Barnett, J. (ed.) *Planning for a New Century*. Washington DC: Island Press.

Rees, M. (1987) *Warren Weaver 1894–1978, A Biographical Memoir*. Washington DC: National Academy of Sciences.

Venturi, R. (1966) *Complexity and Contradiction in Architecture*. New York: The Museum of Modern Art Press.

Weaver, W. (1948) Science and complexity. *American Scientist*, **36**, pp. 536–544. Available at philoscience.unibe.ch/documents/uk/weaver1948.pdf. Accessed 19 February 2012.

Wolfram, S. (2002) *A New Kind of Science*. Champaign, IL: Wolfram Media. Available at http://www.wolframscience.com/nksonline/. Accessed 20 February 2012.

Index